Ergonomics and Business Policies for the Promotion of Well-Being in the Workplace

Mildrend Montoya-Reyes
Autonomous University of Baja California, Mexico

Ismael Mendoza-Muñoz
Autonomous University of Baja California, Mexico

Gabriela Jacobo-Galicia
Autonomous University of Baja California, Mexico

Samantha E. Cruz-Sotelo
Autonomous University of Baja California, Mexico

IGI Global
PUBLISHER of TIMELY KNOWLEDGE

A volume in the Advances in Human Resources Management and Organizational Development (AHRMOD) Book Series

Published in the United States of America by
IGI Global
Business Science Reference (an imprint of IGI Global)
701 E. Chocolate Avenue
Hershey PA, USA 17033
Tel: 717-533-8845
Fax: 717-533-8661
E-mail: cust@igi-global.com
Web site: http://www.igi-global.com

Library of Congress Cataloging-in-Publication Data

Names: Montoya-Reyes, Mildrend, 1979- editor. | Mendoza-Munoz, Ismael, 1986- editor. | Jacobo-Galicia, Gabriela, 1968- editor. | Cruz-Sotelo, Samantha E., editor.
Title: Ergonomics and business policies for the promotion of well-being in the workplace / Mildrend Montoya-Reyes, Ismael Mendoza-Muñoz, Gabriela Jacobo-Galicia and Samantha E. Cruz-Sotelo, editor.
Description: Hershey PA : Business Science Reference, [2022] | Includes bibliographical references and index. | Summary: "The objective of this book is to present the new trends in sustainable work through the analysis and application of methods to evaluate and improve the interaction of human beings with their work, their work area, and their environment"-- Provided by publisher.
Identifiers: LCCN 2021019414 (print) | LCCN 2021019415 (ebook) | ISBN 9781799873969 (hardcover) | ISBN 9781799873976 (paperback) | ISBN 9781799873983 (ebook)
Subjects: LCSH: Work environment--Case studies. | Industrial hygiene--Case studies. | Psychology, Industrial--Case studies. | Human engineering--Case studies. | Sustainable development--Case studies.
Classification: LCC HD7261 E74 2022 (print) | LCC HD7261 (ebook) | DDC 658.3/82--dc23
LC record available at https://lccn.loc.gov/2021019414
LC ebook record available at https://lccn.loc.gov/2021019415

This book is published in the IGI Global book series Advances in Human Resources Management and Organizational Development (AHRMOD) (ISSN: 2327-3372; eISSN: 2327-3380)

British Cataloguing in Publication Data
A Cataloguing in Publication record for this book is available from the British Library.

Advances in Human Resources Management and Organizational Development (AHRMOD) Book Series

Patricia Ordóñez de Pablos
Universidad de Oviedo, Spain

ISSN:2327-3372
EISSN:2327-3380

Mission

A solid foundation is essential to the development and success of any organization and can be accomplished through the effective and careful management of an organization's human capital. Research in human resources management and organizational development is necessary in providing business leaders with the tools and methodologies which will assist in the development and maintenance of their organizational structure.

The **Advances in Human Resources Management and Organizational Development (AHRMOD) Book Series** aims to publish the latest research on all aspects of human resources as well as the latest methodologies, tools, and theories regarding organizational development and sustainability. The **AHRMOD Book Series** intends to provide business professionals, managers, researchers, and students with the necessary resources to effectively develop and implement organizational strategies.

Coverage

- Talent Identification and Management
- Performance Improvement
- E-Human Resources Management
- Job Enrichment
- Employee Relations
- Employee Benefits
- Upward Feedback
- Collaborative Method
- Change Management
- Executive Education

IGI Global is currently accepting manuscripts for publication within this series. To submit a proposal for a volume in this series, please contact our Acquisition Editors at Acquisitions@igi-global.com or visit: http://www.igi-global.com/publish/.

The Advances in Human Resources Management and Organizational Development (AHRMOD) Book Series (ISSN 2327-3372) is published by IGI Global, 701 E. Chocolate Avenue, Hershey, PA 17033-1240, USA, www.igi-global.com. This series is composed of titles available for purchase individually; each title is edited to be contextually exclusive from any other title within the series. For pricing and ordering information please visit http://www.igi-global.com/book-series/advances-human-resources-management-organizational/73670. Postmaster: Send all address changes to above address.

Titles in this Series

For a list of additional titles in this series, please visit: http://www.igi-global.com/book-series/advances-human-resources-management-organizational/73670

Analyzing Telework, Trustworthiness, and Performance Using Leader-Member Exchange COVID-19 Perspective
Michael A. Brown Sr. (Right Fit Communications LLC, USA)
Business Science Reference • © 2022 • 263pp • H/C (ISBN: 9781799889502) • US $215.00

Future Advancements for CSR and the Sustainable Development Goals in a Post-COVID-19 World
Andrea Pérez (University of Cantabria, Spain)
Business Science Reference • © 2022 • 355pp • H/C (ISBN: 9781799880653) • US $225.00

Building Competencies for Organizational Success Emerging Research and Opportunities
Donta S. Harper (University of Washington, USA)
Business Science Reference • © 2021 • 217pp • H/C (ISBN: 9781799865162) • US $195.00

Role of Leadership in Facilitating Healing and Renewal in Times of Organizational Trauma and Change
Lynda Byrd-Poller (Thomas Nelson Community College, USA) Jennifer L. Farmer (Renewed Mindset LLC, USA) and Valerie Ford (ISP Global Communications LLC, USA)
Business Science Reference • © 2021 • 291pp • H/C (ISBN: 9781799870166) • US $195.00

Impact of Infodemic on Organizational Performance
Muhammad Waseem Bari (Government College University, Faisalabad, Pakistan) and Emilia Alaverdov (Georgian Technical University, Georgia)
Business Science Reference • © 2021 • 380pp • H/C (ISBN: 9781799871644) • US $195.00

Handbook of Research on Advancements in Organizational Data Collection and Measurements Strategies for Addressing Attitudes, Beliefs, and Behaviors
Mihai C. Bocarnea (Regent University, USA) Bruce E. Winston (Regent University, USA) and Debra Dean (Regent University, USA)
Business Science Reference • © 2021 • 400pp • H/C (ISBN: 9781799876656) • US $295.00

Effective Strategies for Communicating Insights in Business
Ross Jackson (Wittenberg University, USA) and Amanda Reboulet (Jacoulet, USA)
Business Science Reference • © 2021 • 261pp • H/C (ISBN: 9781799839644) • US $195.00

IGI Global
PUBLISHER of TIMELY KNOWLEDGE

701 East Chocolate Avenue, Hershey, PA 17033, USA
Tel: 717-533-8845 x100 • Fax: 717-533-8661
E-Mail: cust@igi-global.com • www.igi-global.com

Table of Contents

Preface xiv

Chapter 1
Eudaemonic Design to Achieve Well-Being at Work, Wherever That May Be 1
Jenna Mikus, Queensland University of Technology, Australia
Janice Rieger, Queensland University of Technology, Australia
Deanna Grant-Smith, Queensland University of Technology, Australia

Chapter 2
The Impact of Job Demands Variables in the Job Demands Resources Model 33
Henry Milimu Shililu, Excelsia College, Australia

Chapter 3
NOM-035-STPS-2018: Opportunities for Better Implementation – A Review 64
Raul Martinez-Balderrama, Autonomous University of Baja California, Mexico
Gabriela Jacobo Jacobo-Galicia, Autonomous University of Baja California, Mexico
María Elizabeth Ramírez- Barreto, Autonomous University of Baja California, Mexico
Judith M. Paz-Delgadillo, Autonomous University of Baja California, Mexico
Samantha Cruz-Sotelo, Autonomous University of Baja California, Mexico

Chapter 4
Productivity Evaluation in Function of Worker Psychosocial Factors 72
Erick McGregor Roa-Badilla, Autonomous University of Baja California, Mexico
Gabriela Jacobo-Galicia, Autonomous University of Baja California, Mexico
Mildrend Ivett Montoya-Reyes, Autonomous University of Baja California, Mexico
Ismael Mendoza-Muñoz, Autonomous University of Baja California, Mexico
Juan Ceballos- Corral, Autonomous University of Baja California, Mexico

Chapter 5
Evaluation of Working Conditions as a Factor of Well-Being of Workers in an Electronic Industry in Mexicali 107
Carlos Raul Navarro González, Autonomous University of Baja California, Mexico
Yanet Villarreal González, Tecnologico Nacional de Mexico, Instituto Tecnolgico de Mexicali, Mexico
Pedro Alberto Escárcega Zepeda, Tecnologico Nacional de Mexico, Instituto Tecnolgico de Mexicali, Mexico
Ana Laura Sanchez Corona, Autonomous University of Baja California, Mexico
Rigoberto Zamora Alarcon, Autonomous University of Baja California, Mexico
Gustavo Lopez Badilla, UNEA Universidad, Mexico

Chapter 6
Determinants of Employee Motivation: A Comparison of Operational and Non-Operational Staff.. 130
Bikash Basnet, Excelsia College, Australia
Sarah Eyaa, Excelsia College, Australia
Nekpen Euodia Okhawere, University of Benin, Nigeria

Chapter 7
New Model to Promote Well-Being in Work Areas of an Aerospace Industry Facility in Mexicali: Ergonomic Analysis 150
Carlos Raul Navarro Gonzalez, Autonomous University of Baja California, Mexico
Juan Ceballos-Corral, Autonomous University of Baja California, Mexico
Olivia Yessenia Vargas-Bernal, Autonomous University of Baja California, Mexico
Gustavo Lopez Badilla, UNEA University, Mexico
Judith M. Paz-Delgadillo, Autonomous University of Baja California, Mexico

Chapter 8
Model for Determination of Musculoskeletal Disorder Cost/Benefit: Base for Strategy for Implementation of a Preventive DME Program for a Company 173
Juan Alberto Castillo Martinez, Universidad del Rosario, Colombia
Andres Felipe Garcia S., Universidad del Rosario, Colombia

Chapter 9
Comparison of Six Passive Exoskeletons for Upper Limbs Using the TOPSIS Method 193
Pablo Antonio Muñoz Gutierrez, Autonomous University of Ciudad Juarez, Mexico
Juan Luis Hernández-Arellano, Autonomous University of Ciudad Juarez, Mexico
Juan Alberto Castillo Martinez, Universidad del Rosario, Colombia
Aide Aracely Maldonado-Macias, Autonomous University of Ciudad Juarez, Mexico

Chapter 10
Factorial Solution for Determination of Critical Success Factors (CSF) in Deployment of Six Sigma and Its Relation to Sustainability: Case Study – Baja California Aerospace Industry 208
Aida López Guerrero, Autonomous University of Baja California, Mexico
Jesús Andrés Hernández Gómez, Autonomous University of Ciudad Juarez, Mexico
Karla Isabel Velázquez Victorica, Autonomous University of Baja California, Mexico
Mydory Oyuky Nakasima López, Autonomous University of Baja California, Mexico
Luz del Consuelo Olivares Fong, Autonomous University of Baja California, Mexico

Chapter 11
Gradual Technology Development for Ethnic Groups: Ergonomics, Processes, and Education........ 234
Eusebio Jimenez Lopez, Universidad La Salle Noroeste, Mexico
Victor Manuel Martinez Molina, Citi Hall of Cajeme, Mexico
Victoria Moroyoqui Galaviz, Casa Etchohuaquila, Mexico
Lilia Zulema Gaytán Martínez, Universidad Tecnológica del Sur de Sonora, Mexico
José Manuel Luna Nemecio, Centro Universitario CIFE, Mexico
Aldo Augusto Lopez Martínez, Centro de Ingeniería y Diseño Industrial (CIDESI), Mexico

Compilation of References 262

About the Contributors 294

Index 301

Detailed Table of Contents

Preface xiv

Chapter 1
Eudaemonic Design to Achieve Well-Being at Work, Wherever That May Be 1
Jenna Mikus, Queensland University of Technology, Australia
Janice Rieger, Queensland University of Technology, Australia
Deanna Grant-Smith, Queensland University of Technology, Australia

The concept of eudaemonia originates from neo-Aristotelian philosophy and is associated with human flourishing. Self-determination theory, a means to attain eudaemonia, is examined here as a foundational approach to drive Eudaemonic Design--a novel design strategy that aims to achieve holistic physical, mental, and social health, or eudaemonic well-being. This chapter advances Eudaemonic Design as an architectural and organizational approach to create healthful work environments that support employee and business flourishing. The authors argue that the importance of adopting Eudaemonic Design has grown in need and complexity as work is (re)shaped by the constraints and opportunities presented by the pandemic. By contrasting dominant pre-COVID-19 Work from Office expectations against the post-COVID-19 Work from Anywhere model, this chapter explores the application of Eudaemonic Design to deliver holistic workplace well-being, rather than single variable health and wellness alone, now and into the post-COVID-19 future of work.

Chapter 2
The Impact of Job Demands Variables in the Job Demands Resources Model 33
Henry Milimu Shililu, Excelsia College, Australia

The purpose of this chapter is to report on the findings of a study that was conducted by the author to investigate the impact of job demands variables on emotional exhaustion and emotional ill-health. A sample of 173 drawn from employees who worked for different organizations in the Pacific, mainly Australia, the African region, the Indian subcontinent of India, Nepal, Pakistan, Bangladesh, and Sri Lanka, and employees who professed Christian and Hindu religions. A broad range of ages, occupations, ethnicities, religions, and cultures was represented in the sample, that is, the targeted population were employees whose different contexts and characteristics (e.g., attitudes, occupations, ages, marital status, religion, opinions, behaviors, and other defined variables) could be measured and allowed to generalize the results. The study used a quantitative research design. A diversity of findings were established with some findings being consistent with the JD-R theory and previous studies across the cultures while other findings were not consistent with previous studies and the JDR theory.

Chapter 3
NOM-035-STPS-2018: Opportunities for Better Implementation – A Review 64
Raul Martinez-Balderrama, Autonomous University of Baja California, Mexico
Gabriela Jacobo Jacobo-Galicia, Autonomous University of Baja California, Mexico
María Elizabeth Ramírez- Barreto, Autonomous University of Baja California, Mexico
Judith M. Paz-Delgadillo, Autonomous University of Baja California, Mexico
Samantha Cruz-Sotelo, Autonomous University of Baja California, Mexico

Looking at the structure of NOM-035-STPS-2018, there is an assumption that there are areas of opportunity to improve the implementation of the standard. Thus, the purpose of this research is to identify through a review whether there are areas of opportunity that can improve the implementation of NOM-035. For the review, articles addressing the psychosocial risk factors evaluation were selected and analyzed. Four topics of discussion were identified: impact of psychosocial risk factors, policy and regulations, management systems, and evaluation of psychosocial risk factors. Subsequently, a synthesis was made, and it was found that there are three areas of opportunity to improve NOM-035-STPS-2018: it does not have a risk management system, its instruments do not present evidence of statistical validity, and the instruments do not take into account indicators of consequence.

Chapter 4
Productivity Evaluation in Function of Worker Psychosocial Factors.. 72
Erick McGregor Roa-Badilla, Autonomous University of Baja California, Mexico
Gabriela Jacobo-Galicia, Autonomous University of Baja California, Mexico
Mildrend Ivett Montoya-Reyes, Autonomous University of Baja California, Mexico
Ismael Mendoza-Muñoz, Autonomous University of Baja California, Mexico
Juan Ceballos- Corral, Autonomous University of Baja California, Mexico

Workers are exposed to different factors that can be detrimental to their well-being, being the most known safety and hygiene factors. A few years ago, the concepts of harmful factors for workers were updated by adding the psychosocial factors. Although there is literature on psychosocial factors and their effect on health, this work focused specifically on seeking the relationship between productivity and psychosocial factors to know how it impacts the organization. The investigation was applied in a case study for a doorknob locks manufacturing company in its final assembly area. Data collection was done by applying the questionnaire provided by NOM-035-STPS-2018 and the company's productivity databases for the subsequent analysis using statistical tools. The results were that, for the violence factor, its correlation with productivity was R2 = 0.8886, indicating a strong correlation with which it is concluded that there is an influence on productivity.

Chapter 5
Evaluation of Working Conditions as a Factor of Well-Being of Workers in an Electronic Industry in Mexicali 107
Carlos Raul Navarro González, Autonomous University of Baja California, Mexico
Yanet Villarreal González, Tecnologico Nacional de Mexico, Instituto Tecnolgico de Mexicali, Mexico
Pedro Alberto Escárcega Zepeda, Tecnologico Nacional de Mexico, Instituto Tecnolgico de Mexicali, Mexico
Ana Laura Sanchez Corona, Autonomous University of Baja California, Mexico
Rigoberto Zamora Alarcon, Autonomous University of Baja California, Mexico
Gustavo Lopez Badilla, UNEA Universidad, Mexico

The objective of this research was developed to evaluate the working conditions of workers in an electronic industry located in the city of Mexicali, analyzing a process in a work table where welding operations of electronic components are made and certain factors are presented that generated discomfort to the operating personnel of this manufacturing area. The workers frequently visited the company doctor and health institutions in Mexicali due to symptoms of discomfort and pain in the head, neck, back, spine, arms, hands, and shoulders in addition to discomfort in the eyes due to not having a position due to poor structure (work table and chair) and low light intensity, which caused fatigue and stress and discomfort with eyestrain. In addition, certain employees in the production areas presented symptoms of respiratory diseases caused by an environment contaminated by pollutants, essentially derived from sulfur (sulfides), as well as variations in temperature and relative humidity in the four seasons of the year.

Chapter 6
Determinants of Employee Motivation: A Comparison of Operational and Non-Operational Staff.. 130
Bikash Basnet, Excelsia College, Australia
Sarah Eyaa, Excelsia College, Australia
Nekpen Euodia Okhawere, University of Benin, Nigeria

This chapter integrates collectivism with the dimensions of the Expectancy Theory to investigate the direct and indirect impact of horizontal and vertical collectivism on employee motivation of operational and non-operational staff. Data were collected from 205 employees using a cross-sectional survey. Hypotheses were tested with multiple regression analysis. Across both employee categories, horizontal collectivism improves motivation while vertical collectivism does not have a significant impact on motivation. Mediation effects were significant in the relationship between horizontal collectivism across both employee categories. However, there were some variations in the mediation effects on the relationship between vertical collaboration and motivation across the two categories. This chapter contributes to motivation literature by integrating the Expectancy Theory with two under-investigated dimensions of collectivism to compare motivation determinants among operational and non-operational staff. This chapter presents implications for managers and policy for improving employee motivation.

Chapter 7
New Model to Promote Well-Being in Work Areas of an Aerospace Industry Facility in Mexicali: Ergonomic Analysis 150
Carlos Raul Navarro Gonzalez, Autonomous University of Baja California, Mexico
Juan Ceballos-Corral, Autonomous University of Baja California, Mexico
Olivia Yessenia Vargas-Bernal, Autonomous University of Baja California, Mexico
Gustavo Lopez Badilla, UNEA University, Mexico
Judith M. Paz-Delgadillo, Autonomous University of Baja California, Mexico

This investigation was made to evaluate the health and well-being of workers who made activities in the manufacturing processes of an aerospace industry installed in the city of Mexicali and based on the evidence presented in certain stages of a production line. The cost-benefit of applying ergonomic methods was analyzed, developing a descriptive model, which involved important aspects. Said aspects analyzed were (1) work methods, (2) training of employees in the operational area, (3) evaluation of times and movements of industrial operations, and (4) working conditions as the relationship of workers with supervisors and managers.

Chapter 8
Model for Determination of Musculoskeletal Disorder Cost/Benefit: Base for Strategy for Implementation of a Preventive DME Program for a Company 173
Juan Alberto Castillo Martinez, Universidad del Rosario, Colombia
Andres Felipe Garcia S., Universidad del Rosario, Colombia

It is generally considered that the costs related to musculoskeletal disorders (MSDs) stem from absenteeism, medical expenses, reduced productivity, and quality of life. To estimate the costs associated with MSDs in organizations and thus determine the benefits for a company of implementing an effective and sustainable prevention program, it is necessary to consider the need to know the current and future prevalence of MSDs as well as to understand whether these data vary according to the economic sector, geographic location, and demographic aspects. It is also necessary to understand whether there are comorbidities associated with MSDs as well as the direct and indirect impacts in terms of the productive and work capacity of organizations and individuals. In the development of this study, the authors wanted to generate an analysis tool to estimate the incidence of MSDs and their economic costs, which also serves as a baseline to evaluate the possible benefits derived from prevention programs for this type of work-related disease.

Chapter 9
Comparison of Six Passive Exoskeletons for Upper Limbs Using the TOPSIS Method 193
Pablo Antonio Muñoz Gutierrez, Autonomous University of Ciudad Juarez, Mexico
Juan Luis Hernández-Arellano, Autonomous University of Ciudad Juarez, Mexico
Juan Alberto Castillo Martinez, Universidad del Rosario, Colombia
Aide Aracely Maldonado-Macias, Autonomous University of Ciudad Juarez, Mexico

The use of exoskeletons in occupational tasks has increased significantly in the last five years. However, few comparative studies have been conducted to understand the advantages and disadvantages of existing exoskeletons. This chapter presents the comparison of six exoskeletons using the TOPSIS method. Using databases of patents and commercial products, a total of six that were chosen to be compared by experts in the design and/or use of exoskeletons. The criteria evaluated were exoskeleton weight, load capacity, anthropometric adjusts, maintenance, and installation on the user. The Shoulder-X exoskeleton was selected as the best, serving as a reference for the acquisition of characteristics for recommendations for the development of new models for use in occupational tasks.

Chapter 10
Factorial Solution for Determination of Critical Success Factors (CSF) in Deployment of Six Sigma and Its Relation to Sustainability: Case Study – Baja California Aerospace Industry 208
Aida López Guerrero, Autonomous University of Baja California, Mexico
Jesús Andrés Hernández Gómez, Autonomous University of Ciudad Juarez, Mexico
Karla Isabel Velázquez Victorica, Autonomous University of Baja California, Mexico
Mydory Oyuky Nakasima López, Autonomous University of Baja California, Mexico
Luz del Consuelo Olivares Fong, Autonomous University of Baja California, Mexico

Recently, the interest in being part of more competitive companies has increased. For this, organizations apply various strategies of continuous improvement that allow them to maintain high standards of competitiveness. In this sense, organizations make use of various techniques, tools, and methodologies that support the achievement of objectives. This research presents an approach towards the Six Sigma (SS) strategy, one of the main continuous improvement strategies used to achieve competitiveness. On the other hand, organizations currently seek that during manufacture of their products, caring for the environment is naturally part of their objectives, seeking to achieve benefits with a sustainable impact. Therefore, this research seeks to define the CSF for implementation of SS through a factor analysis that allows identifying the relationship between SS and obtaining sustainable benefits (SB) through its implementation.

Chapter 11
Gradual Technology Development for Ethnic Groups: Ergonomics, Processes, and Education........ 234
Eusebio Jimenez Lopez, Universidad La Salle Noroeste, Mexico
Victor Manuel Martinez Molina, Citi Hall of Cajeme, Mexico
Victoria Moroyoqui Galaviz, Casa Etchohuaquila, Mexico
Lilia Zulema Gaytán Martínez, Universidad Tecnológica del Sur de Sonora, Mexico
José Manuel Luna Nemecio, Centro Universitario CIFE, Mexico
Aldo Augusto Lopez Martínez, Centro de Ingeniería y Diseño Industrial (CIDESI), Mexico

This chapter presents the application of the concept of gradual technology to improve and increase the productivity of a workshop for the manufacture of handcrafted furniture owned by a cooperative formed by members of the Guarijía ethnic group, located in San Bernardo, Alamos, Sonora. The production process of the rustic furniture called "stool" was systematized and equipment was designed taking into account basic ergonomic aspects. Production sub-processes of the workshop and equipment were improved, including machinery design, purchase of basic technology, adaptation of electric current, water, and air conditioning systems. The basic inputs for manufacturing the furniture, such as wood and cowhide, were studied to determine whether the production of the stool affected the environment. The operating personnel in charge of the cooperative were trained in the use of the equipment and in the visualization of the improved processes.

Compilation of References 262

About the Contributors 294

Index 301

Preface

AN OVERVIEW OF THE SUBJECT MATTER

Ergonomics is important in the workplace because it increases comfort and in doing so, it improves productivity and reduces stress. When a person is doing a job, their body is affected by it. These effects can be reflected mainly in problems to the musculoskeletal system with symptoms such as: fatigue, discomfort, and pain, caused by an awkward posture, extreme temperature, or repeated movement.

It is well documented that workers frequently visit health institutions and health practitioners due to symptoms of discomfort and pain related to their jobs. So, it is very important that organizations hire or listen to an ergonomist when designing or modifying the workplace in order for it to fit the worker, not the other way around. The goal is to eliminate discomfort and risk of injury due to work.

Although the health effects of poor workplace design have been studied extensively, ergonomic regulations are relatively recent, particularly in emerging countries. Generally speaking, it is the organizations that devise industry standards that have developed regulations on this issue more consistently, and it is these standards that are implemented most regularly in organizations. However, more needs to be done on this area in order to enforce the ergonomic mindset when designing or improving a workplace.

HOW THE TOPIC FITS IN THE WORLD TODAY

Recently, the interest of companies in becoming more competitive has become more relevant. In order to achieve this objective, organizations apply various strategies of continuous improvement that allow them to maintain high efficiency standards. Health problems associated with poor ergonomic design impact disabilities and days lost due to work injury or illness. On the other hand, no matter the age, occupation, ethnicity, religion, and culture, the psychosocial work factors and their effects on health have a strong influence on productivity, resulting in economic losses for both the organization and its employees.

Now into the Post-COVID-19 era of work, organizations should make use of various techniques, tools, and methodologies that support a holistic physical, mental, and social health approach or eudaemonic well-being, to achieve their company objectives. This book presents an approach to how organizations are considering ergonomics as a valuable tool to achieve benefits to the bottom line with a positive impact for the employees.

TARGET AUDIENCE

This book was written for people who are interested in ergonomics: employers that are looking for new methods and strategies that increase the comfort, well-being, and emotional health of workers; students who want to learn more about ergonomics and related information; teachers who want up-to-date information and real cases to share in their classes; and researchers who require sources of information and support for their projects.

CHAPTERS

Chapter 1: Eudaemonic Design to Achieve Well-Being at Work – Wherever That May Be

The term eudaemonia originates from neo-Aristotelian philosophy and is associated with human flourishing. Self-Determination Theory, a means to achieve eudaemonia, is proposed here as a foundational approach to drive Eudaemonic Design to achieve holistic physical, mental, and social health, or eudaemonic well-being. This chapter advances Eudaemonic Design as an architectural and organizational design approach to create healthful work environments that support employee and business flourishing. The authors argue that the importance of adopting Eudaemonic Design has grown in need and complexity as work is (re) shaped by the constraints and opportunities presented by the pandemic. By contrasting dominant Pre-COVID-19 Work from Office expectations against the Post-COVID-19 Work from Anywhere model, this chapter explores the application of Eudaemonic Design to deliver holistic workplace well-being, rather than single variable health and wellness alone, now and into the Post-COVID-19 future of work.

Chapter 2: The Impact of Job Demands Variables in the Job Demands Resources Model

The purpose of this chapter is to report on the findings of a study that was conducted by the author to investigate the impact of job demands variables on emotional exhaustion and emotional ill-health. A sample of 173 was drawn from employees who worked for different organizations in the pacific mainly Australia, the African region, the Indian subcontinent of India, Nepal, Pakistan Bangladesh, and Sri Lanka, and employees who professed Christian and Hindu religions. A broad range of ages, occupations, ethnicities, religions, and cultures was represented in the sample. i.e. the targeted population were employees whose different contexts and characteristics (e.g. attitudes, occupations, ages, marital status, religion, opinions, behaviors, and other defined variables) could be measured and allowed to generalize the results. the study used a quantitative research design. A diversity of findings was established with some findings being consistent with the JD-R theory and previous studies across the cultures while other findings were not consistent with previous studies and the JDR theory.

Chapter 3: NOM-035-STPS-2018 Opportunities for Better Implementation – A Review

Looking at the structure of NOM-035-STPS-2018, there is an assumption that there are areas of opportunity to improve the implementation of the standard. Thus, the purpose of this research is to identify through a review whether there are areas of opportunity that can improve the implementation of NOM-035. For the review, articles addressing the psychosocial risk factors evaluation were selected and analyzed. Four topics of discussion were identified: impact of psychosocial risk factors, policy and regulations, management systems, and evaluation of psychosocial risk factors. Subsequently, a synthesis was made, and it was found that there are 3 areas of opportunity to improve NOM-035-STPS-2018: it does not have a risk management system, its instruments do not present evidence of statistical validity, and the instruments do not take into account indicators of consequence.

Chapter 4: Productivity Evaluation in Function of Worker Psychosocial Factors

Workers are exposed to different factors which can be detrimental to their well-being, being the most known safety and hygiene factors. It is until a few years ago that the concepts of harmful factors for workers have been updated by adding now the psychosocial factors. Although there is literature on psychosocial factors and their effect on health, this work focused specifically on seeking the relationship between productivity and psychosocial factors to know how it impacts the organization. The investigation was applied in a case study for a doorknob locks manufacturing company in its final assembly area. Data collection was done by applying the questionnaire provided by NOM-035-STPS-2018 and the company's productivity databases for the subsequent analysis using statistical tools. The results were that, for the violence factor, its correlation with productivity was $R^2 = 0.8886$, indicating a strong correlation with which it is concluded that there is an influence on productivity.

Chapter 5: Evaluation of Working Conditions as a Factor of Well-Being of Workers in an Electronic Industry in Mexicali

The objective of this research was developed to evaluate the working conditions of workers in an electronic industry located in the city of Mexicali, analyzing a process in a work table where welding operations of electronic components are made and presented certain factors that generated discomfort to the operating personnel of this manufacturing area. The workers frequently visited the company doctor and to health institutions in Mexicali, due to symptoms of discomfort and pain in the head, neck, back, spine, arms, hands, and shoulders; in addition to discomfort in the eyes due to not having a position due to poor structure (work table and chair) and low light intensity, which caused fatigue and stress and discomfort with eyestrain, which caused discomfort in the mentioned parts of the body. In addition, certain employees in the production areas presented symptoms of respiratory diseases, caused by an environment contaminated by pollutants, essentially derived from sulfur (sulfides), as well as variations in temperature and relative humidity in the four seasons of the year.

Chapter 6: Determinants of Employee Motivation – A Comparison of Operational and Non-Operational Staff

The objective of this research was developed to evaluate the working conditions of workers in an electronic industry located in the city of Mexicali, analyzing a process in a work table where welding operations of electronic components are made and presented certain factors that generated discomfort to the operating personnel of this manufacturing area. The workers frequently visited the company doctor and to health institutions in Mexicali, due to symptoms of discomfort and pain in the head, neck, back, spine, arms, hands, and shoulders; in addition to discomfort in the eyes due to not having a position due to poor structure (work table and chair) and low light intensity, which caused fatigue and stress and discomfort with eyestrain, which caused discomfort in the mentioned parts of the body. In addition, certain employees in the production areas presented symptoms of respiratory diseases, caused by an environment contaminated by pollutants, essentially derived from sulfur (sulfides), as well as variations in temperature and relative humidity in the four seasons of the year.

Chapter 7: New Model to Promote Well-Being in Work Areas of the Aerospace Industry in Mexicali – Ergonomic Analysis

This investigation was made to evaluate the health and well-being of workers who made activities in the manufacturing processes of an aerospace industry installed in the city of Mexicali, based on the evidence presented in certain stages of a production line. The cost-benefit of applying ergonomic methods was analyzed, developing a descriptive model, which involved important aspects. Said aspects analyzed were (1) work methods, (2) training of employees in the operational area, (3) evaluation of times and movements of industrial operations, and (4) working conditions as the relationship of workers with supervisors and managers.

Chapter 8: Model for Determination of Musculoskeletal Disorder Cost/Benefit – Base for Strategy for Implementation of a Preventive DME Program for a Company

This study generates an analysis tool to estimate the incidence of Musculoskeletal Disorders (MSDs) and its economic costs, which also serves as a baseline to evaluate the possible benefits derived from the sustainable prevention program for this type of work-related disease, consider the need to know the current and future prevalence of MSDs, as well as understand if these data vary by economic sector, geographic location, and demographics.

Chapter 9: Comparison of Six Passive Exoskeletons for Upper Limbs Using the TOPSIS Method

This chapter presents the comparison of six exoskeletons that are used in occupational tasks through the TOPSIS method, to understand their advantages and disadvantages through databases of patents and commercial products. Experts in the design and / or use of exoskeletons evaluated the criteria: weight of the exoskeleton, load capacity, anthropometric adjustments, maintenance and installation by the user.

Chapter 10: Factorial Solution for Determination of Critical Success Factors (CSF) in Deployment of Six Sigma and Its Relation to Sustainability – Case Study: Baja California Aerospace Industry

Recently, the interest in being part of more competitive companies has increased, for this, organizations apply various strategies of continuous improvement that allow them to maintain high standards of competitiveness. In this sense, organizations make use of various techniques, tools, and methodologies that support the achievement of objectives. This research presents an approach towards the Six Sigma (SS) strategy, one of the main continuous improvement strategies used to achieve competitiveness. On the other hand, organizations currently seek that during the manufacture of their products, caring for the environment is naturally part of their objectives, seeking to achieve benefits with a sustainable impact. Therefore, this research seeks to define the CSF for implementation of SS through a factor analysis that allows identifying the relationship between SS and obtaining Sustainable Benefits (SB) through its implementation.

Chapter 11: Gradual Technology Development for Ethnic Groups – Ergonomics, Processes, and Education

This paper presents the application of the concept of gradual technology to improve and increase the productivity of a workshop for the manufacture of handcrafted furniture owned by a cooperative formed by members of the Guarijía ethnic group, located in San Bernardo, Alamos, Sonora. The production process of the rustic furniture called “stool” was systematized and equipment was designed taking into account basic ergonomic aspects. Production sub-processes of the workshop and equipment were improved, including machinery design, purchase of basic technology, adaptation of electric current, water, and air conditioning systems. The basic inputs for manufacturing the furniture, such as wood and cowhide, were studied to determine whether the production of the stool affected the environment. The operating personnel in charge of the cooperative were trained in the use of the equipment and in the visualization of the improved processes.

CONCLUSION

This book contributes to the ever-growing body of research on the well-being of workers and its relationship to the economic impacts that job-related health problems have on both organizations and the economy in general. By providing information on new and emerging methods to improve conditions in the workplace, this book benefits not only those who read it, but the workers affected by the measures that can be implemented from its review.

It also benefits the field of ergonomics, in particular, and the field of occupational health in general, by showcasing techniques that favor the development of person-centered workplaces.

It is the desire of the editors and authors, that this book favors a better approach to the safe design of workplaces and the consideration of the worker as the center of the work space.

Chapter 1
Eudaemonic Design to Achieve Well-Being at Work, Wherever That May Be

Jenna Mikus
https://orcid.org/0000-0002-2240-7659
Queensland University of Technology, Australia

Janice Rieger
Queensland University of Technology, Australia

Deanna Grant-Smith
https://orcid.org/0000-0001-5935-2690
Queensland University of Technology, Australia

ABSTRACT

The concept of eudaemonia originates from neo-Aristotelian philosophy and is associated with human flourishing. Self-determination theory, a means to attain eudaemonia, is examined here as a foundational approach to drive Eudaemonic Design--a novel design strategy that aims to achieve holistic physical, mental, and social health, or eudaemonic well-being. This chapter advances Eudaemonic Design as an architectural and organizational approach to create healthful work environments that support employee and business flourishing. The authors argue that the importance of adopting Eudaemonic Design has grown in need and complexity as work is (re)shaped by the constraints and opportunities presented by the pandemic. By contrasting dominant pre-COVID-19 Work from Office expectations against the post-COVID-19 Work from Anywhere model, this chapter explores the application of Eudaemonic Design to deliver holistic workplace well-being, rather than single variable health and wellness alone, now and into the post-COVID-19 future of work.

DOI: 10.4018/978-1-7998-7396-9.ch001

INTRODUCTION

In early 2020, design for health became a global priority as the world encountered the COVID-19 pandemic. This reprioritization prompted significant shifts in how and where people live and work (Boland et al., 2020; Thompson, 2020), which in turn highlighted the need to consider the physical, mental, and social dimensions of the places people work, rest, and play (WHO, 2020). This change also precipitated a shift in the range of locations considered legitimate workplaces. Indeed, wherever people worked became their place of work, including their homes. Conversations quickly transitioned from encouraging acceptable levels of health support in homes (Walsh, 2019) and offices (Caramela, 2018; Daum, 2017) to creating environments that not only sought to limit the spread of the disease (CDC, 2020) but also were attentive to meeting physical, mental, and social health needs (Khazan, 2020; Pirschel, 2020; Shade, 2020; Spangler & McLeod, 2020; Weed, 2020). As more homes and non-office environments became workplaces, what was originally envisioned as a temporary strategy quickly morphed into a new reality requiring a sustainable long-term plan. Attention logically shifted toward ensuring that these new places of work were health-protective (Work in Mind, 2020) and health-promoting (Taysom, 2021). This chapter explores the importance of workplace wellness in a Post-COVID-19 world and the contribution of the built environment in promoting wellness at work in the context of these changes.

The challenges and opportunities presented by the global COVID-19 pandemic and its impact on the spatial and temporal dimensions of work and working provide the chance to fundamentally shape understandings of achieving well-being at work. Whether workers find themselves continuing to work from home, returning to work from their Pre-COVID-19 office, or working from a "near home" office, public, or shared coworking place (Ashworth & Martinuzzi, 2020), workplace wellness remains an important consideration for employers. However, despite this recognized significance and push for supporting policy (Timm et al., 2018), there have been few concrete suggestions on how to achieve these aims. A proactive approach to designing for an optimal balance of the World Health Organization's three aspects of health (physical, mental, and social health) (WHO, 2020) is needed—one that puts people first and balances their needs for health and happiness via enhanced well-being. By focusing on designing for the well-being of workers, their workspaces, and their workplaces and the intersection of human, technical, and socio-technical factors, Eudaemonic Design is proposed as a design solution to enhance physical and digital work environments and improve wellness of workers and the organizations in which they work.

This chapter commences by discussing the impact of the built environment on wellness and well-being before discussing the origins of Eudaemonic Design, its differences and similarities to existing approaches for designing for workplace wellness, and its potential for realizing autonomy, competence, and relatedness-driven outcomes derived from Self-Determination Theory (SDT). The potential application of Eudaemonic Design for achieving well-being at work across a wide variety of workplaces is also discussed. The chapter concludes with a discussion of areas for future research, including the potential role of technology in delivering Eudaemonic Design.

THE IMPACT OF THE BUILT ENVIRONMENT ON HEALTH AND WELLNESS

Globally it has been estimated that 98% of people spend 90% of their lifetimes inside buildings (Allen & Macomber, 2020a; Roberts, 2016). Before the COVID-19 pandemic, the amount of time spent indoors was already increasing (Klepeis et al., 2001), and it is expected to have increased further as physical and social distancing practices restricted many to their homes. Considering these trajectories and the impact of COVID-19 in particular, it is apparent that buildings can either help or hinder well-being by "[making] you sick or [keeping] you well" (Allen, 2020, p. 1). If buildings are designed to support health and well-being, they can prevent sickness and support occupants to be healthier and happier.

The human body is a product of its environment. While this chapter does not explore the granular aspects of exposomes (Dai et al., 2017), it recognizes the significant impact built environments have on human health and wellness (Prüss-Üstün & Corvalán, 2006). In recent years, there has been a heightened interest in designing 'healthy' buildings and developing associated standards and certifications to define and regulate the creation of such structures (CfAD, 2021; IWBI, 2021). Because workers spend approximately 25-40% of their lifetimes at work (Campbell, 2017; Vaughn, 2018), there has been an associated emphasis on improving the physical, mental, and social conditions of work environments to harness the power of health-focused design, resulting in healthier bodies and thus less absenteeism, minimized risk of depression and anxiety, enhanced productivity, and heightened morale (BCO, 2018; Burton, 2010; Hatcher, 2018; UKGBC, 2017; WorldGBC, 2016). This improves worker lives and business profitability and performance.

Indeed, it has been noted the built environment matters for both the "health and wealth" of organizations (Allen & Macomber, 2020a, p. 42). Considering that the Wellness Real Estate market was valued at $134 billion in 2017 and is anticipated to reach $197 billion by 2022 (GWI, 2020), there is a tremendous business financial opportunity in improving the quality of the built environment as a means to design for wellness. By doing so, it is possible to significantly impact company recruitment and retention—by enhancing company brand appeal (e.g., depth and breadth of amenities) to recruit new quality applicants (Arruda, 2018; Petersen, 2020) and by designing-in elements of mental health support (e.g., more flexible space, better safety procedures) to benefit current employees (Lass, 2018; Orsini & Rodrigues, 2020), respectively.

Achieving Workplace Wellness Through Health-based Architectural Design

Workplace wellness has been a fundamental consideration for businesses since the *Seoul Declaration on Safety and Health at Work* (ILO, 2008) and the World Health Organization's *Healthy Workplace Framework and Model* (Burton, 2010). The latter document positioned the argument for a global audience, augmenting awareness on the need for better approaches to achieving healthy workplaces and positioning workplace health and wellness as an ethical, operational, and legal obligation (Burton, 2010; WHO, 2020). Despite the pioneering work of the Wellness Council of America and others in advocating for employee empowerment in workspaces (Knight & Haslam, 2010), initial adoption of workplace wellness was slow as organizations instead chose the formerly prevalent approaches of rapid turnover, reallocations, and reductions in force to maintain fresh, seemingly motivated workers (T. Allen, 2018; Society for Human Resource Management (SHRM), 2020). However, in more recent years, organizations have begun to recognize the power of proactive design to infuse energy into existing workforces. Deliberately enhancing the work-related built environment was found to be a successful mechanism of influencing and improving the health of workers via their workspaces and workplaces to promote symbiotic health, while having the added benefit of potentially maintaining the workforce.

In 2014, to encourage the adoption of healthy building work, the World Green Building Council (WorldGBC) assembled a group of 60 experts from 20 countries to discuss the relationship between health and buildings. Together, they documented how a combination of quality air, temperature, humidity, daylight, views, sound, and more could "play a crucial role in creating a healthy, productive workplace" (Alker, 2014, p. 2). The WorldGBC definitively linked health-based design to business finance by approximating that typical real estate costs break down into three parts: energy costs (1%), rental costs (9%), and staff costs (90%). The dominance of staff costs within this model underscores that "a healthy, happy workforce is a vital component of a productive, successful business in the long-term" (WorldGBC, 2016, p. 8). This cost distribution was confirmed by Jones Lang LaSalle (JLL, 2016) through global dissemination of their 3:30:300 rule, which demonstrated an average order of magnitude across company costs associated with utilities, rent, and payroll, respectively, per square foot annually. Just as the WorldGBC report had done, JLL's work highlighted the financial value to organizations in positively impacting the payroll metric by proactively designing for people rather than focusing efforts on saving negligible amounts of money on "green building"-related efforts affecting utility spend-related energy costs or on space allocation efforts impacting rental costs.

Designing for human health via built environment health has become a driving business, especially over the past decade; but that evolution has taken time. Countless books have been written on the subject (Allen & Macomber, 2020a; Channon, 2019; De Botton, 2007; Goldhagen, 2017) and multiple interest groups and professional certifications formulated around it. This collective body of research stemmed from interest initially expressed by architects, public health practitioners, clinicians, and engineers who saw first-hand how published building standards (e.g., American Society of Heating, Refrigerating and Air, Conditioning Engineers) were not adequately supporting human health and wellness. Wellness-focused design accreditation bodies that focus on designing the built environment for human health and wellness, such as the WELL Building Standard (IWBI, 2021) and Fitwel (CfAD, 2019), have raised awareness, promulgated knowledge, and provided guidelines for effective health-driven design.

EUDAEMONIC DESIGN FOR OPTIMAL WELLNESS AND WELL-BEING AT WORK

Despite the upwards trajectory health-based design experienced prior to the pandemic, COVID-19 has transformed the meaning of the term. It is no longer just about designing for protection from the elements. It is now about preventing active pandemic spread, while also "nudging" better health practices (Thaler, 2008). Eudaemonic Design's positive take on designing for optimal well-being while designing out disease may serve as a mechanism to accomplish all goals. By pursuing health-based design more as a means towards flourishing occupant (employee) and organizational (business) health and by centering those concepts around SDT's tenets and values, rather than a defensive means of protection, prevention, and survival, it is possible to accomplish all goals.

Eudaemonic well-being or flourishing human health and wellness has roots in the neo-Aristotelian concept of eudaemonia (i.e., literally combining ideas of *eu*, good or healthy, and *daimon*, true self), which encourages people to be the best versions of themselves. In recent years, a variety of research has explored designing for eudaemonia-related ideals, including flow (Csikszentmihalyi, 2008, 2014), happiness (Channon, 2019; de Botton, 2007; Layard, 2005; Medina, 2019; Stevens et al., 2014), and thriving (Buettner, 2011). However, these explorations have primarily emphasized a subjective well-being focus rather than a comprehensive objective and subjective health approach, such as is offered by eudaemonic well-being (i.e., the eudaemonia-derived concept of well-being that balances optimal physical, mental, and social health, enabling people to be their best selves).

For years, psychologists have built practices on positive psychology and the philosophy of eudaemonic thought to prompt meaningful change for patients (Waterman, 2013). Considering the impact of buildings on occupant health, a similar onus could and arguably should fall on the curators, constructors, and controllers of the built environments (Jones et al., 2019) and on the businesses whose employees occupy those spaces and whose health they should protect (Allen & Macomber, 2020a). It is imperative that Eudaemonic Design be included in architectural design and organizational management plans to manage risk, meet needs, and most importantly prompt flourishing well-being in the workplace.

Applying Self-Determination Theory to Achieve Eudaemonia

Optimal health and wellness in the form of eudaemonia occurs when humans are self-determined to thrive and experience well-being. SDT explores this idea and defines what is needed to prompt intrinsic, or inwardly driven, motivation to enhance health. According to Ryan and Deci (2000), the theory "aims to specify factors that nurture the innate human potentials entailed in growth, integration, and well-being, and to explore the processes and conditions that foster the healthy development and effective functioning of individuals, groups, and communities" (Ryan & Deci, 2000, p. 7).

Figure 1. A Model for Eudaemonic Design
Source: Adapted from (Ryan et al., 2008)

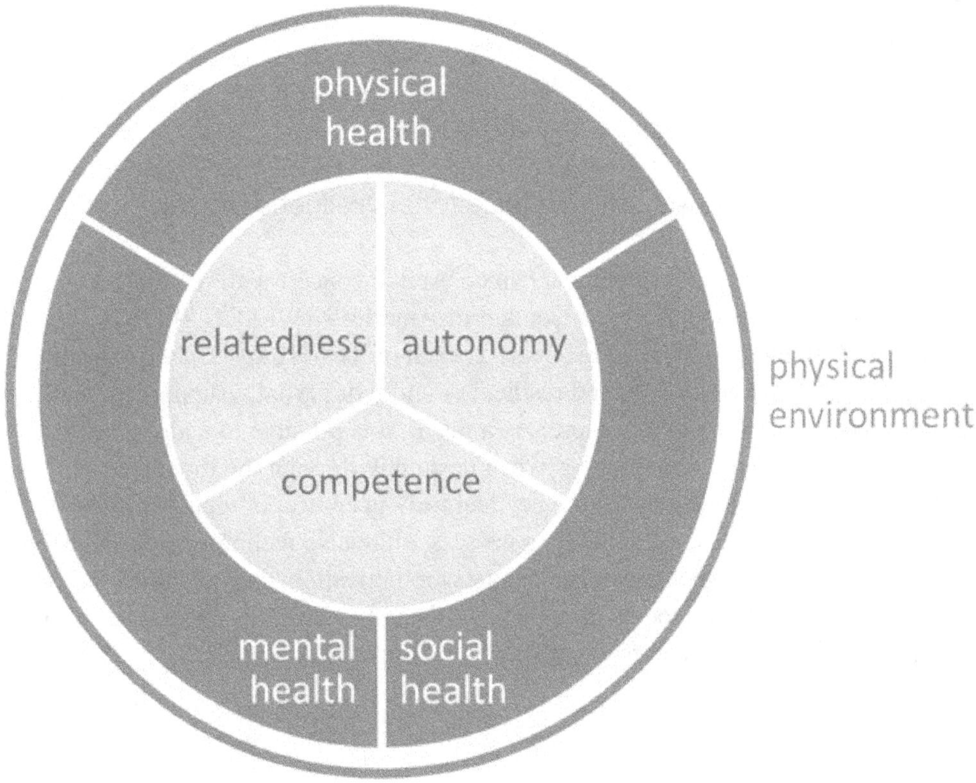

SDT is built on three tenets or needs that must be met for someone to feel engaged, supported, and intrinsically motivated: autonomy (having a feeling of control in life); competence (being able to do enjoyable activities); and relatedness (enjoying good social relations for a sense of belonging) (Deci & Ryan, 2008). This theory can therefore be used to understand people's needs and to design physical environments for those requirements. Therefore, as depicted in Figure 1, SDT-designed environments can prompt experiences of flourishing eudaemonic well-being and consequently be used as a means to design for optimal workplace health.

Eudaemonic Design is by its nature inclusive. It allows a variety of stakeholders to implement ideas supportive of autonomy, competence, and relatedness tactically (bottom-up) or strategically (top-down) (Waterman, 2013). This method of organizational ownership has the potential to improve the likelihood of sustainable success. By focusing on Eudaemonic Design, rather than prescriptive health-based design methods, work environments become less about disjointed perspectives on people, places, and technology and more about the resulting collaborative experience. This means supporting workers to feel, function, and connect with their work, workspaces, workplaces, and colleagues both in-person and remotely. Eudaemonic Design provides an underlying logic or 'why' to environmental design by emphasizing the value in human-centric design, empowering all individuals, and centralizing company purpose. In essence, designing for the individuals via their environments benefits the overarching group, enabling an organization to also be the best version of itself.

Integrating Workplace Wellness Models and Eudaemonic Design

Considering Eudaemonic Design's foundation in SDT, it benefits from the universality of the theory's application (Chen et al., 2015) and can complement and enhance existing models striving for workplace wellness from organizational and architectural wellness perspectives.

A Eudaemonic Comparison with an Organizational Wellness Model

An organizational wellness model example that can be used in concert with the three tenets of SDT to achieve Eudaemonic Design is the Wellness Council of America's (WELCOA) (2021) seven areas of successful workplace wellness. As shown in Figure 2, each of the WELCOA areas—health, meaning, safety, connection, achievement, growth, and resiliency—fully or partially supports at least one of the SDT tenets, with most supporting two or more. As a result, it is possible to address each of the seven areas of organizational wellness best practices when designing through the three tenets. For example, if someone works in an environment in which they feel truly in control of their workload and environment, does something they love using skills they possess while also feeling appropriately challenged, and experiences support and connection with colleagues for motivation, they will likely meet the criteria of organizational wellness-related models like WELCOA's and feel healthy, purpose-driven, safe, connected, accomplished, challenged, and resilient.

Figure 2. The relationship between Self-Determination Theory (SDT) and Wellness Council of America's (WELCOA) Elements of Wellness

A Eudaemonic Comparison with an Architectural Wellness Model

A built environment model that can also be used symbiotically with the three tenets is Harvard's 9 Foundations of a Healthy Building, which include air quality, thermal health, moisture, dust and pests, safety and security, water quality, noise, lighting and views, and ventilation (Allen et al., 2017). As shown in Figure 3, each one of these nine foundations corresponds to at least one of the SDT tenets. This means that, when employing Eudaemonic Design, SDT's three tenets will be satisfied, and all nine foundations will likely be met. In turn, when the 9 Foundations' aspects are considered in a design, those will support SDT and thereby Eudaemonic Design. Therefore, it is possible to address each of the 9 Foundations of a Healthy Building when designing for the three tenets, and experience aspects of Eudaemonic Design if done vice versa.

For the built environment comparative example, those foundations or areas of architectural wellness that align with all three tenets are those that allow for feelings of control, being more functional, and feeling connected. Four such examples include air quality, thermal health, noise, and lighting and views, which are enhanced when built on architectural science best practices mixed with SDT's needs. If these criteria are met, it is likely occupants will be happier, healthier, more productive, and more connected. Research shows that if air quality maintains humidity levels between 30% and 60%, then odor issues are less likely, thus enabling workers to avoid unnecessary distraction (Harvard T. H. Chan, 2021). Optimal thermal health occurs when temperatures are in the low 70s Fahrenheit with humidity levels between 20% and 60% (Rosone, 2019), but maintaining 71.6 degrees Fahrenheit (22 degrees Celsius) indoors results in 6-9% productivity increases (Wyon, 2004). When considering noise, open-plan offices allow for better interaction and socialization, however enclosed private spaces result in better air quality, noise, privacy, control, and therefore less stress (Kim & de Dear, 2013). For lighting and views, access to natural daylighting increases better sleep quality for workers and results in approximately 10% fewer sick days taken (Boubekri et al., 2014), and the incorporation of plants or elements of nature (i.e., to encourage biophilia or human's innate connection with nature) results in increased productivity of approximately 15% (Nieuwenhuis et al., 2014). Therefore, there is a logical correspondence between architectural design and Eudaemonic Design.

Figure 3. The relationship between Self-Determination Theory (SDT) and Harvard University's 9 Foundations of a Healthy Building

Eudaemonic Design is supportive of existing organizational and architectural wellness models. As described in the model examples above, it offers a logical and inclusive alternative to the use of formal standards while upholding the core needs of SDT, thus prompting workers, managers, and executives to feel autonomous, competent, and related.

Designing for Workers, Workspaces, and Workplaces

It is possible to design eudaemonia into an organization through physical and digital design by focusing on the interconnected levels of the worker, the workspace, and the workplace. Eudaemonic Design can be applied outside the standard office environment because it is attentive to these three levels of design need. As all organizations must consider design with respect to workers, their immediate workspaces (e.g., desks, cubicles, offices), and their workplaces (e.g., home, office, public), a robust yet simplified and flexible alternative that targets all three would likely prove useful. Figure 4 visualizes the application of eudaemonia in the workplace by incorporating Eudaemonic Design concepts from the inside out and outside in.

Figure 4. Eudaemonic Design for Well-being at Work

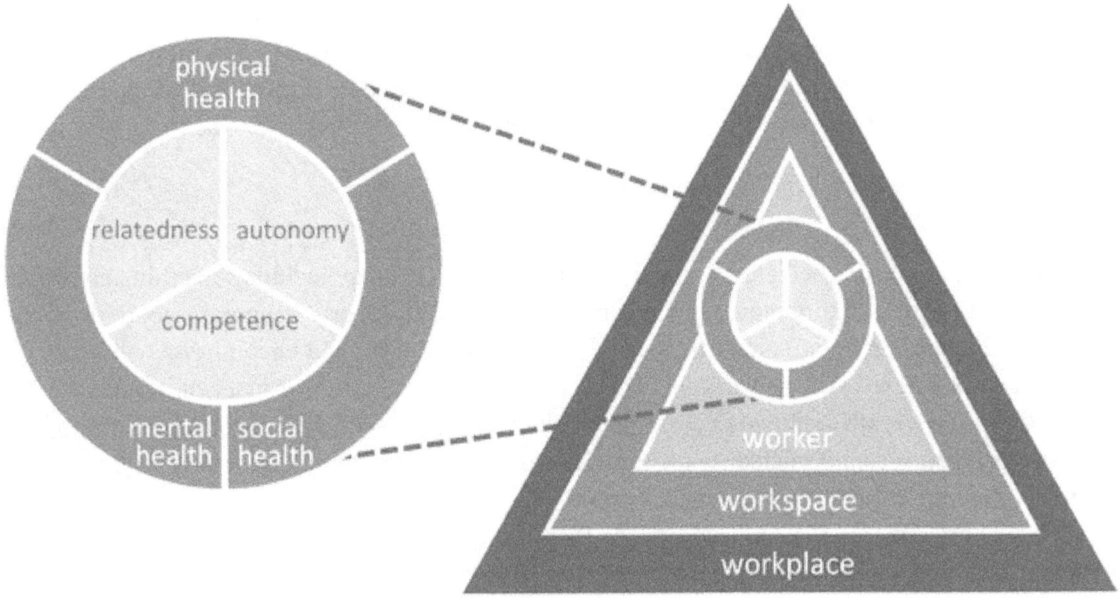

The Eudaemonic Design for Well-being at Work model depicted in Figure 4 is flexible and widely applicable. Its sensitivity to gender, race, and culture among other differences allows application to a variety of workers, workspaces, and workplaces. Psychological research describes that when autonomy, competence, and relatedness are designed for, they contribute to individual, team, and organizational human flourishing (Ryan & Deci, 2017). Further, when all three SDT tenets are addressed on all organizational levels simultaneously, a multiplier effect occurs, encouraging people to be intrinsically motivated to choose to act, to act effectively, and to relate to others while doing so.

The Workplace

The workplace is the comprehensive "office" environment, consisting of individual cubicles or a conglomeration of workspaces or desks in an area of a building, throughout an entire building, or spanning a campus. The workplace has traditionally been narrowly defined to focus on the Work from Office model and associated place of work, but the definition has now been extended to include any areas where workers carry out their day-to-day work. This change has been unprecedented, especially considering having transitioned from a nearly exclusive Work from Office model Pre-COVID-19, when the vast majority (90%) of workers went to a physical office every day (GWI, 2018).

Despite ongoing workplace changes, Eudaemonic Design can be applied to achieve autonomy, competence, and relatedness in every workplace. Some examples of how to enact this include: encouraging autonomy with targeted employee engagement (e.g., occupant surveys) to ensure the organization and workplace are providing workers with what they want and need (Penny, 2020) and inclusive signage for easier, more logical wayfinding for intergenerational and neurodiverse workforces (Barton, 2019); facilitating competence with flexible work schedules based on worker work style, hour, activity, and location preferences and work location options (e.g., providing quiet "library zones" for noise sensitive workers to reduce stress and avoid heightened blood pressure) (Brown, 2020); and providing a variety of social engagement options in "social hubs" to engage workers of varying abilities, engagement styles, and play preferences and prompt relatedness (Deloitte, 2021; Smith, 2020). By providing environmental and organizational support from the outside-in, workplaces facilitate the satisfaction of the SDT tenets. This enables and encourages workers to function as their best selves physically, mentally, and socially.

The Workspace

Workspaces refer to the immediate work areas of employees. This may include something as simple as a desk, outfitted with a laptop, mouse, and chair; a cubicle or office; or a temporary hot desk or phone room. The workspace may no longer be located in an office and instead encompasses physical space wherever a worker happens to be working, whether in an office, at home, or in a near home location.

Just as there are ways to facilitate Eudaemonic Design for workplaces, there are methods of supporting autonomy, competence, and relatedness within the workspace: facilitating autonomy with funding for flexible, ergonomic furniture arrangement options (Knight & Haslam, 2010) and optional "decluttering parties" to organize workspaces and limit excess cortisol production (Lucchesi, 2019); encouraging competence with workspace personalization policies (Byron & Laurence, 2015), personal décor preferences (Kondō & Sonenshein, 2020), and access to natural daylight, fresh air, optimal thermal comfort (Rosone, 2019), and nature via biophilia (Beatley, 2018; Tabb, 2021) to enhance mood and reduce anxiety (Brown, 2020; IWBI, 2021); and providing optional socialization opportunities, both physically and digitally (e.g., enabling Zoom "happy hours"), to accommodate relatedness preferences (Work in Mind, 2021a). As with workplace design, workspace design provides outside-in support for each worker. The difference is that workspaces offer this support on a more granular scale, oftentimes resulting in impact the worker can feel viscerally, given the frequency of and tangible contact with the workspaces they inhabit. By having a eudaemonic workspace, workers can exercise choice—maintaining flexibility in when, where, and how they work and socializing on their preferred terms.

The Worker

Workers are the employees who perform paid or unpaid work on the behalf of an employer, business, or organization. These may be part-time or full-time employees, contractors, or subcontractors. While workers benefit from intentional Eudaemonic Design done for the workplace and workspace, there are ways it can focus on the worker themselves and strengthen flourishing-focused design overall. Workers are central to the Eudaemonic Design philosophy; thus, all design decisions must focus on and support on their needs. Some examples include: ensuring managers support intrinsic, autonomous motivation (e.g., Swiss insurance worker study) (Güntert, 2014) rather than extrinsic, controlled provocation (Orsini & Rodrigues, 2020); empowering workers through competence-supportive training opportunities and validating feedback loops (Reis et al., 2000), not micromanaging or providing burnout-precipitating pressure (Moss, 2019, 2021); and considering biophilic (i.e., nature-referencing) and salutogenic (i.e., health-supporting and stress-suppressing) elements in interior architectural design to enable workers to feel more connected with the world, less overwhelmed, and more motivated to be good-natured and caring (Ryan et al., 2010) with greater feelings of sustainability and beneficence (Martela & Riekki, 2018). This worker-centered approach has the potential to result in healthier, happier workers who are likely to care about their work, workspace, and workplace and have the intrinsic motivation to maintain and improve conditions to facilitate eudaemonia.

THE IMPACT OF COVID-19 ON (RE)SHAPING THE PLACES AND SPACES OF WORK

The effects of COVID-19 can be defined as a set of overlapping eras shaped by risk, pandemic prevalence, time period, and geographical location (refer Figure 5). The COVID-19 era notionally commenced in early 2020, when COVID-19 was recognized as a global pandemic. At this time, utilizing healthy buildings as a means to design for human and business health was already on an upswing. However, as human health became the core priority, health-based design transitioned from being a luxury to becoming an organizational priority (Kehrt, 2020).

Figure 5. The evolution of the COVID-19 eras, progressing from Pre-COVID-19 era through COVID-19 and culminating in the present-future Post-COVID-19 era

Although COVID-19 is still a very real problem as of February 2021, vaccine introduction has prompted a deflection point from which many countries are transitioning from COVID-19 to Post-COVID-19 activities, whether that involves minimal physical distancing measures alone (e.g., Australia) or extreme physical distancing measures with mandatory Personal Protective Equipment (PPE) usage (e.g., United States). Therefore, COVID-19 is likely to extend past February 2021 for many countries, just as Post-COVID-19 is likely to be underway in other countries, with post-vaccine sub-eras occurring as vaccines become available. Regardless, it appears that hybrid work practices will be the preference going forward (Gensler Research Institute, 2021; McLaurin & Barber, 2020; (PwC), 2021; Work in Mind, 2021a).

The Evolution of the COVID-19 Workplace

COVID-19 has reshaped where and how people work. As of late February 2021, COVID-19 has caused over 2.5 million deaths worldwide and continues as a global pandemic with serious public health consequences (WHO, 2021). The world now falls into two evolving groups—those still in an active COVID-19 era and those moving toward the Post-COVID-19 era. Post-COVID-19 countries are considered those with minimal risk of contagion and therefore no longer requiring the mandatory PPE use or large-scale lockdowns. Some of these will include vaccinated countries as those increase in prevalence while others will result from effective lockdown measures. It is likely that this era will overlap with COVID-19 eras of other countries and will be significantly shaped by the widespread uptake of global vaccination programs underway. However, the transitions between eras and the reintroduction of mitigation measures will likely continue to change for some time. Thus, it is important to understand how the workplace evolved from Pre-COVID-19 to the current ongoing COVID-19 and Post-COVID-19 eras to learn from our history to curate a better future.

Pre-COVID-19 to Early COVID-19 Era

When COVID-19 was declared an international pandemic in early 2020, an epic experiment began. To reduce risk of exposure, companies around the globe shuttered offices and transitioned operations to be based at home. As the months elapsed and people became more comfortable in their home environments, many were hesitant to return to office buildings for work. Since then, employees continue to receive notice of Human Resources-related policies allowing and even advocating for working from home temporarily (e.g., Google (Liu, 2020)), part-time going forward (e.g., Salesforce (Rizzi, 2021)), and indefinitely (e.g., United States (US)-based Twitter and Facebook (Liu, 2020), Australia-based Atlassian (Novet, 2020), and most recently US-based Spotify (Gourarie, 2021)).

Prior to COVID-19, workspaces varied from being makeshift (if at home) (Detwiler, 2020) or overly sterile (if in an office) (Mudditt, 2020), both oftentimes ineffective or at least sub-optimal. Many company cultures were considered "toxic", and remote working was the exception (~10% of the workforce) and oftentimes an unacceptable option due to a pervasive lack of trust (Kehrt, 2020). However, once COVID-19 hit, the conversation shifted almost overnight from Pre-COVID-19 talks of maintaining barely adequate levels of health support in homes and offices to COVID-19 discussions focused on proactively curating optimal health-supportive environments for personal and professional use, for the unforeseen future and perhaps forever as a new way of working.

COVID-19 Era

In March 2020, a Harvard Business School report described how COVID-19 was already impacting the future of business only one month into the pandemic (Gerdman, 2020). Allen (a public health practitioner, researcher, and academic) and Macomber (a real estate finance practitioner, researcher, and academic) indicated that people and buildings would need to become significantly healthier in the future—setting higher standards to actively monitor and attain. Just three months after their prediction, a shift occurred emphasizing the interest of tenants and investors in "healthy buildings" for economic organizational survival (Allen & Macomber, 2020b). Websites such as Glassdoor began reporting on office conditions, which factored into workers' decisions relating to their work in general, where they did it (i.e., at home, in an office, or elsewhere), and if they kept or left their jobs.

Looking back on 2020, according to the UK-based Chartered Institute of Personnel and Development's (CIPD) 2020 report, more organizations (44%) were executing a strategic approach to employee well-being, being more proactive (than reactive) in their well-being strategies than those from 2019 and "taking a holistic approach to supporting people's health and well-being, with mental health the most common priority" (CIPD, 2020, p. 7). That is certainly a step in the right direction. In December 2020, WIRED Magazine published an article entitled "The 'Healthy Building' Surge Will Outlast the Pandemic", and indeed it has (Kehrt, 2020). Healthy buildings for workplace wellness are no longer a trend. They are becoming a business strategy and general best practice.

Post-COVID-19 Era

At the time of this book chapter, knowledge about workplace wellness is becoming more widespread, recognized, and respected each day, and the interest in understanding, designing, and learning new ways to facilitate healthy buildings is increasing. Businesses are no longer relying on the 3:30:300 rule to rationalize design for worker health and productivity. They are now seeking simple, smart ways to design for disease-free health-promoting environments that enable employees to feel protected yet autonomous, supported yet competent, and physically distanced yet connected.

The post-pandemic future provides humanity with an opportunity to make impactful changes for people and society (Kehrt, 2020). There has already been talk about how the pandemic offers opportunities to rethink wrongs of the past and rewrite the future (IFTF, 2020). A theory-based, industry-supported approach that is founded on positive psychology, empowerment, and community meets this need while also addressing the desired autonomy, competence, and relatedness tenets. Eudaemonic Design offers this with pragmatic application to intrinsically motivate and empower workers so they can be their best selves while "at work"—be it when working in the office, at home, or elsewhere.

Anticipated Post-COVID-19 Global Trends

Global workplace studies were conducted by Gartner, JLL, and Gensler between mid-2020 and early 2021, identifying anticipated future trends globally but focusing on Australia, the US, and the UK in particular. Each varied in some ways, but there were key themes across all three sets of findings. Gartner's 2020 report (Baker, 2020) highlighted what company leaders were willing to allow in a Post-COVID-19 workplace. This included terms around remote work (82% to permit remote work part of the time and 47% all of the time) and flexibility (40% to support flex hours and days). A follow-up report in 2021 (Baker, 2021) increased these figures to 90% and 65%, respectively, and included the addition of needs-based benefits for 44%. JLL's 2020 report (Murray, 2020; Pradere, 2020) highlighted needs paralleling Eudaemonic Design objectives: flexible working locations and hours (autonomy); improved work-life balance and allowances for work support (competence); and enriched human connection (relatedness). Most people wished to have an opportunity to come to an office, but half wanted to work both in an office and remotely. Locations were said to vary by purpose with each place having its advantages for collaboration, focus, and socializing. Gensler's 2021 reports (Cohen et al., 2021; Gensler, 2021) focused on experience and the desire to reconnect. For workplaces, they emphasized the need for work and place "uncoupling"; a culturally enticing work experience; enhanced "choice, autonomy, health, and well-being"; and flexibility and adaptability (Gensler, 2021, p. 3).

Of the findings, the most compelling and consistent findings related to accommodating hybrid work (McLaurin & Barber, 2020; PwC, 2021); providing choice through flexibility (Parker et al., 2020); curating workplaces with cultural experiences and connections (Davis, 2020); and strengthening meaning and purpose (Gershon, 2017; Leinonen, 2020). Workers expressed a wish to prioritize work-life balance, even if it meant sacrificing approximately 10% salary (Murray, 2020). But companies now know that if they want to be competitive and retain their best employees, they should be proactive in addressing these wishes so employees do not have to make concessions. Good workplaces make for good workers and thus good business.

DESIGNING FOR POST-COVID-19 WELL-BEING AT WORK

There are a variety of Post-COVID-19 workplace models that are anticipated to be part of the future. These include Working from Home (WfH), Working from Near Home (WfNH), Working from Office (WfO), and the all-encompassing Working from Anywhere (WfA) model. Each has evolved as a result of the pandemic and each has its own Eudaemonic Design considerations and unique challenges and opportunities.

Eudaemonic Design Considerations for Working from Home

Working from Home (WfH) is a spatial model of work in which the worker engages in work from their home. It is a type of remote work that originated over the past 10-20 years with the proliferation of high-speed internet and Wi-Fi bandwidth, enabling connection while at home. While up until COVID-19, this was a limited way of work (accounting for between 10% and 20% of the workforce), it has become the "new normal" in the COVID-19 world.

In a US-based FlexJobs survey of 4000 people working remotely during the pandemic, 95% said productivity has been at the same level or greater than that of the past due to fewer interruptions, more focused time, quieter work environments, more comfortable workplaces, and lack of office politics (Pelta, 2020). Two-thirds of this group would like to become full-time remote employees while one-third would prefer a hybrid option. One reason WfH became feasible was because of companies such as Zoom Video Communications, which provides the now well-known remote videoconferencing software that grew thirtyfold in the first half of 2020 (Iqbal, 2020). While collaboration-promoting software like Zoom provided the flexibility appreciated by many early in the COVID-19 era, allowing endless opportunities to address autonomy, competence, and relatedness needs (Pelta, 2020), others experienced negative repercussions such as lack of work-life balance (Boland et al., 2020) and longer hours (Work in Mind, 2021c), an ongoing "cycle of [physical, cognitive, and emotional] fatigue" (Work in Mind, 2021b) or inability to "disconnect" (AP, 2020), as well as "Zoom fatigue" (Franklin, 2021).

There is a tremendous opportunity in learning how to design for WfH effectively. Studies show that most people have enjoyed the flexibility and safety on offer when working from their homes (Baker, 2020; Gensler, 2021; Pradere, 2020); and because workers are assumed to have control over their home environment, it seems possible that they could personalize a workspace to their optimal work specifications without having to compromise with colleagues. Unfortunately, they may not be able to do this easily due to family obligations or financial issues.

Eudaemonic Design can play an important role when incorporated across WfH workplaces, workspaces, and workers. When considering and planning WfH support options, companies should address assumptions early to identify what is needed for each worker to work best when at home. Only then can support mechanisms be put in place, such as providing home care monetary support, establishing flexible working hour policies, providing guidelines of how to set up optimal working conditions, supplementing ergonomic furniture purchases, furnishing technology to ensure seamless co-worker interaction, and conducting training to ensure trust-based collaboration. Workers can augment these workplace initiatives by designating work hours and sticking to them, establishing a family code of conduct when working-from-home, and prioritizing work-life balance. By combining these Eudaemonic Design workplace, workspace, and worker strategies, it is possible to make WfH work.

Eudaemonic Design Considerations for Working from Near Home

Working from Near Home (WfNH) is a spatial model in which the worker engages in work in a location within geographical proximity to where the worker lives, thereby reducing commute time. Options include company satellite offices; public options such as a library, park, or café; or coworking spaces. This model has become popularized over the past five to ten years but only recently been named (Ashworth & Martinuzzi, 2020). Pre-COVID-19 work done from this model commonly involved isolated tactical work, such as finishing a report or conducting a client meeting, rather than entire days of work. The exception was coworking spaces (e.g., WeWork), which people used similar to everyday offices.

While many home workers wish to continue to do remote work, others have expressed interest in returning to a place of work with their colleagues for socialization purposes without necessarily returning to the office of old, per se.

...People don't really want to get back to the office. They want to get out of their apartments, their houses, their parents' houses. They want their children back in school, and also out of the house. They want to see people's faces again, and have conversations with people who are closer than six feet from them. But that doesn't mean that they actually want to be back in the office — at least not the way the office was before. (Petersen, 2020, p. 1)

The WfNH model offers a "happy medium" alternative for people undecided between whether they wish to work from home or from the office. It provides an opportunity to do work the worker wants, when and how they want; to experience location flexibility enabling the worker to choose a place that facilitates activity-based working and background noise and lighting levels of choice; and to socialize with non-work-colleagues if desired.

While WfNH is a good option for working, it does not provide much choice for personalization options that can be maintained. Instead, WfNH locations offer temporary solutions which should be considered when choosing this as a work environment. If someone wishes a change of condition, they may have to choose a new location or even venue, requiring a potentially taxing relocation of workspace hardware and interrupting train of thought. Therefore, when selecting a WfNH location, workers should be cognizant to sit in a position where they will not experience excess noise, smell, glare, or temperature fluctuation and where they anticipate feeling comfortable, at least for the day.

It is difficult to truly personalize WfNH options unless a worker discovers an already curated environment that meets their needs. While this scenario is possible in coworking locations that design for wellness (Bolt, 2019), it is not always an available option, based on cost or location. As an alternative, workers can formulate a "work kit" to customize workspaces. Kits often include ergonomic set-ups such as a laptop shelf for better posture, a comfortable mouse for ergonomic support, and noise-cancelling headphones for noise pollution protection. These kits can be easily constructed and carried, and commonly result in a more work-conducive environment.

A WfNH model works especially well if workers allocate appropriate activities agreeable with the venue. Such activities may include socializing or creating new material—actions that are best suited to times when workers are inspired while comfortable, motivated but not stressed, and connected but not distracted. If workers can strike this balance and deliberatively align work activities suitable to work locations, WfNH options could prove effective for them and for downsizing companies who no longer have the office footprint to accommodate employee needs.

Eudaemonic Design Considerations for the New Working from Office

The new Working from Office (WfO) model is likely to be different in size, shape, and design than that of the past. While a majority of workers spent time in offices Pre-COVID-19, few organizations are expected to grow their office or portfolio footprint Post-COVID-19 (Smith, 2021) and many are already downsizing (Griffiths & Clarence-Smith, 2021). As organizations sacrifice square footage quantity, they are transitioning to focus on quality design solutions instead. Organizations now have the opportunity to entice employees by "[cultivating] an aesthetic and culturally relevant environment that enables people to feel comfortable and reach their potential" (Taysom, 2021).

A variety of studies have been conducted to identify workforce needs for new WfO models (Baker, 2021; Pradere, 2020; Cohen et al., 2021). While some have involved new requirements, many relate to issues prevalent Pre-COVID-19 but exacerbated by the pandemic. Of the five future office trends identified by Gensler (Gensler Research Institute, 2021), all relate to SDT tenets and therefore align to Eudaemonic Design. These include but are not limited to provisions of mobility, choice, privacy, unassigned seating, and health and well-being (McLaurin, 2021).

Most of the identified needs can be met with an agile approach to Eudaemonic Design, allowing for options that meet workers' resounding preferences for choice. Examples include open inclusive entryways, collaborative hot-desking versus library quiet zones, supplemental health support and exercise facilities, as well as flexible workspaces appealing to a variety of workers (Smith, 2021). Adaptable workspaces may include "Zoom Rooms" and Breakout Spaces with whiteboard walls and moveable furniture for collaboration and interactive ideating (Smith, 2021) versus quiet enclosed areas such as library zones or meditation rooms that allow for contemplation, deep thinking, and analysis (IWBI, 2021).

While number of hours and days worked per week have become more flexible over the past five to ten years, a 40-hour work week spread across five days has been the ongoing accepted standard of work. Revisiting this antiquated scheduling model would augment feelings of work choice and promote work hour variations that enable meeting home life responsibilities, provide opportunities for working at times they personally work best and experience "flow" (Csikszentmihalyi, 2008), and decrease risk of unnecessary interaction during high sessions of flu or cold sickness. The office of the future should be a place of inspiration, support, collaboration, and connection (Pradere, 2020) and provide opportunities for excitement, intrigue, and culture for added allure and engagement (Taysom, 2021), not be stuck in illogical standards and protocols that worked poorly in the past. Transformational change through Eudaemonic Design is possible and feasible.

Eudaemonic Design Considerations for the Emerging Work from Anywhere Model

As clearly indicated in the JLL, Gensler, and Gartner reports (Baker, 2021; Pradere, 2020; Cohen et al., 2021), it is likely that the Post-COVID-19 working world will require a hybrid approach to workplaces. One term that has recently gained momentum in industry is the Working from Anywhere (WfA) model, which encompasses working from home, near home, and/or the office, as shown in Figure 6.

Figure 6. The Post-COVID-19 Work from Anywhere (WfA) Model that occurs at the intersection of Work from Home (WfH), Work from Near Home (WfNH), and Work from Office (WfO)

The new WfA model accommodates all work models and is therefore appropriate for all workers, including their range of work preferences, styles, and industries. Though the remote work movement has been most embraced and encouraged by the 18-24-year-old demographic (Work in Mind, 2021a), all generations have the potential to benefit. Whether conducted by design firms (Gensler Research Institute, 2021; McLaurin & Barber, 2020), real estate groups (Deloitte, 2021; Murray, 2020), remote working companies (Pelta, 2020), or research think tanks (Baker, 2020; Parker et al., 2020), all 2020-2021 studies declare that 60% to 70+% of the workforce favor a flexible hybrid workplace future, such as that offered by the WfA model.

This amount of flexibility will require an agile way of thinking and intensive inclusive design efforts, as well as inherent trust among co-workers and between workers and management. Therefore, designing for the WfA of the future must involve a key understanding—"Remote work will have to be viewed as equally important as in-person work" (Petersen, 2020, p. 3). Only with mutually valued recognition can a proper balance of autonomy, competence, and relatedness be realized and therefore organizational eudaemonia achieved. Work models must work seamlessly. This will require physical, organizational, and digital infrastructural support so workers can "plug into" a work environment effortlessly when remote such that they can continue to work from their last stopping point, manage data without issue, and collaborate with colleagues as needed and desired.

Despite the variation across the WfA model, best practices exist when applying Eudaemonic Design. These consider the SDT tenets across the workplace, workspace, worker model in ways that promote WfA flexibility. Having the opportunity to WfA is the best way of encouraging autonomy at work (e.g., enabling workers to fully control when and where they work). Providing workers with the conditions they need to do their work at home (by providing them with funding for ergonomic furniture), when near home (by allowing them to select activity-based near home locations), or at the office (by creating zones of varying light, noise, and temperature levels) encourages competence. Further, identifying policy and physical space protocols that designate social versus library zones allows for intentional or unintentional interaction that supports relatedness but allows for individual preference. As the Post-COVID-19 era evolves to include vaccinations and recurrences of new strains, workplace requirements and worker needs will continue to vary. Workers' work styles, workloads, and preferred working conditions will change. Offices will likely transition to be more social hubs for people to connect and collaborate with colleagues, and homes and near home work locations will continue to offer both opportunities for focus as well as distraction. Change is inevitable, yet it must be planned for and accommodated through adaptable design.

The WfA model provides what workers desire—flexibility, convenience, and support—and what companies are willing to accommodate—worker needs without maintaining a large real estate portfolio in a high-cost central business district location. Companies can lease annex locations outside of the city closer to employee homes or occupy coworking locations in those areas. With this flexible approach, workers and organizational preferences can evolve and be accommodated over time. It is a realistic approach and therefore one likely to succeed.

FUTURE RESEARCH DIRECTIONS

Suggested future work involves building upon the Eudaemonic Design model. Co-design can be used as a methodology to customize user or organization-centric Eudaemonic Design processes and outcomes. Eudaemonic Design as a Service could be explored as a potential offering by WfA affiliates, such as coworking companies, and technology can be utilized to operationalize design protocols that evolve as appropriate and proven.

Developing and Implementing the Model

Future research directions include validating the proposed Eudaemonic Design model and cross-referencing it more closely with existing models to understand implementation efficacy for workplaces and other asset types where health and wellness are of high importance (e.g., healthcare, schools). It may also prove useful to understand how co-design could factor into this process and how coworking companies can meet prime WfA requirements.

Co-Design as a Means of Achieving Work from Anywhere Eudaemonic Design

Co-design has long been considered an effective means of designing with and for a user group, especially when considering health (Slattery et al., 2020). More recently, scholarship has surfaced around research through co-design as a means to understand the process of co-design and how it can inform not only the design it results in but also the process through which that output is derived (Busciantella-Ricci & Scataglini, 2019). One possible way of deriving Eudaemonic Design specific to one company or one workforce is via research through co-design. By building on the core concepts of autonomy, competence, and relatedness, a co-design facilitator could work with user groups to fully develop what they individually desire with respect to work. Doing so will likely result in curated Eudaemonic Design that accounts for current worker to workplace needs and processes that may be repeatable when revisiting Eudaemonic Design at times of flux in the future.

Coworking Companies as Work from Anywhere Eudaemonic Design Service Providers

According to 2020-2021 reports on Post-COVID-19 projections, companies may return to the coworking model as one means towards WfA in the Post-COVID-19 future as they decrease their historical office footprints. Therefore, the new WfA preferred future model could infuse new energy into the coworking spaces that were burgeoning prior to COVID-19 but have since lost momentum (Scruggs, 2021). As workers look for alternative means of socializing on their own terms (outside of their offices and homes), coworking spaces could provide not only that relatedness aspect but also the competence and autonomy desired through choice, not to mention the favorable beauty-related neuroaesthetics that are commonly associated with coworking spaces. Global coworking company WeWork proclaims that "A well-designed workspace is more than just visually appealing—it enables you to get work done, keeps you motivated, and connects you to your team" (Bolt, 2019). That very definition encapsulates what Eudaemonic workspaces can offer. If coworking spaces can be designed with those qualities in mind and offered as a service while corporate culture is maintained and employee experience optimized (Baker, 2020), coworking indeed may offer the next best WfA solution to providing what workers and companies require to thrive.

The Role of Technology in the Post-COVID-19 Workplace

While technology should not be seen as a "panacea" (de Lange, 2013; Wiig, 2015), it does have a place in the Post-COVID-19 future. Its incorporation into work must be done intentionally, with employee health and well-being in mind, and operationalized once optimized.

Applying Technology for Employee Health and Well-Being

According to the UK's CIPD, technology's impact on employee well-being is primarily positive (42%) rather than negative (30%) (CIPD, 2020). However, it is vital that technology be incorporated into Eudaemonic Design with intention and care.

Ultimately, the benchmark for successful technology comes down to whether it's helping the humans in an organization do what they need to do. Businesses that want to continue to deliver value and help ensure enterprise resiliency in this time of rapid change should aim to become Human Enterprises—putting humans and their needs at the center of their strategies, values, processes, and operations, with technology serving as an enabler rather than a driver of change. (Higgins & Bianzino, 2020, p. 4)

If this call for human-centric technology as a necessary centralized concept for the built environment's new normal (Deloitte, 2021) is done right, technology integration can meet Eudaemonic Design's requirements for autonomy (feeling of control), competence (ability to do things), and relatedness (good social relations) and be applied for the worker, their workspace, and the workplace to achieve wellness. Some Eudeamonic Design-supportive technology examples include project management technologies (e.g., Trello) for autonomy, online centralized collaboration tools (e.g., Miro) for competence, and videoconferencing software (e.g., Zoom) for relatedness. From a built environment perspective, these needs can be further accommodated by providing spaces conditioned to worker specifications.

Operationalizing Eudaemonic Design with Smart Building Technology

Smart building technologies have the potential to operationalize Eudaemonic Design-supportive environmental conditions and do so predictively. They have also been recognized as a means to support SDT needs satisfaction (Chirkov et al., 2003). Therefore, while this chapter does not focus on technology's role in Eudaemonic Design, it does recognize the potential for technology to serve as a facilitator of Eudaemonic Design when considering the built environment's role in workplace wellness in the near future, especially as technology becomes less expensive, more attainable, more user friendly, and thereby ubiquitous.

Assuming buildings have Building Management Systems, it is possible to set and ensure delivery of "a workplace that is consistently conducive to health and productivity" (e.g., air quality, light levels, noise levels, temperature and humidity) (Hatcher, 2018). Therefore, once Eudaemonic Design requirements are established for a project, they can be built into the back end building management system algorithms for optimal workplace conditioning and enforced using Fault Detection and Diagnostics notification software to trigger alarms if conditions drift outside of the acceptable thresholds.

Indeed, there is opportunity in employing the technical factor (technology) for the socio-technical factor (environment) to improve the human factor (humans). The Human-Building Interaction field of domain focuses on three similar subjects—computing, built environment, and people (Wiberg, 2020)—and emphasizes the "multifunctional phenomenon of the building" (Alavi et al., 2019, p. 6:4). Given the interaction of these cross-factors, there is potential for exploring Eudaemonic Design in the context of Human-Building Interaction, whichever "workplace" model is being considered—whether the building in question is a home, an office, a local coworking space, or a public library.

Indoor Location Technologies and Occupancy Analytics

As physical distancing continues to be a standard policy for workforce reintegration, one technology that is of interest is occupancy-related technology. Market interest in related analytics was projected to be high before COVID-19 hit but is already accelerating more quickly than anticipated (Memoori, 2020). With indoor location technologies, it is possible to count people anonymously (i.e., to ensure maximum occupancy levels are met); determine distance among occupants (i.e., to confirm social distancing is adhered to); track vaccinated and unvaccinated occupants (Abate, 2021); and machine learn worker, workspace, and workplace activity, including movement and object placement. While much of this data is meant to be anonymous, privacy is at risk if for example identification badges are used for access. Therefore, while it is possible to monitor occupancy using indoor location technologies and dynamic occupancy management software and to measure body temperature levels using infrared kits, these protocols contradict Eudaemonic Design ideals and are therefore discouraged by the authors.

CONCLUSION

The global vaccination programs currently underway may prove to be a turning point from which many countries may transition to a Post-COVID-19 era, whether that involves the continuation of physical distancing measures alone or extreme physical distancing measures associated with the mandatory use of PPE. What is certain is that the pandemic has had a significant impact on the spatial and temporal dimensions of work globally, as workers have developed new preferred ways and locations of working. Physical workplaces have long served a disciplining function where work could be observed while being performed, resulting in toxic cultures based on notions of presenteeism where physical presence was the measure of performance and burnout pervaded work culture (Moss, 2019). COVID-19 has presented the opportunity to rethink how people work and how people design for work.

It is vital that a new design approach be considered to foster flourishing health and well-being in the new agile "workscape" of working from literally anywhere. Like health-based design, Eudeamonic Design can contribute to organizational profitability and sustainability. However, Eudaemonic Design goes beyond wellness to advocate design that not only meets health needs but also meets needs for autonomy, competence, and relatedness and allows for the possibility to extend efforts towards inclusive design. The Eudaemonic Design focus on flourishing and well-being at the level of the worker, the workspace, and the workplace also responds to Petersen's provocation:

If the future of work is flexibility, our challenge now is to make sure that future doesn't just worsen the ever-widening divide in American society between those promised a new vision of the good, balanced life, and those for whom 'flexibility' means effacing your wants and needs and dreams, once again, to the fickle demands of your employer. (2020, p. 4)

Applying Eudaemonic Design to provide flourishing work environments for workers can deliver well-being at work, wherever that might be.

ACKNOWLEDGMENT

This research received no specific grant from any funding agency in the public, commercial, or not-for-profit sectors.

REFERENCES

Abate, D. (2021, February 26). *Hong kong's covid-19 vaccination program: Considerations for employers*. Society for Human Resource Management (SHRM). https://www.shrm.org/resourcesandtools/hr-topics/global-hr/pages/coronavirus-hong-kong-vaccination-program.aspx

Alavi, H. S., Churchill, E. F., Wiberg, M., Lalanne, D., Dalsgaard, P., Schieck, A. F. G., & Rogers, Y. (2019). Introduction to human-building interaction (HBI): Interfacing HCI with architecture and urban design. *ACM Transactions on Computer-Human Interaction, 26*(2), 6:1-6:10.

Alker, J. (2014, September 25). Office buildings are key to workers' health, wellbeing and productivity. *The Guardian*. https://www.theguardian.com/sustainable-business/2014/sep/24/office-building-design-worker-health-wellbeing-productivity

Allen, J. G. (2020, March 4). Your building can make you sick or keep you well. *The New York Times*. https://www.nytimes.com/2020/03/04/opinion/coronavirus-buildings.html

Allen, J. G., Bernstein, A., Cao, X., Eitland, E. S., Flanigan, S., Gokhale, M., Goodman, J., Klager, S., Klingensmith, L., Laurent, J. G. C., Lockley, S. W., MacNaughton, P., Pakpour, S., Spengler, J., Vallarino, J., Williams, A., Young, A., & Yin, J. (2017). *The 9 foundations of a healthy building* (No. 1). Harvard University. https://forhealth.org/9_Foundations_of_a_Healthy_Building.February_2017.pdf

Allen, J. G., & Macomber, J. D. (2020a). Healthy buildings: How indoor spaces drive performance and productivity (3rd ed.). Harvard University Press.

Allen, J. G., & Macomber, J. D. (2020b, June 8). Tenants and investors will be looking for healthy buildings. *Urban Land Magazine*. https://urbanland.uli.org/sustainability/tenants-and-investors-will-be-looking-for-healthy-buildings/

Allen, T. (2018, November 18). Layoffs on the horizon? How to lead through a reduction in force. *Forbes*. https://www.forbes.com/sites/terinaallen/2018/11/28/do-all-of-this-before-you-lay-me-off-how-gm-and-others-can-get-this-right/

Arruda, W. (2018, April 7). 10 employee wellness ideas that will help you attract top talent. *Forbes*. https://www.forbes.com/sites/williamarruda/2018/04/08/10-employee-wellness-ideas-that-will-help-you-attract-top-talent/

Ashworth, M., & Martinuzzi, E. (2020, November 9). *Wfh is old news: The 'near home' office is the next big thing*. https://www.bloomberg.com/opinion/articles/2020-11-09/stanchart-wants-to-go-way-beyond-wfh

Associated Press (AP). (2020, December 2). *EU pushes for "right to disconnect" from work at home*. AP News. https://apnews.com/article/europe-europe-coronavirus-pandemic-f6f56884206c921a379ae5a060511571

Baker, M. (2020, July 14). *Gartner survey reveals 82% of company leaders plan to allow employees to work remotely some of the time*. Gartner. https://www.gartner.com/en/newsroom/press-releases/2020-07-14-gartner-survey-reveals-82-percent-of-company-leaders-plan-to-allow-employees-to-work-remotely-some-of-the-time

Baker, M. (2021, January 4). *9 tips for managing remote employees*. Smarter with Gartner. www.gartner.com/smarterwithgartner/9-tips-for-managing-remote-employees/

Barton, S. (2019, November 20). Why designing for dementia means designing for everyone. *Work in Mind*. https://workinmind.org/2019/11/20/designing-for-dementia/

Beatley, T. (2018). Biophilic flourishing: The role of nature in creating healthy cities. In T. Beatley, C. Jones, & R. Rainey (Eds.), *Healthy Environments, Healing Spaces* (pp. 81–106). University of Virginia Press. doi:10.2307/j.ctv8d5sgp.8

Boland, B., de Smet, A., Palter, R., & Sanghvi, A. (2020, June 8). *Reimagining the office and work life after COVID-19*. https://view.ceros.com/mckinsey/coronavirus-promo-video-desktop

Bolt, L. (2019, May 28). The science behind smart office design. *Ideas*. https://www.wework.com/ideas/office-design-space/the-science-behind-smart-office-design

Boubekri, M., Cheung, I. N., Reid, K. J., Wang, C.-H., & Zee, P. C. (2014). Impact of windows and daylight exposure on overall health and sleep quality of office workers: A case-control pilot study. *Journal of Clinical Sleep Medicine, 10*(6), 603–611. doi:10.5664/jcsm.3780 PMID:24932139

British Council of Offices (BCO). (2018). *Wellness matters: British Council for Offices completes major research study into health and wellbeing in offices*. https://www.bco.org.uk/News/News34396.aspx

Brown, D. (2020, November 17). *Coronavirus: How to be happier while working from home*. BBC. https://www.bbc.com/news/uk-54886125

Buettner, D. (2011). Thrive: Finding happiness the blue zones way (Illustrated ed). National Geographic.

Burton, J. (2010). Who healthy workplace framework and model: Background and supporting literature and practices (No. 1). World Health Organization.

Busciantella-Ricci, D., & Scataglini, S. (2019). A co-model for research through co-design. Academic Press.

Byron, K., & Laurence, G. A. (2015). Diplomas, photos, and tchotchkes as symbolic self-representations: Understanding employees' individual use of symbols. *Academy of Management Journal, 58*(1), 298–323. doi:10.5465/amj.2012.0932

Campbell, L. (2017, October 19). We've broken down your entire life into years spent doing tasks. *Huffington Post*. https://www.huffingtonpost.com.au/2017/10/18/weve-broken-down-your-entire-life-into-years-spent-doing-tasks_a_23248153/

Caramela, S. (2018, February 21). 4 ways to create a healthier workplace for your employees. *Business News Daily*. https://www.businessnewsdaily.com/10065-create-healthy-workplace.html

Center for Active Design (CfAD). (2021, February). *About Fitwel*. https://fitwel.org/

Centers for Disease Control and Prevention (CDC). (2020, July 24). *Communities, schools, workplaces, and events*. https://www.cdc.gov/coronavirus/2019-ncov/community/index.html

Channon, B. (2019). *Happy by design: A guide to architecture and mental wellbeing*. RIBA Publishing. doi:10.4324/9780367814625

Chartered Institute of Personnel and Development (CIPD). (2020). *Health and well-being at work*. https://www.cipd.co.uk/Images/health-and-well-being-2020-report_tcm18-73967.pdf

Chen, B., Vansteenkiste, M., Beyers, W., Boone, L., Deci, E. L., Van der Kaap-Deeder, J., Duriez, B., Lens, W., Matos, L., Mouratidis, A., Ryan, R. M., Sheldon, K. M., Soenens, B., Van Petegem, S., & Verstuyf, J. (2015). Basic psychological need satisfaction, need frustration, and need strength across four cultures. *Motivation and Emotion*, *39*(2), 216–236. doi:10.100711031-014-9450-1

Chirkov, V., Ryan, R. M., Kim, Y., & Kaplan, U. (2003). Differentiating autonomy from individualism and independence: A self-determination theory perspective on internalization of cultural orientations and well-being. *Journal of Personality and Social Psychology*, *84*(1), 97–110. doi:10.1037/0022-3514.84.1.97 PMID:12518973

Cohen, A., Hoskins, D., Shick, R., & Taylor, L. (2021). *Design forecast 2021: Reconnect* (Design Strategies for a Post-COVID World). Gensler.

Csikszentmihalyi, M. (2008). *Flow: The psychology of optimal experience* (1st ed.). Harper Perennial.

Csikszentmihalyi, M. (2014). *Flow and the foundations of positive psychology the collected works of Mihaly Csikszentmihalyi* (1st ed.). Springer.

Dai, D., Prussin, A. J. II, Marr, L. C., Vikesland, P. J., Edwards, M. A., & Pruden, A. (2017). Factors shaping the human exposome in the built environment: Opportunities for engineering control. *Environmental Science & Technology*, *51*(14), 7759–7774. doi:10.1021/acs.est.7b01097 PMID:28677960

Daum, K. (2017, January 20). *25 ways you can make your life healthier in the office*. Inc.Com. https://www.inc.com/kevin-daum/25-ways-you-can-make-your-life-healthier-in-the-office.html

Davis, D. (2020, November). *The workplace beyond 2020*. Hassell. https://www.hassellstudio.com/conversation/the-workplace-beyond-2020

de Botton, A. (2007). *The architecture of happiness*. Penguin.

de Lange, M. (2013). The smart city you love to hate: Exploring the role of affect in hybrid urbanism. *ResearchGate*, 8.

Deci, E. L., & Ryan, R. M. (2008). Hedonia, eudaimonia, and well-being: An introduction. *Journal of Happiness Studies*, *9*(1), 1–11. doi:10.100710902-006-9018-1

Deloitte. (2021, February 17). JLL: Human-centric tech will recast the workplace. *The Wall Street Journal*. https://deloitte.wsj.com/cio/2021/02/17/jll-human-centric-tech-will-recast-the-workplace/

Detwiler, J. (2020, October 23). *You are your workspace*. Medium. https://forge.medium.com/you-are-your-workspace-eede562b36fb

Franklin, N. (2021, March 1). *Zoom fatigue is real and has four basic causes*. Workplace Insight. https://workplaceinsight.net/zoom-fatigue-is-real-and-has-four-basic-causes/

Gensler. (2021). *Design forecast 2021: Places and spaces in a post-covid world*. https://www.gensler.com/research-insight/publications/design-forecast/reconnect?utm_source=gensler-home-dsk

Gensler Research Institute. (2021). *Workplace surveys: Research and insight*. Gensler. https://www.gensler.com/research-insight/workplace-surveys

Gerdman, D. (2020, March 16). *How the coronavirus is already rewriting the future of business*. HBS Working Knowledge. https://hbswk.hbs.edu/item/how-the-coronavirus-is-already-rewriting-the-future-of-business

Gershon, L. (2017, September 12). *Does a job need to be meaningful?* The Orange Dot. https://www.headspace.com/blog/2017/09/12/meaningful-job/

Global Wellness Institute (GWI). (2018). *Build well to live well: Wellness lifestyle real estate & communities*. https://globalwellnessinstitute.org/industry-research/wellness-real-estate-communities-research/

Goldhagen, S. W. (2017). *Welcome to your world: How the built environment shapes our lives* (1st ed.). Harper.

Gourarie, C. (2021, February 12). Spotify will allow its staff to work from anywhere permanently. *Commercial Observer*. https://commercialobserver.com/2021/02/spotify-will-allow-its-staff-to-work-from-anywhere-permanently/

Griffiths, K., & Clarence-Smith, L. (2021, February 24). HSBC to cut office space by 40 per cent. *The Times*. https://www.thetimes.co.uk/article/hsbc-to-cut-office-space-by-40-per-cent-xgg3dxq3w

Güntert, S. (2014). The impact of work design, autonomy support, and strategy on employee outcomes: A differentiated perspective on self-determination at work. *Motivation and Emotion*, *39*(1), 74–87. doi:10.100711031-014-9412-7

GWI. (2020). *Statistics and facts*. https://globalwellnessinstitute.org/press-room/statistics-and-facts/

Harvard, T. H. C. (2021). *9 Foundations of a Healthy Building*. 9 Foundations. https://9foundations.forhealth.org/

Hatcher, J. (2018, November 1). Smart building controls are delivering a way to wellness. *Smart Buildings Magazine*. https://smartbuildingsmagazine.com/features/smart-building-controls-are-delivering-a-way-to-wellness

Higgins, D., & Bianzino, N. M. (2020, October 12). Tech should enable change, not drive it. *Harvard Business Review*, 6.

Institute for the Future (IFTF). (2020). *After the pandemic: Writing the stories of the future*. Writing the Stories of the Future. https://www.iftf.org/our-work/health-self/whathappensnext/writing-the-stories-of-the-future/

International Labour Organization (ILO). (2008). *Seoul declaration on safety and health at work*. https://www.ilo.org/safework/info/promo/WCMS_151736/lang--en/index.htm

International WELL Building Institute (IWBI). (2021). *WELL v2 standard*. https://v2.wellcertified.com/wellv2/en/overview

Iqbal, M. (2020, October 30). *Zoom revenue and usage statistics*. Business of Apps. https://www.businessofapps.com/data/zoom-statistics/

Jones, M., Rice, L., Meraz, F., & ProQuest. (2019). *Designing for health & wellbeing: Home, city, society*. Vernon Press.

Kehrt, S. (2020, December 15). The 'healthy building' surge will outlast the pandemic. *Wired*. https://www.wired.com/story/healthy-building-outlast-pandemic/

Khazan, O. (2020, May 4). Work from home is here to stay. *The Atlantic*. https://www.theatlantic.com/health/archive/2020/05/work-from-home-pandemic/611098/

Kim, J., & de Dear, R. (2013). Workspace satisfaction: The privacy-communication trade-off in open-plan offices. *Journal of Environmental Psychology*, *36*, 18–26. doi:10.1016/j.jenvp.2013.06.007

Klepeis, N. E., Nelson, W. C., Ott, W. R., Robinson, J. P., Tsang, A. M., Switzer, P., Behar, J. V., Hern, S. C., & Engelmann, W. H. (2001). The National Human Activity Pattern Survey (NHAPS): A resource for assessing exposure to environmental pollutants. *Journal of Exposure Science & Environmental Epidemiology*, *11*(3), 231–252. doi:10.1038j.jea.7500165 PMID:11477521

Knight, C., & Haslam, S. A. (2010). The relative merits of lean, enriched, and empowered offices: An experimental examination of the impact of workspace management strategies on well-being and productivity. *Journal of Experimental Psychology. Applied*, *16*(2), 158–172. doi:10.1037/a0019292 PMID:20565201

Kondō, M., & Sonenshein, S. (2020). *Joy at work: Organizing your professional life*. Little, Brown Spark.

Lass, H. (2018). Developing intra-personal skills as a proactive way to personal sustainability. In O. Parodi & K. Tamm (Eds.), *Personal Sustainability: Exploring the Far Side of Sustainable Development* (1st ed., pp. 21–21). Routledge. doi:10.4324/9781315159997-7

Layard, P. R. G. (2005). *Happiness: Lessons from a new science*. Penguin Press.

Leinonen, T. (2020, December 28). Wellbeing of a university community and its members during remote working. *Teemu Leinonen*. https://teemuleinonen.fi/2020/12/28/wellbeing-of-a-university-community-and-its-members-during-remote-working/

Liu, J. (2020, May 27). *So your company has said you can work from home forever—Now what?* CNBC. https://www.cnbc.com/2020/05/27/so-your-company-has-said-you-can-work-from-home-forevernow-what.html

Lucchesi, E. L. B. (2019, January 3). The unbearable heaviness of clutter. *The New York Times*. https://www.nytimes.com/2019/01/03/well/mind/clutter-stress-procrastination-psychology.html

Martela, F., & Riekki, T. J. J. (2018). Autonomy, competence, relatedness, and beneficence: A multicultural comparison of the four pathways to meaningful work. *Frontiers in Psychology*, *9*, 1157. doi:10.3389/fpsyg.2018.01157 PMID:30042710

McLaurin, J. P. (2021). *5 trends driving the new post-pandemic workplace*. Gensler. https://www.gensler.com/research-insight/blog/5-trends-driving-the-new-post-pandemic-workplace

McLaurin, J. P., & Barber, C. (2020, December 8). *Surprising truths about the new hybrid workplace*. Gensler. https://www.gensler.com/research-insight/blog/surprising-truths-about-the-new-hybrid-workplace

Medina, S. (2019, May 7). *How the "happiness industry" is changing architecture*. Metropolis. https://www.metropolismag.com/architecture/cca-happy-life-architecture-exhibition/

Memoori. (2020). *Occupancy analytics and in-building location based services research: Commercial office space 2019 to 2024*. https://memoori.com/portfolio/occupancy-analytics-in-building-location-based-services/

Moss, J. (2019, December 11). Burnout is about your workplace, not your people. *Harvard Business Review*. https://hbr.org/2019/12/burnout-is-about-your-workplace-not-your-people

Moss, J. (2021, February 10). Beyond Burned Out. *Harvard Business Review*. https://hbr.org/2021/02/beyond-burned-out

Mudditt, J. (2020, May). *How offices will change after coronavirus*. BBC. https://www.bbc.com/worklife/article/20200514-how-the-post-pandemic-office-will-change

Murray, B. (2020, November 17). *Tomorrow's office to be a mix of work styles, workspaces: JLL*. Commercial Property Executive. https://www.cpexecutive.com/post/tomorrows-office-to-be-a-mix-of-work-styles-workspaces-jll/

Nieuwenhuis, M., Knight, C., Postmes, T., & Haslam, S. A. (2014). The relative benefits of green versus lean office space: Three field experiments. *Journal of Experimental Psychology. Applied*, *20*(3), 199–214. doi:10.1037/xap0000024 PMID:25068481

Novet, J. (2020, August 7). *Atlassian tells employees they can work from home indefinitely*. CNBC. https://www.cnbc.com/2020/08/07/atlassian-tells-employees-they-can-work-from-home-indefinitely.html

Orsini, C., & Rodrigues, V. (2020). Supporting motivation in teams working remotely: The role of basic psychological needs. *Medical Teacher*, *42*(7), 828–829. doi:10.1080/0142159X.2020.1758305 PMID:32366152

Parker, K., Horowitz, J. M., & Minkin, R. (2020, December 9). How coronavirus has changed the way Americans work. *Pew Research Center's Social & Demographic Trends Project*. https://www.pewresearch.org/social-trends/2020/12/09/how-the-coronavirus-outbreak-has-and-hasnt-changed-the-way-americans-work/

Pelta, R. (2020, September 21). *Survey: Productivity, work-life balance improves during pandemic.* FlexJobs Job Search Tips and Blog. https://www.flexjobs.com/blog/post/survey-productivity-balance-improve-during-pandemic-remote-work/

Penny, J. (2020, November 12). *Five ways buildings can improve mental health (Greenbuild 2020).* Buildings. https://www.buildings.com/articles/42623/buildings-improve-mental-health

Petersen, A. H. (2020, December 23). Are you sure you want to go back to the office? *The New York Times.* https://www.nytimes.com/2020/12/23/opinion/covid-offices-remote-work.html

Pirschel, C. (2020, April 15). *Places matter: Best practices for working from home.* International WELL Building Institute. https://resources.wellcertified.com/articles/places-matter-best-practices-for-working-from-home/

Pradere, F. (2020). *Reimagining Human Experience* (No. 1). Jones Lang LaSalle.

PricewaterhouseCoopers (PwC). (2021, February). *Changing places: How hybrid working is reinventing the Australian CBD.* https://www.pwc.com.au/important-problems/future-of-work-design-for-the-future/changing-places-australian-cbd.html

Prüss-Üstün, A., & Corvalán, C. (2006). *Preventing disease through healthy environments: Towards an estimate of the environmental burden of disease.* World Health Organization.

Reis, H. T., Sheldon, K. M., Gable, S. L., Roscoe, J., & Ryan, R. M. (2000). Daily well-being: The role of autonomy, competence, and relatedness. *Personality and Social Psychology Bulletin, 26*(4), 419–435. doi:10.1177/0146167200266002

Rizzi, N. (2021, February 9). Salesforce to allow remote work for most staff permanently. *Commercial Observer.* https://commercialobserver.com/2021/02/salesforce-to-let-most-staff-work-remote-permanently/

Roberts, T. (2016, December 15). *We spend 90% of our time indoors: Says who?* BuildingGreen. https://www.buildinggreen.com/blog/we-spend-90-our-time-indoors-says-who

Rosone, M. (2019, April 8). *Office temperature and productivity in the workplace.* Arista. https://aristair.com/blog/office-temperature-and-productivity-in-the-workplace/

Ryan, R. M., & Deci, E. L. (2000). Self-Determination Theory and the facilitation of intrinsic motivation, social development, and well-being. *The American Psychologist, 55*(1), 68–78. doi:10.1037/0003-066X.55.1.68 PMID:11392867

Ryan, R. M., & Deci, E. L. (2001). On Happiness and Human Potentials: A Review of Research on Hedonic and Eudaimonic Well-Being. *Annual Review of Psychology, 52*(1), 141–166. doi:10.1146/annurev.psych.52.1.141

Ryan, R. M., & Deci, E. L. (2017). *Self-Determination Theory: Basic Psychological Needs in Motivation, Development, and Wellness.* Guilford Publications. doi:10.1521/978.14625/28806

Ryan, R. M., Huta, V., & Deci, E. L. (2008). Living well: A self-determination theory perspective on eudaimonia. *Journal of Happiness Studies, 9*(1), 139–170. doi:10.100710902-006-9023-4

Ryan, R. M., Weinstein, N., Bernstein, J., Brown, K. W., Mistretta, L., & Gagné, M. (2010). Vitalizing effects of being outdoors and in nature. *Journal of Environmental Psychology, 30*(2), 159–168. doi:10.1016/j.jenvp.2009.10.009

Scruggs, G. (2021, February 28). Co-working companies tap into customers facing work-from-home fatigue. *Washington Post*. https://www.washingtonpost.com/road-to-recovery/2021/02/28/remote-work-flex-office-work-home/

Shade, M. (2020, April 20). *Pro tips for working from home and staying healthy*. CNN. https://www.cnn.com/2020/04/20/health/staying-well-working-from-home/index.html

Slattery, P., Saeri, A. K., & Bragge, P. (2020). Research co-design in health: A rapid overview of reviews. *Health Research Policy and Systems, 17*(1), 1–13.

Smith, J. (2020, November 23). *The workplace to become more human-centric than ever, as priorities change*. Workplace Insight. https://workplaceinsight.net/the-workplace-to-become-more-human-centric-than-ever-as-priorities-change/

Smith, J. (2021, February 19). *'Zoom rooms' and breakout space top of the agenda for post-COVID offices*. Workplace Insight. https://workplaceinsight.net/zoom-rooms-and-breakout-space-top-of-the-agenda-for-post-covid-offices/

Society for Human Resource Management (SHRM). (2020, March 25). *Reduction in force (RIF) strategy and selection checklist*. https://www.shrm.org/resourcesandtools/tools-and-samples/hr-forms/pages/downsizingchecklist.aspx

Spangler, A., & McLeod, V. (2020, April 24). *New rhythms of working: How to work WELL from home*. https://resources.wellcertified.comzh-cn//articles/working-well-from-home

Stevens, R., Petermans, A., & Vanrie, J. (2014). Converting happiness theory into (interior) architectural design missions. Designing for subjective well-being in residential care centers. *Proceedings of the Annual Architectural Research Symposium in Finland*, 53–67.

Tabb, P. J. (2021). *Biophilic urbanism: Designing resilient communities for the future*. Routledge.

Taysom, T. (2021, February 24). *Post-Covid offices will become cultural hubs and even art galleries to tempt staff back to the office*. CityAM. https://www.cityam.com/post-covid-offices-will-become-cultural-hubs-and-even-art-galleries-to-tempt-staff-back-to-the-office/

Thaler, R. H. (2008). *Nudge: Improving decisions about health, wealth, and happiness*. Yale University Press.

Thompson, D. (2020, March 13). The Coronavirus experiment in working from home. *The Atlantic*. https://www.theatlantic.com/ideas/archive/2020/03/coronavirus-creating-huge-stressful-experiment-working-home/607945/

Timm, S., Gray, W. A., Curtis, T., & Chung, S. S. E. (2018). Designing for health: How the physical environment plays a role in workplace wellness. *American Journal of Health Promotion, 32*(6), 1468–1473. doi:10.1177/0890117118779463b PMID:29972070

UK Green Building Council (UKGBC). (2017, September 21). *Health, wellbeing and productivity in offices: The next chapter for green building*. https://www.ukgbc.org/ukgbc-work/health-wellbeing-productivity-offices-next-chapter-green-building/

Vaughn, K. (2018, May 5). *You will spend 90,000 hours of your lifetime at work. Are you happy?* Medium. https://kassandravaughn.medium.com/you-will-spend-90-000-hours-of-your-lifetime-at-work-are-you-happy-5a2b5b0120ff

Walsh, C. (2019, June 20). Harvard researchers outline steps to a healthy home. *Harvard Gazette*. https://news.harvard.edu/gazette/story/2019/06/harvard-researchers-outline-steps-to-a-healthy-home/

Waterman, A. S. (2013). *The best within us: Positive psychology perspectives on eudaimonia* (1st ed.). American Psychological Association. doi:10.1037/14092-000

Weed, J. (2020, June 21). How to succeed in your office job when there is no office. *The New York Times*. https://www.nytimes.com/2020/06/21/business/work-home-coronavirus.html

Wellness Council of America (WELCOA). (2021). *The key to creating thriving organizations*. https://www.welcoa.org/blog/definition-of-wellness/

WHO. (2021, February 27). *WHO Coronavirus Disease (COVID-19) dashboard*. https://covid19.who.int

Wiberg, M. (2020, March-April). Interaction and architecture is dead: Long live architectural interactivity! *Interaction*, *27*(2), 72–75. doi:10.1145/3378567

Wiig, A. (2015). IBM's smart city as techno-utopian policy mobility. *City*, *19*(2–3), 258–273. doi:10.1080/13604813.2015.1016275

Work in Mind. (2020, November 19). *Safety concerns driving continued demand for remote working*. https://workinmind.org/2020/11/19/safety-concerns-driving-continued-demand-for-remote-working/

Work in Mind. (2021a, January 20). *Hybrid working: Hybrid model of work is being led by 18-24-year-olds*. https://workinmind.org/2021/01/20/hybrid-working-hybrid-model-of-work-is-being-led-by-18-24-year-olds/

Work in Mind. (2021b, February 10). *Workers report a cycle of fatigue when working from home*. https://workinmind.org/2021/02/10/pedalling-furiously-workers-report-a-cycle-of-fatigue-when-working-from-home/

Work in Mind. (2021c, February 16). *How do we really feel about working from home? – Microsoft explains*. https://workinmind.org/2021/02/16/how-do-we-really-feel-about-working-from-home-microsoft-has-the-answers/

World Green Building Council (WorldGBC). (2016). *Health, wellbeing and productivity in offices: The next chapter for green building*. World Green Building Council (WorldGBC).

World Health Organization (WHO). (2020, August). *World Health Organization Constitution*. https://www.who.int/about/who-we-are/constitution

Wyon, D. P. (2004). The effects of indoor air quality on performance and productivity. *Indoor Air*, *14*(Suppl 7), 92–101. doi:10.1111/j.1600-0668.2004.00278.x PMID:15330777

ADDITIONAL READING

Allen, J. G., & Macomber, J. D. (2020a). Healthy buildings: How indoor spaces drive performance and productivity (3rd ed.). Harvard University Press.

Baker, M. (2020, July 14). *Gartner survey reveals 82% of company leaders plan to allow employees to work remotely some of the time*. Gartner. https://www.gartner.com/en/newsroom/press-releases/2020-07-14-gartner-survey-reveals-82-percent-of-company-leaders-plan-to-allow-employees-to-work-remotely-some-of-the-time

Cohen, A., Hoskins, D., Shick, R., & Taylor, L. (2021). *Design forecast 2021: Reconnect* (Design Strategies for a Post-COVID World). Gensler.

Deci, E. L., & Ryan, R. M. (2008). Hedonia, eudaimonia, and well-being: An introduction. *Journal of Happiness Studies*, *9*(1), 1–11. doi:10.100710902-006-9018-1

Pradere, F. (2020). *Reimagining Human Experience* (No. 1). Jones Lang LaSalle.

Prüss-Üstün, A., & Corvalán, C. (2006). *Preventing disease through healthy environments: Towards an estimate of the environmental burden of disease*. World Health Organization.

Ryan, R. M., Huta, V., & Deci, E. L. (2008). Living well: A self-determination theory perspective on eudaimonia. *Journal of Happiness Studies*, *9*(1), 139–170. doi:10.100710902-006-9023-4

Waterman, A. S. (2013). *The best within us: Positive psychology perspectives on eudaimonia* (1st ed.). American Psychological Association. doi:10.1037/14092-000

World Green Building Council (WorldGBC). (2016). *Health, wellbeing and productivity in offices: The next chapter for green building*. World Green Building Council (WorldGBC).

KEY TERMS AND DEFINITIONS

Autonomy: One of the three tenets of Self-Determination Theory; refers to the need to have a feeling of control in life, feel ownership of behavior, and maintain volition in actions.

Competence: One of the three tenets of Self-Determination Theory; refers to the need to be able to do enjoyable activities, feel effective in taking action (ideally to the point of mastery), and produce good outcomes and desired results.

COVID-19 Era: The period commencing in early 2020, when COVID-19 was recognized as a global pandemic.

Eudaemonia: Originating from neo-Aristotelian philosophy, refers to flourishing health, happiness, and "living life in a full and deeply satisfying way" (Deci & Ryan, 2008, p. 1). Alternate spelling is Eudaimonia or Eudemonia.

Eudaemonic Well-Being: A perspective on well-being that originated with Ryan and Deci's (2001) take on eudaemonia and evolved into a combined subjective and objective interpretation considered in both narrow (self-realization) and broad (flourishing) terms; this paper recognizes the broad (flourishing) definition by Waterman (2013) that represents a eudaemonia-driven perspective on flourishing physical, mental, and social health (compare to well-being).

Exposome: A measure of all the exposures of an individual in their lifetime and how these relate to health; includes exposures before birth and environmental and occupational sources.

Health: The physical, mental, and social conditions of the body; being free of illness, disease, or injury (compare to well-being).

Miro: A software tool that enables online mind-mapping and a centralized means of team collaboration.

Personal Protective Equipment (PPE): Anything used or worn to minimize risks to workers' health and safety, including face masks.

Post-COVID-19: A term relating to countries or areas considered to be of minimal contagion risk and therefore no longer requiring mandatory personal protective equipment use or large-scale lockdowns; an era that is likely to overlap with COVID-19 eras of other countries and likely to be significantly shaped by the widespread uptake of COVID-19 vaccines.

Pre-COVID-19: The period occurring before the COVID-19 era began in early 2020.

Relatedness: One of the three tenets of Self-Determination Theory; refers to the need to enjoy good social relations, promote effective relationships, and establish a sense of belonging.

Self-Determination Theory (SDT): A theory established by Richard Ryan and Edward Deci (Ryan & Deci, 2000) that is based on empowerment and concepts of intrinsic motivation, centering around three cornerstones: autonomy, competence, and relatedness.

Trello: A software tool that supports individual worker task organizing and collective team project management scheduling.

Well-Being: A holistic balance of optimal physical, mental, and social health dimensions (compare to wellness).

Wellness: The quality or state of being in good health; the process of improving aspects of health to attain well-being (compare to well-being).

Worker: Anyone who performs paid or unpaid work in any capacity for an employer, business, or organization; synonymous with employee and may include contractors and subcontractors.

Working From Anywhere (WfA): The idea that work can occur in any location, including any historical model; encompasses Work from Home, Work from Near Home, and Work from Office workplace models; also known as Work from Anywhere.

Working From Home (WfH): A spatial model of work in which the worker engages in work from their home; also known as Work from Home.

Working From Near Home (WfNH): A spatial model of work that has evolved into a variety of locations within local geographical proximity to the worker's home, reducing the need for significant commuting; includes a company's decentralized or satellite office; local café, public library, or park; or coworking space; also known as Work from Near Home.

Working From Office (WfO): A spatial model of work in which the worker attends a physical corporate workplace, often referred to as the office, to engage in work; also known as Work from Office.

Workplace: The comprehensive "office" environment (e.g., individual cubicle or conglomeration of workspaces); was traditionally defined to focus on the Work from Office model and associated "workplace", but the definition has now been extended to include all Work from Anywhere model places where workers carry out their day-to-day work.

Workplace Wellness: A concept relating to the ongoing improvement of workplace conditions to improve worker and thereby organizational health (compare to wellness).

Workspace: The immediate working area (e.g., desk, chair, computer) of a worker, regardless of physical workplace; may include desk-space alone, a cubicle, or an enclosed office (compare to workplace).

Zoom: A software tool that offers video-conferencing capabilities to remote workers.

Chapter 2
The Impact of Job Demands Variables in the Job Demands Resources Model

Henry Milimu Shililu
Excelsia College, Australia

ABSTRACT

The purpose of this chapter is to report on the findings of a study that was conducted by the author to investigate the impact of job demands variables on emotional exhaustion and emotional ill-health. A sample of 173 drawn from employees who worked for different organizations in the Pacific, mainly Australia, the African region, the Indian subcontinent of India, Nepal, Pakistan, Bangladesh, and Sri Lanka, and employees who professed Christian and Hindu religions. A broad range of ages, occupations, ethnicities, religions, and cultures was represented in the sample, that is, the targeted population were employees whose different contexts and characteristics (e.g., attitudes, occupations, ages, marital status, religion, opinions, behaviors, and other defined variables) could be measured and allowed to generalize the results. The study used a quantitative research design. A diversity of findings were established with some findings being consistent with the JD-R theory and previous studies across the cultures while other findings were not consistent with previous studies and the JDR theory.

INTRODUCTION

The purpose of this chapter is to report on the findings of a study that was conducted to investigate the impact of job demands variables on emotional exhaustion and emotional ill health in diverse workplaces using the job demands-resources (JD-R) model. The chapter commences with the background and rationale of the study followed by a brief overview of the antecedents and consequences of emotional exhaustion and emotional ill-health. This is followed by the theoretical framework, research questions, and hypothesis, the conceptual framework, research methodology, a summary of findings, a summary of the discussion, theoretical contributions, management contribution for practice followed by limitations and recommendations for future study, and finally, a chapter summary.

DOI: 10.4018/978-1-7998-7396-9.ch002

BACKGROUND AND RATIONALE

Anxiety and depression among employees at the workplace have increased at an alarming rate in recent years because of the negative imbalance between job demands and job resources. An estimated 264 million people globally suffer from depression and anxiety (World Health Organization, 2019). According to Maslach and Leiter (2016), employee mental illness is caused by depression and anxiety as a result of high job demands.

In a recent study by the World Health Organization (2019), it is estimated that the global economy loses annually US$ One (1) Trillion in lost productivity due to employee disorders associated with anxiety and depression. The study further revealed that employee mental and physical ill-health is caused by bad working conditions that lead to employee absence from work due to illness that subsequently leads to lost productivity. The study recommended workplaces to promote support for mental health through good working conditions to help reduce workplace illness so that as a consequence, an organization can benefit from the resulting economic growth and productivity (World Health Organization, 2019).

The literature indicates that although a significant number of studies linking job demands or job resources to employee emotional exhaustion and emotional ill-health have been conducted in both Europe and non-European contexts (Schaufeli & Taris, 2014), relatively few studies have directly examined the influence of societal cross-cultural dimensions across geographical and religious contexts.

The rationale of conducting this study was to uncover the influence of culture within the JD-R theory framework with a view of prescribing antidotes to combat emotional ill health in different cultures. Previous research has demonstrated that cross-national heterogeneity in culture has shaped perceptions of job demands–burnout relationships at the individual employee level (Yang et al., 2012). However, it is currently uncertain whether different JD-R variables mean the same thing in different cultures (Luchman & González-Morales, 2013). Despite the JDR theory's universal adoption, limited research has examined whether culture influences relationships within the JD-R model with a view of managing emotional ill health (depression and anxiety) at different individual cultural levels.

RESEARCH ON EMOTIONAL EXHAUSTION AND EMOTIONAL ILL-HEALTH

A review of the literature regarding the antecedents and consequences of emotional exhaustion and emotional ill-health in the health impairment process of the JD-R model is discussed below:

Antecedents of Emotional Exhaustion and Emotional Ill- Health

Traditionally, scholars have classified the antecedents of emotional exhaustion and emotional ill-health in two general categories: personality or individual factors (e.g. Self-efficacy), situational factors e.g., work overload (Xanthopoulou, Bakker, Demerouti, & Schaufeli, 2007).

Situational Factors Antecedents

A meta-analysis by Lee and Ashforth (1996) established that the most prominent predictor of burnout which is the antecedent of emotional exhaustion is job demands. Findings by Lee and Ashforth (1996) concluded that job demands are considered stressors because "meeting such demands requires the investment of valued resources" (p. 129).

Alarcon (2011) in her more recent meta-analysis supported the critical role that job demands play in predicting burnout and emotional exhaustion within the JD-R model. In a review of between 37 and 86 different studies from various career groups, the author established that the significant predictors of burnout and emotional ill health were workload and role ambiguity. Therefore, it is not surprising that psychological costs (e.g., exhaustion that leads to high blood pressure) increases an employee's heart rate, and elevated hormonal activity and are correlated to job demands (Maslach & Leiter, 2016).

Individual Factors

According to Xanthopoulou et al. (2007), individual factors are also referred to as personality traits. Alarcon, Eschleman, and Bowling (2009) established that personality traits may influence burnout through how employees perceive the nature of their work environment. For example, personality may predispose employees to view their jobs positively irrespective of the nature of their work environments (Brunborg, 2008). Employees with high emotional stability may perceive a high workload as a challenge while similar jobs may be perceived as hindrances by staff with low emotional stability. One possible explanation could be that certain personality traits can cope with stressful job demands than others.

Furthermore, Alarcon et al. (2009) established that self-esteem, confidence, optimism, self-efficacy, and positive personality were all negatively correlated with burnout and consequently emotional exhaustion and emotional ill-health. This indicates that variations in human personalities may play a role in the development of burnout and ultimately emotional exhaustion and emotional ill-health. Employees with positive ratings on these individual variables feel that they have control over their workplace environment and can therefore manage their job demands effectively (Bickerton, Miner, Dowson, & Griffin, 2014).

Consequences of Emotional Exhaustion

Traditionally, scholars have classified the consequences of emotional exhaustion into two general categories: health-related outcomes and job-related outcomes (Maslach, Schaufeli, & Leiter, 2001).

Health-Related Outcomes

Studies have established that heavy job demands make employees report more psychological and physical health problems because they are usually emotionally exhausted by persistent job demands (Maslach & Leiter, 2016). Further, Ahola and Hakanen (2008) in their study that used a nationally representative survey sample of the Finnish working population to investigate psychological health problems established that psychological health issues were linked to increased occurrence of depressive and anxiety complaints and alcohol addiction among employees.

Similarly, Hillhouse, Adler, and Walters (2000) in their study among medical staff identified that patient-related exhaustion increased mood disturbance among health care staff. In addition, emotional exhaustion increases the risk of musculoskeletal problems among apparently healthy employees (Armon, Melamed, Shirom, & Shapira, 2010). Additionally, emotional exhaustion among apparently healthy employees increased the likelihood of musculoskeletal problems (Armon et al., 2010). It has also been established that emotional exhaustion condition is an independent risk factor for influenza (e.g., the common cold; (Mohren et al., 2003) and type 2 diabetes (Melamed, Shirom, Toker, Berliner, & Shapira, 2006). Many studies have established that burnout and depression are positively correlated (Renzo. Bianchi, Schonfeld, & Laurent, 2015). Further, in their systematic analysis, Ahola and Hakanen (2014) established that emotional exhaustion–the core component of burnout–was positively associated with depressive symptoms.

Job-Related Outcomes

Specifically, future absence duration from work by employees due to sickness is associated with emotional exhaustion since an increase in emotional exhaustion positively correlates to an increase per year in sick leave (Borritz et al., 2006). Additionally, according to Toppinen-Tanner, Ojajärvi, Väänänen, Kalimo, and Jäppinen (2005), medically certified absences from work is correlated to an increase in emotional exhaustion. Further, Mark and Smith (2012) established that increased levels of anxiety were correlated to extrinsic effort and over-commitment. According to Turnipseed (1998), a state of anxiety is elevated due to the interaction between bad working conditions and individuals' personality traits as this creates and contributes to the onset of psychological health issues.

THEORETICAL FRAMEWORK

This study was anchored on the Job Demands–Resources (JD-R) theory (Bakker & Demerouti, 2017). At the core of the JD-R theory lies the premise that all job characteristics are categorized as either job demands, or job resources, and the concept can be extended to different work settings regardless of the job resources and job demands involved.

The JD-R model has two parallel simultaneous processes, the health impairment process and the motivational process (Bakker & Demerouti, 2018). The health impairment process is when an employee's mental and physical resources are exhausted by high job demands with limited job resources and result in negative health issues while the motivational process is when high job resources with limited job demands foster employee engagement (Bakker & Demerouti, 2018).

Specifically, the study was anchored primarily on the health impairment component of the JD-R model which predicted the potential effects of job demands on employee's wellbeing through everyday experiences of emotions in the workplace. The JD-R model provides a framework that assists in comprehending employees' wellbeing in the workplace. The model assists in elucidating the widely recognized beliefs that employees' stress is caused by job characteristics that result in emotional exhaustion and subsequently emotional ill-health and that such negative effects of job demands may be buffered by job resources (Bakker, Demerouti, & Euwema, 2005).

Figure 1. Below explains the JD-R theory
Source: Schaufeli & Taris (2014)

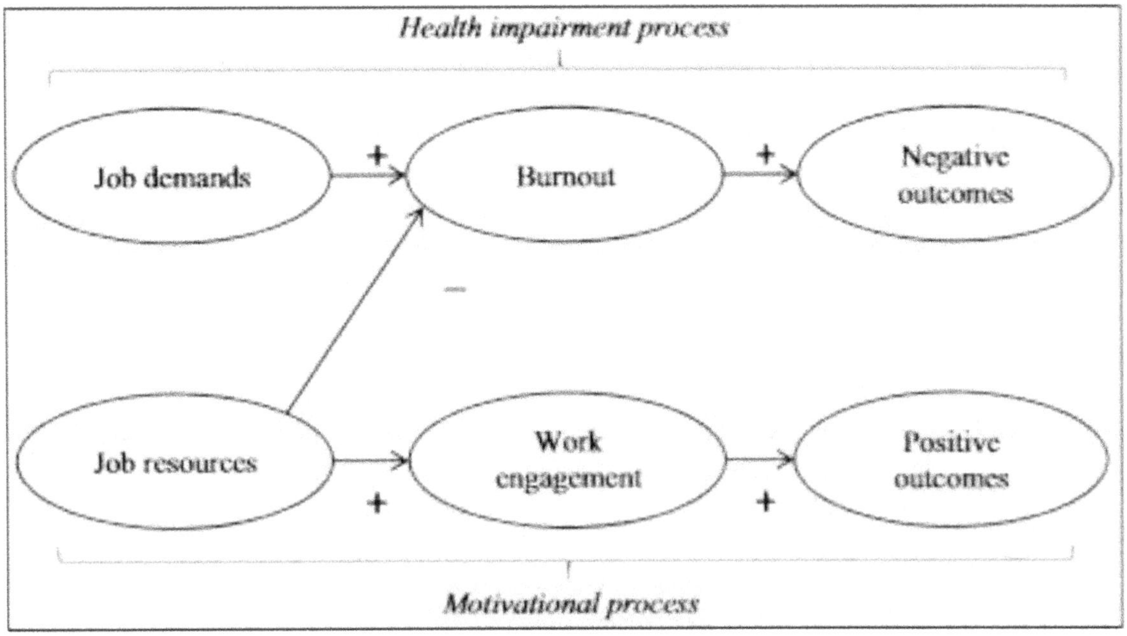

RESEARCH QUESTIONS AND HYPOTHESES

The research questions and hypotheses that were investigated in this study are listed in Table 1 below.

Table 1. Research questions and hypotheses

Research Question	Hypotheses
RQ1 What is the impact of job demands on emotional exhaustion?	H1: Work overload increases emotional exhaustion H2: Work-home interference increases emotional exhaustion H3: Inter-personal conflict increases emotional exhaustion H4: Role ambiguity increases emotional exhaustion
RQ2 What is the impact of job demands, and emotional exhaustion on emotional ill-health?	H5: Work overload increases emotional ill-health H6: Work-home interference increases emotional ill-health H7: Inter-personal conflict increases emotional ill-health H8: Role ambiguity increases emotional ill-health H9: Emotional exhaustion increases emotional ill-health
Dimensions of the variables • Job Demands - Work overload; work-home interference; Inter-personal conflict; Role ambiguity	

CONCEPTUAL FRAMEWORK

Hypotheses linking the variables of job demands and emotional exhaustion and emotional ill health investigated in this study are discussed below:

Job Demands and Emotional Exhaustion

Job demands are "physical, social, or organizational aspects of the job that require sustained physical or mental effort and are therefore associated with certain physiological and psychological costs'' (Demerouti, Bakker, Nachreiner, & Schaufeli, 2001, p. 501). Further, Thisera and Nawaratne (2018) propose that when job demands are very high, employees indulge in greater effort and energy, and subsequently, their efficiency is adversely impacted leading to emotional exhaustion. The dimensions of job demands (work overload, work-home interference, role ambiguity, and interpersonal conflict) are defined and the relationships between them and emotional exhaustion are discussed in the subsequent sections to derive hypotheses H1, H2, H3 and H4 indicated in table 1 above.

Work Overload and Emotional Exhaustion

Work overload refers to jobs characterized by the unreasonable expectation of a heavy workload and doing work that is beyond an employee's capacity within a limited given time and with limited available resources (Altaf & Awan, 2011). Previous studies have established that once work overload depletes the emotional capacity of employees to accomplish the demands of a job, psychological-emotional exhaustion is occasioned (Schaufeli & Taris, 2014). Therefore, the following hypothesis is derived:

H1: Work overload increases emotional exhaustion.

Work - Home Interference and Emotional Exhaustion

Work-home interference refers to situations where expectations from work and family roles are not compatible so that the presence in one role makes it impossible to engage in the other role (Verweij et al., 2017). According to the JD-R theory read together with the work-home resources (W-HR) model by Brummelhuis, Lieke, and Bakker (2012), work-home interference exhausts employees emotionally. Such conflict between work and home responsibilities weakens the cognitive levels of employees making it hard for them to cope emotionally. Involvement in work–home roles induces a depleting process whereby demands in one role drain emotional and mental resources in the other role limiting cognitive resources for optimal functioning (Tayfur & Arslan, 2013).

Previous research has established that work-home interference is one of the main antecedents of emotional exhaustion and that employees who experience work-home interference are at a greater risk of developing emotional exhaustion because the phenomenon is associated with certain physiological and psychological costs (Tayfur & Arslan, 2013). Therefore, based on previous studies and the JD-R theory, the following hypothesis is derived:

H2: Work-home interference increases emotional exhaustion

Role Ambiguity and Emotional Exhaustion

Role ambiguity refers to uncertainty about the expectations involved in performing activities in one's role (Ebbers & Wijnberg, 2017). According to the JD-R theory, Bakker and Demerouti (2017), role ambiguity negatively exerts pressure on employees' physical and emotional level because when employees are uncertain of their roles and their boundaries, they experience frustration that results in emotional exhaustion. Employees who perceive incongruence with their roles may also experience uncertainty and this may result in dissatisfaction resulting in psychological costs that consume emotional and physical energy leading to emotional exhaustion (Panari, Caricati, Pelosi, & Rossi, 2019).

Previous research established a positive association between role ambiguity and emotional exhaustion (Lepine, Podsakoff, & Lepine, 2005; Panari et al., 2019). For example, Tetrick et al, (2000: cited in Sunhee & Wang (2018) surveyed 160 licensed morticians and established that decreased levels of emotional exhaustion were positively correlated to perceived lower levels of role ambiguity. Based on these findings and the JD-R theory, the following hypothesis is derived:

H3: Role ambiguity increases emotional exhaustion

Inter-Personal Conflict and Emotional Exhaustion

Inter-personal conflict is defined as "a dynamic process that occurs between interdependent parties as they experience negative emotional reactions to perceived disagreements and interference with the attainment of their goals" (Barki & Hartwick, 2004, p. 234). Inter-personal conflict at the workplace can occur in many forms, ranging from gossip to physical attacks (Spector & Jex, 1998). According to the JD-R model (Bakker & Demerouti, 2017; Demerouti et al., 2001), inter-personal conflict negatively exerts pressure on the physical and emotional levels of employees. For example, the spreading of office rumors about an employee due to inter-personal conflicts in the office may create anger that may lead to emotional exhaustion for the employee being talked about.

Previous studies Giebels and Janssen (2004) established that inter-personal conflict at the workplace is associated with higher levels of emotional exhaustion. In a study to examine associations between inter-personal conflict in work settings and emotional exhaustion, Fujiwara, Tsukishima, Tsutsumi, Kawakami, and Kishi (2003) investigated home care workers in a cross-sectional survey in Sapporo, Japan. The study established that conflict with clients and their families was strongly associated with emotional exhaustion among home care workers. Conflict with supervisors too was strongly linked to emotional exhaustion. Based on existing research and the JD-R theory, the following hypothesis is derived:

H4: Inter-personal conflict increases emotional exhaustion

Job Demands and Emotional Ill-Health

Consistent with the JD-R theory Bakker and Demerouti (2017), the dimensions of job demands are significantly associated with emotional ill-health and the relationship is mediated through emotional exhaustion. The relationship between the four dimensions of job demands and emotional ill-health to derive hypotheses H5, H6, H7, and H8 are discussed below:

Work Overload and Emotional Ill-Health

According to the JD-R theory, Bakker and Demerouti (2017), work overload increases emotional exhaustion, which in turn increases emotional ill-health. In previous research by Maslach and Leiter (2016), it was established that work overload is significantly related to employees' depressive symptoms. Furthermore, de Beer, Pienaar, and Rothmann (2016) examined the causal associations of the well-being of employees in the JD-R model and the mediating role of emotional exhaustion in the relationship between emotional ill-health and work overload. It was established that emotional ill health was predicted by emotional exhaustion and that emotional exhaustion was predicted by work overload. Indirect relationships were established between emotional ill-health and work overload via emotional exhaustion.

The findings were consistent with the JD-R theory Bakker and Demerouti (2017) where emotional exhaustion had a causal mediation mechanism between emotional ill-health and work overload in the JD-R model. Therefore, the following hypothesis is derived:

H5: Work overload increases emotional ill-health

Work-Home Interference and Emotional Ill-Health

According to the JD-R theory Bakker and Demerouti (2017), work-home interference being a dimension of job demands increases emotional exhaustion which subsequently increases emotional ill-health due to the depletion of emotional energy at work and home. For example, if an employee is exhausted at the end of the day, he or she will be less likely to engage in his or her family duties at home which may result in work-home interference (Ilies, Huth, Ryan, & Dimotakis, 2015). Previous research studies Blom et al. (2014) established that an imbalance between the roles of work and home was correlated with sub-optimal wellbeing in employees including mental health. Therefore, the following hypothesis is derived:

H6: Work-home interference increases emotional ill-health

Inter-Personal Conflict and Emotional Ill-Health

According to the JD-R theory, Bakker and Demerouti (2017) inter-personal conflict as a dimension of job demands increases emotional ill-health with emotional exhaustion as the mediator. For example, inter-personal conflict at the workplace may lead to decreased individual well-being through increased alcohol intake and low-quality sleep, which are all manifestations of emotional ill-health (Danna & Griffin, 1999).

A longitudinal study by Nixon, Mazzola, Bauer, Krueger, and Spector (2011) established that inter-personal conflict at work is associated with higher levels of gastrointestinal problems and sleep disturbances, resulting in doctor visits by employees. In addition, Stoetzer et al. (2009) investigated a cohort of Swedish employees over two years and established that inter-personal conflict at work increased employee depression levels. Therefore, the following hypothesis is derived:

H7: Inter-personal conflict increases emotional ill-health

Role Ambiguity and Emotional Ill-Health

According to the JD-R theory Bakker and Demerouti (2017), role ambiguity influences emotional exhaustion and subsequently emotional ill-health. Further, in a study by Wu, Hu, and Zheng (2019) on contractors, subcontractors, and supervisors in the Chinese construction industry, it was established that role ambiguity caused employees to develop negative emotional experiences including increased stress, extreme internal tensions, and anxiety. Therefore, the following hypothesis is derived:

H8: Role ambiguity increases emotional ill-health

Emotional Exhaustion and Emotional Ill-Health

Emotional exhaustion refers to human wear and energy loss and is characterized by a feeling of being over-extended emotionally by job-related activities (Maslach & Leiter, 2016). Emotional exhaustion, being the most important dimension of burnout exhibits the depletion of emotional resources and energy leading to depression and anxiety (Maslach & Leiter, 2016). Chronic fatigue, emotional distress, and cognitive dysfunction are among the clinical signs and symptoms of emotional exhaustion (Maslach & Leiter, 2016; Sharpe & Wilks, 2002).

Emotional ill-health is a ''psychological-emotional disorder characterized by irrational and uncontrollable fears, persistent anxiety, or extreme hostility related to a psychological-emotional disorder'' (American Psychological Association, 2018). Further, (American Psychological Association, 2018; Maslach & Leiter, 2016) argue that emotional ill-health is characterized by depression and anxiety.

Occupational depression is a component of emotional ill-health and is characterized by the lack of motivation or enjoyment, dejected mood, tiredness or energy loss, diminished focus, worthless feelings, reduced or elevated appetite, sleep disturbances, and suicidal thoughts (Maslach & Leiter, 2016). According to Maslach and Leiter (2016), there is evidence in the literature that ties occupational depression to occupational burnout which is further linked to job demands as the main cause.

Anxiety according to the American Psychological Association (2018) is defined as emotions marked by an emotional state of strain, worries, and elevated blood pressure among employees. Further, anxiety is also described as a normal psychological disorder that serves as a defensive protective mechanism against threatening condition however, chronic anxiety can contribute to psychological distress impacting an employee's daily functioning (Cole, 2014)

Consistent with the JD-R theory, Bakker and Demerouti (2017), employees who continuously work under stressful or demanding conditions may increase their risk of developing long-term psychological conditions such as depression and panic attacks which impair employees' psychological functioning (Maslach & Leiter, 2016). Previous research has further established that emotional exhaustion may lead to serious mental and physical health problems according to Ruotsalainen, Verbeek, Mariné, and Serra (2014), often leading to several forms of withdrawal, such as absenteeism from work due to ill-health (Fernet, Torrès, Austin, & St-Pierre, 2016). Finally, emotional exhaustion fully mediates the relationship between job demands and depression (Alarcon, 2011; Renzo Bianchi, Schonfeld, & Laurent, 2014). Therefore, based on previous studies and the JD-R theory, the following hypothesis is derived:

H9: Emotional exhaustion increases emotional ill-health

RESEARCH METHODOLOGY

Details of the methods applied to collect and analyze the data are presented as follows: Research philosophy and design; sampling and sampling procedure, data collection followed by a brief discussion of survey instruments, measurement of variables, instrument reliability, and validity, and finally data analysis.

Research Philosophy and Design

To address the two research questions and to objectively quantify defined variables to generalize the findings, the study used a quantitative research design. The JD-R model was tested quantitively in the cultures of Africa, Asia, the Pacific, and the religions of Christianity and Hinduism. A diversity of findings were established with some findings being consistent with the JD-R theory and previous studies across the cultures while other findings were not consistent with previous studies and the JDR theory. The positivism cross-sectional design was chosen as the main philosophical stance for the study

Sampling and Sampling Procedure

Non-random sampling techniques (convenience and snowballing) were used to sample the respondents. A perfect representative sample was to be at least 30% of the total population sampled (Borg, Gall, & Gall, 2007). To comply with that assumption, five hundred (500) invitations were sent out but 173 (34.6%) responses were received back for analysis which was above 30% of the total population sampled. The criterion was fulfilled. The study's primary representation was drawn from employees who worked for different organizations and occupations in the regions of the Pacific (mainly Australia and New Zealand). Africa, Asia (Indian sub-continent of India, Pakistan, Nepal, Bangladesh, Siri-Lanka), and the religions of Christianity and Hindus. A broad range of ages, occupations, ethnicities, religions, and cultures was represented in the sample. The sample included mainly employees over the age of 18 from any occupation, religion, and region.

Data Collection

The data was collected using a survey instrument that was sent out electronically to the entire sampled population. To address privacy, a password was employed to protect the web-based survey platform with further measures taken to increase participant anonymity. Participants were to provide consent once they accessed the survey instrument so that they could continue filling the questionnaire. After consent, participants were required to answer qualifying questions, such as "what is your occupation, age, and sex?

Survey Instruments

The first part of the survey instrument captured the respondent's demographic characteristics while the other sections were organized in line with the main study themes. Instruments were selected considering two main criteria: (1) whether the tools fulfilled acceptable criteria of reliability and validity (2) whether the questions were concise and realistic to answer in terms of the time required to complete them. All the above two criteria regarding the instruments were fulfilled. The scales had been validated in other studies undertaken by (Bickerton et al., 2014). There were a total of 40 items in the instrument used in this study and it was estimated that it would take less than 15 minutes to finish completing the questionnaire.

Although the reliability and validity of the four scales of measures (job demands, emotional exhaustion, and emotional ill-health) had been established in previous studies (Bickerton et al., 2014; Bickerton, Miner, Dowson, & Griffin, 2015; Demerouti et al., 2001; Miner, Bickerton, Dowson, & Sterland, 2015; Schaufeli & Bakker, 2004), this study's sample was used by the researcher to estimate the reliability and cross-validated all the scales. All items (job demands, emotional exhaustion) were scored on a seven-point Likert scale (1=strongly disagree, 7= strongly agree) except emotional ill-health which was scored on a four-point Likert scale (1 = strongly disagree, 4= strongly agree).

Table 2. Variables and the Likert scale type

No	Variables	Items	Likert Scale
1.	Work overload	3	Seven-point Likert scale
2.	Work-home interference	3	Seven-point Likert scale
3.	Inter-personal conflict	3	Seven-point Likert scale
4.	Role Ambiguity	3	Seven-point Likert scale
5.	Emotional Exhaustion	5	Seven-point Likert scale
6.	Emotional Ill Heath	4	Four-point Likert scale

Measurement of Variables

Measurement items for the variables investigated in this study are presented in this section in the following order: work overload, role ambiguity, inter-personal conflict, and work-home interference, emotional exhaustion, and emotional ill-health.

Work Overload

Two items drawn from Zohar (1999) subscale and a third item drawn from Peterson et al. (1995) subscale were used to assess work overload. These scales were used to assess the impact of work overload on self-assessments of work quality on employees (Beebe, 2007). The scales were preferred because their validity and reliability were tested in previous research by Bickerton et al. (2015) and were found to be stable. Measurement items for work overload are listed below:

1. *There is not enough time for me to finish my work.*
2. *I am responsible for an unmanageable number of tasks at the same time.*
3. *The amount of work I must do interferes with the quality of my work.*

Role Ambiguity

Three items adapted from Ivancevich and Matteson (1980) subscale were used to measure role ambiguity. These scales were preferred because their validity and reliability were tested in previous research by Bickerton et al. (2014) and were found to be stable. Measurement items for role ambiguity are listed below:

1. *My work duties and objectives are unclear to me.*
2. *I do not know what the people I work with expect of me.*
3. *I must act without knowing exactly what is expected of me.*

Inter-Personal Conflict

Inter-personal conflict was assessed using three items adapted from Pearson, Ensley, and Amason (2002) Intragroup Conflict subscale These scales were preferred because their validity and reliability were tested in previous research by Bickerton et al. (2014) and were found to be stable. Measurement items for inter-personal conflict are listed below:

1. *Others are critical of me and the things I do at work.*
2. *I experience personal friction with others at work.*
3. *There are tensions at work when making group decisions.*

Work-Home Interference

Three items adapted from Netemeyer, Boles, and McMurrian (1996) work-family conflict subscale were used to measure work-home interference. These scales were preferred because their validity and reliability were tested in previous research by Bickerton et al. (2014) and were found to be stable. Measurement items for work-home interference are listed below:

1. *The demands of my work interfere with my home/family life.*
2. *My work schedule stops me from fulfilling my domestic obligations.*
3. *My work leaves little time for other activities.*

Emotional Exhaustion

The five-item exhaustion subscale of the Maslach Burnout Inventory–General Survey (MBI-GS) Emotional exhaustion was used to assess emotional exhaustion (Schaufeli, Leiter, Maslach, & Jackson, 1996). This subscale was selected because their validity and reliability was tested in previous research by Bickerton et al. (2014) and was found to be stable. Measurement items for emotional exhaustion are listed below:

1. *I feel used up at the end of the workday*
2. *I feel tired when I get up in the morning and must face another day on the job*
3. *I feel emotionally drained from my work*
4. *Working all day is a strain for me*
5. *I feel burned out from my work*

Emotional Ill-Health

Four items from the 12-item version of the General Health Questionnaire (GHQ-12) were used to measure emotional ill-health (Goldberg & Williams, 1988). This subscale was selected because their validity and reliability was tested in previous research by Bickerton et al. (2014) and was found to be stable. Measurement items for emotional ill-health are listed below:

1. *Lost much sleep over worry*
2. *Felt constantly under strain*
3. *Felt you could not overcome difficulties*
4. *Been feeling unhappy and depressed*

Instrument Reliability and Validity

The reliability of the scales was based on Cronbach Alpha Coefficients while instrument validity was based on Pearson's correlation coefficient to validate the degree to which the measuring scales accurately measured the constructs (job demands, emotional exhaustion, and emotional ill-health). A discussion regarding instrument reliability and validity is presented below:

Instrument Reliability

A generally accepted rule according to Hulin, Netemeyer, and Cudeck (2001) is that a Cronbach Alpha Coefficient of between 0.6 - 0.7 implies a reasonable degree of reliability, and 0.8 or greater is a very strong level. However, values higher than 0.95 aren't inherently good, since they may strongly indicate redundancy. In this study, none of the Cronbach's alpha Coefficients for both the independent and dependent variables were under 0.6 and above 0.95 suggesting an acceptable level of reliability (Hulin et al., 2001). The results of the Cronbach Alpha Coefficients are provided in Table 3 below.

Table 3. Variables and the Likert scale type/reliability Statistics

Variable	Items	Cronbach Alpha Coefficient
Work overload	3	0.652
Work-home interference	3	0.755
Inter-personal conflict	3	0.692
Role ambiguity	3	0.756
Emotional exhaustion	5	0.816
Emotional ill heath	4	0.851

Overall, the scales demonstrated a satisfactory reliability.

Instrument Validity

The validity of Pearson's correlation coefficient is a number between 0 and 1.00 which shows the magnitude of the relationship "r," between the test and the measure of criterion. The confidence of the researcher in the predictions from the test scores is greater when the coefficient is high. The degree to which the test is associated with the criterion shows a reliable predictor of the criterion measured. Below are the Pearson's correlation coefficient (r) and the *p-values* as presented in Table 4 below.

Table 4. Correlation statistics

Variables	Correlation Coefficients (r)	p- value
Workover load and Emotional Exhaustion	0.477**	0.000
Workover load and emotional ill-health	0.455**	0.000
Work-home interference and Emotional Exhaust.	0.435**	0.000
Work-home interference and emotional ill-health	0.434**	0.000
Inter-personal conflict and Emotional Exhaustion	0.407**	0.000
Inter-personal conflict and emotional ill-health	0.490**	0.000
Role Ambiguity and Emotional Exhaustion	0353**	0.000
Role Ambiguity and emotional ill-health	0.383**	0.000
Emotional Exhaustion and emotional ill-health	0.541	0.000

**. Correlation is significant at the 0.01 level (2-tailed).
*. Correlation is significant at the 0.05 level (2-tailed).

According to Table 4 above, the correlation coefficients between the dimensions of job demands and emotional exhaustion and emotional ill-health and the correlation coefficients between emotional exhaustion and emotional ill-health were high above 0.3 indicating that the researcher had a lot of confidence in the predictions made from the test scores and the tests were valid.

Data Analysis

Path analysis modeling was used to represent the hypotheses of the model. Each of the variables in the model was included as a latent factor operationalized by the observed variables. M-plus 7 (Muthen & Muthen, 2013) was used to test the measurement model, and latent-variable hypothesized structural relationships through regression analysis. Data analysis was conducted in one single step where all paths were simultaneously tested, and significant beta weights were identified and reported.

Descriptive statistics including coding and quality checks were done in Statistical Package for Social Sciences (SPSS) Windows Version 26 (2019). Data entry quality was not of concern because the survey was entered by respondents directly online, so there were no errors in data entry anticipated.

SUMMARY OF THE FINDINGS

Findings on hypotheses investigating the impact of the dimensions of job demands on emotional exhaustion and emotional ill health are presented in this section. Table 5 below summarizes the coefficients results of the hypotheses tests and significant ones indicated by an (*).

*Table 5. Summary of path analysis significant coefficients indicated with**

Research Question	Hypotheses	Hypotheses supported?					
		All respondents	**Christians**	**Hindus**	**Asia**	**Africa**	**Pacific Region**
RQ1 What is the impact of job demands on emotional exhaustion?	H1: Work overload increases emotional exhaustion	**0.007***	0.125	0.301	**0.034***	**0.025***	**0.088****
	H2: Work-home interference increases emotional exhaustion	**0.028***	**0.007***	0.546	**0.521**	**0.366**	**0.000***
	H3: Inter-personal conflict increases emotional exhaustion	0.622	0.143	0.774	0.925	0.495	0.695
	H4: Role ambiguity increases emotional exhaustion	0.209	0.300	**0.086****	**0.087****	0.806	**0.002***
RQ2 What is the impact of job demands, and emotional exhaustion on emotional ill-health?	H5: Work overload increases emotional ill-health	0.354	0.601	**0.065****	**0.026***	0.568	0.810
	H6: Work-home interference increases emotional ill-health	0.107	0.375	0.128	0.277	0.580	0.202
	H7: Inter-personal conflict increases emotional ill-health	**0.067****	0.538	**0.085****	**0.012***	0.248	0.771
	H8: Role ambiguity increases emotional ill-health	0.547	0.124	0.360	0.830	0.415	0.689
	H9: Emotional exhaustion increases emotional ill-health	**0.000***	**0.000***	0.170	**0.039***	**0.000***	0.693

Dimensions of the variables
Job Demands - Work overload; work-home interference; Inter-personal conflict; Role ambiguity
* Beta coefficient is significant at the 0.05 level (2-tailed)
** Beta coefficient is significant at 0.1 level (2-tailed)

CONCLUSION AND DISCUSSION

The concluding discussion to the findings of this study regarding the impact of the dimensions of job demands on emotional exhaustion and emotional ill health are presented below:

Job Demands and Emotional Exhaustion

To answer the first research question, findings investigated the impact of the dimensions of job demands on emotional exhaustion and are discussed below.

Work Overload and Emotional Exhaustion

The findings were supported across the overall respondent category and within the three geographical regions namely, Asia, Africa, and the Pacific. The findings were consistent with the JD-R theory Bakker and Demerouti (2017) and were also supported by previous studies (Schaufeli & Taris, 2014; Thuynsma & de Beer, 2016) who established that work overload predicted emotional exhaustion. However, the findings were not supported among Christians and Hindus indicating that work overload does not predict emotional exhaustion in the religious realm. Overall, however, the findings indicated that work overload predicted emotional exhaustion.

The findings according to Munroe and Munroe (1972) are attributable to the culture of obedience in Africa and Asia where employees take on more jobs beyond their capacity as it is culturally disrespectful to disobey a person in authority. This is unlike the culture of disobedience in the United States of America where employees do not take on more jobs citing abuse of human rights (Munroe & Munroe, 1972). Due to the culture in Africa and Asia, the effects of such a heavy workload lead to emotional exhaustion (Munroe & Munroe, 1972). In most cases in Africa, Asia, China, and Latin America employees take on more jobs without adequate compensation, such as the lack of overtime payments including non-fully paid holiday leave, and inadequate job resources such as training to upskill. This leads to frustration and employee emotional disturbance

Further, according to (Asia Society, 2020; BBC News, 2019), the caste system in the Indian subcontinent has contributed to bad working conditions and relations at the workplace because employees are looked down upon by their employers because they are not regarded as members of their club in status and class. Employees feel emotionally disturbed with such pathetic attitudes by employers.

In the Pacific region mainly in Australia and New Zealand, the British/European culture is practiced where working conditions are good and working long hours is compensated under normal circumstances. However, work overload in this region is manifested in employees' perceptions regarding the amount of work and the job characteristics of work to be performed (Ryan & Deci, 2000). Intrinsic employees may find solace in routine jobs and any change in job design may cause emotional exhaustion (Ryan & Deci, 2000).

The British/European culture is also practiced in the United States of America and Canada where working conditions are good and working long hours is also compensated under normal circumstances. Work overload in this region is manifested in employees' perceptions regarding the amount of work and the job characteristics of work to be performed (Ryan & Deci, 2000). Intrinsic employees may find solace in routine jobs and any change in job design may cause emotional exhaustion (Ryan & Deci, 2000)

Work-Home Interference and Emotional Exhaustion

The finding was supported across the overall respondent's category and the respondents within the geographical region of the Pacific and those who profess Christianity. The findings are consistent with the JD-R model Bakker and Demerouti (2017) and previous studies (Bakker et al., 2011; Yunsoo & Eissenstat, 2018) which established that work-home interference predicted emotional exhaustion. However, the finding was not supported among Hindus and the regions of Asia and Africa indicating that work-home interference does not predict emotional exhaustion in those categories. Overall, however, the findings indicate that work-home interference predicts emotional exhaustion.

In the Pacific region which includes Australia and New Zealand, for example, according to Kashima, Halloran, Yuki, and Kashima (2004), this finding could be attributable to the British and European individualistic conservative culture where it is generally known to emphasize individual goals at the expense of group or community goals. This individualistic mindset contributes to the negative attitude of "my problem not anyone else's business'' in that neighbors do not share, for example, child nanny responsibilities on a rotation basis while working on shifts. The other attributing factor is the high cost of nannies and childcare centers in the Pacific region to relieve working parents to concentrate on work. All these factors combined leave employees mainly female employees with children at home frustrated and exhausted while combining work and family roles.

Similar British and European individualistic conservative culture is shared in the United States of America which often places a greater emphasis on characteristics such as assertiveness and independence (William, 2007). Americans are more likely to prioritize themselves over a group and they value independence and autonomy (William, 2007). For example, a reasonable request like wearing a face mask in exchange for saving thousands of lives because of the effects of COVID 19 is met with skepticism by employees in the U.S.A. There are those American employees who rail against being told what to do by employers. This is so that the employees sacrifice a minor inconvenience for the greater good (Matthew, 2020). Such an individualistic culture has made employees frustrated and exhausted.

In the Hindu faith, Africa, and Asia, the finding was not supported for this category of respondents and this could be attributable to employees not having children at home. This finding supports the view that having children at home may cause work-home interference that subsequently increases emotional exhaustion among employees in all cultures (Hubert & Aujoulat, 2018). Further, the finding could be attributable to the Hindu faith and African culture where women remain at home to take care of children and family (Sharma, Pandit, Pathak, & Sharma, 2013). This support by the wife to the husband is assumed to buffer the negative effects of work-home interference on emotional exhaustion since the husband concentrates on work while the wife looks after the home (Flood & Genadek, 2016).

This is contrasted in the United States of America, Canada, and Australia who follow the European way of life where both husband and wife work and leave children in childcare centers (William, 2007). This practice reduces emotional exhaustion among couples who have children at home. Additionally, the Hindu, Christian, and African cultures encourage married couples to share roles and those who share family roles do not feel emotionally exhausted (Sharma et al., 2013). This sharing of roles among couples is also supported in the United States of America, Canada, and Australia including China and Latin America (Flood & Genadek, 2016).

This finding may also be attributable for example to the culture where Asians including the Chinese just like Africans and Latinos live in a collectivist structure where the ''problem of a neighbor is a problem for us'' (Hui & Triandis, 1986). Hence, aunties and uncles assist in taking care of children when parents go to work. Also because of high unemployment in Asia and Africa and the Latino world, well-learned house helps (nannies) are employed to take care of the home and children while the parents are busy working.

Inter-Personal Conflict and Emotional Exhaustion

The finding was not supported across all the respondent's category, Africa, Pacific, Asia, Christians, and Hindus indicating that inter-personal conflict did not predict emotional exhaustion in all the categories of respondents This finding is not consistent with the JD-R theory Bakker and Demerouti (2017) which proposes that inter-personal conflict as a dimension of job demands predicts emotional exhaustion.

Further, this finding is not consistent with previous studies (Barki & Hartwick, 2004; De Dreu, van Dierendonck, & Dijkstra, 2004; Fujiwara et al., 2003; Giebels & Janssen, 2004) which established that inter-personal conflict as a dimension of job demands is associated with higher levels of emotional exhaustion. These findings were not expected, and further research using a larger sample is recommended. Overall, however, the findings indicate that inter-personal conflict does not predict emotional exhaustion. The reasons for the predictions are listed below:

In the Pacific region, the finding although not expected may be attributable to well-established rules and conflict management procedures and policies at the workplaces in Australia (NSW, 2021). Australia has relied extensively on a scheme of mutual conciliation and arbitration to deal with workplace interpersonal conflicts. Such processes have been encouraged to facilitate the responsibility of each party (Hancock, Polites, & Fitzgibbon, 1985). The realization by employees that conflict resolution mechanisms are in place in workplaces in the Pacific region influences positive work mentality (Hancock et al., 1985). This mutual conciliation and arbitration to deal with workplace interpersonal conflicts are also practiced in the European Union countries including Britain (Sverdrup, 2021).

The cultural Asian, African, Christian, and Hindu orientation propagates the value of love and a collectivist culture where the responsibilities and obligations of an individual are to a group and any misunderstanding within a work environment is solved within a cultural group context (Chadda & Deb, 2013). This realization of duty of care and respect within a group setting reduces the negative effects of inter-personal conflict on emotional exhaustion by increasing positive work relations and hope (Bickerton et al., 2015). Further, the fear of being psychologically expelled or punished by the group initiates positive behavior within an employment group contributing to less inter-personal conflict (Chadda & Deb, 2013).

The value of love and a collectivist culture where the responsibilities and obligations of an individual are to a group setting to sort out misunderstanding in the workplace is also practiced in Latin countries of South America (Velez-Calle, Robledo-Ardila, & Rodriguez-Rios, 2015). Similarly, inter-personal resolution mechanisms are practiced in the Muslim Arab world and China who also practice a collectivist culture. The three regions show common trends in their societal patterns oriented toward collectivism in resolving conflicts at the workplace (Velez-Calle et al., 2015).

Role Ambiguity and Emotional Exhaustion

The finding was not supported across the overall respondent's category, Christian and among Africans indicating that role ambiguity did not predict emotional exhaustion in those categories. This is not in line with the JD-R theory Bakker and Demerouti (2017) which proposes that role ambiguity as a dimension of job demands predicts emotional exhaustion. These findings were not expected and further research using a larger sample is recommended.

However, the finding was supported in Asia, the Pacific and among the Hindus, indicating that role ambiguity predicted emotional exhaustion in those categories. These findings are consistent with the JD-R theory Bakker and Demerouti (2017) which proposes that role ambiguity as a dimension of job demands predicts emotional exhaustion. The finding is also aligned with previous studies conducted by (Erica & Barak, 2015; Panari et al., 2019) who established that emotional exhaustion was positively correlated to role ambiguity.

The findings relating to Asia, Pacific, and among the Hindus could be attributable to perceived employees incongruence with their roles which make them experience uncertainty and this may result in dissatisfaction resulting in psychological costs that consume emotional and physical energy leading to emotional exhaustion (Ngo, Foley, & Loi, 2005; Panari et al., 2019). Overall, however, the findings indicate that role ambiguity does not increase emotional exhaustion.

Job Demands and Emotional Ill-Health

To answer the second research question, findings investigated the impact of the dimensions of job demands on emotional exhaustion and are discussed below.

Work Overload and Emotional Ill-Health

The finding was not supported across the overall respondent's category, among Christians, Africans, and respondents from the Pacific indicating that work overload did not directly predict emotional ill-health. The findings were consistent with the JD-R theory (Bakker & Demerouti, 2017) which proposes that work overload does not directly increase emotional ill-health but indirectly predicts emotional ill-health through emotional exhaustion. The findings were also consistent with previous studies (Bickerton et al., 2015) indicating that work overload does not directly increase emotional ill-health. This could be attributable to Christian religious beliefs in the Pacific and African regions and among Christians where work is seen as a calling and a benefit to humanity and nature (Bickerton et al., 2015). Such beliefs about work may not lead directly to emotional ill-health as confirmed by the JD-R theory (Bakker & Demerouti, 2017).

However, the finding was supported in Asia and among Hindus suggesting that work overload directly predicts emotional ill-health. This finding could be attributable to Hindu religious beliefs where people are very emotional and do not compromise on their beliefs be it work or otherwise (Richardsone, Sinha, & Yaapar, 2014). It follows therefore that work-related stress will sometimes directly influence emotional ill-health without being mediated through emotional exhaustion.

Work-Home Interference and Emotional Ill-Health

The finding was not supported among the overall respondents' category, Africa, Asia, Pacific, Christians, and Hindus, suggesting that work-home interference as a job demand does not directly predict emotional ill-health. These findings are consistent with the JD-R Theory of Bakker and Demerouti (2017) which proposes that work-home interference as a job demand does not directly predict emotional ill-health but is influenced through emotional exhaustion as a mediating variable. However, this finding is not consistent with previous studies by (Huang, Ribeiro, Musacchio, & Franklin, 2017; Thuynsma & de Beer,

2016) who established that work-home interference was found to be significantly related to employees' depressive symptoms.

However, Peeters, Montgomery, Bakker, and Schaufeli (2005) disagreed, arguing that the mismatch between work–home is triggered by certain occupational stressors which lead to emotional exhaustion and subsequently depression and anxiety (emotional ill-health). Further, it should be remembered that working people with concurrent family responsibilities have shown to experience higher levels of stress and exhaustion. (Kinnunen & Mauno, 1998). Therefore overall, work-home interference did not directly predict emotional ill-health.

This is attributable for example to the culture where Asians just like Africans live in a collectivist structure where the ''problem of a neighbor is a problem for us'' (Hui & Triandis, 1986). Hence, aunties and uncles assist in taking care of children when parents go to work. Also because of high unemployment in Asia, well-learned house helps (nannies) are employed to take care of the home and children while the parents are busy working. Also, culturally Asia and African, women take care of the home and children while men work (Sharma et al., 2013). This causes low incidences of work-home interference that lead directly to emotional ill-health.

Role Ambiguity and Emotional Ill-Health

The finding was not supported among the overall respondents' category, Africa, Asia, Pacific, Christians, and Hindus suggesting that role ambiguity as a job demand does not directly predict emotional ill-health. These findings are consistent with the JD-R Theory of Bakker and Demerouti (2017) which proposes that role ambiguity as a job demand does not predict emotional ill-health directly but through the mediation of emotional exhaustion. However, this finding is not consistent with previous studies by (Huang et al., 2017; Mañas et al., 2018; Thuynsma & de Beer, 2016) who found that role ambiguity as an emotional job demand was found to be significantly related to employees' depressive symptoms. Therefore overall, role ambiguity does not directly increase emotional ill-health. This could be attributable to employees being unable to predict a workload and strategize a work plan causing confusion and frustration and subsequently causing emotional exhaustion and subsequently emotional ill-health (Ngo et al., 2005; Panari et al., 2019).

Inter-Personal Conflict Increases Emotional Ill-Health

The finding was supported indicating that inter-personal conflict significantly predicted emotional ill-health in the overall respondent category, Asia, and among the Hindus. However, these findings were not consistent with JD-R Theory Bakker and Demerouti (2017) which proposes that inter-personal conflict as a job demand does not predict emotional ill-health directly but through the mediation of emotional exhaustion. This finding is aligned with previous studies Raeve, Jansen, Brandt, Vasse, and Kant (2009) which established that inter-personal conflict had a direct positive effect on emotional ill-health.

This finding is also consistent with previous studies by (Huang et al., 2017; Mañas et al., 2018; Thuynsma & de Beer, 2016) which established that job demands (Inter-personal conflict) was found to be significantly related to employees' depressive symptoms. This finding could be attributable to Hindu religious beliefs where people are very emotional and do not compromise on their beliefs be it work or otherwise (Richardsone et al., 2014). It follows therefore that work-related stress will sometimes directly influence emotional ill-health without being mediated through emotional exhaustion.

However, the finding was not supported among the respondents who were Christians, Africa, and the Pacific indicating that inter-personal conflict did not predict emotional ill-health directly in those categories. This could be due to having conflict resolution mechanisms in place in workplaces in this category of respondents that may reduce the negative effects of job demands on emotional ill health by increasing positive work orientation. Such processes have been encouraged as a way to facilitate the responsibility of each party (Hancock et al., 1985). Further, the cultures of African, the pacific mainly Australia, and the Christian orientation propagates the value of love. This realization of duty of care and respect within a group setting reduces the negative effects of inter-personal conflict on emotional exhaustion by increasing positive work relations and hope (Bickerton et al., 2015)

The findings from these categories are consistent with the JD-R Theory of Bakker and Demerouti (2017) but are not aligned with previous studies of Raeve et al. (2009) which established that inter-personal conflict had a direct positive effect on emotional ill-health. Further, this finding is also not consistent with several previous studies that established that job demands (inter-personal conflict) were found to be significantly related to employees' depressive symptoms (Huang et al., 2017; Mañas et al., 2018; Thuynsma & de Beer, 2016).

Emotional Exhaustion and Emotional Ill-Health

The finding was supported in the overall respondent category, Africa, Asia, and among Christians indicating that emotional exhaustion increased emotional ill-health. The findings are consistent with previous research findings by Bickerton et al. (2014) who established that emotional exhaustion directly influenced emotional ill-health. Further, in previous studies, burnout (exhaustion) fully mediated the relationship between job strain and depression (Ahola & Hakanen, 2008, 2014; Ahola, Hakanen, Perhoniemi, & Mutanen, 2014). The findings are also consistent with the JD-R theory Bakker and Demerouti (2017) which proposes that emotional exhaustion directly influences emotional ill-health.

However, the finding was not supported among the Hindus and the Pacific indicating that emotional exhaustion does not increase emotional ill-health. This finding is not consistent with the JD-R theory Bakker and Demerouti (2017) which proposes that emotional exhaustion increased emotional ill-health. The finding was not consistent with previous research findings either by (Bickerton et al., 2014; Maslach & Leiter, 2016) who established that emotional exhaustion predicted emotional ill-health. This finding was not expected, and further research is recommended with a larger sample. Therefore overall, emotional exhaustion reduces emotional ill-health.

Theoretical Contributions of the Study

The study represented a novel investigation of the effects of job demands on emotional exhaustion and emotional ill-health thus extending the health impairment process of the JD-R model in the context of the cultures of Asia, Africa, and Pacific and the Christian and Hindu religions thus providing valuable lessons on the universality of the JD-R model. The design of this study was based on the theoretical framework of the JD-R theory (Bakker & Demerouti, 2017). The study established two main contributions to the JD-R theory:

Firstly, the study provided valuable insight into the potential impacts of each dimension of job demands on emotional exhaustion or emotional ill-health in the context of the cultures of Asia, Africa, Pacific, the Christian and Hindu religions in the health impairment component of the

JD-R theory (Bakker & Demerouti, 2017). In this study, the universality of the JD-R theory was tested, and mixed findings were established within the cultures under review. It can be concluded from the findings that different cultures influence the outcomes of the health impairment process of the JD-R theory differently. Therefore, regarding the findings, job demands positively predicted emotional exhaustion and emotional ill health in some cultures and not others. This means that job demands regardless of the combinations of the dimensions could exert harmful effects on employee's health.

The findings also collaborated with previous studies on the outcomes of job demands and extend the theory of the health impairment process of the JD-R model (Bakker & Demerouti, 2014, 2017; Demerouti et al., 2001). However, based on the contrasting outcomes of this study, the JD-R theory can be used by practitioners to combine specific dimensions of job demands applicable to different cultures hence extending the robustness of the theory and providing valuable insights on the mechanism of emotional exhaustion and emotional ill-health. This is a theoretical contribution to the literature as each job demand dimension predicts differently in each culture.

Secondly, the study provided valuable insight into the potential impacts of emotional exhaustion on emotional ill-health in the context of the cultures of Asia, Africa, and the Pacific and the Christian and Hindu religions. Overall, the findings confirmed the JD-R theory (Bakker & Demerouti, 2017). However, some findings within the cultures returned mixed results. It can be concluded from the findings that different cultures influence differently the operation of the JD-R theory. Significantly, emotional exhaustion did not predict emotional ill-health in the Pacific region and Hindu religion. This finding was not consistent with the JD-R theory and previous studies and was not expected. Further studies are recommended.

Managerial Contributions of the Study

The findings have some implications for human resource practitioners, for example, investment in JD-R interventions may offer organizations the opportunity to meet employee expectations by providing high-quality working environments compatible with the type of job demands in their culture. The study suggested that work overload had a positive significant relationship with exhaustion and multiple regression analysis showed that work overload was a statistically significant predictor of employee exhaustion and subsequently emotional ill-health. Therefore, practitioners need to know that, having high workloads, the need to meet deadlines, and working under tight time pressure significantly creates employee exhaustion and subsequently emotional ill-health. Practitioners must moderate the amount of work allocated to each employee since the moderation significantly decreases emotional exhaustion directly and subsequently emotional ill-health.

The findings further suggested that work-home interference created a conflict that aggravated emotional exhaustion and subsequently emotional ill-health These findings support the conclusion that work-home interference is positively related to emotional exhaustion and subsequently emotional ill-health. Therefore, to curtail employees' feelings of exhaustion, practitioners should design and prioritize organizational interventions to decrease work-home interference to manageable levels, for example, creating a fine balance in the way in which work is assigned to employees and also designing working from home rosters. In addition, it would be beneficial to determine the minimum, maximum, and optimal number of hours an employee should work per week while making sure that employees equally share the workload, not only quantitatively but qualitatively. Other programs could include assisting membership fees in childcare centers. Such incentives could contribute to employee wellbeing that could see a reduction in work-home interference. This may increase employee emotional nourishment.

Practitioners should also pay attention to gender differences, practitioners need to know that married employees with children at home might experience higher levels of job demands, thus resulting in emotional exhaustion and subsequently, emotional ill-health Practitioners should also keep in mind that such employees take many days of sick leave meaning they have higher levels of exhaustion. Practitioners should work to resolve these work situations by moderating the workload as this may affect employee performance.

The study further established that role ambiguity was positively related to emotional exhaustion subsequently emotional ill-health This is because if the role of an employee is uncertain, the workload cannot be strategized or predicted. To eliminate incompetence and psychological concerns resulting from role ambiguity, organizations should inform employees about their roles and the expectations of the organizations regarding their roles and these should be properly documented.

The study further established that interpersonal conflict in the workplace was positively related to emotional exhaustion and subsequently to emotional ill-health. To reduce conflict, organizations should establish conflict resolution mechanisms and rules, and these should be properly documented.

Overall, this study demonstrated the potential predictive power of the JD-R model (Bakker & Demerouti, 2014, 2017; Demerouti et al., 2001). Therefore, the study contributed to the literature by assessing the different effects of the dimensions of job demands in different cultures within the context of the JD-R theory. The findings indicate that organizations may use different combinations and approaches of interventions based on the dimensions that relate to each culture to reduce exhaustion and emotional ill health and improve labor laws of each culture.

LIMITATIONS/RECOMMENDATIONS FOR FUTURE STUDY

The researcher relied on self-completed questionnaires which depended on the perception of respondents. However, there is a possibility that common method bias could affect the strength of the contributions (Podsakoff, MacKenzie, Lee, & Podsakoff, 2003). Nevertheless, the researcher did not expect this to be a problem because common method bias generally declines when studying interactions (Siemsen, Roth, & Oliveira, 2010). Further, the instruments had direct questions which could not obtain objective answers. The study further did not include success cases by organizations where they had done well in maintaining a conducive work environment.

Future studies could change the questions so that objective answers are obtained. Further, future studies could include success cases by organizations where they had done well in maintaining a conducive work environment. Additionally, future studies could minimize this potential effect by collecting data across different periods (longitudinal study) including collecting data from multiple sources (e.g., conducting semi-structured interviews). Further, this study utilized non-random sampling methods. For practical reasons, this sampling design was chosen because of time constraints and a limited budget. A major disadvantage of this design method is that the results might not be representative. It is recommended that future studies use larger samples selected through random sampling methods to make the findings more representative.

CHAPTER SUMMARY

The chapter explored the effects of job demands on emotional exhaustion and emotional ill-health on employee's wellbeing in the health impairment process of the JD-R model. Overall, the findings largely confirmed the JD-R health impairment process hypothesis. The study further confirmed that job demands variables are seen to be directly associated with emotional exhaustion but indirectly associated with emotional ill heath with emotional exhaustion as a mediator. The findings also suggested that the effects of the work environment factors such as job demands (work overload, interpersonal conflict, role ambiguity, and work-home interference) on emotional exhaustion and emotional ill health may differ across cultures.

REFERENCES

Ahola, K., & Hakanen, J. J. (2008). Job strain, burnout, and depressive symptoms: A prospective study among dentists. *Journal of Affective Disorders*, *104*(1-3), 103–110. doi:10.1016/j.jad.2007.03.004 PMID:17448543

Ahola, K., & Hakanen, J. J. (2014). Burnout and health. In *Burnout at work: A psychological perspective* (pp. 10–31). Psychology Press.

Ahola, K., Hakanen, J. J., Perhoniemi, R., & Mutanen, P. (2014). Relationship between burnout and depressive symptoms: A study using the person-centred approach. *Burnout Research*, *1*(1), 29–37. doi:10.1016/j.burn.2014.03.003

Alarcon, G. M. (2011). A meta-analysis of burnout with job demands, resources, and attitudes. *Journal of Vocational Behavior*, *79*(2), 549–562. doi:10.1016/j.jvb.2011.03.007

Alarcon, G. M., Eschleman, K. J., & Bowling, N. A. (2009). Relationships between personality variables and burnout: A meta-analysis. *Work and Stress*, *23*(3), 244–263. doi:10.1080/02678370903282600

Altaf, A., & Awan, M. A. (2011). Moderating Affect of Workplace Spirituality on the Relationship of Job Overload and Job Satisfaction. *Journal of Business Ethics*, *104*(1), 93–99. doi:10.100710551-011-0891-0

American Psychological Association. (2018). *Treating Depression, Anxiety, and Stress in Ethnic and Racial Groups: Cognitive Behavioral Approaches*. The American Psychological Association. doi:https://www.apa.org/topics/depression/

Armon, G., Melamed, S., Shirom, A., & Shapira, I. (2010). Elevated Burnout Predicts the Onset of Musculoskeletal Pain Among Apparently Healthy Employees. *Journal of Occupational Health Psychology*, *15*(4), 399–408. doi:10.1037/a0020726 PMID:21058854

Asia Society. (2020). *Jati: The Caste System in India*. Author.

Bakker, A. B., ten Brummelhuis, L. L., Prins, J. T., & der Heijden, F. M. M. A. (2011). Applying the job demands–resources model to the work–home interface: A study among medical residents and their partners. *Journal of Vocational Behavior*, *79*(1), 170–180. doi:10.1016/j.jvb.2010.12.004

Bakker, A. B., & Demerouti, E. (2014). Job demands-resources theory. In *Work and wellbeing: A Complete Reference Guide* (Vol. 3, pp. 37–64). Wiley-Blackwell. doi:10.1002/9781118539415.wbwell019

Bakker, A. B., & Demerouti, E. (2017). Job demands–resources theory: Taking stock and looking forward. *Journal of Occupational Health Psychology, 22*(3), 273–285. doi:10.1037/ocp0000056 PMID:27732008

Bakker, A. B., & Demerouti, E. (2018). *Multiple levels in job demands-resources theory: Implications for employee well-being and performance*. DEF Publishers.

Bakker, A. B., Demerouti, E., & Euwema, M. C. (2005). Job Resources Buffer the Impact of Job Demands on Burnout. *Journal of Occupational Health Psychology, 10*(2), 170–180. doi:10.1037/1076-8998.10.2.170 PMID:15826226

Barki, H., & Hartwick, J. (2004). Conceptualizing The Construct of Interpersonal Conflict. *International Journal of Conflict Management, 15*(3), 216–244. doi:10.1108/eb022913

BBC News. (2019). *What is India's caste system?* BBC News.

Beebe, R. S. (2007). Predicting Burnout, Conflict Management Style, and Turnover Among Clergy. *Journal of Career Assessment, 15*(2), 257–275. doi:10.1177/1069072706298157

Bianchi, R., Schonfeld, I., & Laurent, E. (2014). Is burnout a depressive disorder? A reexamination with special focus on atypical depression. *International Journal of Stress Management, 21*, 307-324. doi:10.1037/a0037906

Bianchi, R., Schonfeld, I., & Laurent, E. (2015). Burnout-depression overlap: A review. *Clinical Psychology Review, 36*, 28-41. doi:10.1016/j.cpr.2015.01.004

Bickerton, G. R., Miner, M. H., Dowson, M., & Griffin, B. (2014). Spiritual resources and work engagement among religous workers: A three - wave longitudinal study. *Journal of Occupational Psychology, 87*(2), 370–391. doi:10.1111/joop.12052

Bickerton, G. R., Miner, M. H., Dowson, M., & Griffin, B. (2015). Incremental validity of spiritual resources in the job demands-resources model. *Psychology of Religion and Spirituality, 7*(2), 162–172. doi:10.1037/rel0000012

Blom, V., Sverke, M., Bodin, L., Bergström, G., Lindfors, P., & Svedberg, P. (2014). Work–home interference and burnout: A study based on swedish twins. *Journal of Occupational and Environmental Medicine, 56*(4), 361–366. doi:10.1097/JOM.0000000000000128 PMID:24709761

Borg, W. R., Gall, M. D., & Gall, J. P. (2007). Educational Research: An Introduction (8th ed.). New York: Longman.

Borritz, M., Rugulies, R., Bjorner, J. B., Villadsen, E., Mikkelsen, O. A., & Kristensen, T. S. (2006). Burnout among employees in human service work: Design and baseline findings of the PUMA study. *Scandinavian Journal of Public Health, 34*(1), 49–58. doi:10.1080/14034940510032275 PMID:16449044

Brummelhuis, T., Lieke, L., & Bakker, A. B. (2012). A resource perspective on the work–home interface: The work–home resources model. *American Psychologist, 67*(7), 545-556. doi:10.1037/a0027974

Brunborg, G. (2008). Core Self-Evaluations: A Predictor Variable for Job Stress. *European Psychologist, 13*(2), 96–102. doi:10.1027/1016-9040.13.2.96

Chadda, R. K., & Deb, K. S. (2013). Indian family systems, collectivistic society and psychotherapy. *Indian Journal of Psychiatry, 55*(6, Suppl 2), S299–S309. doi:10.4103/0019-5545.105555 PMID:23858272

Cole, A. H. (2014). Anxiety. In Encyclopedia of Psychology and Religion. Boston, MA: Springer. doi:10.1007/978-1-4614-6086-2_38

Danna, K., & Griffin, R. W. (1999). Health and Well-Being in the Workplace: A Review and Synthesis of the Literature. *Journal of Management, 25*(3), 357–384. doi:10.1177/014920639902500305

de Beer, L. T., Pienaar, J., & Rothmann, S. Jr. (2016). Work overload, burnout, and psychological ill-health symptoms: A three-wave mediation model of the employee health impairment process. *Anxiety, Stress, and Coping, 29*(4), 387–399. doi:10.1080/10615806.2015.1061123 PMID:26079200

De Dreu, C., van Dierendonck, D., & Dijkstra, M. (2004). Conflict at work and individual well-being. *International Journal of Conflict Management, 15*(1), 6–26. doi:10.1108/eb022905

Demerouti, E., Bakker, A. B., Nachreiner, F., & Schaufeli, W. B. (2001). The job demands-resources model of burnout. *Journal of Applied Psychology, 86*(3), 499-512. http://dx.doi.org.excelsia.idm.oclc.org/10.1037/0021-9010.86.3.499

Ebbers, J. J., & Wijnberg, N. M. (2017). Betwixt and between: Role conflict, role ambiguity and role definition in project-based dual-leadership structures. *Human Relations, 70*(11), 001872671769285. doi:10.1177/0018726717692852 PMID:29081536

Erica, L., & Barak, M. M. (2015). *Job burnout and affective wellbeing: A longitudinal study of burnout and job satisfaction among public child welfare workers*. doi:10.1016/j.childyouth.2015.05.005

Fernet, C., Torrès, O., Austin, S., & St-Pierre, J. (2016). The psychological costs of owning and managing an SME: Linking job stressors, occupational loneliness, entrepreneurial orientation, and burnout. *Burnout Research, 3*(2), 45–53. doi:10.1016/j.burn.2016.03.002

Flood, S. M., & Genadek, K. R. (2016). Time for Each Other: Work and Family Constraints Among Couples. *Journal of Marriage and Family, 78*(1), 142–164. doi:10.1111/jomf.12255 PMID:26778856

Fujiwara, K., Tsukishima, E., Tsutsumi, A., Kawakami, N., & Kishi, R. (2003). Interpersonal conflict, social support, and burnout among home care workers in Japan. *Journal of Occupational Health, 45*(5), 313–320. doi:10.1539/joh.45.313 PMID:14646273

Giebels, E., & Janssen, O. (2004). Conflict Stress and Reduced Wellbeing at Work: The Buffering Effect of Third-Party Help. *European Journal of Work and Organizational Psychology, 14*. Advance online publication. doi:10.2139srn.602063

Goldberg, D., & Williams, P. (1988). *A User's Guide to the General health Questionnaire*. NFER-Nelson.

Hancock, K., Polites, G., & Fitzgibbon, C. (1985). *Report of Committee of Review into Australian Industrial Relations Law and Systems*. Commonwealth Government Printer.

Hillhouse, J., Adler, C., & Walters, D. (2000). A simple model of stress, burnout and symptomatology in medical residents: A longitudinal study. *Psychology Health and Medicine*, *5*(1), 63–73. doi:10.1080/135485000106016

Huang, X., Ribeiro, J. D., Musacchio, K. M., & Franklin, J. C. (2017). Demographics as predictors of suicidal thoughts and behaviors: A meta-analysis. *PLoS ONE, 12*(7). doi:10.1371/journal.pone.0180793

Hubert, S., & Aujoulat, I. (2018). Parental Burnout: When Exhausted Mothers Open Up. *Frontiers in Psychology*, *9*, 1021–1021. doi:10.3389/fpsyg.2018.01021 PMID:29997543

Hui, C. H., & Triandis, C. H. (1986). Individualism -Collectivism- A study of cross cultural researchers. *A Study of Cross Cultural Psychology, 17*(2), 225-248.

Hulin, C., Netemeyer, R., & Cudeck, R. (2001). Can a Reliability Coefficient Be Too High? *Journal of Consumer Psychology*, *10*, 55–58. doi:10.1207/S15327663JCP1001&2_05

Ilies, R., Huth, M., Ryan, A. M., & Dimotakis, N. E. (2015). Explaining the links between workload, distress, and wor‹ family conflict among school employees: Physical, cognitive, and emotional fatigue. *Journal of Educational Psychology*, *107*(4), 1136–1149. doi:10.1037/edu0000029

Ivancevich, J. M., & Matteson, M. T. (1980). Optimizing Human Resources: A Case for Preventive Health and Stress Management. *Organizational Dynamics*, *9*(2), 5–25. doi:10.1016/0090-2616(80)90037-6 PMID:10249451

Kashima, E. S., Halloran, M., Yuki, M., & Kashima, Y. (2004). The effects of personal and collective mortality salience on individualism: Comparing Australians and Japanese with higher and lower self-esteem. *Journal of Experimental Social Psychology*, *40*(3), 384–392. doi:10.1016/j.jesp.2003.07.007

Kinnunen, U., & Mauno, S. (1998). Antecedents and outcomes of work-family conflict among employed women and men in Finland. *Human Relations*, *51*(2), 157–177. doi:10.1177/001872679805100203

Lee, & Ashforth, B. (1996). A meta-analytic examination of the correlates of the three dimensions of job burnout. *J. Appl. Psychol., 81*(2), 123-133. doi:10.1037/0021-9010.81.2.123

Lepine, J. A., Podsakoff, N. P., & Lepine, M. A. (2005). A meta-analytic test of the challenge stressor-hindrance stressor framework: An explanation for inconsistent relationships among stressors and performance. *Academy of Management Journal*, *48*(5), 764–775. doi:10.5465/amj.2005.18803921

Luchman, J. N., & González-Morales, M. G. (2013). Demands, control, and support: A meta-analytic review of work characteristics interrelationships. *Journal of Occupational Health Psychology, 19*(3), 376–384. doi:10.1037/a0030541

Mañas, M. A., Díaz-Fúnez, P., Pecino, V., López-Liria, R., Padilla, D., & Aguilar-Parra, J. M. (2018). Consequences of Team Job Demands: Role Ambiguity Climate, Affective Engagement, and Extra-Role Performance. *Frontiers in Psychology*, *8*(2292). Advance online publication. doi:10.3389/fpsyg.2017.02292292 PMID:29375424

Mark, G., & Smith, A. P. (2012). Occupational stress, job characteristics, coping, and the mental health of nurses. *British Journal of Health Psychology*, *17*(3), 505–521. doi:10.1111/j.2044-8287.2011.02051.x PMID:22107162

Maslach, C., & Leiter, M. P. (2016). Understanding the burnout experience: Recent research and its implications for psychiatry. *World Psychiatry; Official Journal of the World Psychiatric Association (WPA), 15*(2), 103–111. doi:10.1002/wps.20311 PMID:27265691

Maslach, C., Schaufeli, W. B., & Leiter, M. P. (2001). Job burnout. *Annual Review of Psychology, 52*(1), 397–422. doi:10.1146/annurev.psych.52.1.397 PMID:11148311

Matthew, M. F. M. (2020). *The Radical Individualism Raging Throughout America.* Academic Press.

Melamed, S., Shirom, A., Toker, S., Berliner, S., & Shapira, I. (2006). Burnout and Risk of Cardiovascular Disease: Evidence, Possible Causal Paths, and Promising Research Directions. *Psychological Bulletin, 132*(3), 327–353. doi:10.1037/0033-2909.132.3.327 PMID:16719565

Miner, M. H., Bickerton, G. R., Dowson, M., & Sterland, S. (2015). Spirituality and work engagement among church leaders. *Mental Health, Religion & Culture, 18*(1), 57–71. doi:10.1080/13674676.2014.1003168

Mohren, D., Swaen, G., Kant, I., Amelsvoort, L., Borm, P., & Galama, J. (2003). Common infections and the role of burnout in a Dutch working population. *Journal of Psychosomatic Research, 55*(3), 201–208. doi:10.1016/S0022-3999(02)00517-2 PMID:12932792

Munroe, R. L., & Munroe, R. H. (1972). Obedience Among Children in an East African Society. *Journal of Cross-Cultural Psychology, 3*(4), 395–399. doi:10.1177/002202217200300408

Netemeyer, R. G., Boles, J. S., & McMurrian, R. (1996). Development and validation of work–family conflict and family–work conflict scales. *The Journal of Applied Psychology, 81*(4), 400–410. doi:10.1037/0021-9010.81.4.400

Ngo, H.-Y., Foley, S., & Loi, R. (2005). Work role stressors and turnover intentions: A study of professional clergy in Hong Kong. *International Journal of Human Resource Management, 16*(11), 2133–2146. doi:10.1080/09585190500315141

Nixon, A., Mazzola, J., Bauer, J., Krueger, J., & Spector, P. (2011). Can Work Make You Sick? A Meta-Analysis of the Relationships Between Job Stressors and Physical Symptoms. *Work and Stress, 25*(1), 1–22. doi:10.1080/02678373.2011.569175

NSW. (2021). *Workplace Policies and Procedures Checklist.* doi:https://www.industrialrelations.nsw.gov.au/employers/nsw-employer-best-practice/workplace-policies-and-procedures-checklist/

Panari, C., Caricati, L., Pelosi, A., & Rossi, C. (2019). Emotional exhaustion among healthcare professionals: The effects of role ambiguity, work engagement and professional commitment. *Acta bio-medica. Atenei Parmensis, 90*(6-S), 60–67. doi:10.23750/abm.v90i6-S.8481 PMID:31292416

Pearson, A., Ensley, M., & Amason, A. (2002). An assessment and refinement of Jehn's Intragroup Conflict Scale. *International Journal of Conflict Management, 13*(2), 110–126. doi:10.1108/eb022870

Peeters, M. C. W., Montgomery, A. J., Bakker, A. B., & Schaufeli, W. B. (2005). Balancing Work and Home: How Job and Home Demands Are Related to Burnout. *International Journal of Stress Management, 12*(1), 43–61. doi:10.1037/1072-5245.12.1.43

Peterson, S., Smith, P. B., Akande, A., Ayestaran, S., Bochner, S., Callan, V., Jesuino, J. C., D'Amorim, M., Francois, P.-H., Hofmann, K., Koopman, P. L., Mortazavi, S., Munene, J., Radford, M., Ropo, A., Savage, G., & Setiadi, B. (1995). Role conflict, ambiguity, and overload: A 21-nation study. *Academy of Management Journal, 38*(2), 429–452. doi:10.2307/256687

Podsakoff, P., MacKenzie, S., Lee, J.-Y., & Podsakoff, N. (2003). Common Method Biases in Behavioral Research: A Critical Review of the Literature and Recommended Remedies. *The Journal of Applied Psychology, 88*(5), 879–903. doi:10.1037/0021-9010.88.5.879 PMID:14516251

Raeve, L., Jansen, N., Brandt, P., Vasse, R., & Kant, I. (2009). Interpersonal conflicts at work as a predictor of self-reported health outcomes and occupational mobility. *Occupational and Environmental Medicine, 66*(1), 16–22. doi:10.1136/oem.2007.037655 PMID:19095708

Richardsone, C., Sinha, L., & Yaapar, S. (2014). Work ethics from the Islamic and Hindu traditions: In quest of common ground. *Journal of Management, Spirituality & Religion, 11*(1), 65–90. doi:10.1080/14766086.2013.801025

Ruotsalainen, J., Verbeek, J., Mariné, A., & Serra, C. (2014). Preventing occupational stress in healthcare workers. *Cochrane Database of Systematic Reviews, 134*. Advance online publication. doi:10.1590/1516-3180.20161341T1

Ryan, R. M., & Deci, E. L. (2000). Self-determination theory and the facilitation of intrinsic motivation, social development, and well-being. *The American Psychologist, 55*(1), 68–78. doi:10.1037/0003-066X.55.1.68 PMID:11392867

Schaufeli, W. B., & Bakker, A. B. (2004). Job demands, job resources, and their relationship with burnout and engagement: A multi-sample study. *Journal of Organizational Behavior, 25*(3), 293–315. doi:10.1002/job.248

Schaufeli, W. B., Leiter, M. P., Maslach, C., & Jackson, S. E. (1996). MBI-General survey. Mashlach Burnout Inventory, 3.

Schaufeli, W. B., & Taris, T. (2014). A Critical Review of the Job Demands-Resources Model: Implications for Improving Work and Health. *Bridging Occupational, Organizational and Public Health, A Transdisciplinary Approach*, 43-65. , doi:10.1007/978-94-007-5640-3_4

Sharma, I., Pandit, B., Pathak, A., & Sharma, R. (2013). Hinduism, marriage and mental illness. *Indian Journal of Psychiatry, 55*(6, Suppl 2), S243–S249. doi:10.4103/0019-5545.105544 PMID:23858262

Sharpe, M., & Wilks, D. (2002). Fatigue. *BMJ (Clinical Research Ed.), 325*(7362), 480–483. doi:10.1136/bmj.325.7362.480 PMID:12202331

Siemsen, E., Roth, A., & Oliveira, P. (2010). Common Method Bias in Regression Models With Linear, Quadratic, and Interaction Effects. *Organizational Research Methods, 13*(3), 456–476. doi:10.1177/1094428109351241

Spector, P. E., & Jex, S. M. (1998). Development of four self-report measures of job stressors and strain: Interpersonal Conflict at Work Scale, Organizational Constraints Scale, Quantitative Workload Inventory, and Physical Symptoms Inventory. *Journal of Occupational Health Psychology*, *3*(4), 356–367. doi:10.1037/1076-8998.3.4.356 PMID:9805281

Stoetzer, U., Ahlberg, G., Johansson, G., Bergman, P., Hallsten, L., Forsell, Y., & Lundberg, I. (2009). Problematic Interpersonal Relationships at Work and Depression: A Swedish Prospective Cohort Study. *Journal of Occupational Health*, *51*(2), 144–151. doi:10.1539/joh.L8134 PMID:19225218

Sverdrup, U. (2021). *Compliance and styles of conflict management in Europe.* Arena Working Papers. https://www.sv.uio.no/arena/english/research/publications/arena-working-papers/2001-2010/2003/wp03_8.pdf

Tayfur, O., & Arslan, M. (2013). The role of lack of reciprocity, supervisory support, workload and work–family conflict on exhaustion: Evidence from physicians. *Psychology Health and Medicine*, *18*(5), 564–575. doi:10.1080/13548506.2012.756535 PMID:23330970

Thisera, T. J. R., & Nawaratne, N. N. J. (2018). Job demands and exposure to workplace bullying: A study of state universities in Sri Lanka. *Asian Journal of Empirical Research*, *8*(6), 195–207. doi:10.18488/journal.1007/2018.8.6/1007.6.195.207

Thuynsma, C., & de Beer, L. T. (2016). Burnout, depressive symptoms, job demands and satisfaction with life: Discriminant validity and explained variance. *South African Journal of Psychology. Suid-Afrikaanse Tydskrif vir Sielkunde*, *47*(1), 46–59. doi:10.1177/0081246316638564

Toppinen-Tanner, S., Ojajärvi, A., Väänänen, A., Kalimo, R., & Jäppinen, P. (2005). Burnout as a Predictor of Medically Certified Sick-Leave Absences and Their Diagnosed Causes. *Behavioral Medicine (Washington, D.C.)*, *31*(1), 18–27. doi:10.3200/BMED.31.1.18-32 PMID:16078523

Turnipseed, D. L. (1998). Anxiety and Burnout in the Health Care Work Environment. *Psychological Reports*, *82*(2), 627–642. doi:10.2466/pr0.1998.82.2.627 PMID:9621740

Velez-Calle, A., Robledo-Ardila, C., & Rodriguez-Rios, J.-D. (2015). On the Influence of Interpersonal Relations on Business Practices in Latin America: A Comparison with the Chinese Guanxi and the Arab Wasta. *Thunderbird International Business Review*, *57*(4), 281–293. Advance online publication. doi:10.1002/tie.21669

Verweij, H., van Hooff, M. L. M., van der Heijden, F. M. M. A., Prins, J. T., Lagro-Janssen, A. L. M., van Ravesteijn, H., & Speckens, A. E. M. (2017). The relationship between work and home characteristics and work engagement in medical residents. *Perspectives on Medical Education*, *6*(4), 227–236. doi:10.100740037-017-0364-y PMID:28677047

William, H. (2007). America's individualist culture influences the ability to view others' perspectives. *The University of Chicago Chronicles, 26*(19). doi:http://chronicle.uchicago.edu/070712/perspectives.shtml

Wu, Hu, & Zheng. (2019). Mental health in the workplace-Information sheet. World Health Organization.

Wu, G., Hu, Z., & Zheng, J. (2019). Role Stress, Job Burnout, and Job Performance in Construction Project Managers: The Moderating Role of Career Calling. *International Journal of Environmental Research and Public Health*, *16*(13), 2394. doi:10.3390/ijerph16132394

Xanthopoulou, D., Bakker, A. B., Demerouti, E., & Schaufeli, W. B. (2007). The role of personal resources in the job demands-resources model. *International Journal of Stress Management*, *14*(2), 121–141. doi:10.1037/1072-5245.14.2.121

Yang, L.-Q., Spector, P., Sanchez, J., Allen, T., Poelmans, S., Cooper, C., Lapierre, L. M., O'Driscoll, M. P., Abarca, N., Alexandrova, M., Antoniou, A.-S., Beham, B., Brough, P., Çarikçi, I., Ferreiro, P., Fraile, G., Geurts, S., Kinnunen, U., Lu, C., ... Woo, J.-M. (2012). Individualism–collectivism as a moderator of the work demands–strains relationship: A cross-level and cross-national examination. *Journal of International Business Studies*, *43*(4), 424–443. Advance online publication. doi:10.1057/jibs.2011.58

Yunsoo, L., & Eissenstat, S. J. (2018). A longitudinal examination of the causes and effects of burnout based on the job demands-resources model. *International Journal for Educational and Vocational Guidance*, *18*(3), 337–354. doi:10.100710775-018-9364-7

Zohar, D. (1999). Predicting burnout with a hassle-based measure of role demands. *Journal of Organizational Behavior*, *18*(2), 101–115. doi:10.1002/(SICI)1099-1379(199703)18:2<101::AID-JOB788>3.0.CO;2-Y

Chapter 3

NOM-035-STPS-2018: Opportunities for Better Implementation – A Review

Raul Martinez-Balderrama
Autonomous University of Baja California, Mexico

Gabriela Jacobo Jacobo-Galicia
Autonomous University of Baja California, Mexico

María Elizabeth Ramírez- Barreto
Autonomous University of Baja California, Mexico

Judith M. Paz-Delgadillo
https://orcid.org/0000-0003-3468-5071
Autonomous University of Baja California, Mexico

Samantha Cruz-Sotelo
https://orcid.org/0000-0001-8224-0101
Autonomous University of Baja California, Mexico

ABSTRACT

Looking at the structure of NOM-035-STPS-2018, there is an assumption that there are areas of opportunity to improve the implementation of the standard. Thus, the purpose of this research is to identify through a review whether there are areas of opportunity that can improve the implementation of NOM-035. For the review, articles addressing the psychosocial risk factors evaluation were selected and analyzed. Four topics of discussion were identified: impact of psychosocial risk factors, policy and regulations, management systems, and evaluation of psychosocial risk factors. Subsequently, a synthesis was made, and it was found that there are three areas of opportunity to improve NOM-035-STPS-2018: it does not have a risk management system, its instruments do not present evidence of statistical validity, and the instruments do not take into account indicators of consequence.

DOI: 10.4018/978-1-7998-7396-9.ch003

INTRODUCTION

In recent years, studies have found that the impact of psychosocial risk factors such as work stress, anxiety, and depression, affect the mental health and well-being of a significant percentage of the working population (Cruz, López, Cruz, & Llanillo, 2016; Memish, Martin, Bartlett, Dawkins, & Sanderson, 2017; Meunier, Roberge, Coulombe, & Houle, 2019; ILO, 2016). Epidemiological studies also point to the positive association between occupational psychosocial risks and physiological damage such as cardiovascular disease and musculoskeletal disorders [MSDS] (Navinés, Martín-Santos, Olivé, & Valdés, 2016; ILO, 2016). In this regard, a growing body of research has demonstrated the socio-economic impact that psychosocial risk factors and their various psychosocial consequences have had on productivity, direct and indirect manufacturing costs, and the competitiveness of organizations (Cruz et al., 2016; Leka, Jain, Iavicoli, Vartia, & Ertel, 2011; Meunier et al., 2019; ILO, 2016; R. Potter, O'Keeffe, Leka, Webber, & Dollard, 2019; Víctor H. Charria O, Kewy V. Sarsosa P, 2011). As a result of this research, many policy efforts have been made around the world to counter this issue. In particular, Mexico has recently developed a Mexican Official Standard NOM-035-STPS-2018. It is a regulatory instrument that requires mental health care in the workplace through specifications and guidelines for the identification, analysis, and prevention of psychosocial risk factors (Uribe-Prado, Gutiérrez-Amador, & Amézquita-Pino, 2020). Since this new standard has not been yet fully implemented, it may be relevant to identify, through a systematic review, the most significant topics of discussion concerning the study of psychosocial risk factors, as well as to analyze the good practices that exist in the literature for their evaluation, to find areas of opportunity that may have the possibility to improve the implementation of NOM-035-STPS-2018.

METHODOLOGY

A systematic review of the literature was performed through Google Scholar and the Elsevier database. The keywords used were: Management, Evaluation, Psychosocial Risk Factors, Labor, Industry/Management, Assessment, Psychosocial risk factors, Workplace, and Industry. To gather as many potential topics of discussion as possible, articles that were thought to address the topic of psychosocial risk factors evaluation were selected regardless of the approach applied by the article, and no exclusion criteria were considered in regards to publication date or the article´s subject. The first selection was made through a title and summary analysis. The chosen articles were subsequently reviewed in full to identify whether they contained useful information regarding potential topics of discussion. The search was conducted for 4 months, from August 2019 to November 2019. A comparative table to list the different articles by author and topic of discussion identified was created. Then, the articles were grouped according to the main topic of discussion identified. Finally, a second review was performed to identify the necessary measures to be taken to address psychosocial risks that the NOM-035 does not currently consider to designate them as areas of opportunity.

FINDINGS

After the review was completed, 30 articles were included that coincided with the eligibility criteria. From these, 4 main topics of discussion regarding the study and evaluation of psychosocial risk factors were identified: 1) impact of psychosocial risks, 2) policy and policy regulation, 3) risk management systems, and 4) evaluation of psychosocial risk factors. Table 1 shows the identified discussion topics. It is important to note that there are articles that consider more than one of these topics.

Table 1. Main topics of discussion per Author

Authors	Impact of psychosocial risks	Policy and policy regulation	Risk management systems	Evaluation of psychosocial risk factors
Potter, O'Keeffe, Leka, Webber & Dollard, 2019	X	X		
Ribeiro, Teixeira & Ambiel, 2019				X
Metzler, Groeling-Muller & Bellingrath, 2019				X
Da Silva & Amaral, 2019		X	X	
Llorens et. al, 2019				X
Meunier et. al, 2019	X			
Uribe Prado et.al, 2019				X
Hohnen et. al, 2018		X		
Aminian, Moradi & Efteqhari, 2018				X
Oakman et. al, 2018			X	
Bergh et.al, 2018			X	X
Ncube, 2018	X			
Potter, Dollard, Owen, O'Keeffe, Bailey & Leka, 2017	X	X	X	X
Memish et. al, 2017	X		X	
Kyaw-Myint et.al, 2017			X	X
Nordlöf et.al, 2017			X	
Jespersen et. al, 2016		X		
Unda et.al, 2016				X
Navinés et.al, 2016	X			
Vera-Calzaretta et. al, 2015				X
Sivris & Leka, 2015			X	
Reavley et. al, 2014	X		X	
Aranda, Pando & Ronquillo, 2014				X
Lucchini, 2014	X			
Persechino et. al, 2013		X	X	
Zoni & Lucchini, 2012		X	X	
Leka, Jain, Cox & Kortum, 2011	X		X	
Leka, Jain, Iavicoli, Vartia & Ertel, 2011		X	X	
Charria, Sarsosa & Arenas, 2011	X	X	X	X

Source: Self made

Figure 1 shows the number of papers that belong to each area of discussion identified. It was found that the main topic addressed was risk management systems with 14 articles. It is followed by psychosocial risk factors evaluation with 12 articles, impact of psychosocial risks with 10 articles, and regulations and policies with 9 articles.

Figure 1. Number of papers per topic
Source: Self made

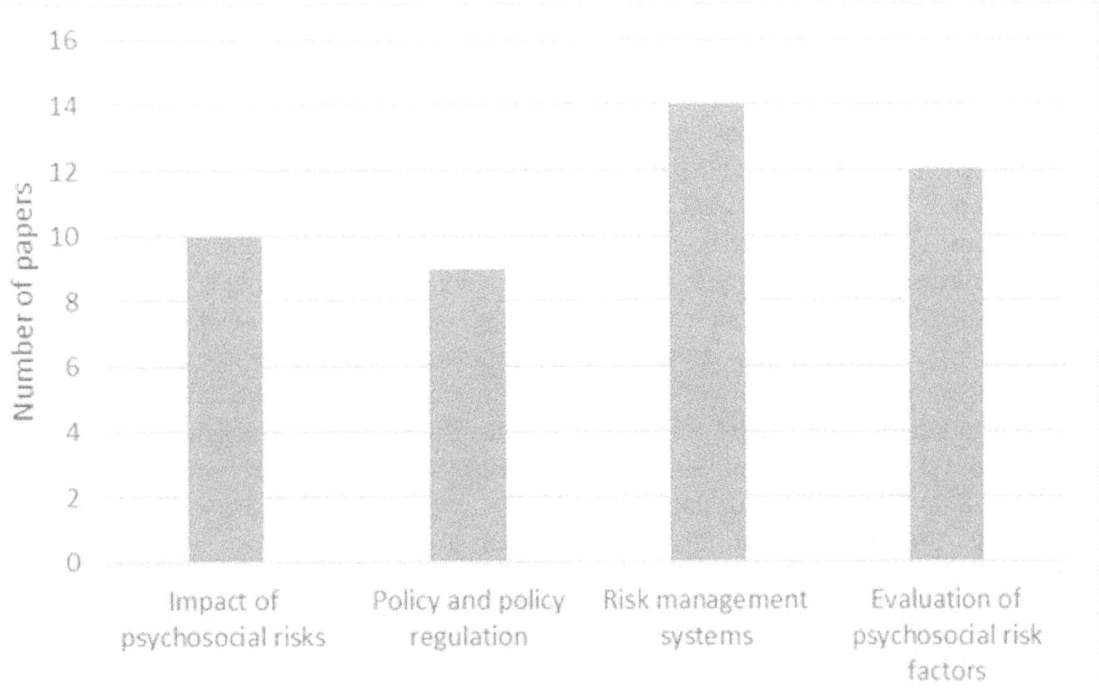

DISCUSSION

Four main topics emerged from the review, here each of them is discussed in more detail. First, many authors talk about the impact that psychosocial risks generate on an individual level as well as on a large scale. There is a wealth of evidence to indicate that psychosocial risk factors are associated with the emergence of various mental and physiological conditions, such as depressive disorders, anxiety disorders, and musculoskeletal and cardiovascular problems. Also, a considerable economic impact of the various psychosocial risk factors has been found. A large number of studies consider psychosocial risk factors-related expenditures to be approximately 4% of countries' Gross Domestic Product [GDP] (Leka, Jain, Cox, & Kortum, 2011; Lucchini & London, 2014; Memish et al., 2017; Meunier et al., 2019; Navinés et al., 2016; Ncube & Kanda, 2018; R. E. Potter et al., 2017; R. Potter et al., 2019; Reavley, Ross, Martin, LaMontagne, & Jorm, 2014; Víctor H. Charria O, Kewy V. Sarsosa P, 2011).

On the other hand, several authors indicate the importance of creating regulations and policies for the management of psychosocial risk factors. Various authors consider it necessary for working conditions to remain standardized through legislative guidelines to lessen the impact of poor mental health on workers. It is noted that Occupational Health and Safety [OSH] policies, including psychosocial risks, play a critical role in leading organizations to accept responsibility for meeting specific requirements relevant to employee health, primarily by delineating specific duties and regulations. However, it is ensured that OSH regulations do not indicate how requirements should be implemented, but will be addressed at the convenience of each case, i.e. the requirements of the regulations are what is standardized, while the implementation will depend on each situation (Da Silva & Amaral, 2019; Hohnen & Hasle, 2018; Jespersen, Hohnen, & Hasle, 2016; Leka, Jain, Iavicoli, et al., 2011; Persechino et al., 2013; R. E. Potter et al., 2017; R. Potter et al., 2019; Víctor H. Charria O, Kewy V. Sarsosa P, 2011; Zoni & Lucchini, 2012).

In a different perspective, many authors point out the importance of also having management systems for the OSH department, including the management of psychosocial risk factors. On this issue, it is argued that risk assessment should be included in a process that considers interrelated phases that are generally comprised of three main stages: risk identification and measurement, risk assessment or classification, and risk reduction. It is emphasized that this process should be integrated into the management systems and strategic policies of the organization. In this sense, the assessment of psychosocial factors should be treated from a systemic perspective, considering its relationship with the organizational environment, its internal processes, and the people that comprise it. In addition, several examples of existing management models for the assessment and management of psychosocial risks use a holistic, comprehensive, interdisciplinary, and participatory approach, always emphasizing the active role and need for worker participation, as well as the practice of continuous improvement (Bergh, Leka, & Zwetsloot, 2018; Da Silva & Amaral, 2019; Kyaw-Myint, Strazdins, Clements, Butterworth, & Gallagher, 2017; Leka, Jain, Cox, et al., 2011; Leka, Jain, Iavicoli, et al., 2011; Memish et al., 2017; Nordlöf, Wiitavaara, Högberg, & Westerling, 2017; Oakman, Macdonald, Bartram, Keegel, & Kinsman, 2018; Persechino et al., 2013; R. E. Potter et al., 2017; Reavley et al., 2014; Sivris & Leka, 2015; Víctor H. Charria O, Kewy V. Sarsosa P, 2011; Zoni & Lucchini, 2012).

Last but not least, several considerations have been discussed about the assessment of psychosocial risk. Several authors indicate that it is necessary to take into account health-related variables to calculate psychosocial risk, to establish whether the calculated exposure levels of psychosocial risk factors are effectively affecting the health of the worker. In this way, the psychosocial risk assessment should distinguish two indicators: exposure indicators and consequence indicators. Exposure indicators correspond to the elements surrounding the worker that trigger responses in workers, i. e. psychosocial risk factors; and consequence indicators are reactive indicators, that measure the exposure-response, which can include the various health problems that have already been mentioned, such as work stress. About the identification and measurement of psychosocial risk factors, many authors stipulate the need to statistically validate the instruments that measure these factors, i.e. that psychosocial risk factors evaluation instruments must have adequate reliability and validity tests, as well as standardization processes for the specific application of these (Bergh et al., 2018; Kyaw-Myint et al., 2017; Llorens, Navarro, Salas, Utzet, & Moncada, 2019; Moreno, 2014; R. E. Potter et al., 2017; Ribeiro, Teixeira, & Ambiel, 2019; Unda et al., 2016; Uribe-Prado et al., 2020; Vera-Calzaretta, Carrasco-Dájer, Da Costa, & Páez-Rovira, 2015; Víctor H. Charria O, Kewy V. Sarsosa P, 2011).

According to the findings of this review, it may be suggested that establishing a management process aimed at psychosocial risk factors and, in turn, conducting a statistically validated psychosocial risk factors assessment and proactively focusing on consequence indicators, are the most important aspects to consider in the management, analysis, and prevention of psychosocial risks. In this regard, three areas of opportunity were established that can enrich the application of NOM-035-STPS-2018.

First, on the issue of risk management systems, it was found that the formulation of the standard does not consider any systematic method for carrying out the management of psychosocial risk factors. It is therefore suggested that a more comprehensive analysis of the literature be developed about proposals for management systems already in use around the world, to adapt and build an appropriate management system for the implementation of NOM-035 about the management of psychosocial risks.

In addition, two niches of opportunity to improve NOM-035 were identified on specific psychosocial risk measurements and assessments. The first concerns the lack of evidence of reliable data and statistical validity due to the recent publication of the standard's instruments. This means that, once they begin to be implemented, it will be essential that all possible data be reported and stored for statistical validity testing, to generate evidence to ensure that the instruments function properly.

Finally, the second gap in NOM-035 on the specific assessment of psychosocial risks concerns the fact that the instruments of the standard do not present evidence that they take into account health-associated indicators of consequences for the assessment of psychosocial risk. This means that measurements of current versions of NOM-035 instruments only focus on assessing exposure to certain psychosocial risk factors, without actually analyzing whether these exposures are in any way influencing the health of the worker. This is why it is considered necessary to build evaluative alternatives from the NOM-035 instruments so that they can take measurements both at the level of exposure to certain psychosocial risk factors and the possible consequences of these, thus allowing to determine the potential risk of harm associated with the health and well-being of workers.

CONCLUSION

From the results of this review, it can be concluded that, while it is true that the recent development of the NOM-035 regulation represents a considerable advance in psychosocial risk management in Mexico, the scope of the standard today is still quite limited and with ample room for improvement. Having said that, it will be of great importance that works shortly be done on the development of solutions for these areas of opportunity, since, according to the discussion built here, these guidelines can be interpreted as representing a minimum standard of what good practice should look like to the management of psychosocial risks.

REFERENCES

Bergh, L. I. V., Leka, S., & Zwetsloot, G. I. J. M. (2018). Tailoring Psychosocial Risk Assessment in the Oil and Gas Industry by Exploring Specific and Common Psychosocial Risks. *Safety and Health at Work*, *9*(1), 63–70. doi:10.1016/j.shaw.2017.05.001 PMID:30363066

Cruz, M., López, E., Cruz, R., & Llanillo, M. E. (2016). *El estrés laboral en México. La Micro y Pequeña Empresa: Un Análisis Desde La Perspectiva Economico-Administrativa*. Retrieved from https://www.ecorfan.org/actas/A_1/32.pdf

Da Silva, S. L. C., & Amaral, F. G. (2019, August 1). Critical factors of success and barriers to the implementation of occupational health and safety management systems: A systematic review of literature. In *Safety Science*. Elsevier B.V. doi:10.1016/j.ssci.2019.03.026

Hohnen, P., & Hasle, P. (2018). Third party audits of the psychosocial work environment in occupational health and safety management systems. *Safety Science*, *109*, 76–85. doi:10.1016/j.ssci.2018.04.028

Jespersen, A. H., Hohnen, P., & Hasle, P. (2016). Internal audits of psychosocial risks at workplaces with certified OHS management systems. *Safety Science*, *84*, 201–209. doi:10.1016/j.ssci.2015.12.013

Kyaw-Myint, S. M., Strazdins, L., Clements, M., Butterworth, P., & Gallagher, L. (2017). A method of identifying health-based benchmarks for psychosocial risks at work: A tool for risk assessment. *Safety Science*, *93*, 143–151. doi:10.1016/j.ssci.2016.11.016

Leka, S., Jain, A., Cox, T., & Kortum, E. (2011). The development of the European framework for psychosocial risk management: PRIMA-EF. *Journal of Occupational Health*, *53*. doi:10.1539/joh.O10010

Leka, S., Jain, A., Iavicoli, S., Vartia, M., & Ertel, M. (2011). The role of policy for the management of psychosocial risks at the workplace in the European Union. *Safety Science*, *49*(4), 558–564. doi:10.1016/j.ssci.2010.02.002

Llorens, C., Navarro, A., Salas, S., Utzet, M., & Moncada, S. (2019). For better or for worse? Psychosocial work environment and direct participation practices. *Safety Science*, *116*, 78–85. doi:10.1016/j.ssci.2019.02.028

Lucchini, R. G., & London, L. (2014, July 1). Global occupational health: Current challenges and the need for urgent action. *Annals of Global Health*. doi:10.1016/j.aogh.2014.09.006

Memish, K., Martin, A., Bartlett, L., Dawkins, S., & Sanderson, K. (2017, August 1). Workplace mental health: An international review of guidelines. In *Preventive Medicine*. Academic Press Inc. doi:10.1016/j.ypmed.2017.03.017

Meunier, S., Roberge, C., Coulombe, S., & Houle, J. (2019). Feeling better at work! Mental health self-management strategies for workers with depressive and anxiety symptoms. *Journal of Affective Disorders*, *254*, 7–14. doi:10.1016/j.jad.2019.05.011 PMID:31082629

Moreno, M. P. (2014). *De Diversos Giros Laborales Reliability and Validity of an Identification Guide on Psychosocial*. Academic Press.

Navinés, R., Martín-Santos, R., Olivé, V., & Valdés, M. (2016). Estrés laboral: Implicaciones para la salud física y mental. *Medicina Clínica*, *146*(8), 359–366. doi:10.1016/j.medcli.2015.11.023 PMID:26806767

Ncube, F., & Kanda, A. (2018, December 1). Current Status and the Future of Occupational Safety and Health Legislation in Low- and Middle-Income Countries. In *Safety and Health at Work*. Elsevier Science B.V. doi:10.1016/j.shaw.2018.01.007

Nordlöf, H., Wiitavaara, B., Högberg, H., & Westerling, R. (2017). A cross-sectional study of factors influencing occupational health and safety management practices in companies. *Safety Science*, *95*, 92–103. doi:10.1016/j.ssci.2017.02.008

Oakman, J., Macdonald, W., Bartram, T., Keegel, T., & Kinsman, N. (2018). Workplace risk management practices to prevent musculoskeletal and mental health disorders: What are the gaps? *Safety Science*, *101*, 220–230. doi:10.1016/j.ssci.2017.09.004

Organización Internacional del Trabajo (OIT). (2016). *Estrés en el trabajo*. Retrieved from www.ilo.org/safeday

Persechino, B., Valenti, A., Ronchetti, M., Rondinone, B. M., Di Tecco, C., Vitali, S., & Iavicoli, S. (2013). Work-related stress risk assessment in Italy: A methodological proposal adapted to regulatory guidelines. *Safety and Health at Work*, *4*(2), 95–99. doi:10.1016/j.shaw.2013.05.002 PMID:23961332

Potter, R., O'Keeffe, V., Leka, S., Webber, M., & Dollard, M. (2019). Analytical review of the Australian policy context for work-related psychological health and psychosocial risks. *Safety Science*, *111*, 37–48. doi:10.1016/j.ssci.2018.09.012

Potter, R. E., Dollard, M. F., Owen, M. S., O'Keeffe, V., Bailey, T., & Leka, S. (2017). Assessing a national work health and safety policy intervention using the psychosocial safety climate framework. *Safety Science*, *100*, 91–102. doi:10.1016/j.ssci.2017.05.011

Reavley, N. J., Ross, A., Martin, A., LaMontagne, A. D., & Jorm, A. F. (2014). Development of guidelines for workplace prevention of mental health problems: A Delphi consensus study with Australian professionals and employees. *Mental Health & Prevention*, *2*(1–2), 26–34. doi:10.1016/j.mhp.2014.07.002

Ribeiro, M. A., Teixeira, M. A. P., & Ambiel, R. A. M. (2019). Decent work in Brazil: Context, conceptualization, and assessment. *Journal of Vocational Behavior*, *112*, 229–240. doi:10.1016/j.jvb.2019.03.006

Sivris, K. C., & Leka, S. (2015). Examples of holistic good practices in promoting and protecting mental health in the workplace: Current and future challenges. *Safety and Health at Work*, *6*(4), 295–304. doi:10.1016/j.shaw.2015.07.002 PMID:26929841

Unda, S., Uribe, F., Jurado, S., García, M., Tovalín, H., & Juárez, A. (2016). Elaboración de una escala para valorar los factores de riesgo psicosocial en el trabajo de profesores universitarios. *Revista de Psicología del Trabajo y de las Organizaciones*, *32*(2), 67–74. doi:10.1016/j.rpto.2016.04.004

Uribe-Prado, J., Gutiérrez-Amador, J., & Amézquita-Pino, J. (2020). Crítica a las Propiedades Psicométricas de una Escala de Medición de Factores de Riesgo Psicosocial Propuesta en la NOM 035 de la STPS en México. *Contaduría y Administración*, *64*(1), 1–35.

Vera-Calzaretta, A., Carrasco-Dájer, C., Da Costa, S., & Páez-Rovira, D. (2015). Factores psicosociales del presentismo en trabajadores del Sistema de Salud chileno. *Revista de Psicología del Trabajo y de las Organizaciones*, *31*(2), 119–128. doi:10.1016/j.rpto.2015.03.004

Víctor, Charria, Kewy, & Sarsosa. (2011). Factores de riesgo psicosocial laboral : Métodos e instrumentos de evaluación. *Revista Facultad Nacional de Salud Pública*, *29*(4), 380–391.

Zoni, S., & Lucchini, R. G. (2012). *European approaches to work-related stress: A critical review on risk evaluation. Safety and Health at Work*. Elsevier Science B.V. doi:10.5491/SHAW.2012.3.1.43

Chapter 4
Productivity Evaluation in Function of Worker Psychosocial Factors

Erick McGregor Roa-Badilla
Autonomous University of Baja California, Mexico

Gabriela Jacobo-Galicia
Autonomous University of Baja California, Mexico

Mildrend Ivett Montoya-Reyes
https://orcid.org/0000-0001-5575-8060
Autonomous University of Baja California, Mexico

Ismael Mendoza-Muñoz
https://orcid.org/0000-0002-0810-2090
Autonomous University of Baja California, Mexico

Juan Ceballos- Corral
Autonomous University of Baja California, Mexico

ABSTRACT

Workers are exposed to different factors that can be detrimental to their well-being, being the most known safety and hygiene factors. A few years ago, the concepts of harmful factors for workers were updated by adding the psychosocial factors. Although there is literature on psychosocial factors and their effect on health, this work focused specifically on seeking the relationship between productivity and psychosocial factors to know how it impacts the organization. The investigation was applied in a case study for a doorknob locks manufacturing company in its final assembly area. Data collection was done by applying the questionnaire provided by NOM-035-STPS-2018 and the company's productivity databases for the subsequent analysis using statistical tools. The results were that, for the violence factor, its correlation with productivity was $R^2 = 0.8886$, indicating a strong correlation with which it is concluded that there is an influence on productivity.

DOI: 10.4018/978-1-7998-7396-9.ch004

INTRODUCTION

The International Labour Organization [ILO] was created in 1919, as part of the Treaty of Versailles when the First World War ended, and it reflected the conviction on how social justice is essential to achieve universal peace (Lecca, Guevara & Boza, 2013). In 2013, this organization pointed that, even though some traditional risks have diminished due to safety, technological advances, and better normativity, although, some still affect workers while an increase has been registered in a new type of professional illness without them been prevented or controlled adequately, these risks been called psychosocial risk factors (Secretaría del Trabajo y Prevención Social, 2016).

Different authors have taken the task to learn more about the psychosocial factors using evaluation and prevention tools, for example, the ones being used by the Instituto Nacional de Seguridad e Higiene en el Trabajo [INSHT] in Spain, who since 1987 started applying surveys that included elements about psychosocial analysis, like the one from 2011 which showed how several indicators relative to the work demands have worsened over the years (INSHT, 2011).

ISSUES, CONTROVERSIES, PROBLEMS

At a global level, psychosocial risks are more likely to cause harm to workers' health and affect their productivity in the company. Such is the case of work stress, which is considered a current pandemic (Moreno, 2011; Benavides et al., 2002).

This is how this research work seeks to identify, from a case study within the production area of a manufacturing company, the relationship between psychosocial factors of workers and their productivity to know how both interact with each other.

HYPOTHESIS

There is a correlation between psychosocial factors and the productivity of manufacturing companies.

GENERAL OBJECTIVE

Analyze and evaluate the psychosocial factors of a manufacturing company located at Circuito, Siglo XXI #1926, Rivera, 21259, in Mexicali, B.C., México, and their relationship with productivity.

SPECIFIC OBJECTIVES

1. Identify the psychosocial factors to study in the research.
2. Evaluate existing instruments that measure psychosocial factors.
3. Select the instrument that best suits the problem studied.
4. Select a manufacturing company to apply the instrument. Obtain information on the productivity of the company.

5. Using statistical tools to determine if there is a relationship between psychosocial factors and productivity
6. Analyze and evaluate the results.
7. Propose solutions to control, eliminate or minimize the psychosocial factor (s) present, using tools from industrial engineering, ergonomics, and psychology, among other sciences.

BACKGROUND

The psychosocial risk factors topic has been expanded over years thanks to a great variety of authors from all around the world.

Work is defined as the means through which human beings relate and interact with the environment to obtain the goods and services necessary to live (Acevedo, Farias, Sánchez, Astegiano & Fernández, 2012). At present, far from constituting exclusively a means of subsistence, work is an important element of social appreciation and development of a creative activity, as it represents a right and a duty of the person (Díaz, 2007).

It is impossible to imagine organizations without humans, even with technological advances the human resource is who gives life and humanizes the relation between client-company (Muñoz, Orellano & Hernández, 2018).

The concept of psychosocial factors has been used to point out conditions that present themselves in work situations and that are directly related to the organization and work content, being these able to affect the well-being or health [physical, psychic, or social] of the employee, as well the completion of the task (Pando M., Aranda C., Parra L. & Ruiz D., 2013). The concept is relatively recent and probably originates in the last quarter of the past century, it is when the first official reference comes in 1984 with the title of "The psychosocial factors in work: acknowledgment and control" published by the ILO (Jiménez, 2011).

These psychosocial factors at work are inherent to the act of working; they can become risky or protective for health according to how they are conceptualized, identified, measured, and controlled (Ortiz, Jaramillo, 2013).

By now considering the employee as the main actor in the organization, recent studies expose psychosocial factors that cause socioeconomic problems by causing absenteeism, low efficiency, psychological and heart diseases, there is solid scientific evidence that assesses the adverse effects of stress as a source of disease coronary arteries in people who are in constant environments of hostility, urgencies against time and strict fulfillment of goals (RB Williams, JC Barefoot, N. Schneiderman, 2003).

Given this approach, it is important to solve these problems that directly impact both the health of the worker and the organization.

The task of researchers and professionals has been to reveal the psychosocial aspects that play a role in the way in which people currently establish their relationship with work, and how the labor market demands certain ways of working (Ortiz, Jaramillo, 2013).

Although the delimitation between psychosocial risk factors and psychosocial risks is not always clear, there is a tendency to recognize as psychosocial risks situations such as violence and aggression at work, workplace and sexual harassment, chronic work stress, burnout or professional burnout, and contractual insecurity (Izquierdo, 2012).

Health, Job Accidents, and Psychosocial Factors

This relation between health and psychosocial factors has been studied for decades, a consensus has been that at a greater number of psychosocial factors higher the influence in the development of skeletal muscle problems in men (Silva & Gontijo, 2017). Some Venezuelan industries also had a relation of skeletal muscle problems with insecurity and esteem, since more than 50% of the workers perceived them negatively (Márquez Gómez & Márquez Robledo, 2015). This has made researchers focus their attention on organizational variables and job risks as sources of illnesses and anguish in the population (Salazar & Ruvalcaba, 2012).

Authors have related their investigations to labor accidents and psychosocial risk factors. Holland studied these in two types of industries: construction and health. The study showed that occupational accidents in the construction industry typically involved physical damage, while the health sector relatively resulted in mental damage (van der Klauw, Hengel, Roozeboom, Koppes & Venema, 2016). The United States has also done research aimed at their workforce and found that factors as hostile work environment, job insecurity, and family-work unbalance, were associated with work injuries, being hostile work environment the most significant among all, suggesting workers health could be improved if psychosocial risks are worked on (Farnacio, Pratt, Marshall & Graber, 2017).

The United States approaches the subject of psychosocial factors to find the relationship between stressful occupations and psychosocial symptoms against injuries in the construction industry, which resulted in associations between the occurrence of injuries with job control, training, job certainty, organizational climate, and responsibility for the safety of others (Abbe, Harvey, Ikuma, & Aghazadeh, 2011).

Also in the United States, a study aimed at the American workforce was carried out to examine whether psychosocial risk factors were related to occupational injuries and it was found that the occupational factors studied - hostile work environment, job insecurity, and family imbalance -work- were all positively associated with work-related injuries, with the hostile work environment being the most significantly associated with injuries, suggesting then that workers' health can be improved if any of the psychosocial risks in the work environment are addressed (Farnacio, Pratt, Marshall, & Graber, 2017).

On the other hand, Abbe et al. (2011) find that all the variables in charge of measuring occupational stress do not infer the result of injuries due to psychosocial factors, the only possible factor of creating occupational injuries being feeling sad, which can cause headaches or strain the worker what has to do with workplace injuries.

Karasek´s Study

One of the most known and utilized works in the topic of the psychosocial factors is the "Job Demands, Job Decision Latitude, and Mental Strain: Implications for Job Redesign" and the Job Content Questionnaire authored by Robert Karasek in 1979 (Gomes, 2015, Neffa, 2002, Souza et al., 2006, Alavinia et al., 2008, Salazar & Ruvalcaba, 2012, Astudillo, 2003, Gontijo, et al., 2017, Meerding et al., 2005, Abbe et al., 2011, Moreno & Báez, 2011, Law et al., 2011, Ocampo et al., 2015, Awang et al., 2012, Ortiz & Jaramillo, 2013, Umeda et al., 2015).

Karasek shows in his work a model that predicts mental tension according to the interaction between job demand and job decision latitude. He represents it like the following figure.

Figure 1. Job Demands
Source: Karasek (1979)

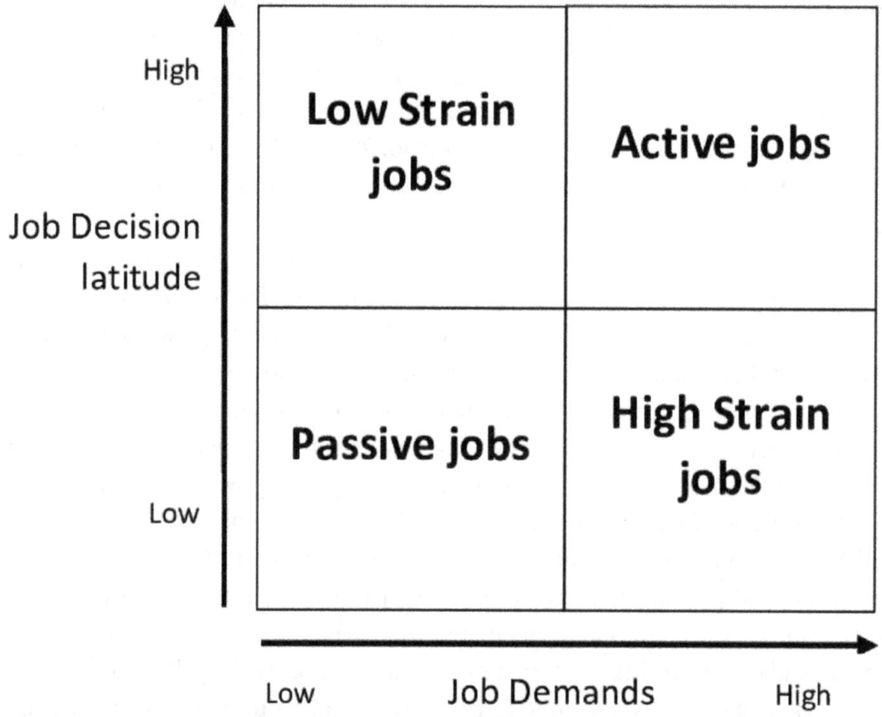

Also, Karasek with Brisson, Kawakami, Houtman, Bongers, and Amick made the Job Content Questionnaire [JCQ] in 1998. This instrument has been used by several authors to study psychosocial factors (Gómes, 2015, Estrada et al., 2013, Souza et al., 2006, Alavinia et al., 2008, García et al., 2014, Neffa, 2002, Espeleta, 2015, Salazar & Ruvalcaba, 2012, Gontijo et al., 2017, Law et al., 2011, Ocampo et al., 2015, Awang et al., 2012, Umeda et al., 2015). JCQ will evaluate five scales: job decision latitude, psychological demand, social support, physical demand, and job insecurity, all within 49 questions (Karasek et al., 1988).

Demographic Differences

Japan is known for being a country with a high job demand, where their workers suffer constantly from psychosocial risks especially from social pressure; studies in this country indicate how woman when they better their job status, their mental health could be at risk due to social unbalances and not because of the work itself (Umeda et al., 2015).

Another aspect that has been related is the education level since it has high-level depersonalization in personal with lower education, which is most likely due to the presence of operational-level jobs that involve, multiple routines, repetitive activities and with reduces responsibility and decision making, which translates in a risk factor of the depersonalization of the worker (Pérez, 2013). A similar study found the same relation where uncompleted elementary education was predominant (Original, 2014). More demographic statistics indicate that women have higher emotional exhaustion compared to men.

This situation is explained by several authors as a consequence of the multiple roles that women cover by attending job demands and home demands (Gil-Monte, 2002; Maslach, 2009).

This cultural perception changes in countries from Latin America and Spain, where a study researched the perception of innovation in organizations, being this negatively associated, the results indicated that meanwhile autonomy is positively perceived in the work role and individual auto efficiency workers will be motivated (Gondim, Mazzieri & Torres, 2016).

Productivity and Psychosocial Factors

When talking about productivity in companies, healthy organizations do systematic work to benefit their workers' well-being, as well as higher productivity, being achieved with good workstation design, support channels, career development, and equal opportunities so a balanced of work and private life can happen (Wilson, DeJoy, Vandenbert, Richardson & McGrath, 2004).

As Barrios (2013) points out interactions between organizational components, worker abilities, synergy in work relationships, and work conditions can provoke employees to develop work exhaustion and lower productivity levels. At the same time, Enrique Díaz, Kotzab, Sytch & Frieling (2012) found when increasing production, a perceived psychosocial risk also increases, although, if work tasks are combined with social interactions and ergonomic factors, it is possible to increase productivity without negative impacts in psychosocial risks.

A negative individual perception has been found due to performance and low motivational activity, related to organizational factors, in workplaces where lack of incentives, job insecurity, missing job recognition, low salary, and insufficient training exists (Salazar, Beltrán, Moreno & Romero, 2014).

Solutions for these risks have been fomenting communication strategies between structural levels, establishing systems for conflict resolutions, improving motivation on workers, facilitate internal group cohesion, impulse creativity and promote support groups for workers (Aranda et al., 2013).

In this sense, it is important that directives of any company compensate adequately their employees, as well as take measures to lower controlling supervision and job insecurity since it is common to find these psychosocial risks (Ocampo, Juárez, Arias & Hindrichs, 2015).

Productivity must be seen as the result of the human talent performance, being surrounded by conditions and basic safety measures and work comfortably in the organization, can offer all of their efforts to produce goods and services efficiently, meaning that every intervention to better productivity has its genesis in the people (Cox, 2000).

Psychosocial Factors Evaluation

When it comes to the identification and evaluation of psychosocial factors, give the nature of the phenomenon and the amplitude, the evaluation of these risks has implicated some difficulties to the professionals in charge of the prevention in organizations since it requires a different methodology from the commonly used to evaluate psychical risks, ergonomics, hygiene, and mechanicals (Artacoz y Molinero, 2004; Blanch, Sahagún y Cervantes, 2010; Charria et al., 2011; Meliá, 2006; Villalobos, 2005).

Blanch (2010) points out that, contrary to other types of risks, this evaluation must be made through questionnaires that lets people's perception be captured over the workplace conditions and workers experience in their psychosocial dimensions.

The proposal of algorithms seems like an effective tool to design rotative schedules as temporal alternatives to support critical positions with high repetitively, in such a way that risks can be balanced, preventing workers from high risks levels and higher recuperation, although proposals like these are simply temporal and do not eliminate the risk itself ((Asensio Cuesta, Diego Mas, Cremades Oliver, & González Cruz, 2012).

Other solutions are methods to manage psychosocial risks comprehensively and that helps leaders with information to be prepared (Mathisen, Brønnick, Arntzen, & Bergh, 2016).

Studies have helped to have a first approach to psychosocial risks in different types of industries, with tools like the Copenhagen Psychosocial Questionnaire [COPSOQ] that let research find job dissatisfaction, discrimination, and burnout syndrome.

MAIN FOCUS OF THE CHAPTER

Methodology

The research strategy employed was a case study applied to a manufacturing company that makes knob locks for doors in their final assembly area, ubicated in the city of Mexicali, Baja California, México. This company has been operating for over 30 years in the city, offering over 1350 jobs, and has been taking security and well-being more seriously. The employees that will take part in this study will be the ones in the final assembly area since the research aims to study both productivity and psychosocial risks; they are all adults and of both genders. A case study was chosen given the intention is to gain knowledge of a real situation, since modifying factor levels may originate a result that does not represent reality.

Exploration and analysis of existing literature about psychosocial factors and data gathering tools

Literature findings were made using three databases, primordially: EBSCOHost, ELSEVIER, and SPRINGER. The next step was an advanced search prioritizing documents that included psychosocial factors in industries. Also, only arbitrated, and complete texts were utilized. Of all found results, they all were analyzed for this research utility.

In the end, only 46 articles complied with the established requisites, showing what factors and instruments they used and why.

The 22 factors found in the studies is the next:

1. Job stability
2. Workplace harassment
3. Work-Family interference
4. Organizational climate
5. Leadership
6. Work rythm
7. Recognition
8. Role definition
9. Authonomy
10. Job satisfaction
11. Training
12. Psychological demand

13. Depersonalization
14. Work overload
15. Hability
16. Extra time
17. Physical load
18. Stress
19. Labour conditions
20. Growth
21. Support
22. Fatigue

PSYCHOSOCIAL FACTORS AND INSTRUMENTS SELECTIONS UTILIZED FOR THE CASE STUDY

In the investigation process, a large number of factors and instruments were found, like the General Health Questionnaire [GHQ], Job Content Questionnaire [JCQ], ISTAS21, and more. However, while investigating, the past October 23 of 2018 an Official Mexican Norm [NOM] was approved, called Norma Oficial Mexicana: Factores de riesgo psicosocial en el trabajo - Identificaci6n, análisis y prevenci6n [NOM 035], which translates to Psychosocial risk factors at Work-Identification, analysis, and prevention. These norms are mandatory in Mexico, so it was opted to utilize the instrument provided by the norm.

MEASURING INSTRUMENT

The questionnaire to Identify the Psychosocial Risk Factors and Evaluate Organizational Environments in Work Centers has 2 types of questionnaires depending on the number of workers studied.

For organizations with less than 50 employees, guide reference II is used, which counts 46 questions and evaluates the fields of work environment conditions, job load, lack of work control, working hours, interference in work-family relation, leadership, work relations, and violence.

For organizations with more than 50 employees, guide reference III is used, it has 72 questions and evaluates the fields of work environment conditions, job load, lack of work control, working hours, interference in work-family relation, work relations, violence, performance recognition and insufficient sense of belonging and instability.

In the case study, the final assembly area counts 272 employees, for this reason, guide reference III was utilized.

The instrument comes with its evaluation method, which generates a result classified in one of five levels:

1. Null: The risk results negligible.
2. Low: Better psychosocial factors prevention.
3. Medium: Intervention programs are needed.
4. High: Sensitization campaigns are needed.
5. Very high: Specific actions needed to stop or prevent risks.

It was also added to the questionnaire a demographic section to know age, antiquity, assembly line, work shift, and gender.

INSTRUMENT APPLICATION

An agreement with the company was made, 3 dates were scheduled to apply the questionnaire. For better results, it was opted to not use a sample and instead survey all workers. The questionnaire was applied in person, appointments were made for all employees to assist and all the questions were read to them. Each reactive manages a scale from 0 to 4, where the value depends on what question they are answering.

Productivity measurements were taken from a production history, where the engineering department registered a production plan and real production day by day. This plan-reality relation was utilized as a productivity percentage, by dividing the volume by the production plan [this was done to each production lane].

The data collected was put in a database and analyzed through the NOM 035 evaluation. The averages were calculated by production lane, and with the results from the norm and with the production data a correlation analysis was made. Table 1 exemplifies the database that was used for productivity; the whole database is confidential to keep company privacy.

Table 1. Productivity by assembly line example

Lane	Production plan (pieces)	Produced volume (pieces)	Productivity %
1	11525	10740	93%
3	11300	12124	107%
4	11000	10080	92%
5	6045	6078	101%
6	11023	11550	105%
7	4318	5292	123%
8	8995	8928	99%
9	8781	6564	75%

Table 1.2 exemplifies the database that resulted from the nom 035 questionnaire, where the number represents the average risk level for each psychosocial risk. For example, the first row shows the first questionnaire applied, which corresponds to assembly line number 1. For the work environment factor, the questionnaire sums up the results of the corresponding questions and depending on where the value locates within a range, it will be its score.

Table 2. Example of psychosocial factors average levels by questionnaire

Lane	Questionnaire Number	Work environment conditions	Job load	Leadership
1	1	10	37	17
1	2	9	18	4
7	3	7	20	19

RESULTS

Descriptive Statistic

The following are the results obtained from polling 272 employees. There were 158 females and 92 males; ages ranged from 18 to 28 years (74 persons), 29 to 38 years (53 persons), 39 to 48 years (74 persons), and 49 years and older (71 persons). When it comes to antiquity, it ranged from 0 to 1 year (106 persons), up to 5 years (67 persons), up to 10 years (8 persons), and above 10 years (91 persons).

Figure 2. Population by gender

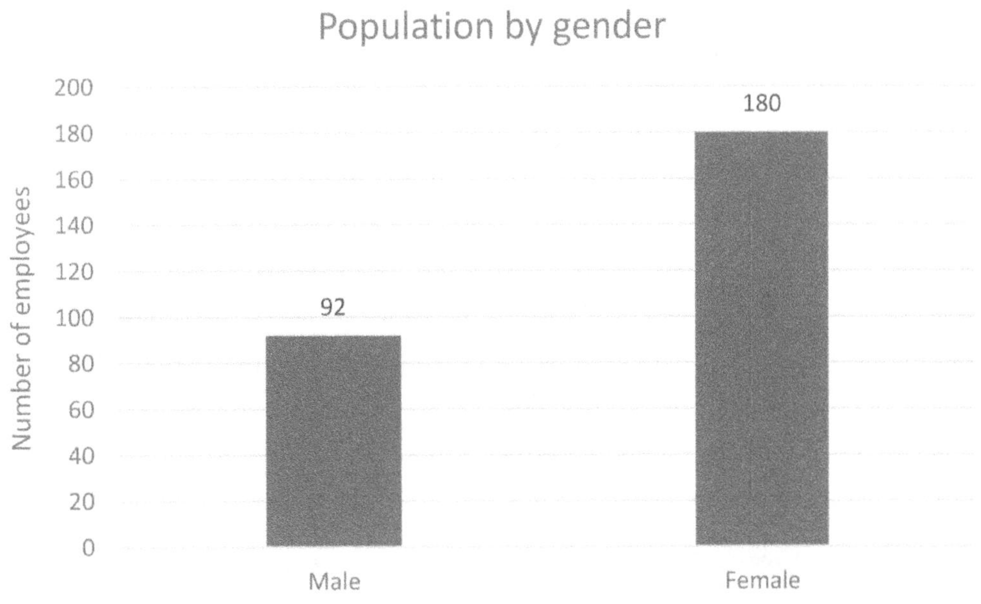

Figure 3. Population by ages

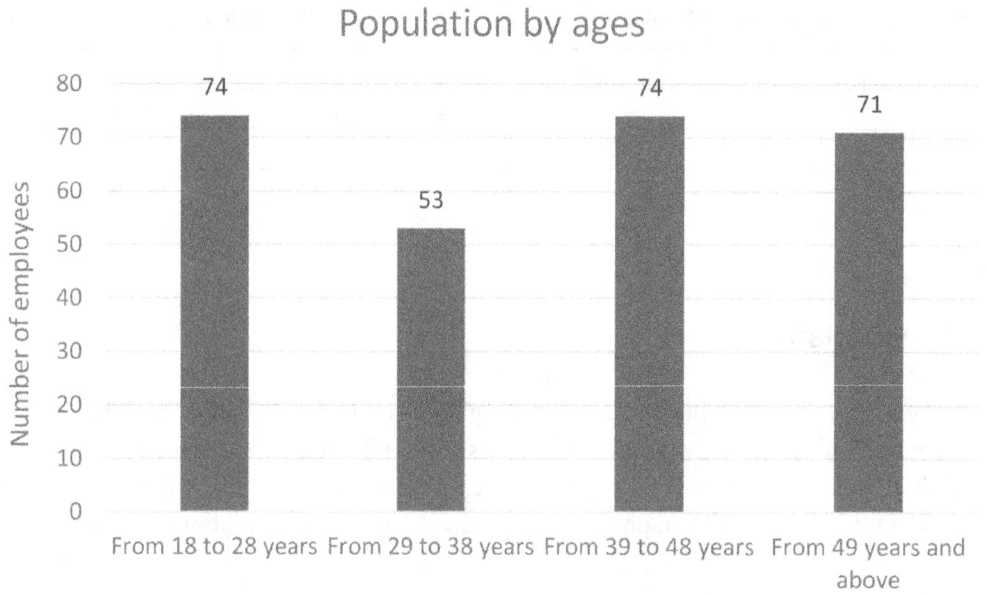

Figure 4. Population by antiquity

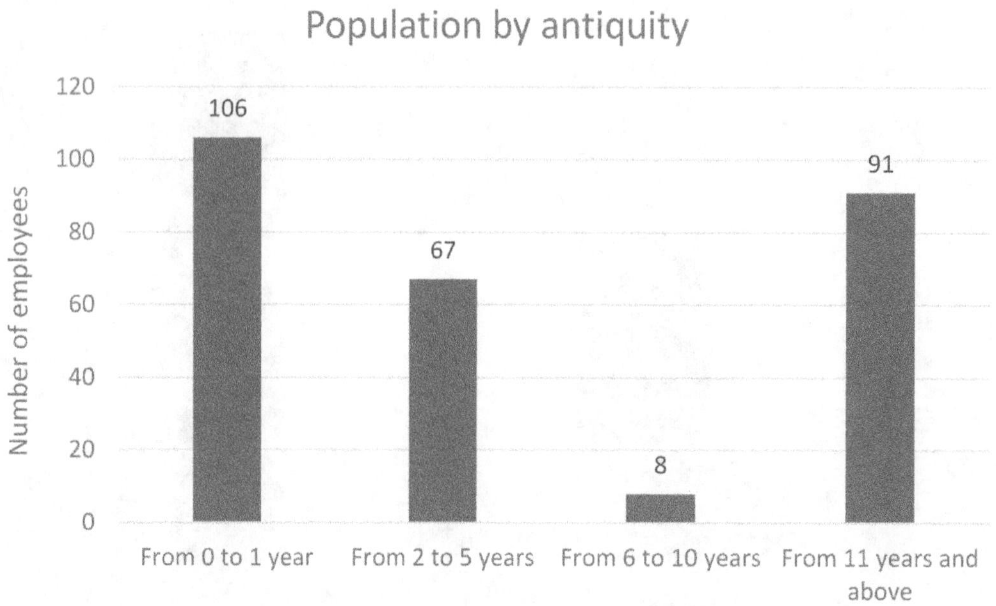

Figure 5. Population by marital status

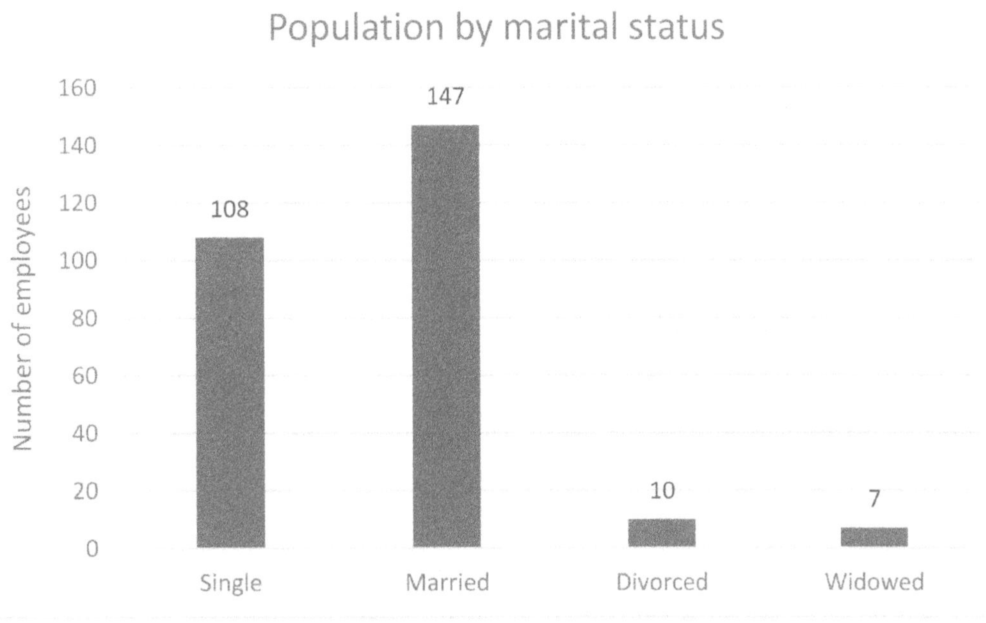

NOM-035 QUESTIONNAIRE RESULTS

The following factors were rated: Conditions in the work environment, Workload, Lack of control over work, Work shift, Interference in the work-family relationship, Leadership, Work relationships, Violence, Recognition of performance, and Insufficient sense of belonging and instability, based on the score table by NOM 035. The results were divided by the assembly line and the overall result. A color code is used to symbolize the risk levels: zero [blue], low [green], medium [yellow], high [orange], and very high [red].

The average scores of all the lines are those shown in table 2. As it can be seen, the two factors that show a high risk are the lack of control overwork and the recognition of performance, while only leadership and violence present a medium level, however, not risky.

Table 2. Average levels of the global psychosocial factors

Psychosocial factors				
Work Environment	**Workload**	**Lack of control overwork**	**Work shift**	**Interference in the work-family relationship**
7.12	17.58	23.18	0.76	4.74
Psychosocial factors				
Leadership	Work relationships	Violence	Recognition of performance	Insufficient sense of belonging and instability
14.75	10.73	11.43	13.76	5.69

Next are the bar graphs for each factor broken down by the final assembly line and their respective percentage of responses.

STACKED BAR CHART (100%)

The following graphs will be used to compare by final assembly line (Y-Axis) where the data is most concentrated and find out in greater detail where there is a greater or lesser percentage of psychosocial risk (X-Axis).

Looking at figure 6 highlights the low level of psychosocial risk, and even only three assembly lines show a small hint of high risk, which can represent very specific cases.

Figure 6. Work Environment, general

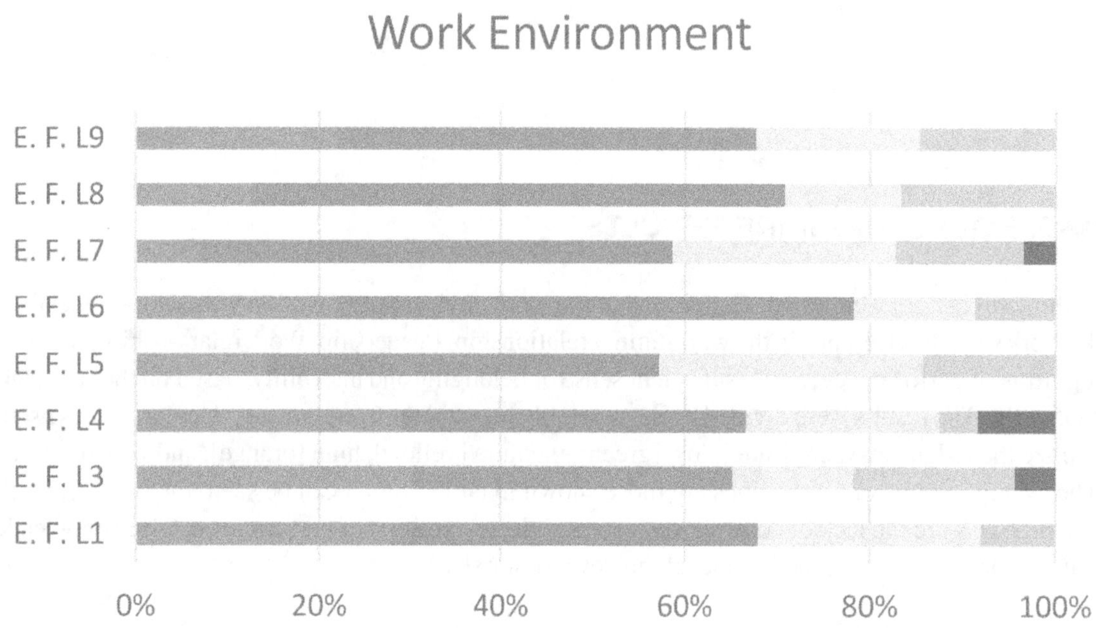

In figure 7 the risk percentage is almost zero, however, it does reach a low level. This shows how the company does not overload its employees or that employees are not affected by the workload assigned to them.

Figure 7. Workload, general

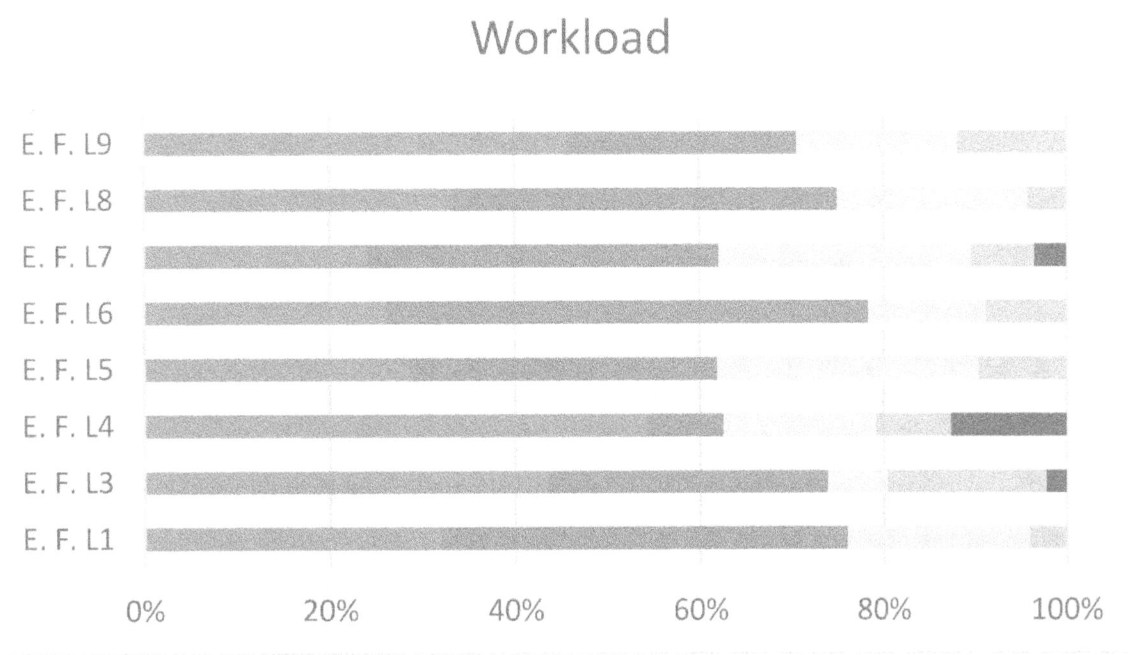

In figure 8 most lines show a high level of risk and even three lines show their mean at a very high level. This indicates little freedom for workers to make decisions.

Figure 8. Lack of control over work, general

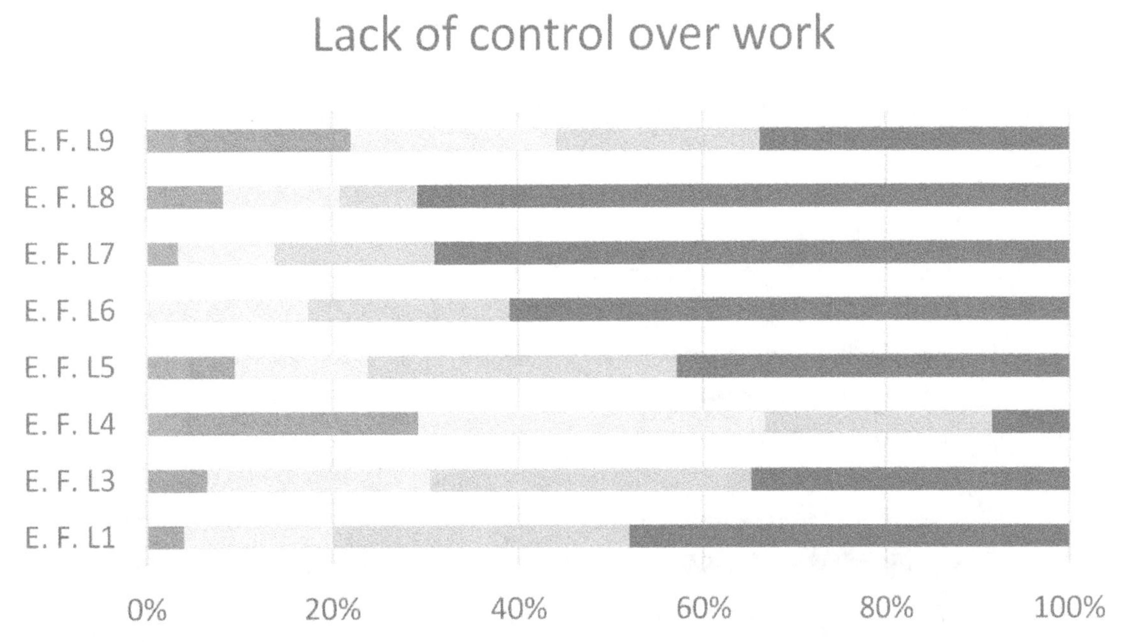

For the working day, figure 9 indicates that this factor does not present any risk for most of the personnel.

Figure 9. Work shift, general

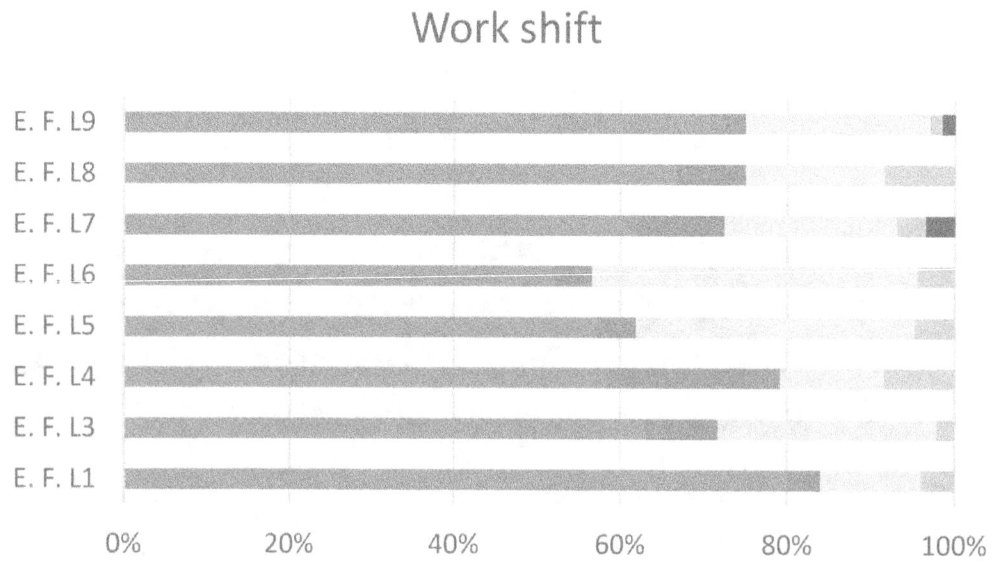

In figure 10 there is a low risk for the most part, only with two assembly lines showing a medium level, which shows that the risk is largely controlled, only a few cases were reported where work interferes with the family or vice versa, but not at a high level.

Figure 10. Interference in the work-family relationship, general

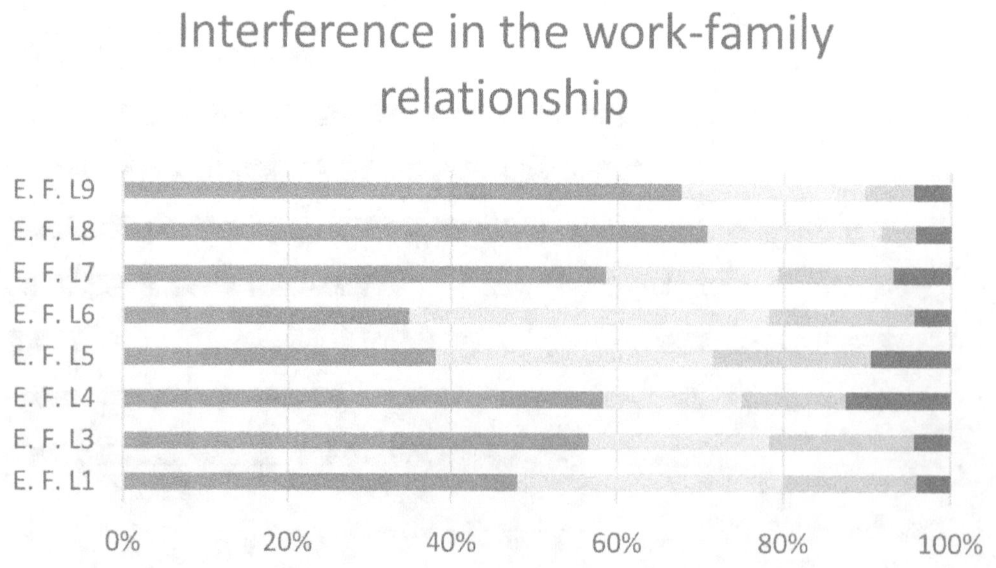

Unlike the previous figures, figure 11 shows a clear variety in the results and how each assembly line views its leaders differently. While in one assembly line there is a low level, in another it reaches the highest level of risk. However, globally speaking as an assembly area, the risk reaches medium levels.

Figure 11. Leadership, general

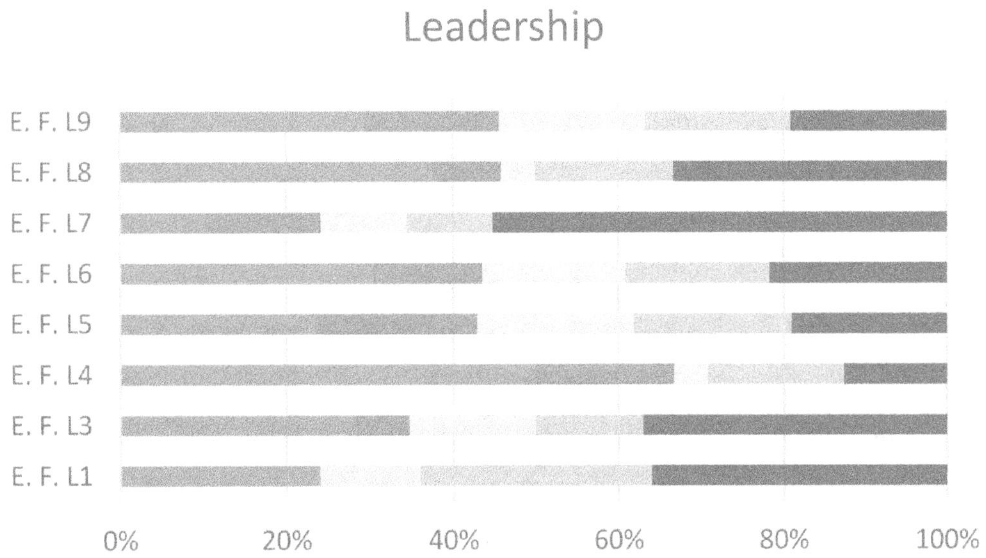

Figure 12 shows the existence of violence at a medium to a high level for certain assembly lines and a line at a mostly null level. This can lead to problematic relationships with coworkers, among other possibilities. Even so, at the assembly area level, the risk is seen at a medium risk level.

Figure 12. Violence, general

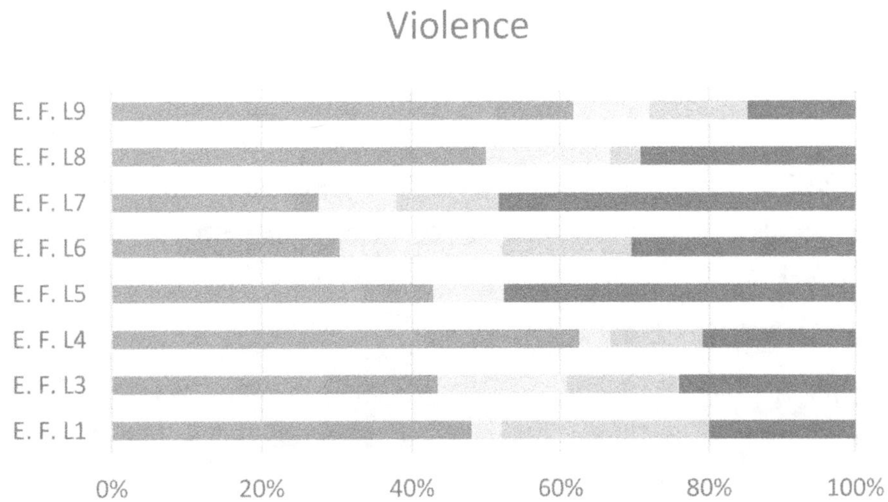

For figure 13, the risks are low or null, demonstrating a healthy employment relationship between the different work areas, not representing any psychosocial risk.

Figure 13. Work relationships, general

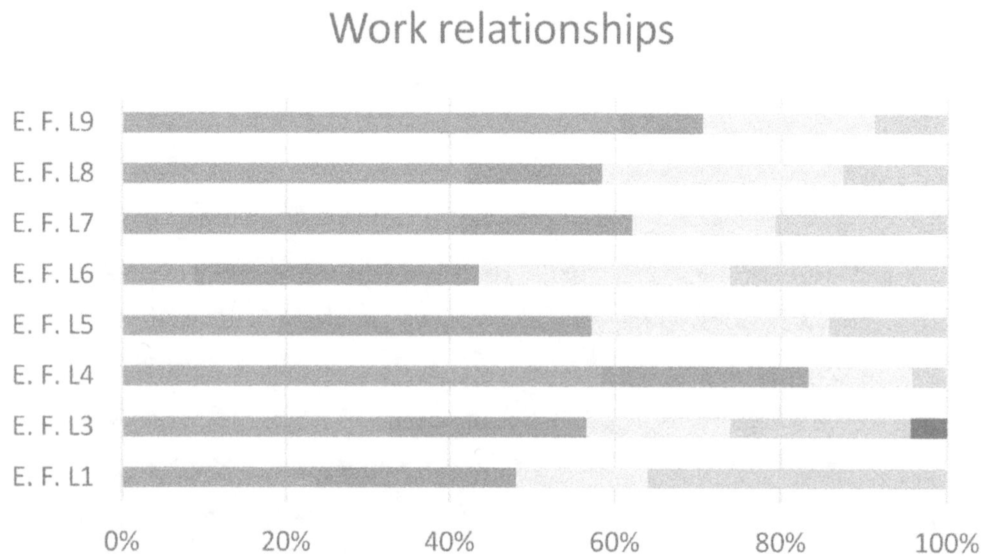

Figure 14, the psychosocial risk it presents is visible. At the area level, the risk shows a medium level, however, the graph shows a trend of few results for low or no risk levels, and more loaded at medium, high and very high levels.

Figure 14. Recognition of performance, general

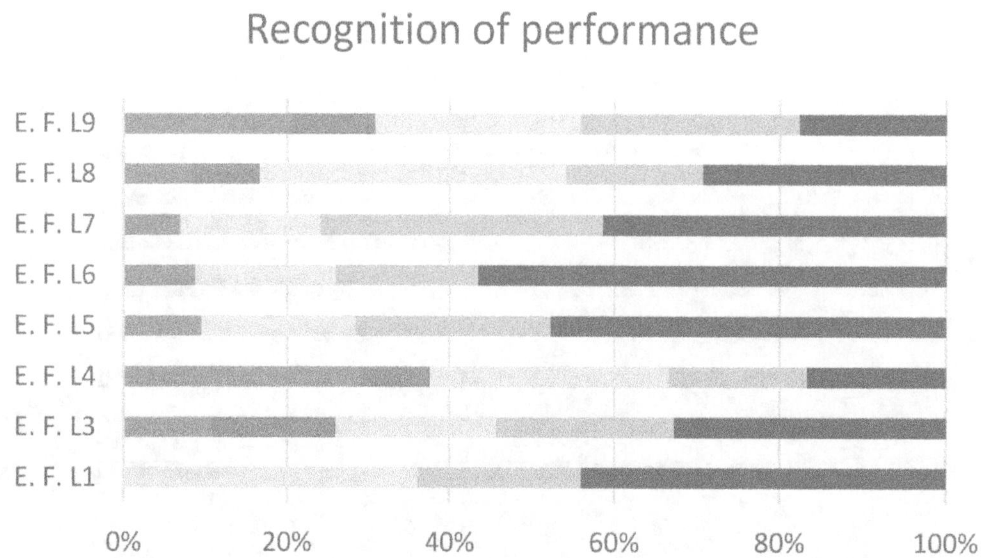

As can be seen in figure 15, the sense of belonging and instability does not show high risks that can affect the worker. Most of the results show low levels for most assembly lines.

Figure 15. Insufficient sense of belonging and instability, general

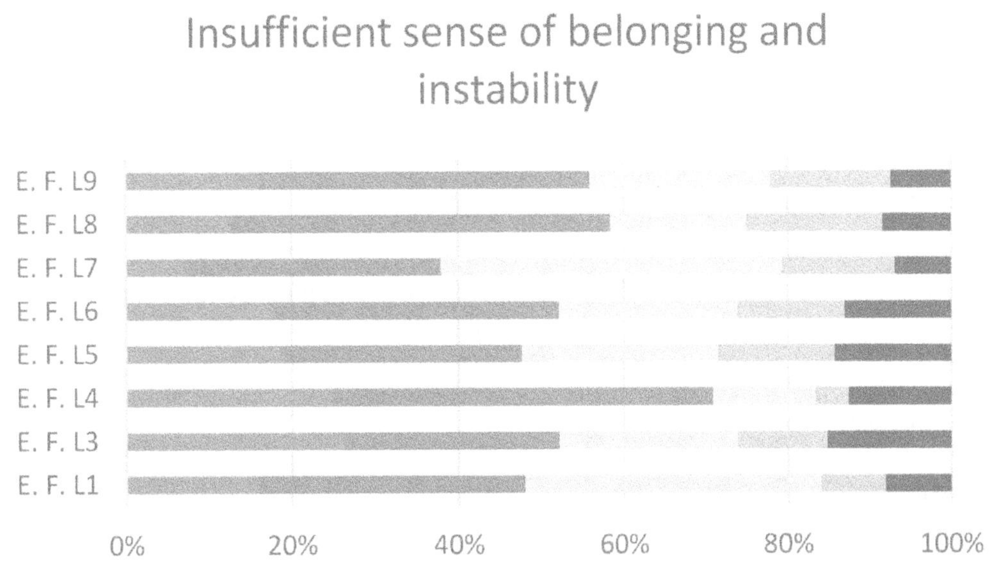

Visualizing the ten graphs, those of Lack of control over work, Recognition of performance are those that present the highest levels of risk; Leadership and Violence are what are found at medium levels, while the others have low to zero levels. This should be considered when relating these results with their respective coefficients of determination R^2.

THE DETERMINATION COEFFICIENT (R^2)

When applying this coefficient, the correlation between 'Psychosocial risk factor' and 'Productivity' is sought to find out if the higher the level of the psychosocial factor, the lower or the higher productivity. To find this number, the scatter charts in Excel were used, where the level of psychosocial risk per assembly line was related in a column with its respective percentage of productivity to find the correlation of both factors.

Table 3. Results of work environment psychosocial risk and productivity

Assembly line	Risk level	Productivity percentage
1	6.96	97%
3	6.8	101%
4	6.95	95%
5	7.52	109%
6	6.7	103%
7	7.96	130%
8	7.7	98%
9	6.97	91%

Figure 16 shows a value for R^2 of 0.4528 with a slight positive inclination, this indicates a medium correlation showing that the factor does not significantly influence the productivity response.

Figure 16. Work environment and productivity

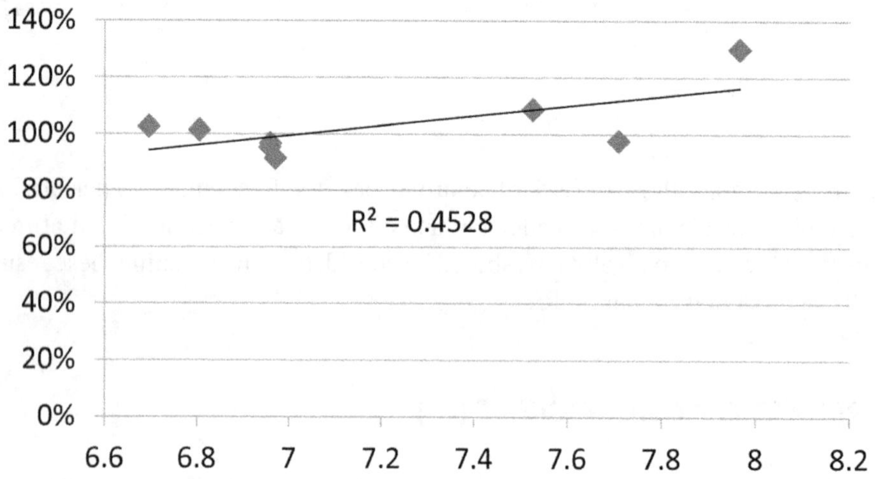

Table 4. Results of psychosocial risk, workload, and productivity

Assembly line	Risk level	Productivity percentage
1	17.56	96%
3	17.11	101%
4	21.11	91%
5	18.52	101%
6	16.6	105%
7	19	91%
8	17.41	97%
9	19.41	84%

For the graph shown in figure 17, a negative trend and a median correlation due to the R^2 of 0.528 are shown, indicating that there is no significant influence on the productivity response.

Figure 17. Workload and productivity

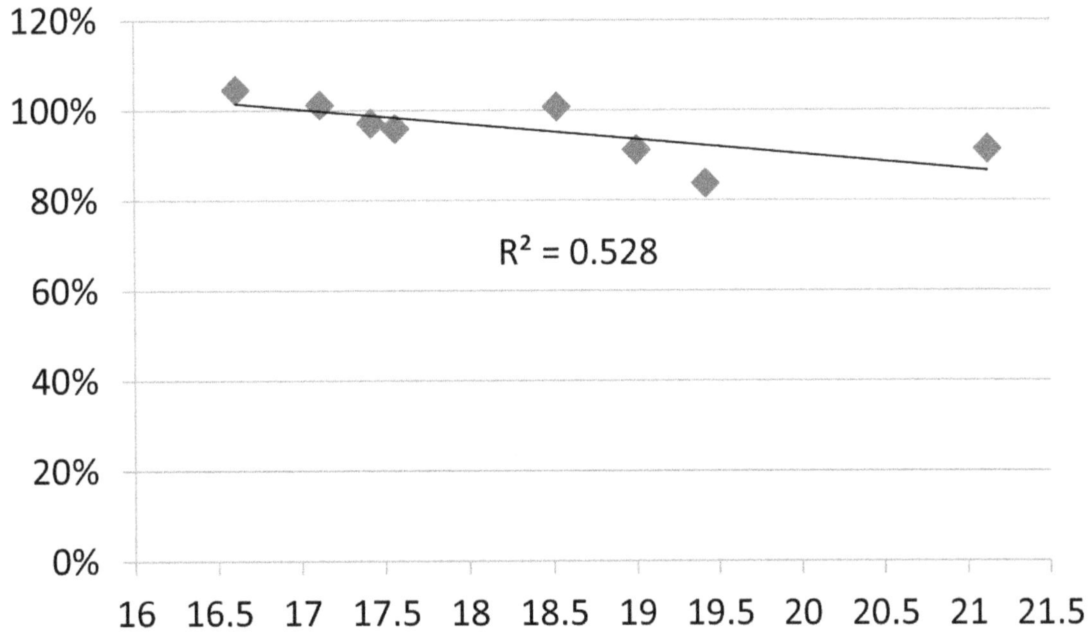

Table 5. Results of psychosocial risk, lack of control overwork, and productivity

Assembly line	Risk level	Productivity percentage
1	24.36	96%
3	23.13	105%
4	18.11	93%
5	22.8	111%
6	25.52	107%
7	26.79	113%
8	26.58	96%
9	19.38	88%

In figure 18 the R^2 result of 0.3516 shows a low and positive correlation. Similarly, this indicates that there is no significant influence on the productivity response.

Figure 18. Lack of control over work and productivity

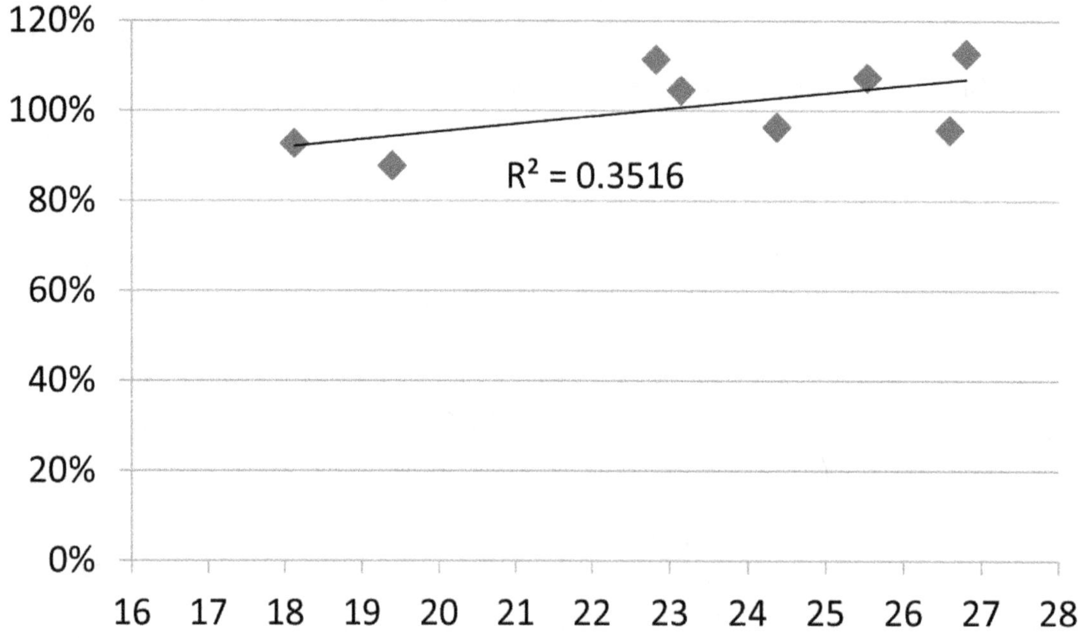

Table 6. Results of psychosocial risk, workday, and productivity

Assembly line	Risk level	Productivity percentage
1	0.48	98%
3	0.77	97%
4	1.05	88%
5	0.90	97%
6	1	98%
7	0.93	80%
8	0.83	101%
9	0.94	95%

Of the graphs with the lowest correlation, figure 19 shows an R^2 of 0.1714, with a slight negative trend, with practically no influence on the productivity response.

Figure 19. Work shift and productivity

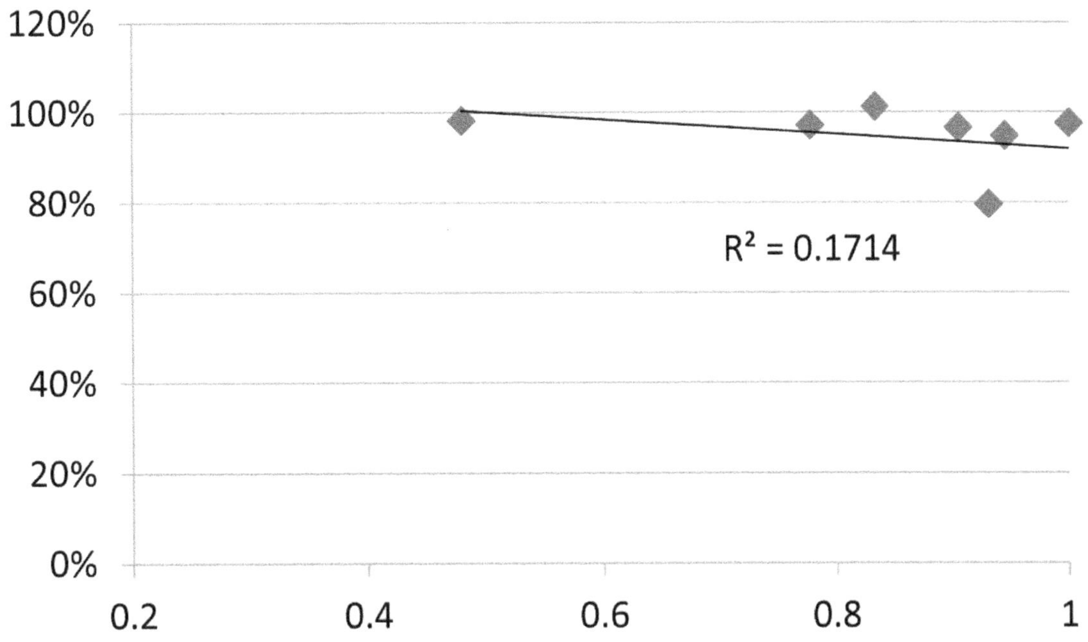

Table 7. Results of psychosocial risk, interference in the work-family relationship, and productivity

Assembly line	Risk level	Productivity percentage
1	5.08	96%
3	4.77	105%
4	3.94	93%
5	6.04	111%
6	5.91	107%
7	4.89	113%
8	3.83	96%
9	3.86	88%

Within figure 20, the positive trend shown by the graph gives a moderate indication that the greater the interference in the work-family relationship has a positive influence on the productivity response, however, the correlation is medium, so this result does not it is significantly correlated.

Figure 20. Interference in the work-family relationship and productivity

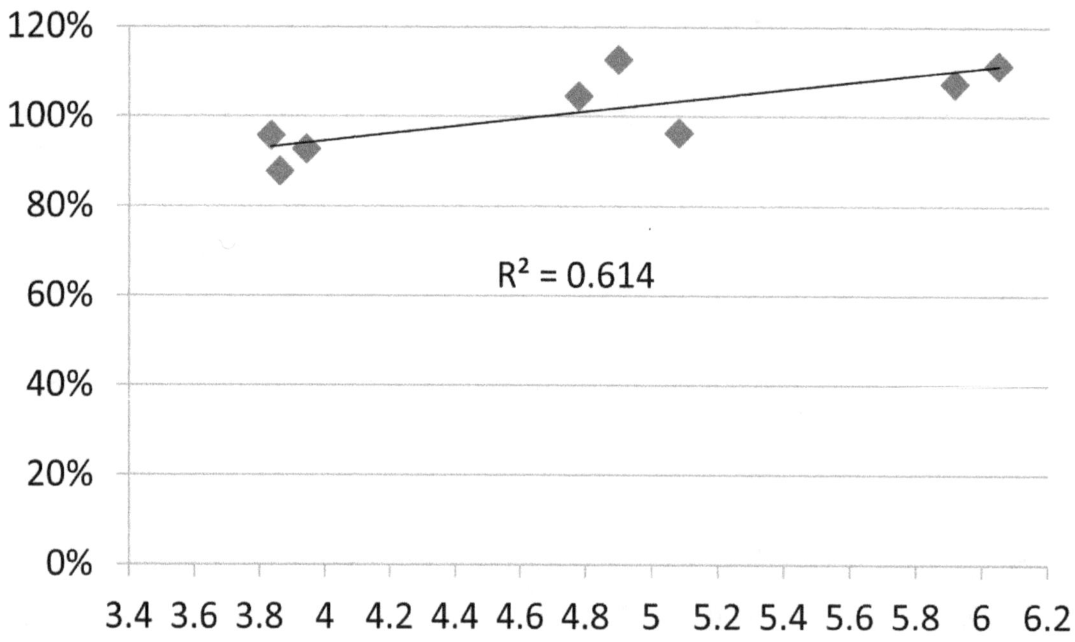

Table 8. Results of psychosocial risk, leadership, and productivity

Assembly line	Risk level	Productivity percentage
1	17.36	97%
3	15.11	101%
4	9.64	95%
5	14.23	109%
6	13.69	103%
7	19.93	130%
8	14.08	98%
9	10.88	91%

For the leadership factor shown in figure 21, the R^2 of 0.5575 shows a moderate and positive correlation, so that there is a medium influence on productivity with better leadership.

Figure 21. Leadership and productivity

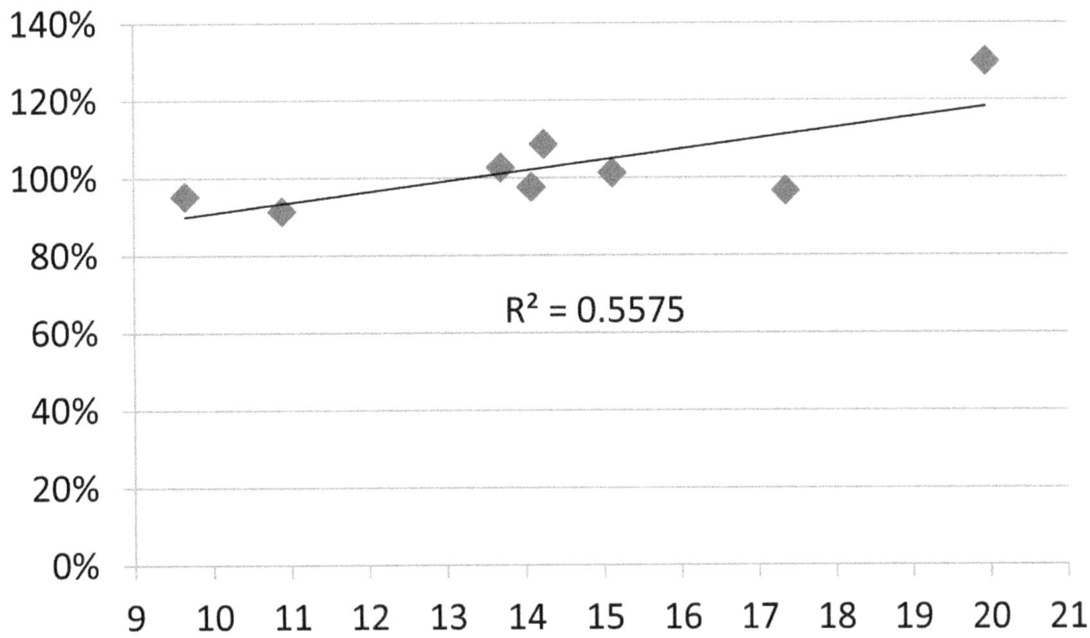

Table 9. Results of psychosocial risk, relationships at work, and productivity

Assembly line	Risk level	Productivity percentage
1	13.4	96%
3	11.82	101%
4	5	91%
5	12.28	101%
6	13.95	105%
7	11.10	91%
8	10.58	97%
9	6.94	84%

The graph of relationships at work shown in figure 22 shows a median positive correlation, therefore, it does not significantly influence productivity.

Figure 22. Work relationships and productivity

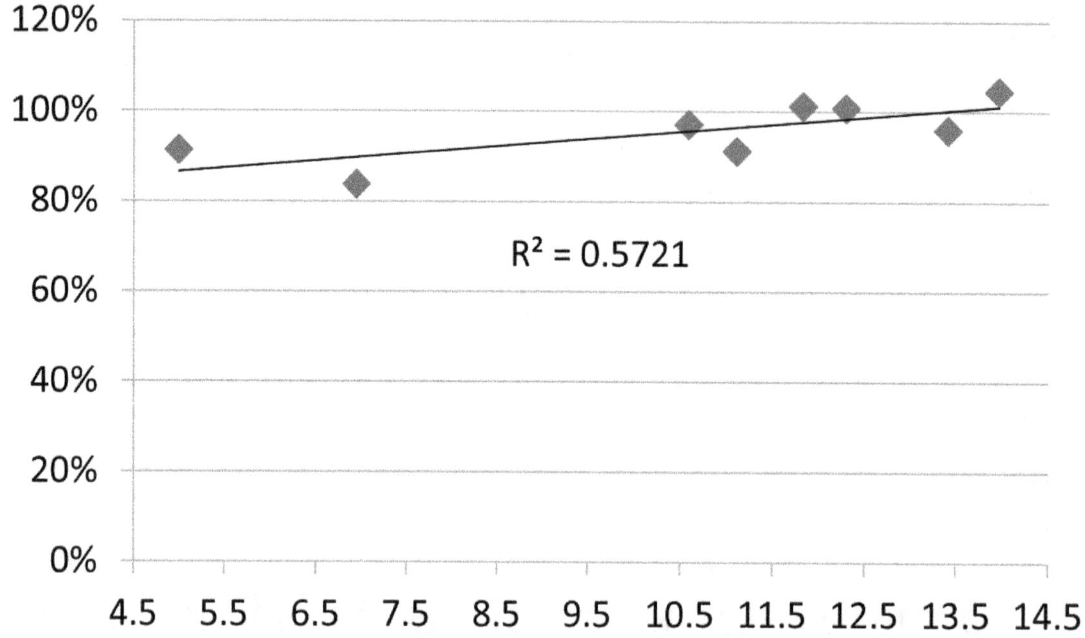

Table 10. Results of psychosocial risk, violence, and productivity

Assembly line	Risk level	Productivity percentage
1	11.04	96%
3	11.37	105%
4	10.41	93%
5	14.14	111%
6	14.04	107%
7	14.58	113%
8	11.70	96%
9	9.19	88%

Of all the R^2 graphs, figure 23 stands out as it shows a significant positive correlation, indicating that the more violence there is an influence on the higher productivity. This factor will be specifically discussed later.

Figure 23. Violence and productivity

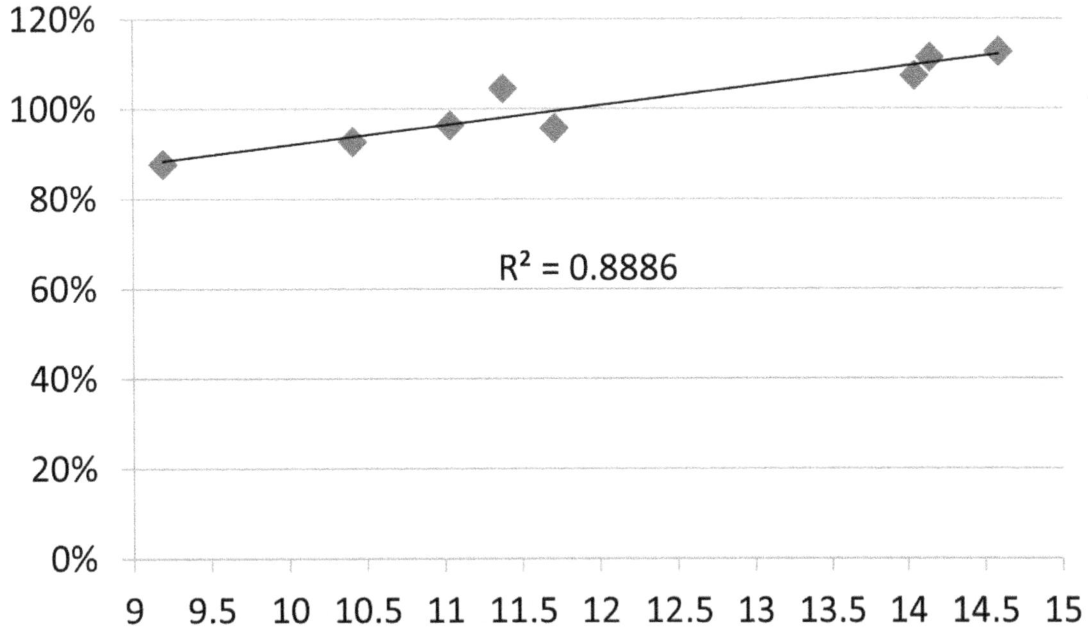

Table 11. Results of psychosocial risk, recognition of performance, and productivity

Assembly line	Risk level	Productivity percentage
1	16.04	96%
3	13.55	105%
4	9.52	93%
5	15.90	111%
6	16.13	107%
7	15.58	113%
8	13.5	96%
9	10.75	88%

Figure 24 shows a slight positive trend, but with a median R^2, again indicating that there is no significant influence on productivity.

Figure 24. Recognition of performance and productivity

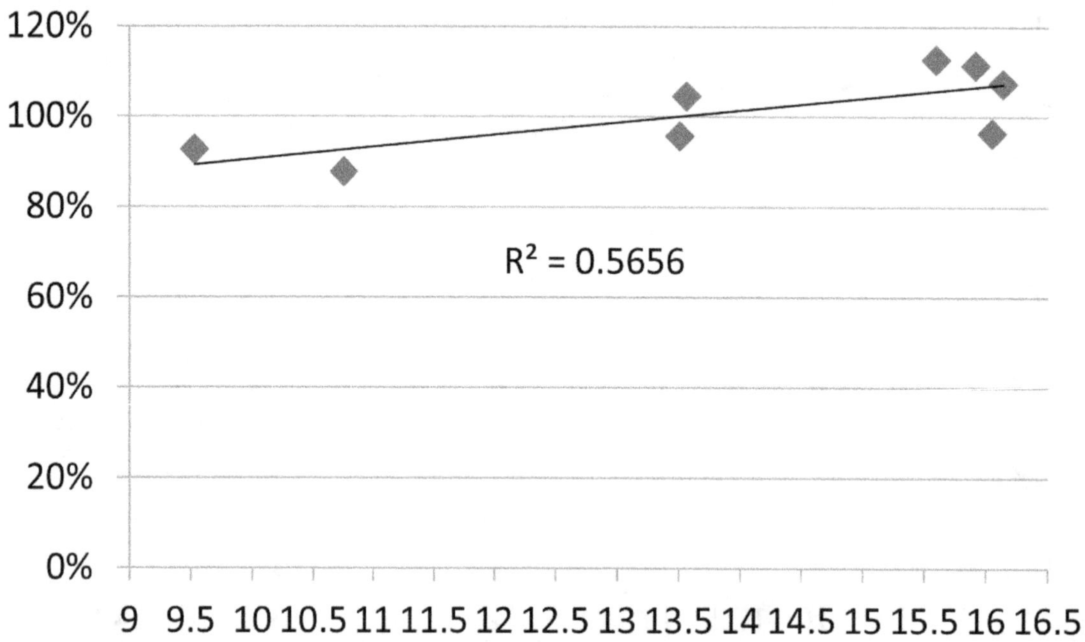

Table 12. Results of psychosocial risk, insufficient sense of belonging and instability, and productivity

Assembly line	Risk level	Productivity percentage
1	5.52	98%
3	5.66	97%
4	6.17	88%
5	6.09	97%
6	5.86	98%
7	6	80%
8	5.45	101%
9	5.47	95%

Finally, for figure 25, having an R^2 of 0.3574, it can be concluded that the factor of insufficient sense of belonging and instability does not influence the response more than moderately.

Figure 25. Insufficient sense of belonging and instability and productivity

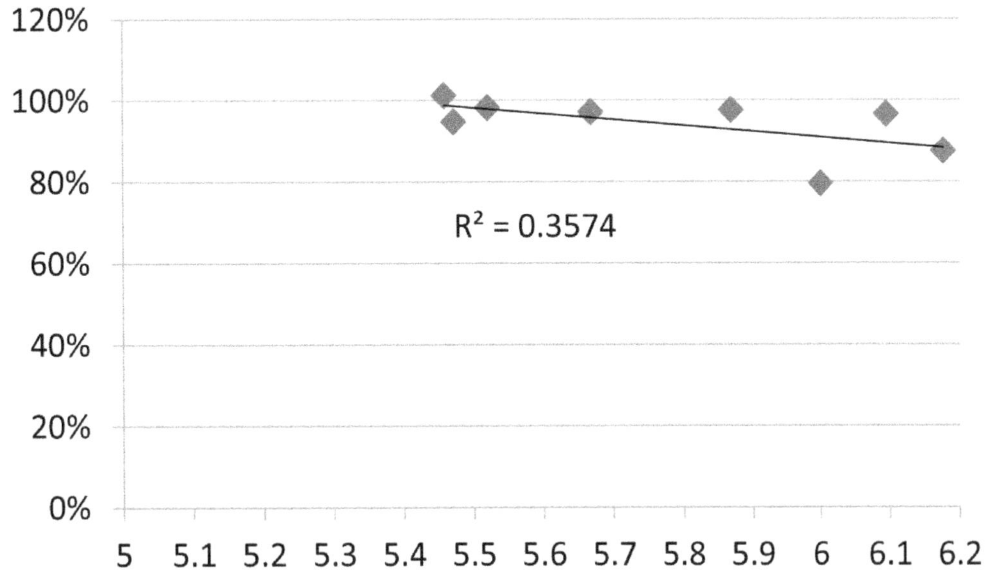

DEMOGRAPHIC RESULTS

Productivity behavior was analyzed depending on gender, age, and work shift, in addition to its qualification according to NOM 035.

It was found in the ratings by gender that both men and women share the lack of control over work with a high or very high level of risk. In the recognition of performance factor, both genders have similar risk levels, with only a slight increase in risk for women.

Figure 26. Lack of control over work, morning shift

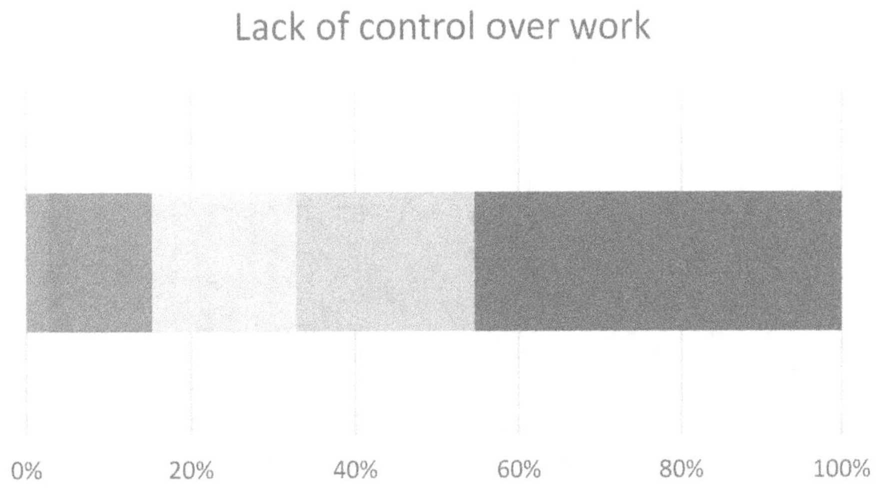

For the results by work shift, again the lack of control over work indicates high and very high levels of risk for both shifts, as shown in figures 26 and 527, however, it is clear that the evening shift is the main group that is affected by having its staff at high and very high risks. Also in what is violence (figures 28 and 28) for the morning shift, the risk is slightly higher than that of the evening shift, which may mean that it is in a specific shift where a greater number of violent acts occur. The next section will discuss this factor in more detail.

Figure 27. Lack of control over work, evening shift

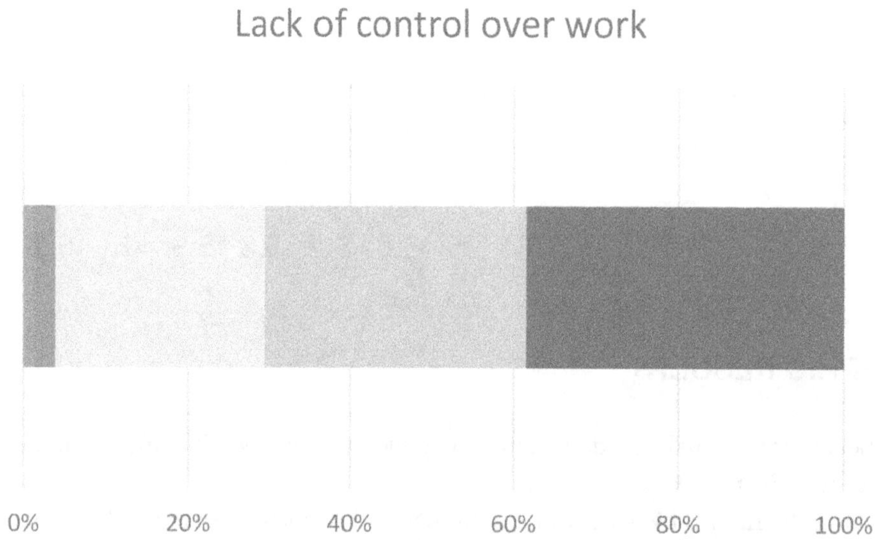

Figure 28. Violence, morning shift

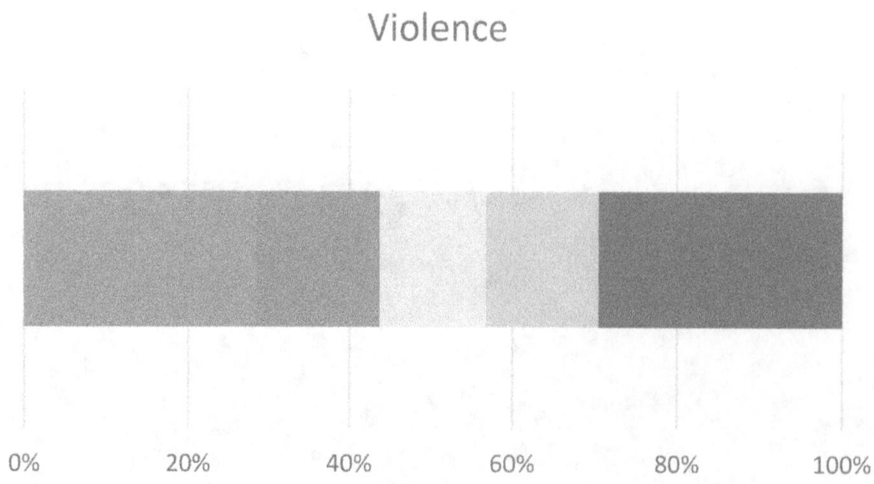

Figure 29. Violence, evening shift

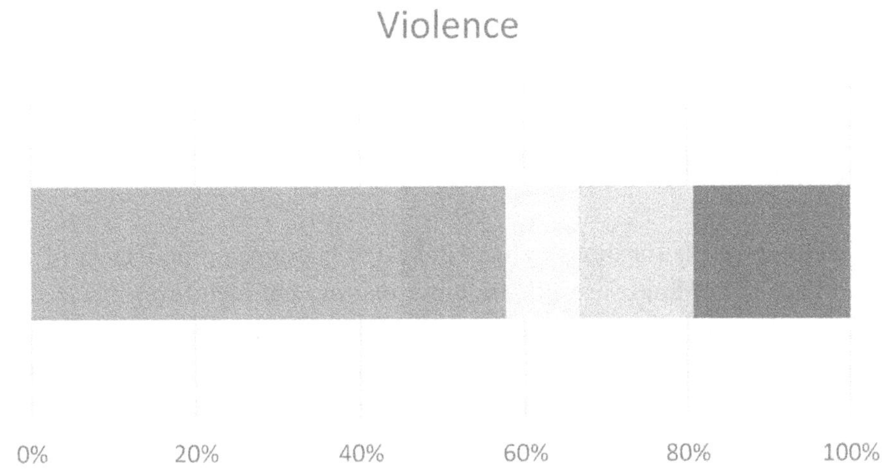

Finally, for people 39 years of age and older, there is an increase in the level of risk of violence to the medium level.

VIOLENCE FACTOR ANALYSIS

It was decided to break down the items that make up the violence factor to visualize in detail what kind of violence the employees perceive the most since it is the factor that obtained the higher R^2 result and contrary to the literature, the higher the violence the indicator had a productivity improvement.

The violence factor is made up of eight items:

1. In my work I can express myself freely without interruptions.
2. I receive constant criticism of my person and/or work.
3. I receive teasing, slander, defamation, humiliation, or ridicule.
4. My presence is ignored, or I am excluded from work meetings and decision-making.
5. Work situations are manipulated to make me look like a bad worker.
6. My job successes are ignored and attributed to other workers.
7. They block or impede my opportunities for promotion or improvement in my job.
8. I have witnessed acts of violence in my workplace.

The results of average levels per reagent are as follows:

Table 13.

Average level	2.04	1.72	1.19	1.32	1.15	1.24	1.03	1.73
Question	1	2	3	4	5	6	7	8

As it can be seen by the results, expressing freely without interruptions does not always happen and this contributes to violence ending up at a high-risk level. Also, workers feel like they receive critics of their person and/or work on a medium scale plus having witnessed acts of violence in their workplace. All other items had a low average level, so employees do not consider this when talking about violence.

DISCUSSION AND CONCLUSION

When viewing the general qualifications by the NOM-035 instrument, the factors of Recognition of performance and Lack of control over work are those that present high levels perceived by workers. These are the factors that possibly significantly influence productivity.

For this, using the correlation coefficient R ^ 2, the factors that are significantly influencing productivity can be appreciated. In this way, the following factors are found with a medium correlation: Conditions in the work environment, Workload, Leadership, Relationships at work, and Recognition of performance. While the Workday, Lack of control overwork, and Insufficient sense of belonging show a low correlation. The low correlation workday maybe because overtime is not allowed in the study company and the employees are used to it.

The high correlation factors were violence and interference in the work-family relationship, both showing a positive correlation. This is unusual because, according to the literature, both factors are detrimental to the worker (Amor, 2014). Analyzing these same factors with the instrument of NOM 035, both factors are found at low and medium levels respectively, which shows that there is no great risk for the worker based on the standards of the norm, even so, it will be interesting in future studies will show if this correlation continues at higher risk levels for both factors, or if productivity decreases after a certain level. Possibly workers are already familiar with minimal acts of violence that do not negatively affect work, on the contrary, they drive them to work.

When delving into the violence factor, it is visualized how employees consider violence mainly for three reasons: they cannot express themselves freely, they receive constant criticism and violent (physical) acts have been witnessed. Although this type of practice is not considered acceptable in a healthy work environment, somehow employees have become accustomed to a slightly hostile treatment that causes the worker to pay no attention to anything other than their work and end up being more productive.

The relationship at work and leadership also shows an interesting result, since an increase in productivity is demonstrated while both factors deteriorate. This may mean that people in this area prefer to work without having to constantly interact with others since relationships at work present a low level of risk according to the norm.

On the other hand, Workload shows a trend that, with the greater workload, whether mental or physical, productivity tends to decrease and inversely, the Performance Recognition factor tends to improve productivity in the face of improvements in both factors.

Taking into account the demographic variables of gender, both men and women show medium and high-risk levels for Lack of control over work, Leadership, Violence, and Recognition of performance, the only difference is in the Recognition of performance, with women being the increase the risk level to high.

For the work shift variables, while the evening shift suffers mainly from Leadership and Lack of control over work, the morning shift maintains the risk level for Lack of control, but increases violence, relationships at work, and recognition performance significantly, marking a notable difference between shifts that may be due to poor practices by morning staff.

Finally, the age variables did not have any difference between them, only people in the 49-year-old range did have high levels of risk for 5 factors. This allows us to see the situation from another perspective, since it may be that the people who have the greatest influence on increasing risk levels are the older personnel, but in turn, these are the people who are increasing productivity, as seen above that these factors are the ones that influence the response.

Then there are enough elements to conclude that the psychosocial factors of Violence and Interference in the work-family relationship do show a correlation with the productivity result of 88.86% and 61.4% respectively.

SOLUTIONS AND RECOMMENDATIONS

In general, the company treats its employees with care, it is only recommended to train line supervisors in conflict management to take care of attitudes that can cause violence out of control, in addition to some type of reward for being a distinguished worker or with values. In this way, physical or mental risks for employees can be prevented and at the same time continue with efficient productivity.

FUTURE RESEARCH DIRECTIONS

Future studies are recommended that visualize individual productivity and another instrument that allows the analysis of psychosocial factors in an individualized and non-group way, to have even more precise results.

REFERENCES

Abbe, O. O., Harvey, C. M., Ikuma, L. H., & Aghazadeh, F. (2011). Modeling the relationship between occupational stressors, psychosocial/physical symptoms, and injuries in the construction industry. *International Journal of Industrial Ergonomics*, *41*(2), 106–117. doi:10.1016/j.ergon.2010.12.002

Acevedo, G., Farias, M., Sanchez, J. & Astegiano, C. (2012). *Condiciones de trabajo del equipo de salud en centros de atención primaria desde la perspectiva del trabajo decente*. Academic Press.

Alavinia, S. M., Molenaar, D., & Burdorf, A. (2008). Productivity Loss in the Workforce: Associations with Health, Work Demands, and Individual Characteristics. *American Journal of Industrial Medicine*. PMID:18942667

Amor, A. (2014). *La violencia laboral*. Defensoría Del Pueblo.

Aranda, C., López, J., & Barraza, J. (2013). Factores psicosociales y síndrome de burnout en trabajadores de la industria de la transformación de la masa, Tepic, México. *Revista Colombiana de Psiquiatría*, *42*(2), 167–172. doi:10.1016/S0034-7450(13)70003-9 PMID:26572811

Artacoz, L., & Molinero, E. (2004). Evaluación de los factores de riesgo psicosocial, combinando metodología cuantitativa y cualitativa. *Archivos de Prevencion de Riesgos Laborales*, *7*(4), 134–142.

Asensio-Cuesta, S., Diego-Mas, J. A., Cremades-Oliver, L. V., & González-Cruz, M. C. (2012). A method to design job rotation schedules to prevent work-related musculoskeletal disorders in repetitive work. *International Journal of Production Research*, *50*(24), 7467–7478. https://doi.org/10.1080/00207543.2011.653452

Astudillo, P. (2003). *Factores psicosociales en el trabajo: ¿Cómo comprender las tensiones psicosociales para regularlas?* Departamento de Salud Ocupacional Instituto de Salud Pública de Chile.

Awang, M., Dollard, M., Coward, J., & Dormann, C. (2012). Psychosocial safety climate: Conceptual distinctiveness and effect on job demands and worker psychological health. *Safety Science*, *50*, 19–28.

Barrios & Illada. (2013). Valoración del desgaste laboral como riesgo psicosocial. *Revista ingeniería industrial.*

Blanch, J., Sahagún, M., & Cervantes, G. (2010). Estructura factorial del cuestionario de condiciones de trabajo. *Revista de Psicología del Trabajo y de las Organizaciones*, *26*(3), 175–189.

Chappell, D., & Di Martino, V. (1998). *Violence at work*. Organización Internacional del Trabajo.

Charria, V., Sarsosa, K., & Arenas, F. (2011). Factores de riesgo psicosocial laboral: Métodos e instrumentos de evaluación. *RevistaFacultad Nacional SaludPública*, *29*(4), 380–391.

Cox, T. (2000). Work-related stress, risk management, and management standards. *Work and Stress*, *18*(3), 89–90.

D'Souza, R., Strazdins, L., Broom, D., Rodgers, B., & Berry, H. (2006). Work demands, job insecurity, and sickness absence from work. How productive is the new, flexible labour force? *Australian and New Zealand Journal of Public Health*, *30*(3), 205–212.

da Silva, J. M. N., da Silva, L. B., & Gontijo, L. A. (2017). Relationship between psychosocial factors and musculoskeletal disorders in footwear industry workers. *Production*, *27*(0), 1–13. doi:10.1590/0103-6513.231516

Díaz, J. M. C. (2007). *Técnicas de prevención de riesgos laborales*. TÉBAR.

Enriquez Diaz, J. A., Kotzab, D., Sytch, A., & Frieling, E. (2012). Impact of increasing productivity on work content and psychosocial work characteristics in Chaku-Chaku assembly lines – A follow-up study in a German automotive manufacturing company. *Work (Reading, Mass.)*, *41*(Suppl.1), 5121–5128. https://doi.org/10.3233/WOR-2012-0803-5121

Paola Espeleta, C. (2015). Los riesgos psicosociales: causas, consecuencias y posibles soluciones. *Facultad de Ciencias Empresariales Y Del Trabajo*, 77.

Estrada, J., & Romero, N. (2014). Factores psicosociales del trabajador en la industria manufacturera en México. *Trabajo Y Sociedad, 20*, 119–129. www.unse.edu.ar/trabajoysociedad/20SALAZARROMEROtrabajadormanufactura mexico.pdf

Farnacio, Y., Pratt, M. E., Marshall, E. G., & Graber, J. M. (2017). Are Workplace Psychosocial Factors Associated With Work-Related Injury in the US Workforce? *Journal of Occupational and Environmental Medicine*, *59*(10), e164–e171. https://doi.org/10.1097/JOM.0000000000001143

Gil-Monte, P. R. (2002). Influencia del género sobre el proceso de desarrollo del síndrome de quemarse por el trabajo (Burnout) en profesionales de enfermería. *Psicologia em Estudo*, *7*(1), 3–10. https://doi.org/10.1590/S1413-73722002000100003

Gomes Carrana, P. (2015). *Evaluación de riesgos psicosociales en los trabajadores de la industria de la limpieza*. Academic Press.

Gondim, S., Mazzieri, S., & Torres, A. (2016). *Percepción de innovación en las organizaciones. Percepción de innovación en organizaciones de España y Latinoamérica*. Academic Press.

Instituto Nacional de Seguridad e Higiene en el Trabajo. (2011). *Vii encuesta nacional de condiciones de trabajo 2011*. Ministerio De Empleo Y Seguridad Social.

Izquierdo, F. M. (2012). *Manual de Riesgos Psicosociales en el trabajo: Teoría y Práctica*. Editorial Académica Española.

Jiménez, B. (2011). Factores y riesgos laborales psicosociales: Conceptualización, historia y cambios actuales. Academic Press.

Karasek, R. A. (1979). Job demands, job decision latitude, and mental strain: Implications for job redesign. *Administrative Science Quarterly*, *24*, 285–308.

Karasek, R. A., Theorell, T., Schwartz, J., Schnall, P., Pieper, C., & Michela, J. (1988). Job characteristics in relation to the prevalence of myocardial infarction in the U.S. HES and HANES. *American Journal of Public Health*, *78*, 910–918.

Law, R., Dollard, M., Tuckey, M., & Dormann, C. (2011). Psychosocial safety climate as a lead indicator of workplace bullying and harassment, job resources, psychological health, and employee engagement. *Accident; Analysis and Prevention*, *43*, 1782–1793.

Leiter, M. P., & Maslach, C. (2009). Nurse turnover: The mediating role of burnout. *Journal of Nursing Management*, *17*, 331–339. doi:10.1111/j.1365-2834.2009.01004.x

Mathisen, G. E., Brønnick, K., Arntzen, K. J., & Bergh, L. I. V. (2016). Identifying and managing psychosocial risks during organizational restructuring: It's what you do and how you do it. *Safety Science*, *100*, 20–29. https://doi.org/10.1016/j.ssci.2016.12.007

Meerding, W. J., Ijzelenberg, W., Koopmanschap, M. A., Severens, J. L., & Burdorf, A. (2005). Health problems lead to considerable productivity loss at work among workers with high physical load jobs. *JournalofClinicalEpidemiology*, *58*, 517–523.

Meliá, J. (2006). *¿Cómo evaluar los riesgos psicosociales en la empresa? Metodologías, oportunidades y tendencias*. Ponencia presentada en el IV Congreso Internacional de Prevención y Riesgos Laborales, Sevilla, España. Recuperado de: http://www.acosomoral.org/ pdf/sevilla06/0303.pdf

Moreno-Jiménez, B., & Báez León, C. (2011). Factores y riesgos psicosociales, formas, consecuencias, medidas y buenas prácticas. *Instituto Nacional de Seguridad E Higiene En El Trabajo*, 4–144. doi:10.1016/0277-9536(85)90255-2

Muñoz, R. D., Nataly, O., & Hernández, P. H. (2018). *Riesgo psicosocial: tendencias y nuevas orientaciones laborales*. Psicogente.

Neffa, J. C. (2002). *Cómo evaluar los riesgos psicosociales en el trabajo?Prevención*. Recuperado de.

NOM-035. (2018). *NORMA Oficial Mexicana NOM-035-STPS-2018, Factores de riesgo psicosocial en el trabajo-Identificación, análisis y prevención*. Secretaría de Gobernación.

Ocampo, R., Juárez, A., Arias, L., & Hindrichs, I. (2015). Factores psicosociales asociados al engagement en empleados de un restaurante de Morelos, México. *Revista Liberabit, 21*|(2), 207–219.

Ortiz, F., & Jaramillo, V. (2013). Factores de riesgo psicosocial en una industria alimenticia de la ciudad de Cali. *Pensamiento Psicológico, 11*(1), 99–113.

Pando, M., Aranda, C., Parra, L., & Ruiz, D. (2013). *Eugenesia Laboral: Salud Mental Positiva en el Trabajo*. Editorial Universidad Libre Seccional.

Pérez, J. (2013). Efecto del burnout y la sobrecarga en la calidad de vida en el trabajo. *Estudios Gerenciales*, *29*, 445–455.

Raffo Lecca, E., Ráez Guevara, L., & Cachay Boza, O. (2013). *Riesgos psicosociales*. Industrial Data.

Salazar, E. & Ruvalcaba, R. (2012). Factores psicosociales del trabajador en la industria manufacturera en México. *Trabajo y Sociedad, 20*, 119-129.

Secretaría del Trabajo y Prevención Social. (2016). PROYECTO de Norma Oficial Mexicana PROY-NOM-035-STPS-2016, Factores de riesgo psicosocial-Identificación y prevención. *Diario Oficial de la Federación*.

Umeda, M., McMunn, A., Cable, N., Hashimoto, H., Kawakami, N., & Marmot, M. (2015). Does an advantageous occupational position make women happier in contemporary Japan? Findings from the Japanese Study of Health, Occupation, and Psychosocial Factors Related Equity (J-HOPE). *SSM - Population Health*, *1*, 8–15. doi:10.1016/j.ssmph.2015.09.002 PMID:29349116

Van der Klauw, M., Hengel, K. O., Roozeboom, M. B., Koppes, L. L., & Venema, A. (2016). Occupational accidents in the Netherlands: Incidence, mental harm, and their relationship with psychosocial factors at work. *International Journal of Injury Control and Safety Promotion*, *23*(1), 79–84. doi:10.1080/17457300.2014.966119 PMID:25531558

Villalobos, G. (2005). *Diseño de un sistema de vigilancia epidemiológica de factores de riesgo psicosocial en el trabajo (Tesis de doctorado)*. Escuela Nacional de Salud Pública.

Williams, R. B., Barefoot, J. C., & Schneiderman, N. (2003). Psychosocial Risk Factors for Cardiovascular Disease More Than One Culprit at Work. *Journal of the American Medical Association*, 2190–2192.

Wilson, M. G., DeJoy, D. M., Vandenbert, R. J., Richardson, H. A., & McGrath, A. L. (2004). Work characteristics and employee health and well-being: Test of a model of healthy work organization. *Journal of Occupational and Organizational Psychology*, *77*(4), 565–588. doi:10.1348/0963179042596522

Chapter 5
Evaluation of Working Conditions as a Factor of Well-Being of Workers in an Electronic Industry in Mexicali

Carlos Raul Navarro González
https://orcid.org/0000-0003-3873-3800
Autonomous University of Baja California, Mexico

Yanet Villarreal González
Tecnologico Nacional de Mexico, Instituto Tecnolgico de Mexicali, Mexico

Pedro Alberto Escárcega Zepeda
Tecnologico Nacional de Mexico, Instituto Tecnolgico de Mexicali, Mexico

Ana Laura Sanchez Corona
Autonomous University of Baja California, Mexico

Rigoberto Zamora Alarcon
Autonomous University of Baja California, Mexico

Gustavo Lopez Badilla
UNEA Universidad, Mexico

ABSTRACT

The objective of this research was developed to evaluate the working conditions of workers in an electronic industry located in the city of Mexicali, analyzing a process in a work table where welding operations of electronic components are made and certain factors are presented that generated discomfort to the operating personnel of this manufacturing area. The workers frequently visited the company doctor and health institutions in Mexicali due to symptoms of discomfort and pain in the head, neck, back, spine, arms, hands, and shoulders in addition to discomfort in the eyes due to not having a position due to poor structure (work table and chair) and low light intensity, which caused fatigue and stress and discomfort with eyestrain. In addition, certain employees in the production areas presented symptoms of respiratory diseases caused by an environment contaminated by pollutants, essentially derived from sulfur (sulfides), as well as variations in temperature and relative humidity in the four seasons of the year.

DOI: 10.4018/978-1-7998-7396-9.ch005

INTRODUCTION

One of the important aspects in a workplace is to maintain working conditions, especially for workers in the manufacturing areas, because this is an index of the levels of productivity and quality in any type of industry at the level global (Bruzzonne, et al, 2012). Throughout the world, there are laws that regulate the working conditions of all industrial companies, in addition to the fact that in the region and country, other types of laws are adhered to according to environmental factors (climate and pollution), as well as being based on equal participation of men and women, ethnic origin, religion and nationality (customs), social levels, people with disabilities, health conditions and family responsibilities; being important aspects in the performance of operating personnel in each industry (Loss, et al, 2016). In the legislation, the rights and obligations are defined according to each activity, so it is necessary to constantly supervise industrial operations; to determine the satisfactory working conditions that lead to generate a cordial environment among the workers in the manufacturing areas, supervisors and managers (Grosse, et al, 2015). Usually, in all industries, it is desired to maintain a good working relationship, with which the development of activities are optimally developed; only that sometimes the way of thinking of certain people in the operational area (workers, supervision and managers) of each industrial company, act in surprising ways, wanting to force the operational workers to made unnecessary, constantly repetitive, uncomfortable, heavy activities no tools or work equipment; and sometimes pregnant women are forced to work in areas where certain industrial equipment or machines emit air pollutants or need to lift heavy items, which are harmful to the health of women and the fetus (Arunesh Ch, et al, 2009). Figure 1 shows the main factors of working conditions in industrial plants in the city of Mexicali; where the relationship between these is observed. In this city are around 150 industrial companies of manufacturing sector where 70% are of electronic area (INDEX, 2020).

Figure 1. Principal factor of labor conditions

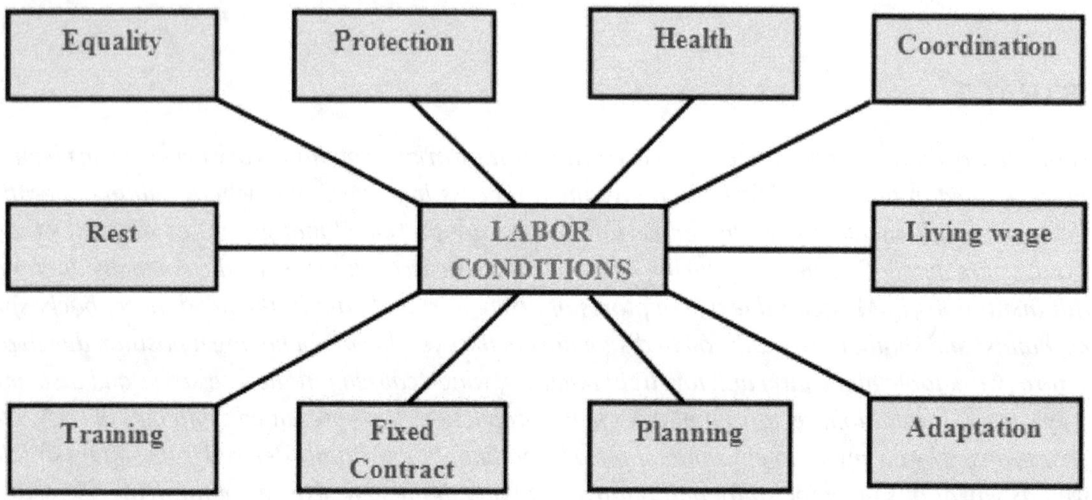

All the factors are of vital interest and each one must be evaluated with the same level of importance, to avoid some kind of problematic situation.

NECESSITY OF MADE INVESTIGATION OF ERGONOMICS IN THE INDUSTRY

Most of the objectives that focus on the manufacturing areas are to increase productivity and quality levels, without considering ergonomic aspects, which are fundamental in the productive performance of operating personnel. Analysis prepared by specialists on the subject of ergonomics in industries of the city of Mexicali (Carlos Raúl Navarro González et al, 2020), recommend preparing scientific studies of basic and specialized times and movements to avoid some type of injury or health symptom of the operating personnel of areas of manufacturing that generates low performance of the workers of the industrial processes and visits to the doctor that could originate some type of fine to the industries.

Labor Laws and Conditions

This concept is defined worldwide, only that in each region of the world, certain aspects that are added to international laws are considered, according to the characteristics of each population, because each area of each country may have different ways of thinking for work activities, being an example in eastern countries where they can work up to twelve hours a day, being that the normal working day is usually eight hours (Ahram, et al, 2014). In addition, the circumstances of rest periods in work activities are considered, in order to have relaxation times that promote the motivation to develop work operations with greater optimism and operational performance. In certain industries worldwide and some in the city of Mexicali, where this study was carried out, the practice of labor gymnastics is considered, where actions are carried out to separate from their work areas, achieve stretching of the extremities of the human body and develop movements relaxing; with the aim of eliminating stress in parts of the human body where work activities suffer the most, especially when they are repetitive, inadequate or without tools or work equipment. This is why regulatory bodies of working conditions in each region of the world, at certain times supervise the work areas of any type of industry, where the way in which manufacturing activities are developed, as well as the environments to which they are made, were evaluated those that are exposed the operational workers and the labor relationship with those in charge of the manufacturing processes (supervisors, personnel specialized in certain operations and managers) (Kuhlang, et al, 2011).

Figure 2. Relation of labor and law conditions

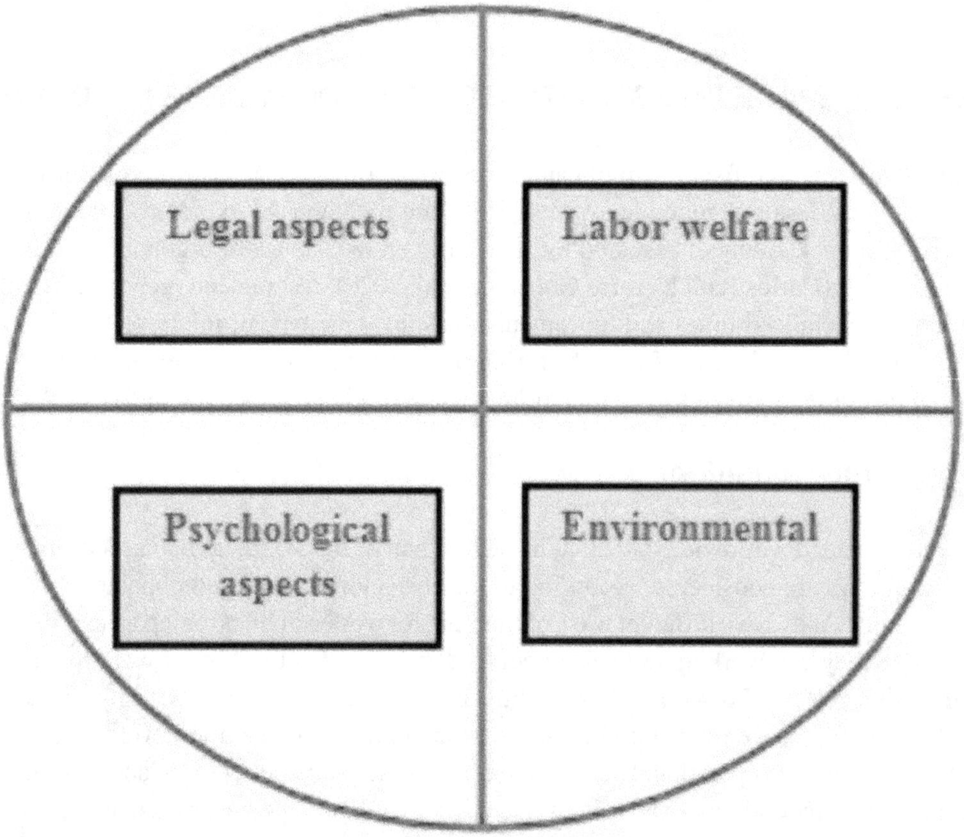

Figure 2 shows the factors of labor and legal conditions, where legal aspects are important in the labor processes of any industry or workplace, which sometimes in certain industrial companies, are not explained in detail to workers of the conditions where they should be made their industrial activities (Kalpakjian, 2014).

Industrial Ergonomics

Currently, one of the aspects of interest in industrial plants around the world is the evaluation of the issue of occupational health, achieving great progress in improving working conditions. This was, to have industrial operations in the most adaptable way possible to made operations in a comfortable way, achieving maximum operational efficiency. Since the beginning of the 21st century, efforts have been duplicated to be very attentive to the working conditions of operational employees in manufacturing areas, with the creation of departments dedicated to this process and the improvement of industrial activities, including personnel specialized in health, manufacturing, engineering, and ergonomics topics (Wilson, et al, 2009). The main objective of this department in each industrial plant is to prevent accidents or health symptoms that cause severe damage to workers in industrial plants. This can be, in work or subsequent periods that lead to inactivity actions in some limbs or organs of the human body, as has been generated in certain industries installed around the world. On some occasions, a situation of severe discomfort or pain can occur, and cause a temporary or permanent disability of a worker, causing a person not to return to work throughout their life (Thatcher, 2013). The theme of industrial ergonomics has been strengthened in the last twenty years, in all industrial activities, where a large number of operating employees in manufacturing areas have suffered mild and severe symptoms in their limbs and organs. Most of the time, industrial plants, including those established in the city of Mexicali, are not aware of the seriousness of not applying ergonomic methods in industrial processes, or are not aware of this. That is why the Mexican authorities of the health and labor sector (Secretaria del Trabajo y Prevision Social-STPS) have acted with great firmness regarding these events (Carrasco Martínez 2010). According to the Mexicali health authorities, in the last ten years, a considerable increase in accidents and illnesses has been observed, mainly due to work stress, with symptoms of discomfort and pain in the head, neck, shoulders, arms, hands, back and hips of workers in the manufacturing area of industrial plants installed in this city, as showed in figure 3, observed as men suffered when try to lift a heavy box. The main causes of the occurrence of these events, is to develop inappropriate operations and without adequate ergonomic methods and tools, with the greatest presence of manual activities and in some cases when operating employees interact with automated industrial equipment and machines (Saniog, et al, 2015). That is why those in charge of the industries from the directive, managerial level, and even the supervisory and specialized personnel to support analysis and improvement of working conditions, have been making great efforts to prevent their employees from operating areas, leaving to go to work, generating extra expenses due to health symptoms and also avoid the large turnover of personnel that is generated in industrial plants in Mexicali. The high turnover of personnel in industry in this city, causes that the industrial operations are developed by inexperienced workers because the people who have the experience, are in situations of deteriorated health due to accidents or diseases by not having the optimal working conditions. This originated in the evaluated industrial company, that errors were generated due to inexperience of its workers, in addition to an increase in accidents and illnesses due to not giving the correct follow-up to industrial activities and not having adequate working conditions, causing a low level of productivity and quality in the evaluated industry (Aven, et al, 2013).

An aspect of interest in the industries is to determine the economic amount that is dedicated to the health of their workers and when it is caused by inadequate working conditions in manufacturing areas, where workers can quickly suffer some health symptoms (Salvendy, 2012) which can damage the finances of industrial companies. In addition to the payment for recovery in the health of the operational personnel, where the investigation was required to pay fines for a large amount of money to Mexican health authorities, which is known as a risk premium, for the large amount of workers treated in public health clinics mostly and private on certain occasions. One of the relevant factors considered in industrial activities is that the city of Mexicali is located in an arid zone with extreme temperatures (in summer up to 45 °C and in winter close to 0 °C), being an important factor in comfort of workers, to develop industrial operations (López, 2008). This was considered from 2000 to date, as an aspect of interest in the analysis of occupational health by the World Health Organization (WHO), which is part of ergonomic issues. This aspect is very relevant in the manufacturing areas of industrial plants, to preserve the good health of workers (López Torres et al. 2012). That is why analyzes have been developed in the manufacturing processes in manual and automated operations, evaluating the times and movements of workers in each industrial activity, to determine if there is any type of risk that causes a negative effect on the health of the personnel that works. . in industrial plants. That is why evaluations in industrial processes include activities that analyze operations development factors to determine if any of these may cause a risk to the health of workers in the manufacturing area. In addition, the productivity and quality indices of the manufactured products are evaluated, balancing these two factors with the manufacturing processes of the manufacturing personnel activities (Chandra, et al, 2009).

Figure 3. Action of man injured by improperly lifting a heavy box
Source: https://es.familydoctor.org/seguridad-al-levantar-consejos-para-prevenir-lesiones-en-la-espalda/

Electronics Industry

The electronics industry is a very important sector with the manufacture of a great diversity of products that are marketed in all regions of the world, being a factor of interest in the economy of each country. This type of industry had its greatest boom in the 1970s of the last century, being televisions, computers, cell phones, control of various equipment for industrial manufacturing areas, in addition to means of transport such as cars, buses, boats and motorcycles (López, et al, 2010). The wide variety of products manufactured in the electronics industry is to achieve better comfort in daily activities, noting that they are used in all regions of the world, being mainly the digital type the most used and in some cases, they remain constantly on, without having rest periods. The electronics industry also manufactures sensors for detecting objects, as well as indices of weight, mass, volume (liquid levels) in industrial and commercial companies, as well as in health institutions, which is very important in the gross domestic product (GDP) of each country. The electronics industry has contributed enormously for ten years to the economy of each country and region, generating profits of several billion dollars each year. For the manufacturing process of electronic devices, equipment and systems, various chemical substances are required that can generate polluting gases in the manufacturing areas, which can cause complicated situations in the internal environment of each industry (López, 2008). This could have a negative effect on the health of workers, where every day we seek to have favorable conditions for the optimal performance of employees in the operational area. That is, from the safety and hygiene departments of industrial plants installed anywhere in the world, and this factor was evaluated in this research as part of the aspects of analysis of working conditions, in the electronics industry, where the scientific study. These atmospheric gases, can penetrate the respiratory tract of workers, they can suffer health symptoms such as a simple flu or cough, can cause side effects in some organs of the body such as the heart, and causing problems of respiratory arrest and being an expense not contemplated in the planning of each industry. For this reason, as part of the investigation, an analysis was developed with specialized equipment, of the monitoring of pollutants generated by industrial processes with chemical substances in the interiors of the evaluated industry and abroad emitted by vehicular traffic and industrial companies of the city of Mexicali, and that penetrate the interior through cracks or holes in the buildings and generate aggressive environments in the manufacturing areas and originate health symptoms that have incalculable costs, and for this reason, the working conditions in the industries located in Mexicali are not presented (Carlos Navarro, et al, 2020). There are basic and complex industrial processes, where certain types of work methods, tools and equipment are required. This is important in planning, where the types of process flow are also considered, to determine the number of operating personnel in the manufacturing areas. In addition, in the last decade, working conditions have been taken into account with greater strength, applying ergonomic and manufacturing methods, contemplating innovations developed by experts from various engineering areas that participate in all industries in the world, including those located in industrial parks from the city of Mexicali (INDEX, 2020).

Health Symptoms by Inadequate Movements in Industrial Processes

Occupational risks are events that can occur in activities of any kind, focusing in this research on the operations carried out in industrial companies located in Mexicali, specifically in an electronic industry, where according to the health authorities of this city (Carlos Navarro, et al, 2020). This scientific study refers to a problematic situation, which was reflected in the presence of an increase in health cases in reference to work stress, discomfort and pain in shoulders, arms, hands, back and neck. This generated lack of attendance at work, errors of inexperienced personnel causing low levels of productivity and quality of manufactured products. In addition to costs to the company evaluated by labor risks, where the concept of risk premium is fundamentally considered, where it is considered as a process where the employer (in this case the industrial plant evaluated), must protect its workers from possible occupational risks. One of the causes was due to the inadequate method of performing the functions when holding the soldering iron as shown in the following in figure 4:

Figure 4. Forms to make the in soldering process of electronic components: (a) inadequate and (b) adequate
Source Analysis of the investigation

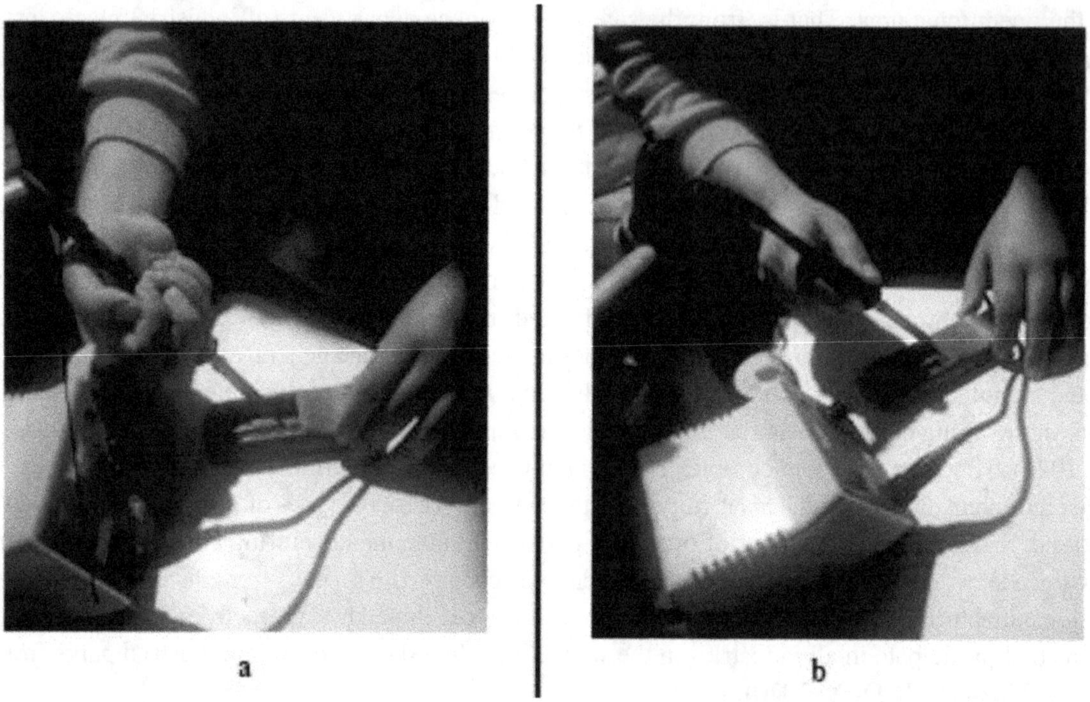

a b

In the last figure was detected that the soldering iron was showed the forms to make the soldering process as inadequate in figure 4a and adequate in figure 4b. In figure 4a, was generated a tension in the hands, arms and shoulders; and in figure 4b the tension disappeared. It causes discomfort in few short periods of work and intense pain in long periods of activity, which is why it was necessary to visit to medical assistance in indoor of the evaluated electronics industry and also the health authorities. This caused the industrial company where the investigation was carried out, to receive fines from the Mexican authorities of regulation of working conditions, for the lack of prevention of health symptoms, such as accidents and illnesses of the operating personnel of the manufacturing areas of this analyzed industry, and there will be health consequences for workers, also affecting the productivity and quality indices of manufactured products. The health symptoms that occurred in industrial operations workers are called musculoskeletal disorders, the soft tissues, muscles, tendons, ligaments, nerves, joints and blood vessels being affected (Bevan, 2015). The muscles have the function of providing energy for the movements of the arms, shoulders and hands; and being injured, they cannot exert the necessary force to make the activities of the industrial processes. The tendons are the pulleys that have the function of joining the muscles to the bones of the human body for the arms, hands and shoulders; elaborate the operational activities. The ligaments generate the union of the bones for an efficient and adequate performance of the functions. The articles are considered as the joints between the bones, for optimal functionality. The nerves have the function of sending information to and from the brain to the muscles to carry out operational activities in a coordinated way. In addition, the vertebral discs are considered in any operation generated by the human body, which are the arm-absorbers for the spinal column. Based on this, the appropriate way to apply the prevention of occupational hazards in the manufacturing areas of the evaluated electronics industry is analyzed. It was observed from the beginning of the investigation that the way of elaborating the operations in the work tables attached to the production line, generated discomfort on the shoulders of the operational workers (Aven, 2015). The necessary measures were developed, such as the change of method and work equipment, such as taking the soldering iron in a suitable way, to avoid discomfort, as well as the times and movements of the performance of the welding functions of electronic components in electronic boards of products manufactured in the evaluated industry (López, 2008).

Mexican Normativity

In addition to consultations for work-related stress, certain serious health symptoms of workers in industries located in Mexicali sometimes occur, such as medical treatments and surgeries that health institutions support operational employees who made out activities in industrial processes. Said health institutions prepare charges to industrial plants, for the risk premium factor, which is due to the generation of accidents or illnesses due to inadequate working conditions. In the Mexican Republic, there is a regulation called the Labor Risk Prevention Law (LPRL); whose antecedent is the Federal Labor Law (LFT) elaborated in 1970 and the Federal Regulation of Safety and Health at Work (RFSST) documented in 2014 (NOM 172, 2019, NOM 011, 2001, NOM 015, 2001, NOM, 024, 2001, NOM 025, 2008). The LPRL gave rise to the generation of the Official Mexican Standards (NOM) in the labor aspect, which is what protects the worker from what executives, managers and supervisors of industrial plants throughout the country do, supporting the operating personnel of manufacturing areas. Also, was used an international normativity as OHSAS (OHSAS, 2007).

METHODOLOGY

Methods

The development of the research consisted of evaluating the working conditions in which there were four work tables located in a production line of the electronic sector company where the scientific study was prepared, located in Mexicali. With the analysis process, a problematic situation was detected that generated low levels of productivity and quality of the manufactured products. This was due to the fact that the operating personnel of the manufacturing areas did not present the maximum performance due to suffering from discomfort and pain in the upper extremities, due to the lack of understanding of how to elaborate the welding functions of electronic components in electronic boards (Carlos Navarro, et al, 220). Experimental tests were conducted to determine possible causes by means of an Ishikawa cause-effect analysis. Based on this, it was observed that the industrial process workers at the work tables elaborated their activities in an uncomfortable way, explaining in detail below the six factors of the Ishikawa diagram (López, et al, 2012):

a) Material. On certain occasions the electronic components were a little larger than their normal size, even though they had the same characteristics, such as the value of each component in each unit of measurement (ohms for resistance, volts for diodes, farads for capacitors, henry for coils; being the most used electronic devices), as well as the operating power in watts. Sometimes, the solder used in joining the electronic components to the electronic boards is of low quality, and it is difficult for the joint to be made, generating poorly joined electronic components, poor connection and lack of electrical conductivity. In addition, there were areas in the electronic boards with missing electronic components, originating a low level of productivity and quality of the manufactured products.

b) Method. A detailed analysis was made of each step (times of each function and movements of the upper extremities (arms, hands, shoulders)) of the process of how to develop the welding activity, with the aim of taking the necessary actions and generating actions comfortable for workers in the manufacturing area of the evaluated electronics industry.

c) Workforce. Several experts and inexperienced people in the activity of soldering electronic components in electronic boards were evaluated in the four work tables. With this analysis, it was observed that inexperienced people did the activity inadequately and suffered more frequently from discomfort and pain in the sections of the upper extremities (hands, arms and shoulders). This also generated tension in the neck, head and back, causing the health symptoms that originated the assistance to the doctor within the evaluated industrial company and to the public health centers outside this industry.

d) Environment. Climate and pollution parameters were evaluated as part of the atmospheric environment, in addition to the work environment, linking the relationship of directive personnel, managers and supervisors with the operational personnel of the manufacturing area. The first evaluation showed that the climate levels (temperature and relative humidity (RH) measured in °C and% respectively, were not adequate at certain times, especially in the summer periods, with temperatures and relative humidity greater than 45 °C in the welding zone due to the soldering iron, and 70% (in July and August) and winter, with temperatures close to 0 °C and greater than 70% RH (in December and January). Regarding the work environment, a detailed analysis was made of the way in which all the people in the manufacturing area were related, in the period of the investigation, where it was observed that at times a very tense environment was generated, due to the increase in production rates. This action generated concern on the part of the management and supervision staff, thinking that the production goal could not be met (AHRAE, 1999).

e) Measurement. The way to evaluate if the electronic components were installed in the electronic boards was visually elaborated by the same workers who carried out the welding activity. This was not adequate, because with the same process of the welding functions of the four people of this activity, generated a tired view, a tension to perform the two operations in a single activity and with it even boredom that was not adequate. This caused that the workers of these steps of the industrial processes, did not perform their functions optimally and with it, the presence of errors and defective products, causing defective by-products and with it low levels of productivity and quality. For this, an analysis guide was developed to be placed on electronic boards to detect incorrectly installed or missing electronic components.

f) Machine. At this stage of the industrial processes of the analyzed production line, the way to prepare the welding operation was evaluated, focusing on the welding equipment (soldering iron), considering that it was in good condition to generate the necessary heat to produce the proper union of electronic components in electronic boards, and avoid defective by-products with more installed or missing electronic components. Another important aspect was the use of the guide designed and tested by specialized personnel for continuous improvement to generate a better comfort for the operational workers to detect the aforementioned failures.

Materials and Equipment

The scientific study carried out in an electronic industry located in the city of Mexicali, was developed with the cooperation of the personnel of this industry and expert researchers from two higher level educational institutions, with a research project. In this analysis process, numerical data were obtained during 2018 and 2019, from the various stages of a production line of the analyzed industrial plant, with the instruments, equipment or specialized industrial machines provided by this electronic industry. In addition, educational institutions provided some types of systems or guides developed in previous research projects and in this research. With these evaluations, the pertinent studies were elaborated to evaluate the working conditions of the evaluated industrial plant. In addition, the company relied on two desktop computers to capture numerical data from the evaluations carried out at each step of the manufacturing process. The research staff provided two laptops to have the supporting information, in addition to carrying out the mathematical analysis between four researchers with different sections of the information, and thus obtaining the analysis of the results of what happened in the manufacturing process as quickly as possible processes. The computer programs required for the research were MATLAB (Magrab, et al, 2011) and Excel (Alexander et al 2016), which were provided and used by the staff of the participating educational institutions. With these programming systems, the capture of numerical data and its evaluation were prepared to determine what was happening in each stage of the industrial processes analyzed. The instruments used to obtain numerical data that were organized and represented in tables and graphs were used based on the six aspects evaluated with the cause-effect diagram. Each aspect generated an analysis process that is described below:

1. Evaluation of materials. Various analyzes were made of the materials used in the four work tables of the electronic components welding activity, evaluating operating characteristics and material handling methods for this stage of the industrial process of a production line, managing to understand how to use them, to prevent operating workers from suffering any health symptoms. In this phase, no instrument was used, only observations from the company manager and supervisory personnel specialized in the development of continuous improvement.
2. Analysis of the work method. Evaluations of the times and movements of the upper extremities and positions of the workers were performed, using Notch sensors with their respective analysis methodology and this instrument provided by an educational institution. With this analysis, the position angles of the operating personnel were determined, as well as the angles of the extremities at the time of the welding activity. In this way, it was possible to obtain better positions and with it a comfort to carry out operations in this manufacturing stage, and achieve maximum operational performance of the workers of the four work tables considered as a manufacturing cell.
3. Workforce evaluation. An analysis was carried out on how to obtain the right people for each specific function, where this process was developed in two aspects. The first was an evaluation of experience and skills in pilot testing of manufacturing stages. The second was an analysis of discussions in certain work periods of different shifts, to know the possible problematic situations of this stage of the industrial process and to give them quick solutions to have the adequate working conditions for the operative person.
4. Evaluation of the work environment. In this phase, five variables that are part of the work environment were evaluated, being the levels of climate (temperature and humidity) and air pollution (chemicals). The humidity and temperature measurements were prepared according to the

NOM-015-STPS-2001 (NOM015 2001) standard with a CW-T20WIFITH Model Datalogger Wifi thermohygrometer with temperature ranges from -40ºC to + 80ºC (± 0.3 ºC) and humidity from 0% to 100% RH (± 2RH%) and with wireless internet connection to quickly and easily send data to a computer for analysis. The contamination levels according to NOM-172-SEMARNAT-2019 (NOM172 2019), were evaluated with a multiple gas monitor that detects oxygen, carbon monoxide, hydrogen sulfide, sulfides and nitrogen oxides. Grainger Model 337WY5.

5. Analysis of the measurement activity. This activity was developed with specific instruments determining the use of a high-quality stopwatch H5671, with a countdown timer, step marker and programmable memory, to measure time and movements, and the speed of industrial machines to be manufactured. at every step.
6. Evaluation of the operation of industrial machines. The workers worked with the welding equipment (soldering iron). In this phase, a high-quality H5671 stopwatch, with countdown timer, step marker and programmable memory, was used to measure the speed of this great machine at each step.

RESULTS

The investigation made included detailed evaluations of the six mentioned factors of the cause-effect diagram, where relevant numerical data were generated, to determine the main causes and quickly and efficiently develop the solutions that originated comfort in the welding activities in the four work tables.

Materials Analysis

An analysis of the use of the materials required for the welding processes of electronic components in electronic boards was carried out, to determine by evaluated periods (spring, summer, autumn and winter, from 2018 to 2019), being observed in figure 6 illustrating a comparison by color of the four factors that generated a bottleneck in this stage of the manufacturing area. These four factors, which are explained below, were related to the attitude of the workers, which were an effect of inadequate working conditions, at the beginning of the investigation:

1. Damaged material. When electronic components were received, it was considered that they were fractured, scratched, with some incomplete section and wet from being exposed to rain or humid environments. This caused that this material was discarded and with it generate waste, causing an increase in garbage.
2. Incomplete material. It was the material that was received with the least amount of electronic components in the shipping boxes, as well as not receiving a full box of an electronic component in a production batch.
3. Inappropriate material. At the time of receiving electronic components, it was considered that it was not the one that should be attached to the electronic boards, being those with a different power value than those required.
4. Misused material. It was the material that was misused by the workers due to inappropriate attitudes, damaging them in the welding process and generating waste from electronic components and boards.

In all four cases, there were unnecessary expenses for requesting more material and preparing production stoppages and thus late delivery to the customer and fines for breaches of contract. The dates of the times of the year, considered in the evaluation processes were: spring (March 21, 2018 to June 21, 2018), summer 2018 (June 21, 2018 to September 21, 2018), fall 2018 (September 21, 2018 to December 21, 2018) and winter (December 21, 2018 to March 21, 2019); shown in figure 5.

Figure 5. Analysis of materials used in the soldering process

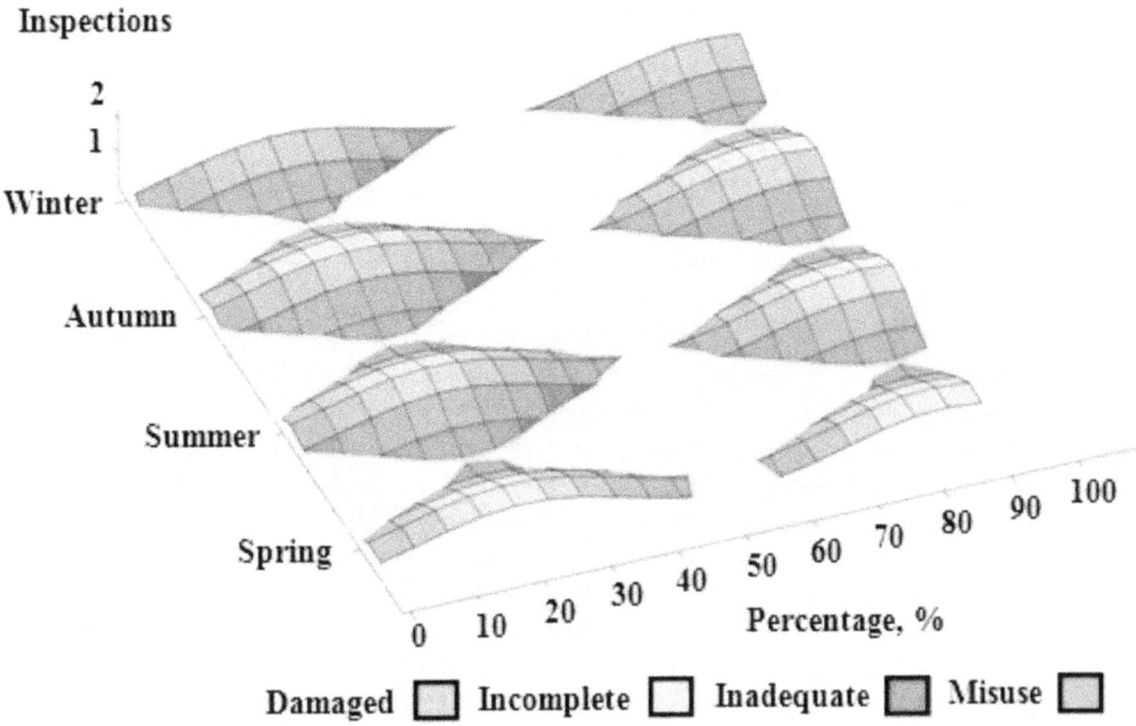

The previous figure shows an evaluation of the four factors of how materials are affected, being observed in the four seasons of the year with the aforementioned factors, identified by colors, being the orange color for the damaged material, the yellow color for the incomplete material, the sky blue color inappropriate material and light green color material misused by workers improper attitudes. These factors were evaluated with percentage levels (from 0% to 100%), with 0% to 50% being the first inspection process that was developed, the first inspection being at 6AM and the second at 2PM each business day. to obtain a better quality of the materials used. Yellow was the color with the greatest presence, followed by blue, green and finally orange. From 50% to 100%, the yellow color continued as the one with the highest incidence, followed by blue, orange and green.

Work Method Evaluation

The evaluation of aspects of interest of the use of the work method that was used before elaborated the investigation in the electronic industry analyzed and located in the city of Mexicali was developed. Two important factors were evaluated in this section, being the amount of movements of each operating personnel of this manufacturing area and rest periods in a period of eight hours, to determine if any type of health symptom could be presented with the method used, as shown in figure 6.

Figure 6. Evaluation of factors of Work method used in the soldering process

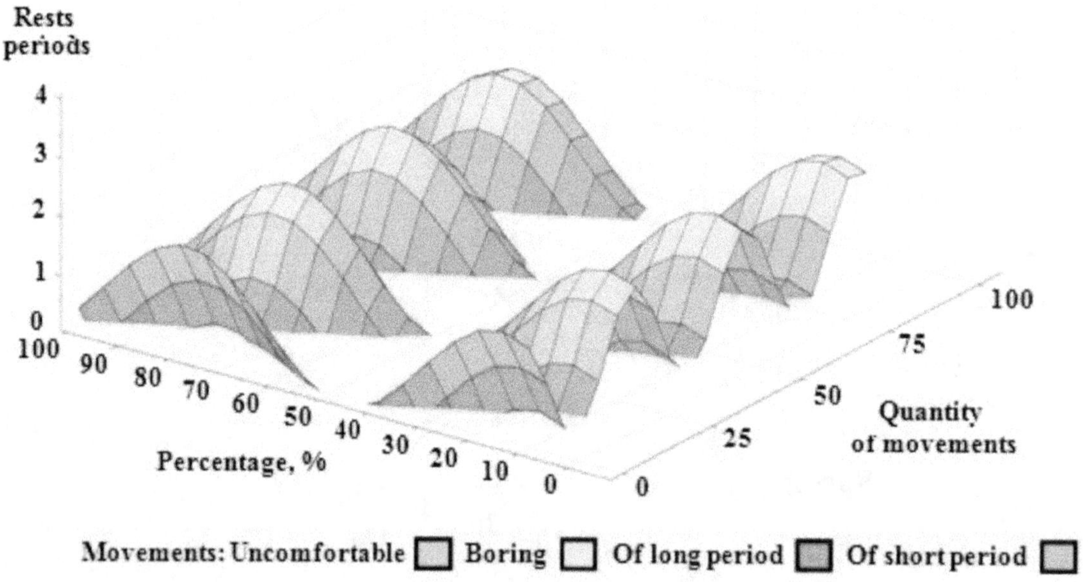

In the previous figure, the aspects that are considered in a process of analysis of work methods are observed, with the amount of movements, rest periods and ways of elaborating the activities with uncomfortable, boring movements, of long or short periods; To thereby determine if there is the possibility of some type of health symptom. In figure 7, it is illustrated how from an analysis of 100 movements with four rest periods, the yellow color in an evaluation from 0% to 50%, being repetitive movements that as the hourly period of each day passed, it was observed as the of higher incidence, and the same happened from 50% to 100%. This aspect was followed by the orange color representing uncomfortable movements, that from 0% to 50% and from 50% to 100%, the same incidence occurred. Later the blue color is illustrated and finally the green color, as well as in the range from 0% to 50% and from 50% to 100%.

ATMOSPHERIC AND HUMAN ENVIRONMENTAL

Atmospheric Evaluation

An analysis of climatic factors (temperature and relative humidity) and air pollutants, essentially those derived from sulfur, nitrogen and carbon was carried out; that are emitted by the vehicular traffic and industries of the city of Mexicali and that must be regulated by Mexican environmental authorities. Air quality standards are determined by the Secretary of Environment and Natural Resources (SEMARNAT) of Mexico and the Environmental Protection Agency (EPA) of the United States, mainly in the border areas between the two countries. The analysis showed that in certain periods of the year, the quality standards indexes are exceeded, where the pollutants derived from the mentioned agents (SOX, NOX, CO); and penetrated through holes and cracks into the evaluated electronics industry, generating an environment not suitable for workers in the manufacturing areas of the evaluated industrial company. Due to this, there were work periods in which the operating personnel presented discomfort with a headache and a tense environment was generated that decreased their operating performance. The aforementioned is observed in table 1, where the levels of pollution and climate in the part of the production line analyzed are illustrated, in addition to the health symptoms presented by the people in this manufacturing cell evaluated.

Table 1. Evaluation of atmospheric factors in indoor of electronics industry (2018)

Levels	Average			Average		Health symptoms
Month	SO_2	NO_2	CO	T, °C	RH%,	
January	0.99	223	58	11	47	Headache and nausea
February	0.84	199	51	16	43	Headache and nausea
March	0.76	186	45	20	40	Headache
April	0.64	158	39	25	37	Headache
May	0.53	134	29	29	34	Headache
June	0.48	105	23	32	39	Headache and nausea
July	0.45	96	31	35	43	Headache and nausea
August	0.58	99	36	37	49	Headache and nausea
September	0.62	113	40	31	42	Headache
October	0.77	146	45	28	37	Headache
November	0.89	179	49	15	32	Headache and nausea
December	0.96	214	58	13	40	Headache and nausea

*Air quality standard: https://www.epa.gov/criteria-air-pollutants/naaqs-table. (a) SO_2: 0.5 ppm in 3 hours, (b) NO_2:100 ppb in 1 hour and (c) CO: 35 ppm in 1 hour.

**Climatic factors: file:///C:/Users/Irene/Downloads/publication---public-health-advice-on-protecting-health-effects-of-heat.pdf. T, °C: From 20°C- to 28°C as a confortable range and RH%: From 30% to 50% as a confortable range, in both parameters in close rooms as the electronics industry evaluated.

The table above shows the levels obtained from the evaluated air pollutants and climate, as well as some health symptoms that generated discomfort in the operating workers, which required visits to the medical area inside the evaluated industrial plant and the outside of this in Mexican public health centers. It is illustrated that in most of the months of 2018, the air quality and climate indices are not in the desired ranges, which is why they caused at least headaches and nausea and especially in pregnant women.

Employee Attitude Evaluation

This aspect is of vital importance in the development of operations and in the analysis of the levels of productivity and quality of the manufactured products. In this research, various types of attitudes were presented that were evaluated as part of the ergonomics theme, being observed in Table 2 those with the highest incidence, reflected in percentage levels of six months (from April to September of 2018) evaluated of 30 workers that was participating in the soldering process of the manufacturing cell analyzed.

Table 2. Analysis of attitude of workers (2018)

Level Attitude	Percentage, %	Level Attitude	Percentage, %	Level Attitude	Percentage, %
Submissive	4	Manipulative	9	Collaborative	14
Positive	6	Sardonic	4	Emphatic	11
Negative	7	Confident	6	Suspicious	5
Analytical	5	Aggressive	3	Emotional	6
Flexible	6	Pessimistic	6	Uncompromising	8

As the first part of the analysis in the aforementioned period, it was determined as positive attitude with 53% and negative with 47%, to later elaborate a more detailed evaluation with 15 types of attitudes, which was carried out in this way because in the Six months of analysis, 30 people were in the work tables, being 70% women (21) and 30% men (9), for being an activity of patience and tolerance, where women have more frequency. The 15 types of attitudes were organized based on the behavior of the 30 people evaluated, holding talks with the operational workers, as well as observations from continuous improvement specialists, determining the types of attitudes. The highest percentage was people with a collaborative attitude with 14%, followed by workers with empathy with 11%. These two types of attitude are positive. Subsequently, people with a manipulative attitude are illustrated, this being a negative aspect, followed by workers with an inflexible attitude. And so the negative (7%), positive (6%), flexible (6%), pessimistic (6%), emotional (6%), analytical (5%), suspicious (5%), submissive (4%) attitudes continue %), sardonic (4%) and finally the aggressive attitude (3%). It should be noted that people presented various types of attitudes, where a worker came to present up to four types of attitudes; whose behavior varied on emotional days, family and economic problems, being female.

Evaluation of Measurement Processes

In the process of the investigation, it was observed that observations were made visually to detect poorly joined or missing electronic components, only that the workers' eyesight was not the same at the beginning of each work period, than at the middle or at the end, for the decision to support with a plastic guide to detect more easily and avoid any health symptoms, especially with the eyes, which generated tension and discomfort in the head, neck and back, due to the different positions taken to inspect the electronic boards and strain your eyes. Based on this, an analysis of the difference between using and not using the guide developed in the research to improve working conditions was developed, as a continuous improvement and expressing the information in table 3. This table represents the evaluation of the levels of discomfort and pain in the head, neck and back; Due to the fact that depending on the analysis period without and with the guide, an effort was made by each person who made the inspection of the electronic components in the electronic boards. These levels are listed from 1 to 5, observing that in the inspection process without guidance, levels from level 2 to 5 were presented in all months, and with guidance from level 1 to 3, information was also obtained from the main health symptoms which were headache, neck and back pain; Most of the headaches were present and in some months together with neck and back pain and from May to July 2018, pain in the head, neck and back, and later once the improvement with the guide was applied, they were reduced the levels of discomfort and the only cases of pain were headaches. For 2019, this activity continued to be evaluated and this health symptom was eliminated.

Table 3. Evaluation of measurement processes (2018)

Levels	Without guide			With guide			Health symptoms
Month	A	B	C	A	B	C	
January	2	2	2	1	1	1	Headache
February	2	2	2	1	1	1	Headache, Neck pain
March	3	3	4	1	1	2	Headache Back pain
April	3	3	3	1	2	2	Headache, Back pain
May	3	4	4	2	2	2	Headache, Neck pain, Back pain
June	4	4	4	2	2	2	Headache, Neck pain, Back pain
July	4	4	4	2	2	2	Headache, Neck pain
August	4	4	4	2	2	2	Headache, Back pain
September	4	4	5	2	2	3	Headache
October	4	5	5	2	3	3	Headache
November	5	5	5	3	3	3	Headache
December	5	5	5	3	3	3	Headache

A. Discomfort and headache, B. Neck pain and discomfort, C. Back pain and discomfort
1-No pain; 2-Mild; 3-Moderate; 4-Severe; 5-Worst.

Welding Equipment Analysis

An analysis of the use of the welding equipment used (soldering iron) was developed, with the times and movements, as well as the way to take the soldering iron, where the information in the inadequate and adequate way on how to take the soldering is represented in Table 4, where soldering iron, as well as the time periods in which each welding operation was made and the amount of movements made.

Table 4. Analysis of soldering processes (2018)

Management of iron	Inadequate		Adequate		Consequences in health of workers
Month	**A**	**B**	**A**	**B**	
January	5	200	X	X	Discomfort and pain in the hands, arms, shoulders, head, neck and back
February	5	200	X	X	Discomfort and pain in the hands, arms, shoulders, head, neck and back
March	5	200	X	X	Discomfort and pain in the hands, arms, shoulders, head, neck and back
April	X	X	3	150	Discomfort and pain in the hands, arms, shoulders and head
May	X	X	3	150	Discomfort and pain in the hands, arms, shoulders and head
June	X	X	3	150	Discomfort and pain in the hands, arms and shoulders
July	X	X	3	120	Discomfort and pain in the hands, arms and shoulders
August	X	X	3	120	Discomfort and pain in the hands and arms
September	X	X	3	120	Discomfort and pain in the hands and arms
October	X	X	3	100	Only mild discomfort in hands, shoulders and arms, generating tiredness
November	X	X	3	100	Only mild discomfort in hands, shoulders and arms, generating tiredness
December	X	X	3	100	Only mild discomfort in hands, shoulders and arms, generating tiredness

The table 4 shows the information on the times and movements of the welding process, where the electronic components are joined in the electronic boards, illustrating that from January to Marc2018, which was in the month of January of this year, When the investigation began and once the improvements to the welding method were made, the working conditions were improved from the method, climate, with minimal contamination; with the aim of avoiding inconvenience to workers in these manufacturing areas. From April to December 2018, continuous improvement was applied and it continued to be evaluated to continue improving the working conditions of this stage of the evaluated production line. One of the aspects of interest was the reduction of times and movements and health symptoms, which were presented at the beginning of the scientific study, with a total of six symptoms (discomfort and pain in the arms, shoulders, shoulders, head, neck and back) and reduce it to only having mild discomfort in the arms, shoulders and hands, which occurred due to repetitive and constant movements; generating fatigue. The times and movements were reduced from 200 seconds to 100 seconds, and from five movements to three movements.

Assessment of Health Symptoms

With this investigation, it was observed that the working conditions in the evaluated electronics industry were not adequate, so this company had high risk premium costs. Due to this, the evaluation was made with which the main causes and health consequences of the workers in this manufacturing area were determined. This information obtained was very useful for directive, managerial, supervisory and specialized personnel in continuous improvement; to make decisions and improve working conditions that will generate a better industrial operation process in a more comfortable way for operating personnel and thereby obtain maximum operational performance. Table 5 shows the information obtained in this scientific study.

Table 5. Evaluation of health symptoms in the soldering processes (2018-2019)

Year	2018		2019		Upper extremities with discomfort and pain	
Month	**A**	**B**	**A**	**B**	**2018**	**2019**
January	1,2, 3	1,2,3	1	1,2	Arms, back, hands, head, neck and shoulders (B24, B2,5)	Arms and hands (B21, B22)
February	1,2,3	1,2,3	1	1,2	Arms, back, hands, head, neck and shoulders (B24, B2,5)	Arms and hands (B21, B22)
March	1,2, 3	1, 2,3	1	1,2	Arms, back, hands, head, neck and shoulders (B23, B24)	Arms and hands (B21, B22)
April	1,2	1,2	1	1,2	Arms, hands, head and shoulders (B22, B23)	Arms and hands (B21, B22)
May	1,2	1,2	1	1,2	Hands, arms, shoulders and head (B22, B23)	Arms and hands (B21, B22)
June	1,2	1,2	1	1,2	Arms, hands and shoulders (B21, B22)	Arms and hands (B21, B22)
July	1,2	1,2	1	1,2	Arms, hands and shoulders (B21, B22)	Arms and hands (B21, B22)
August	1,2	1,2	1	1,2	Arms and hands (B21, B22)	Arms and hands (B21, B22)
September	1	1	1	1,2	Arms and hands (B21, B22)	Arms and hands (B21, B22)
October	1	1	1	1,2	Arms and hands (B21, B22)	Arms and hands (B21, B22)
November	1	1	1	1,2	Arms and hands (B21, B22)	Arms and hands (B21, B22)
December	1	1	1	1,2	Arms and hands (B21, B22)	Arms and hands (B21, B22)

A. Causes; B. Consequences
A1-Inadequate movement; A2-Repetitive movement, A3-Fast movement.
B1-Fatigue; B2-Discomfort; B3-Pain: B21-No pain; B22-Mild; B23-Moderate; B24-Severe; B25-Worst.

Table 5 shows a relevant evaluation where the causes of the activities carried out in the soldering iron process are illustrated and the consequences that are represented by the health symptoms of the upper extremities of the human body, in addition to the head, neck and back. This information greatly supported the development of the relevant improvements and thus have the optimal working conditions in this industrial process. In Table 5, it was observed that in the first three months of initiation of the investigation, the three analyzed causes were presented and as the analysis period passed, eliminating repetitive and rapid movements and until September 2019 until the whole year of 2019. Regarding the consequences, the three evaluated causes and the five levels of discomfort and pain were presented at the beginning of the scientific study; coupled with the parts of the human body with some health complication.

DISCUSSIONS

The development of ergonomics research in the industry is of great importance for the development of systems, equipment, structures and adapted machines, so that the operating personnel of the manufacturing areas develop their functions in a comfortable way and based on this, you can get the maximum operational performance from each worker. The results obtained from the research show the need to evaluate the industrial processes of each manufacturing stage, to determine the activities that require the need to apply continuous improvement to increase productivity and quality levels. In this chapter that integrates the book entitled "Ergonomics and Business Policies for the Promotion of Well-Being in the Workplace", provides a detailed analysis of what is required in manufacturing areas with regard to ergonomic factors, with the objective to improve the functionality of workers in these areas of industries. The development of this research is of great importance to evaluate the problematic situations that occur daily in the industries of this city of Mexicali and companies in any sector around the world. This book chapter can be improved by analyzing the application of automated electronic equipment to improve the working conditions of operating personnel in manufacturing areas. The weaknesses of this research reflected in this chapter was the obtaining of the information on the industrial processes of the industry where the scientific study was made. This chapter is aimed at anyone who wishes to evaluate the information from ergonomic analysis, where improvements are observed in working conditions in industrial companies. For the development of this chapter, the references made in an industry in the city of Mexicali.

CONCLUSION

In the last five years there has been a growing increase in the turnover of personnel in the machining industry installed in the city of Mexicali, of any type of sector, originating a setback in the retention of trained people in industrial plants. These people want to change companies constantly due to salary increases or the inadequate working conditions where they are working, even when they have received specialized training that makes them have a better value as a worker in the labor market. This has created problematic situations in the manufacturing areas of various types of industries, where these companies have considerable expenses due to specialized training processes. In addition to the fact that when making personnel changes in some industrial processes, errors and failures are generated, causing low productivity and quality of manufactured products. It is considered that since ergonomic methods were applied in industrial plants, occupational risks began to be reduced, reducing the ailments suffered by workers in industrial operations. Prior to this, the number of cases of operating personnel injured by work activities and the presence of work stress had increased. This had happened due to the increase in the pace of industrial operations, which increased from the presence of industrial machinery, due to advances in technology, especially since the beginning of the 21st century, forcing operating personnel to a greater number of functions, faster and harder, causing the presence of accidents and diseases. The generation of illnesses or minor accidents, such as work stress, has caused in several people, the birth of serious diseases such as diabetes and cardiovascular disease, mainly. This has caused that once having this type of illness, industrial companies, whether national or foreign, are not interested in this type of aspect, condoning that if a worker can no longer work, there will always be. The generation of illnesses or minor accidents, such as work stress, has caused in several people, the birth of serious diseases such as diabetes and cardiovascular disease, mainly. This has caused that once having this type of illness, industrial companies, whether national or foreign, are not interested in this type of aspect, condoning that if a worker can no longer work, there will always be. This is due to the fact that in specialized manufacturing activities, or in no part of the production lines of the manufacturing areas; who do not have the application of ergonomic methods, and do not have suitable working conditions. Because of this, discomfort or pain arises when operating workers perform their duties. Another aspect of interest is that on certain occasions, the number of personnel has decreased, in some industrial operations, which has generated greater functions for operating personnel and with it more stress due to rapid, repetitive and inappropriate movements. This caused the joints and certain parts of the human body of the workers to be forced, making it necessary to visit the doctor inside the industrial plants located in Mexicali and abroad, mainly in Mexican public clinics. What is the risk premium is also considered, being an important factor in the economic stability of each industry located anywhere in the world. In this investigation, it was observed that the four workstations located in the evaluated manufacturing cell, even with the improvements developed by specialized personnel, physical and mental fatigue was present in the workers, convincing directors, managers and supervisory personnel to have increased number of rest periods. This was modified, being four in periods of eight working hours, where previously there were only two, and thus achieving a better physical and mental condition of the workers and obtaining the maximum operational performance of. This helped to increase the levels of productivity and quality, and thereby obtain the planned goals and even achieve weekly, monthly and annual productivity bonuses. In a scientific study, it was observed that sometimes some workers with experience in industrial processes want to miss their work activities, due to inadequate working conditions, so they had to change inexperienced personnel, which caused errors, causing economic losses for rework actions, paying overtime in wages to workers. By developing the improvements in the four workstations, the number of visits to the doctor inside and outside the evaluated electronics industry was reduced, reducing the risk premium. With this, the operating personnel were working with greater comfort and a favorable attitude for the company where the investigation was made. At the beginning of this scientific study, it was considered by managers and supervisory personnel that the comments of the workers of these industrial processes were only complaints, without paying attention to the opinion of the operating personnel. But once information was obtained from the evaluations that was considered of great interest, they made it possible to elaborate the necessary improvements and the relationship between the workforce between both parties was considerably improved, being very cordial and each worker developing their functions efficiently.

REFERENCES

AHRAE. (1999). *Handbook, Heating, Ventilating and Ari-Conditioning; applications*. American Society of Heating, Refrigerating, and Air-Conditioning Engineers Inc.

Ahram, T., & Jang, R. (2014). Advances in Physical Ergonomics and human factors. *Proceedings of the AHFE Conference*, 403.

Arunesh, C., Surinder, D., Pankaj, Ch., & Randejer, K. (2009). Ergonomics in the Office Environment: A Review. *Int. Conf. on Energy and Environment,* 43-56.

Aven, T. (2015). Risk assessment and risk management: Review of recent advances on their foundation. *European Journal of Operational Research*, *253*(1), 1–13.

Aven, T., & Zio, E. (2013). Model output uncertainty in risk assessment. *International Journal of Performability Engineering*, *9*(5), 475–486.

Bevan, S. (2015). Impacto económico de los trastornos musculoesqueléticos (TME) en el trabajo en Europa. *Best Practice & Research Clinical Rheumatology Journal*, *29*(3), 356–373. doi:10.1016/j.berh.2015.08.002

Bruzzonne, A., Anghinoli, D., Paolucci, M., & Tonelli, F. (2012). Energy-aware scheduling for improving manufacturing process sustainability: A mathematical model for flexible flow shops. *CIRP Annals Journal, 61*(1), 459–462. doi:10.1016/j.cirp.2012.03.084

Carlos, R. N. G., González, Y. V., Pedro, A. E. Z., Ana, L. S. C., Robledo, V. A., Mildrend, I. M. R., Moreno, E. M., Margarita, G. S. R., & Olivia, Y. V. B. (2020, July-September). Analysis of Ergonomic Methods used to Prevent Negative Effect in the Health of Workers in a Metallic Industry in Mexicali, Mexico. *Mediterranean Journal of Basic and Applied Sciences, 4*(3), 33–41. doi:10.46382/MJBAS.2020.4304

Carrasco Martínez, A. C. (2010). *Estudio ergonómico en la estación de trabajo PT0780 de la empresa S-Mex, S.A de C.V. León. México*. Tesis de Ingeniería Industrial. Universidad Tecnológica de la Mixteca. Huajuapan de Leóm.

Chandra, A., Chandna, P., Deswal, S., & Kumar, R. (2009). Ergonomics in the Office Environment: A Review. *Proceedings of World Academy of Science: Engineering & Technology,* 51(1), 913-919.

Grosse, E., Christoph, H., Glock, M., Mohamed, J., & Patrick, N. (2015). Incorporating human factors in order picking planning models: Framework and research opportunities. *International Journal of Production Research, 3*(3), 695–717. doi:10.1080/00207543.2014.919424

Harshal, T. (2017). Historical Milestones of Ergonomics: From Ancient Human to Modern Human. *Journal of Economics, 7*(4), 65–78.

INDEX-Mexicali. (2020). *Reporte de empresas de manufactura de Mexicali, 45*. Author.

Kalpakjian, S. (2014). Manufacturing engineering and technology. Prentice Hall.

Kuhlang, P., Edtmayr, T., & Sihn, W. (2011). Methodical approach to increase productivity and reduce lead time in assembly and production-logistic processes. *CIRP Journal of Manufacturing Science and Technology, 4*(1), 24–32. doi:10.1016/j.cirpj.2011.02.001

Ley Federal del Trabajo-Diario Oficial de la Federación (DOF) de México. (2019). *Regulaciones de condiciones laborales*. STPS-SSA.

Loos, M., Merino, E., & Taboada, C. (2016). Mapping the state of the art of ergonomics within logistics. *Scientometrics Journal, 109*(1), 85–101. doi:10.100711192-016-1960-z

López, G. (2008). Caracterización de la corrosión en materiales metálicos de la industria electrónica en Mexicali, BC (Tesis de doctorado). UABC, Instituto de Ingeniería, Mexicali.

López, V., Marín, E., & Cornejo, R. (2011). Riesgos de Trabajo en Una Planta Maquiladora: Un Análisis Longitudinal. *Revista International Administración & Finanzas., 3*(2), 103–115.

Magrab, E., Azarm, S., Balachandran, B., Duncan, J., Herold, K., & Walsh, G. (2011). An Engineer's Guide to MATLAB: with Applications from Mechanical, Aerospace, Electrical, and Civil Engineering. Prentice Hall.

Neumann, W., & Medbo, L. (2010). Ergonomic and technical aspects in the redesign of material supply systems: Big boxes vs. narrow bins. *International Journal of Industrial.*

Norma NOM-011-STPS-2001 (2001) Condiciones de seguridad e higiene en los centros de trabajo donde se genere ruido

Norma NOM-015-STPS-2001 (2001) Condiciones térmicas elevadas o abatidas-Condiciones de seguridad e higiene

Norma NOM-024-STPS-2001 (2001) Vibraciones-Condiciones de seguridad e higiene en los centros de trabajo

Norma NOM-025-STPS-2008 (2008) Condiciones de iluminación en los centros de trabajo.

Norma NOM-172-SEMARNAT-2019 (2019) Lineamientos para la obtención y comunicación del Índice de Calidad del Aire y Riesgos a la Salud

OHSAS 18:000 (OHSAS 18:000-2007) Gestión de la Seguridad y Salud Ocupacional.

Salvendy, G. (2012). Handbook of Human Factors and Ergonomics (4th ed.). Wiley. doi:10.1002/9781118131350

Saniog, J., Karmakar, S., Patel, T., & Chowdhury, A. (2015). Towards virtual ergonomics: Aviation and aerospace. *Aircraft Engineering and Aerospace Technology Journal*, *87*(3), 266–273. doi:10.1108/AEAT-05-2013-0094

Thatcher, A. (2012). Gr3en ergonomics: Definition and scope. *Ergonomics Journal*, *56*(1), 389–398. PMID:22928500

Wilson, J., Ryan, B., Schock, A., Ferreira, P., Smith, S., & Pitsopoulos, J. (2009). Understanding safety and production risks in rail engineering planning and protection. *Ergonomics Journal*, *52*(1), 774–790. doi:10.1080/00140130802642211 PMID:19562589

Chapter 6

Determinants of Employee Motivation:
A Comparison of Operational and Non-Operational Staff

Bikash Basnet
Excelsia College, Australia

Sarah Eyaa
https://orcid.org/0000-0002-3330-1374
Excelsia College, Australia

Nekpen Euodia Okhawere
https://orcid.org/0000-0002-1492-4277
University of Benin, Nigeria

ABSTRACT

This chapter integrates collectivism with the dimensions of the Expectancy Theory to investigate the direct and indirect impact of horizontal and vertical collectivism on employee motivation of operational and non-operational staff. Data were collected from 205 employees using a cross-sectional survey. Hypotheses were tested with multiple regression analysis. Across both employee categories, horizontal collectivism improves motivation while vertical collectivism does not have a significant impact on motivation. Mediation effects were significant in the relationship between horizontal collectivism across both employee categories. However, there were some variations in the mediation effects on the relationship between vertical collaboration and motivation across the two categories. This chapter contributes to motivation literature by integrating the Expectancy Theory with two under-investigated dimensions of collectivism to compare motivation determinants among operational and non-operational staff. This chapter presents implications for managers and policy for improving employee motivation.

DOI: 10.4018/978-1-7998-7396-9.ch006

INTRODUCTION

Given the increasingly difficult times in which contemporary organisations operate, there is increasing pressure on managers to keep employees motivated to ensure that work obligations are met (Esther, Christian, & Jürgen, 2020). Employees are motivated when they have the drive and will to perform their duties as stated in the terms and conditions of their employment (Sultana, Salman, & Irfan, 2020). Market environment conditions such as global economy uncertainties, policy changes or rapid technological advancements leave organisations and employees overwhelmed with increased workloads, unrealistic work expectations and often, difficult working conditions (Habanik, Martosova, Letkova, & Dubček, 2020). Usually, employees end up demotivated by such workplace conditions (Ann & Blum, 2020). Demotivation has negative consequences for both organisations and the economy (Parker, Jimmieson, & Amiot, 2017).

Within organisations, demotivated employees may engage in absenteeism, avoid additional responsibilities, have poor inter-personal relationships or put minimum effort into their work (Al-Tkhayneh, Kot, & Shestak, 2019; Antosz, Rembiasz, & Verhagen, 2020). At the economic level, employee demotivation leads to losses. For instance, a 2016 report indicated that the Australian economy had lost 34 Billion Dollars due to lost productivity (Carter, 2016). An article published in 2021 showed that 56% of 2000 employees that were surveyed felt demotivated at work and maintained their jobs for the sole reason of paying bills (Doraisamy, 2021). Additionally, 74% of the surveyed workers recommended that employers should implement more initiatives to support and motivate workers better to minimise the negative effects of work-related stress. Given the negative effects of employee demotivation, it is important for organisations to identify effective strategies to motivate employees, otherwise the companies risk failure as companies cannot survive without motivated staff (Kanfer, Frese, & Johnson 2017). When employees are motivated using appropriate strategies, employees will always make an effort to positively contribute to the organisation (Bani-Melhem, Zeffane, & Albaity, 2018).

Existing research has widely investigated the determinants and consequences of employee motivation or demotivation by applying a range of theories such as Expectancy Theory, Maslow's Hierarchy of Needs, Herzberg's Motivation-Hygiene Theory, McClelland's Needs Theory, Self-Determination Theory and Motivation Crowding Theory (AkdemİR, 2020; van der Kolk, van Veen-Dirks, & ter Bogt, 2019). Findings show that motivation is determined by a range of antecedents in the workplace that include, but are not limited to rewards, expectancy, opportunities for improvement, perceptions of acceptance and culture (Cerasoli, Nicklin, & Ford, 2014). Furthermore, the findings on the impact of the determinants on motivation are mixed, hence requiring further research to understand the relationships better (Franco, Bennett, Kanfer, & Stubblebine, 2004; Hanaysha & Majid, 2018; Kuvaas, Buch, Weibel, Dysvik, & Nerstad, 2017).

Additionally, the limited focus on comparing the impact of motivation determinants across different employee categories calls for additional research to shed more light on the specific motivation enhancers for various employee categories to support the design of customised motivation strategies (Chiang & Jang, 2008; Chiang, Jang, Canter, & Prince, 2008; Sultana et al., 2020). Because the contextual factors across employee categories vary, the impact of motivation determinants may be different as well. Understanding the different contextual factors of different employee groups is important for identifying relevant solution strategies and achieving efficient and rewarding results (AkdemİR, 2020). Another area that has not received significant attention in motivation literature despite its significance, is the integration of cultural factors in motivation theories to explain motivation (Ritz, Brewer, & Neumann,

2016). Cultural dimensions influence behaviour in the workplace as well, and it is important that their impact is widely investigated to support informed decisions (Islam & Ismail, 2008)

This chapter addresses these limitations in motivation literature by investigating employee motivation across two employee categories, operational and non-operational. Based on the Cultural Dimensions Theory and Expectancy Theory, this study makes two propositions. First, horizontal collectivism and vertical collectivism improve employee motivation. Second, the relationships between horizontal and vertical collectivism and employee motivation are mediated by expectancy, extrinsic instrumentality, intrinsic instrumentality, extrinsic valence, and intrinsic valence. This study seeks to answer the following questions:

RQ1: What is the impact of horizontal collectivism and vertical collectivism on employee motivation?
RQ2: What is the mediation effect of expectancy, extrinsic instrumentality, intrinsic instrumentality, extrinsic valence, and intrinsic valence on the relationships between horizontal collectivism and vertical collectivism and employee motivation?
RQ3: What are the implications for managers regarding employee motivation?

This chapter contributes to employee motivation literature by extending the testing of the collectivism, a dimension of Hofstede's Cultural Dimensions Theory and Expectancy Theory across employee categories of operational and non-operational staff. Additionally, the study identifies company strategies for improving the motivation of operational and non-operational staff. The chapter comprises four sections. The theoretical framework and hypotheses are presented in the first section, followed by the conceptual framework. The third section discusses the research methods and findings. The last section is the conclusion, summarising the theoretical contribution, managerial and policy implications, limitations, and future research direction.

THEORETICAL FRAMEWORK

Employee motivation is the degree of dedication, creativity and dynamism that employees apply in their jobs (Shahzadi, Javed, Pirzada, Nasreen, & Khanam, 2014). While several theories have been applied to explain employee motivation, the Expectancy Theory proposed by Vroom (1964) is one of the dominant theories (H.-W. Lee, 2019). This theory assumes rationality in individuals and suggests that employee motivation is the outcome of three components, namely expectancy, instrumentality, and valance (Chiang et al., 2008; H.-W. Lee, 2019). Expectancy is the belief that exerting effort in tasks and responsibilities results in good performance (Ghoddousi, Bahrami, Chileshe, & Hosseini, 2014a). Organisations apply the expectancy principle when rewards are given to employees who meet or exceed performance targets that are usually defined in the Key Performance Indicators (KPIs) (HemaMalini & Washington, 2014). Thus, employees are motivated to do their best in order to realise the benefits associated with good performance (Baciu, 2018). The positive impact of expectancy on motivation is confirmed in empirical studies (e.g Abadi, Jalilvand, Sharif, Salimi, & Khanzadeh, 2011; Chiang & Jang, 2008; Chiang et al., 2008; De Simone, 2015).

Instrumentality is the belief that exerting effort in tasks and responsibilities at work leads to good performance (Nimri, Bdair, & Al Bitar, 2015). According to Chiang & Jang (2008), instrumentality may be extrinsic or intrinsic and both categories have the potential to inspire employee to do their best.

Extrinsic instrumentality is the perception that good performance will lead to external rewards such as increased salary, bonuses, or promotion opportunities while intrinsic instrumentality is the belief that good performance yields internal rewards such as a deep sense of accomplishment or satisfaction (Chiang & Jang, 2008). While studies such as Harris, Murphy, DiPietro, & Line (2017) find a positive relationship between extrinsic instrumentality and motivation, other studies (e.g., Abadi et al., 2011; Chiang & Jang, 2008) find a negative relationship. Furthermore, the positive relationship between intrinsic instrumentality and motivation is confirmed in empirical studies (e.g. Abadi et al., 2011; Harris et al., 2017).

Valence is the value that an individual places on rewards or benefits that are provided when performance goals are met or exceeded (H.-W. Lee, 2019). Employees will be motivated to work hard in their jobs to receive valued rewards (Parijat & Bagga, 2014). Like instrumentality, valence has two categorisations, extrinsic and intrinsic. (Chiang & Jang, 2008). While extrinsic valence is the significance attached to external rewards in the workplace, intrinsic valance is the significance attached to internal rewards. Existing studies (e.g., Abadi et al., 2011; Chiang & Jang, 2008) have confirmed that valence influences employee motivation. In summary, the Expectancy Theory argues that high levels of expectancy, instrumentality, and valance enhance employee motivation (De Simone, 2015). Thus, a work environment that improves and maintains motivation should have robust expectancies, instrumentalities, and valence (Baciu, 2018).

While the Expectancy Theory is a relevant framework for explaining employee motivation and has received considerable support (e.g. Abadi et al., 2011; Y. Chen & Lou, 2002; Chiang & Jang, 2008; Chiang et al., 2008; Chopra, 2019; De Simone, 2015; Ghoddousi, Bahrami, Chileshe, & Hosseini, 2014b; H.-W. Lee, 2019), one limitation applies to the theory. This shortcoming arises from the fact that this theory does not consider external or environmental factors that may influence expectancy, instrumentality, and valance to determine motivation in the workplace. Understanding the role of these factors is vital for a more comprehensive understanding and application of the Expectancy Theory. Existing studies (e.g. Chiang & Jang, 2008; Chiang et al., 2008; Ghoddousi et al., 2014b) have emphasized the need for further research to address some of the shortcomings of the Expectancy Theory to extend its application and relevance. This study addresses the identified limitation by incorporating Hofstede's Cultural Dimensions Theory (Hofstede, 1980) to investigate the impact of cultural factors on expectancy, instrumentality, valance and motivation. Culture, is one of the strongest determinants of perceptions, beliefs, values and behaviour yet its impact on motivation remains understudied (Chopra, 2019). Thus, our knowledge of the extent to which culture influences motivation is constrained due to the limited empirical studies undertaken on this relationship.

Hofstede's Cultural Dimensions Theory identifies six cultural dimensions that influence behaviour (Hofstede, 1980, 2011). The dimensions are power distance, uncertainty avoidance, individualism versus collectivism, masculinity versus femininity, long term versus short term orientation and indulgence (Litvin, 2019). Power distance is the degree to which less powerful individuals or institutions acknowledge and believe that power is unequally distributed while uncertainty avoidance is the extent to which individuals feel threatened by uncertain or unfamiliar circumstances (Hofstede, 2001). Individualism focuses on one's self and independence while collectivism focuses on inter-dependence and the well-being of others (Hofstede, 2011). Under masculinity, individuals are motivated by the desire to be the best whereas under femininity, individuals are inspired by what they do (De Mooij & Hofstede, 2010). Long-term orientation refers to the strategies implemented by communities to maintain links with the past while managing present and forthcoming challenges (Erdman, 2018). Indulgence is the degree to which individuals attempt to regulate their longings, based on how they were raised (Minkov & Hofstede, 2011). While the initial focus of the cultural dimensions was at national level, they are applicable at individual level too based on existing literature (Gabor, Conţiu, & Oltean, 2012; Litvin, 2019; Minkov & Hofstede, 2011). Hence the application of the Cultural Dimensions Theory in this study.

For this study, the selected dimension was collectivism because it was deemed the most relevant given that it focusses on inter-dependence while thinking about other people, therefore delivering positive benefits (C. C. Chen, Meindl, & Hunt, 1997; Rhee, Zhao, Jun, & Kim, 2017). This is in line with the argument proposed by Hofstede (1980) that in some contexts, some cultural dimensions are more influential than others. These are key because they align with other theories of motivation such as Maslow's Hierarchy of Needs and Needs Theory that argue that individuals are motivated in the workplace when there is a sense of belonging. Furthermore, inter-dependence is key for today's work environment where collaboration and teamwork are encouraged both online and in person. Collectivism will deliver the desired benefits. Collectivism is categorised in two dimensions, horizontal and vertical (Triandis & Gelfand, 1998). Horizontal collectivism emphasizes inter-dependence, equality, cooperation, and positive relationship norms within groups to create a good feeling amongst team members such that they are inspired to keep working towards their work goals (Triandis & Singelis, 1998). Vertical collectivism stresses the sacrificing personal gain for group gain and preservation of group integrity (Singelis, Triandis, Bhawuk, & Gelfand, 1995; Triandis & Gelfand, 1998). This in turn creates a sense of collective responsibility to aspire members to work towards improving performance (W.-N. Lee & Choi, 2005). Therefore, the following hypotheses are derived:

H1: Horizontal collectivism improves employee motivation.
H2: Vertical collectivism improves employee motivation.

When individuals work together and make group effort, it is expected that performance will improve, and this will in turn enhance motivation to work hard. Also, groups work harder when they believe that their efforts will be recognised to created external and internal rewards which will in turn increase motivation. Thus, the following hypotheses are derived:

Expectancy, extrinsic instrumentality, intrinsic instrumentality, extrinsic valence, and intrinsic valence have a positive meditation effect on the relationship between horizontal collectivism and motivation. (H1a, H1b, H1c, H1d, H1e)

Expectancy, extrinsic instrumentality, intrinsic instrumentality, extrinsic valence, and intrinsic valence have a positive meditation effect on the relationship between vertical collectivism and motivation. (H2a, H2b, H2c, H2d, H2e)

CONCEPTUAL FRAMEWORK

The hypotheses derived in Section 4.0 are illustrated in the conceptual framework in Figure 1. The conceptual framework comprises two independent variables, five mediating variables and one dependent variable. Gender, employment tenure and number of hours worked per week were incorporated in the conceptual framework as control variables based on the argument that motivation levels may vary based on these aspects (Hitka, Kozubíková, & Potkány, 2018; Ližbetinová & Hitka, 2020).

Figure 1. Conceptual framework

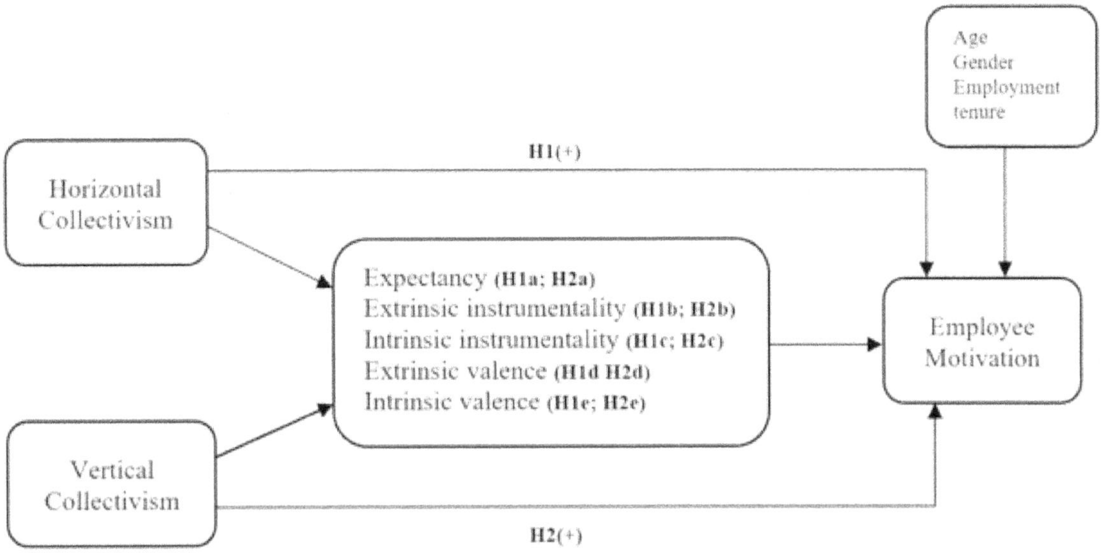

RESEARCH METHODS

The research methods used in this study are discussed in the following order: data collection and sample, measurement, tests for validity, reliability, common methods variance and multi-collinearity, hypotheses testing and findings.

Data Collection and Sample

Data was collected in Australia using an online survey administered via the Google Forms. An overview of the study was provided along with the survey link. For a wider reach, the survey was shared via email and social media platforms such as Facebook and WhatsApp. The survey comprised nine (9) parts. Part A comprised questions on demographic characteristics such as age, gender, highest qualification, hierarchical level at work, number of hours worked per week and employment tenure. Parts B and C comprised items assessing expectancy and extrinsic instrumentality. Items for intrinsic instrumentality were in Part D, followed by items for extrinsic intrinsic valance in Parts E and F. Parts G and H contained measurement items for vertical and horizontal collectivism, respectively. Part I contained measurement items for motivation. The survey did not contain any identification requirements for the respondents, thus ensuring privacy. Furthermore, given that the survey was anonymous, completing the survey implied respondent consent.

The targeted respondents for this study were employed individuals, aged 18 years and above to appropriately provide responses related to motivation in a workplace environment. Respondents were selected using convenience sampling, a non-probability sampling technique. This sampling approach was preferred because it would guarantee a wider reach of respondents within the researchers' networks in a short period of time with limited costs incurred (Taherdoost, 2016). The targeted number of respondents was 300 and this size was determined based on Roscoe's (1975) criteria which proposes that an adequate sample should be ten times or more the number of variables investigated in a study. Since this study investigated eight variables, a sample size of 80 respondents was deemed adequate. The number of usable responses received was 205, yielding a response rate of 68%. As per the Roscoe (1975) criteria, the received number of responses was an adequate sample because it is greater than the recommended number of 80 for this study. The demographic characteristics of the 205 respondents are presented in Table 1. Majority of the respondents were in the 20 – 30-year-old age range and the minority were in the 41 – 50-year-old age range. Respondent distribution across genders was also equal and majority of the respondents had a bachelor's degree qualification. The largest proportion of the respondents worked in operational positions, had been employed for 1 – 5 years and worked between 21 – 30 hours per week.

Table 1. Demographic characteristics

Demographic characteristics	Category	Frequency	Percentage
Age	Below 20 years	39	19.0
	20 – 30 years	109	53.2
	31 – 40 years	56	27.3
	41 – 50 years	1	0.5
Gender	Female	94	45.9
	Male	105	51.2
	Prefer not to say	6	2.9
Highest qualification	High School	9	4.4
	Certificate	16	7.8
	Diploma	41	20.0
	Bachelor's degree	71	34.6
	Postgraduate degree (Honours, Masters, Diploma, Doctorate)	68	33.2
Hierarchical level	Operational	121	59.0
	Non-operational	84	41.0
Number of hours worked per week	1 – 10 hours	12	0.5
	11 – 20 hours	86	5.9
	21 – 30 hours	18	42.0
	31 – 40 hours	74	8.8
	More than 40 hours	14	36.1
	Did not indicate	1	6.8
Employment tenure	Less than 1 year	59	28.8
	1 – 5 years	124	60.5
	6 – 10 years	22	10.7

Measurement

Items adapted from existing studies were used to measure the variables investigated in this study. Thus, content validity content was met in this study. Vertical and horizontal collectivism were each measured using eight items adapted from Lu, Chang, & Yu (2013). Measurements for the remaining variables were adapted from C. F. Chiang & S. S Jang (2008). Expectancy, extrinsic instrumentality, intrinsic instrumentality, and motivation were each measured using four items while extrinsic valance and intrinsic valance were each evaluated using three items. See Table 2 for the measurement items, their sources, means and standard deviations. A five-point Likert scale ranging from 1-strongly disagree to agree 5-strongly was used for responses to the measurement items. Given that measurement items were obtained from existing studies, face validity was met (Sekaran & Bougie, 2016). Content validity was ascertained by pre-testing the survey to get feedback on the adapted measurement items (Sekaran & Bougie, 2016). Following the pre-test, revisions were made to the survey to make it suitable for the respondents.

Validity, Reliability, Common Methods Variance and Multi-Collinearity Tests

The significant Bartlett's test of sphericity (approximate chi-square = 5892, df = 703) and Kaiser-Meyer-Olkin (KMO) measure of adequacy (0.919) confirmed the suitability of the sample for factor analysis. As shown in Tables 2 and 4, convergent validity was met because all factor loadings for all measurement items and Average Variance Extracted (AVE) for all variables were greater than 0.50 (Fornell & Larcker, 1981). Also, the composite reliability for all variables was greater than 0.70 further confirming convergent validity. Discriminant validity is met based on two factors. First, all item loadings on the parent variables were greater than cross-loadings on other variables (see Table 3) (Hair, Black, Babin, Anderson, & Tatham, 2006). Second the square root of the AVE for each variable is greater than all correlations between the variable and other variables (Fornell & Larcker, 1981).

Instrument reliability was assessed using Cronbach's alpha co-efficient and item-to-total correlations (Nunnally & Bernstein, 1994). For the Cronbach alpha co-efficient, the acceptable level is 0.70, while for the item-to-total correlation it is 0.30 (Nunnally, 1978). Reliability criteria was met because Cronbach alpha co-efficient for all variables were greater than 0.70, ranging from 0.82 to 0.89 (see Table 2). Furthermore, all item-to-total correlations were greater than 0.30, ranging from 0.42 to 0.80.

Common Methods Variance (CMV) was assessed using Harman's (1976) single-factor method (Harman, 1976; Podsakoff, MacKenzie, Lee, & Podsakoff, 2003). CMV was ruled out because the first factor that emerged from the Principal Component Analysis accounted for 26.2% of the variance. As a rule, CMV is present when the first extracted factor explains 50% of the variance (Podsakoff & Organ, 1986). Furthermore, as shown in Table 5, multicollinearity was ruled out because for all variables, the Variance Inflation Factor (VIF) were less than 10 and the tolerance statistics greater than 0.20 (Myers & Myers, 1990).

Table 2. Measurement items, descriptive, validity and reliability statistics

Variable	Measurement Items	Indicator	Mean	SD	Mean SD	Factor Loadings	Item-to-total Correlation	Cronbach Alpha
Horizontal collectivism (Lu et al., 2013)	The well-being of my co-worker is important to me	HC1	4.00	0.67	3.69 0.65	0.75	0.63	0.86
	If a co-worker gets a prize, I would feel proud	HC2	3.80	0.84		0.67	0.54	
	If a relative were in financial difficulty, I would help within my means	HC3	3.73	0.69		0.76	0.65	
	It is important to maintain harmony within my group	HC4	4.07	0.83		0.77	0.63	
	I like sharing little things with my neighbours	HC5	3.00	1.16		0.71	0.66	
	I feel good when I cooperate with others	HC6	3.93	0.80		0.79	0.69	
	My happiness depends very much on the happiness of those around me	HC7	3.72	0.95		0.76	0.68	
	To me, pleasure is spending time with others	HC7	3.29	1.15		0.62	0.55	
Vertical collectivism (C. F. Chiang & S. S Jang, 2008)	I would sacrifice an activity that I enjoy very much if my family did not approve it	VC1	2.98	0.97	3.31 0.66	0.66	0.53	0.82
	I would do what would please my family, even if I detested that activity	VC2	2.97	1.01		0.72	0.60	
	Before taking a major trip, I consult with most members of my family and many friends	VC3	3.44	1.10		0.74	0.61	
	I usually sacrifice my self-interest for the benefit of my group	VC4	3.12	1.00		0.80	0.70	
	Children should be taught to place duty before pleasure	VC5	3.45	0.88		0.72	0.60	
	I hate to disagree with others in my group	VC6	3.04	1.03		0.58	0.44	
	We should keep our aging parents with us at home	VC7	3.74	0.95		0.59	0.47	
	Children should feel honoured if their parents receive a distinguished award	VC8	3.75	0.91		0.54	0.42	
Expectancy (C. F. Chiang & S. S Jang, 2008)	If I work hard, my job performance will improve	EX1	4.04	0.89	3.99 0.74	0.79	0.64	0.86
	If I work hard, I will get accomplished	EX2	3.98	0.89		0.86	0.74	
	If I put more effort into my job, my productivity will improve	EX3	3.99	0.90		0.86	0.74	
	If I put more effort into my job, I will be regarded as an effective employee	EX4	3.95	0.87		0.85	0.71	
Extrinsic instrumentality (C. F. Chiang & S. S Jang, 2008)	Performing well in my work will result in getting good pay	EI1	3.33	0.96	3.38 0.81	0.90	0.79	0.88
	Performing well in my work will result	EI2	3.19	0.95		0.85	0.73	
	Performing well in my work will result in getting pay increases in getting monetary bonuses	EI3	3.34	0.90		0.90	0.80	
	Performing well in my work will result in having more opportunities for promotion	EI4	3.67	0.96		0.77	0.62	

Continued on following page

Table 2. Continued

Variable	Measurement Items	Indicator	Mean	SD	Mean SD	Factor Loadings	Item-to-total Correlation	Cronbach Alpha
Intrinsic instrumentality (C. F. Chiang & S. S Jang, 2008)	Performing well in my work will result in having feelings of accomplishment	II1	3.79	0.89	3.87 0.78	0.86	0.74	0.88
	Performing well in my work will result in feeling very good about myself	II2	4.03	0.91		0.88	0.78	
	Performing well in my work will make me feel like a high achiever	II3	3.72	0.95		0.82	0.68	
	Performing well in my work will make me aspire to do better	II4	3.96	0.93		0.88	0.76	
Extrinsic valence (C. F. Chiang & S. S Jang, 2008)	Performing well in my work will result in a good salary/wage	EV1	3.34	0.86	3.26 0.81	0.91	0.78	0.89
	Performing well in my work will result in more monetary bonuses	EV2	3.16	0.88		0.90	0.77	
	Performing well in my work will result in more pay increases	EV3	3.28	0.93		0.91	0.80	
Intrinsic valence (C. F. Chiang & S. S Jang, 2008)	Performing well in my work will result more in responsibility/control over my job	IV1	3.74	0.85	3.80 0.79	0.86	0.69	0.83
	Performing well in my work will result in full use my skills and abilities	IV2	3.81	0.98		0.87	0.70	
	Performing well in my work will result in feelings of accomplishment	IV3	3.87	0.93		0.86	0.69	
Motivation (C. F. Chiang & S. S Jang, 2008)	I expend more effort on my job	MO1	3.85	0.73	3.93 0.71	0.85	0.73	0.88
	I work hard to enhance the quality of my job performance	MO2	4.00	0.87		0.85	0.73	
	I work hard to increase my productivity in my job	MO3	3.99	0.87		0.87	0.76	
	I am always willing to be more involved in my job	MO4	3.90	0.83		0.87	0.75	

Hypotheses Testing and Findings

Hypotheses were tested using Jamovi software. Hypotheses investigating the direct effects were tested using regression analysis while hypotheses investigating mediation effects were tested using mediation analysis. Results of the hypotheses tests are presented in Tables 6 and 7. During the regression analysis, three factors namely age, gender and employment tenure were included as control variables during the regression analysis. While age and employment tenure do not have a significant impact on motivation across both employment categories, gender had a significant impact on motivation among operational staff.

Among both operational ($\beta = 0.654$; $p = <0.001$) and non-operational staff ($\beta = 0.664$; $p = <0.001$) horizontal collectivism improves motivation, providing support for H1 across both employee categories. Vertical collectivism however does not have a significant impact on motivation among both the operational ($\beta = 0.160$; $p = <0.109$) and non-operational staff ($\beta = 0.047$; $p = 0.644$). Thus, H2 is not

Table 3. Cross loadings

Item	HC	VC	EX	EI	II	EV	IV	MO
HC1	**0.77**	0.42	0.47	0.33	0.51	0.32	0.52	0.55
HC2	**0.68**	0.31	0.39	0.24	0.39	0.28	0.45	0.50
HC3	**0.77**	0.52	0.52	0.39	0.47	0.34	0.53	0.58
HC4	**0.78**	0.60	0.54	0.30	0.53	0.25	0.59	0.59
HC5	**0.69**	0.52	0.36	0.29	0.40	0.28	0.40	0.43
HC6	**0.79**	0.44	0.50	0.34	0.49	0.26	0.59	0.54
HC7	**0.75**	0.50	0.44	0.26	0.45	0.21	0.54	0.44
HC8	**0.60**	0.47	0.29	0.26	0.41	0.25	0.36	0.41
VC1	0.30	**0.58**	0.14	0.19	0.21	0.20	0.18	0.24
VC2	0.34	**0.66**	0.25	0.23	0.32	0.21	0.23	0.29
VC3	0.56	**0.73**	0.37	0.24	0.37	0.18	0.35	0.37
VC4	0.49	**0.78**	0.38	0.33	0.37	0.26	0.35	0.40
VC5	0.47	**0.76**	0.40	0.34	0.40	0.27	0.41	0.38
VC6	0.28	**0.52**	0.24	0.17	0.25	0.14	0.19	0.21
VC7	0.43	**0.63**	0.24	0.16	0.32	0.13	0.36	0.33
VC8	0.50	**0.64**	0.42	0.26	0.43	0.19	0.48	0.42
EX1	0.50	0.45	**0.80**	0.48	0.65	0.36	0.64	0.62
EX2	0.54	0.38	**0.86**	0.52	0.67	0.44	0.70	0.62
EX3	0.50	0.37	**0.86**	0.51	0.59	0.42	0.63	0.64
EX4	0.51	0.41	**0.84**	0.56	0.54	0.55	0.61	0.59
EI1	0.28	0.28	0.43	**0.87**	0.48	0.75	0.50	0.40
EI2	0.35	0.34	0.46	**0.85**	0.51	0.74	0.55	0.44
EI3	0.28	0.27	0.50	**0.88**	0.49	0.78	0.55	0.39
EI4	0.46	0.35	0.65	**0.82**	0.62	0.63	0.62	0.53
II1	0.50	0.41	0.64	0.56	**0.85**	0.45	0.75	0.60
II2	0.60	0.48	0.65	0.49	**0.89**	0.46	0.69	0.70
II3	0.52	0.45	0.59	0.60	**0.81**	0.56	0.68	0.56
II4	0.53	0.43	0.62	0.52	**0.87**	0.40	0.70	0.63
EV1	0.29	0.26	0.44	0.73	0.47	**0.89**	0.48	0.40
EV2	0.40	0.29	0.50	0.77	0.47	**0.91**	0.53	0.47
EV3	0.31	0.26	0.50	0.78	0.52	**0.91**	0.53	0.44
IV1	0.59	0.49	0.68	0.55	0.66	0.43	**0.86**	0.63
IV2	0.57	0.42	0.65	0.57	0.73	0.51	**0.86**	0.59
IV3	0.63	0.39	0.66	0.59	0.74	0.53	**0.87**	0.68
MO1	0.54	0.33	0.60	0.45	0.61	0.42	0.60	**0.85**
MO2	0.67	0.52	0.65	0.54	0.72	0.41	0.73	**0.86**
MO3	0.62	0.46	0.64	0.41	0.61	0.39	0.62	**0.87**
MO4	0.56	0.43	0.62	0.41	0.55	0.45	0.56	**0.86**

- **Numbers in bold are item loadings on the parent constructs**
- *** Significant at $p < 0.001$**

Table 4. Reliability, Average Variance Extracted (AVEs) and correlation coefficients

Variable	Composite Reliability	AVE	1	2	3	4	5	6	7	8
Horizontal Collectivism (1)	0.90	0.54	**0.73**							
Vertical Collectivism (2)	0.87	0.50	0.64	**0.71**						
Expectancy (3)	0.91	0.71	0.58	0.45	**0.84**					
Extrinsic Instrumentality (4)	0.92	0.73	0.39	0.35	0.60	**0.85**				
Intrinsic Instrumentality (5)	0.92	0.74	0.62	0.50	0.73	0.62	**0.86**			
Extrinsic Valence (6)	0.932	0.82	0.36	0.29	0.53	0.85	0.54	**0.91**		
Intrinsic Valence (7)	0.90	0.75	0.67	0.47	0.77	0.65	0.82	0.57	**0.87**	
Motivation (8)	0.92	0.74	0.68	0.49	0.73	0.52	0.72	0.48	0.73	**0.86**

- **Bold numbers in diagonal – square root of AVE**
- **Numbers beneath the square roots of the AVE are variable correlations**

Table 5. Multi-collinearity statistics

Variable	VIF	Tolerance
Horizontal collectivism	2.59	0.386
Vertical collectivism	1.82	0.549
Expectancy	2.75	0.363
Extrinsic instrumentality	4.36	0.229
Intrinsic instrumentality	3.56	0.281
Extrinsic valence	3.58	0.280
Intrinsic valence	4.68	0.214

Table 6. Regression analysis results for direct effects across operational and non-operational staff

Category	Antecedent/Control Variable	Standardized Beta Coefficient	Std. Error	t	Sig.		Hypothesis Supported?
Operational staff	Age	0.016	0.091	0.177	0.860	F = 17.1 Sig. = < 0.001 Adj.R^2 = 0.446	
	Gender	-0.174	0.094	-1.850	0.067*		
	Employment tenure	0.131	0.101	1.301	0.196		
	Hours worked per week	0.091	0.060	1.517	0.132		
	Horizontal collectivism	0.654	0.101	6.466	<0.001*		Yes
	Vertical collectivism	0.160	0.099	1.616	0.109		No
Non-operational staff	Age	-0.006	0.0905	-0.0616	0.951	F = 12.9 Sig. = < 0.001 Adj.R^2 = 0.468	
	Gender	-0.009	0.0962	-0.0978	0.922		
	Employment tenure	0.107	0.1000	1.0674	0.289		
	Hours worked per week	0.054	0.0549	0.9852	0.328		
	Horizontal collectivism	0.664	0.1140	5.8244	<0.001*		Yes
	Vertical collectivism	0.047	0.1010	0.4640	0.644		No

Dependent Variable: ***opportunism***
***$p \leq 0.05$**

supported across both categories. The model accounts for 44.6% of the variation in motivation among operational staff and 46.8% of the variation in motivation among non-operational staff.

Hypotheses H1a, H1b, H1c H1d and H1e are supported across both employee categories, implying that horizontal collectivism improves expectancy, extrinsic instrumentality, intrinsic instrumentality, and intrinsic valence to improve employee motivation (see Table 7). Expectancy, intrinsic instrumentality, and intrinsic valance have positive mediation effects on the relationship between vertical collectivism and motivations across both employee categories. Therefore, hypotheses H2a, H2c and H2e are supported for both operational and non-operational staff. Across both employee categories, extrinsic instrumentality is does not mediate the relationship between vertical collectivism and motivation. Thus, hypothesis H2b is not supported across both employee categories. Extrinsic valence mediates the relationship between

Table 7. Mediation effects across operational and non-operational staff

Category	Hypothesis	Mediation Effect (ab)	Std. Error	LLCI 95%	ULCI 95%	Sig.	Hypothesis Supported?
	H1a: HC > EX > MO	0.354	0.087	0.192	0.529	<0.001*	Yes
	H1b: HC > EI > MO	0.091	0.044	0.016	0.195	0.037*	Yes
Operational staff	H1c: HC > II > MO	0.340	0.102	0.148	0.535	<0.001*	Yes
	H1d: HC > EV > MO	0.072	0.037	0.012	0.152	0.047*	Yes
	H1e: HC > IV > MO	0.355	0.091	0.176	0.548	<0.001*	Yes
	H1a: HC > EX > MO	0.236	0.100	0.0556	0.437	0.019*	Yes
	H1b: HC > EI > MO	0.129	0.065	0.0247	0.267	0.046*	Yes
Non-operational staff	H1c: HC > II > MO	0.219	0.083	0.0545	0.373	0.008*	Yes
	H1d: HC > EV > MO	0.109	0.056	0.0899	0.222	0.053**	Yes
	H1e: HC > IV > MO	0.311	0.093	0.151	0.488	<0.001*	Yes
	H2a: VC > EX > MO	0.318	0.095	0.127	0.495	<0.001*	Yes
	H2b: VC > EI > MO	0.105	0.048	0.024	0.210	0.029	No
Operational staff	H2c: VC > II > MO	0.311	0.101	0.108	0.488	0.002*	Yes
	H2d: VC > EV > MO	0.084	0.044	0.015	0.180	0.056**	Yes
	H2e: VC > IV > MO	0.263	0.092	0.075	0.445	0.004*	Yes
	H2a: VC > EX > MO	0.245	0.118	0.0524	0.491	0.038*	Yes
	H2b: VC > EI > MO	0.158	0.088	0.0301	0.355	0.071	No
Non-operational staff	H2c: VC > II > MO	0.288	0.120	0.083	0.545	0.017*	Yes
	H2d: VC > EV > MO	0.107	0.071	0.0067	0.282	0.130	No
	H2e: VC > IV > MO	0.362	0.124	0.151	0.618	0.003*	Yes

Dependent variable – MO - Motivation
Independent variables – HC – Horizontal collectivism; VC – Vertical Collectivism
Mediators – EX- Expectancy; EI – Extrinsic Instrumentality; II – Intrinsic Instrumentality; EV – Extrinsic Valence; IV – Intrinsic valence
LLCI – Lower Limit Confidence Interval; **ULCI** – Upper Limit Confidence Interval
SE – Standard Error
Bootstrapped sample size = 1000;*p ≤ 0.05; **p≤ 0.1

vertical collectivism and motivation among operational staff but not operational staff. Consequently, hypotheses H2d is supported for operational staff but not non-operational staff.

CONCLUSION

This section comprises the following: theoretical contribution, managerial and policy implications, limitations, and future research directions.

Theoretical Contribution

This study has contributed to employee motivation literature by investigating the direct and indirect effects of the two dimensions of collectivism, namely horizontal and vertical collectivism on motivation across operational and non-operational staff. Findings have shown no variations in the direct and indirect effects across the employee categories, thus demonstrating that the impact of both horizontal and vertical collectivism on motivation may not always vary across the two employee categories. Hence, when motivating staff from both categories in the context of collectivism, managers can apply similar strategies. However, in designing motivation strategies for operational staff, gender aspects need to be taken into consideration, given that gender has a positive significant impact on motivation in this employee category. While the positive relationship between horizontal collectivism and motivation is consistent with studies that have found that horizontal collectivism creates positive workplace behaviour (e.g. Moorman & Blakely, 1995; Rhee et al., 2017; Van Dyne, Vandewalle, Kostova, Latham, & Cummings, 2000), the finding on the impact of vertical collectivism is inconsistent with these studies. This difference in the direct impact of the collectivism dimensions has confirmed the distinctiveness of the aspects of collectivism proposed by Triandis & Gelfand (1998), thereby validating the concept and its application across diverse contexts.

Additionally, this study has extended the Expectancy Theory by incorporating the cultural dimension of collectivism, to respond to calls for more empirical studies on cultural factors and motivation across diverse employee categories (Chiang & Jang, 2008; Chiang et al., 2008; Ghoddousi et al., 2014b). Furthermore, regarding mediation effects, this study finds no variations in the mediation effects of the Expectancy Theory dimensions on the relationship between horizontal collectivism and motivation across both employee categories. One difference is identified in the mediation effect of extrinsic valence in the relationship between vertical collectivism and motivation. While this mediation effect is significant among operational staff, it is insignificant among non-operational staff. This difference may be attributed to differences in the level and extent of interaction among staff in the two categories. Operational staff tend to interact a bit more, therefore creating an environment where more value is attached to the rewards received within the organisation. Non-operational staff, on the other hand do not interact as much, implying that vertical collectivism would not have a significant impact on extrinsic valence to improve motivation.

Managerial and Policy Implications

Given the positive impact of horizontal collectivism on motivation, organisations should put in place systems and resources that support aspects such as inter-dependence, cooperation, mutual relational norms, and equality. These norms are characteristics of horizontal collectivism and can be promoted through organisational awareness campaigns, team building initiatives and exercises. Also, the positive mediation effects of expectancy, instrumentality and valance implies that these dimensions need to be enhanced to improve employee motivation. Therefore, management should build policies that empower employees to improve their performance based on trainings received and reward the good performance attained with benefits that are valued by employees. It should be noted that the value attached to some benefits will vary among employees, even within the same organisation for different reasons. Therefore, context needs to be considered when deciding on the benefits that will be tied to performance. Since policies serve as guides and foundations to determining organisational culture, management can utilise their implementation as the first step towards creating a desired state of employee motivation within organisations. In this case, policies should clearly state the aims, processes, and requirements from each employee such that each employee's attitude and behaviour at work are reconstituted towards the managerial agenda of enhancing motivation.

Management should take a further step to create engaging work formats that are motivation focused. Such work formats should structure work processes to indicate specific work expectations and accountability, either manually or electronically from each employee. This will provide a platform for measuring work effort and outcomes to support the evaluation of effort/performance to assign relevant rewards. When this happens, employees become aware of what they should be doing, making it possible for a self-evaluation of work performance. In addition, since there is accountability for work done, managers should ensure that work done is identified, recognised, and rewarded.

Managers should consider implementing social support systems in the workplace through initiatives such as team building exercises, collaborative ventures, inter-disciplinary teams, networking sessions or social events. These help to promote positive relationship norms to enhance horizonal collectivism, which will in turn improve motivation. When challenges arise between employees, support services such as counselling or conflict resolution should be availed to allow for the quick resolution of conflict to avoid damaging workplace relationships. The effectiveness of the social support systems will be enhanced by feedback systems that make it possible for managers and employees to discuss any challenges related to work expectations, targets, or teamwork.

Limitations and Future Research Directions

Although this study makes a significant contribution to motivation literature by investigating the determinants of employee motivation across operational and non-operational staff, some limitations remain. Given that this study has investigated only one dimension of Hofstede's Cultural Dimensions Theory, i.e., collectivism, future studies should consider investigating the impact of the other dimensions of this theory on motivation as well as variables derived from other cultural theories. Furthermore, this study investigated employee motivation determinants across operational and non-operational staff categories, implying that the findings may not be generalised to other staff categories. Forthcoming studies can compare employee motivation across other employee categorisations such as sectors, occupations, education levels, employment tenure, nationality, or age groups.

Research undertaken in future can also consider analysing motivation from the perspective of managers as opposed to employees only to get a more comprehensive understanding of motivation. Where possible, future studies can compare employee motivation perspectives of managers and employees to identify any differences or similarities between those being governed and those undertaking the role of governing in organisations. While this study has investigated the mediation effects of expectancy, extrinsic instrumentality, intrinsic instrumentality, extrinsic valence, intrinsic valence, future research can consider investigating other mediators as well as moderators. More specifically, future mediation and moderation effects can be evaluated across cultures. Upcoming studies can take on a longitudinal focus to determine if there are any variations on the effects of motivation determinants over a period.

REFERENCES

Abadi, F. E., Jalilvand, M. R., Sharif, M., Salimi, G. A., & Khanzadeh, S. A. (2011). A study of influential factors on employees' motivation for participating in the in-service training courses based on modified expectancy theory. *International Business Management*, *2*(1), 157–169.

Akdem, ir, E. (2020). The Determination of Teachers' Motivation Based on Herzberg's Motivation Theory. *The Turkish Online Journal of Educational Technology*, *19*(4).

Al-Tkhayneh, K., Kot, S., & Shestak, V. (2019). Motivation and demotivation factors affecting productivity in public sector. *Administratie si Management Public*, *1*(33), 77–102. doi:10.24818/amp/2019.33-05.

Ann, S., & Blum, S. C. (2020). Motivating senior employees in the hospitality industry. *International Journal of Contemporary Hospitality Management*, *32*(1), 324–346. doi:10.1108/IJCHM-08-2018-0685

Antosz, P., Rembiasz, T., & Verhagen, H. (2020). Employee shirking and overworking: Modelling the unintended consequences of work organisation. *Ergonomics*, *63*(8), 997–1009. doi:10.1080/00140139.2020.1744710 PMID:32188339

Baciu, L. E. (2018). Expectancy Theory Explaining Civil Servants' work Motivation. Evidence from A Romanian City Hall. *The USV Annals of Economics and Public Administration*, *17*(2 (26)), 146–160.

Bani-Melhem, S., Zeffane, R., & Albaity, M. (2018). Determinants of employees' innovative behavior. *International Journal of Contemporary Hospitality Management*, *30*(3), 1601–1620. doi:10.1108/IJCHM-02-2017-0079

Carter, L. (2016). *Presenteeism costs economy $34 billion a year through lost productivity, report shows*. Retrieved from https://www.abc.net.au/news/2016-04-12/presenteeism-costing-the-economy-billions/7318832

Cerasoli, C. P., Nicklin, J. M., & Ford, M. T. (2014). Intrinsic motivation and extrinsic incentives jointly predict performance: A 40-year meta-analysis. *Psychological Bulletin*, *140*(4), 980–1008. doi:10.1037/a0035661 PMID:24491020

Chen, C. C., Meindl, J. R., & Hunt, R. G. (1997). Testing the effects of vertical and horizontal collectivism: A study of reward allocation preferences in China. *Journal of Cross-Cultural Psychology*, *28*(1), 44–70. doi:10.1177/0022022197281003

Chen, Y., & Lou, H. (2002). Toward an understanding of the behavioral intention to use a groupware application. *Journal of Organizational and End User Computing*, *14*(4), 1–16. doi:10.4018/joeuc.2002100101

Chiang, C.-F., & Jang, S. (2008). An expectancy theory model for hotel employee motivation. *International Journal of Hospitality Management*, *27*(2), 313–322. doi:10.1016/j.ijhm.2007.07.017

Chiang, C.-F., Jang, S., Canter, D., & Prince, B. (2008). An expectancy theory model for hotel employee motivation: Examining the moderating role of communication satisfaction. *International Journal of Hospitality & Tourism Administration*, *9*(4), 327–351. doi:10.1080/15256480802427263

Chopra, K. (2019). Indian shopper motivation to use artificial intelligence: Generating Vroom's expectancy theory of motivation using grounded theory approach. *International Journal of Retail & Distribution Management*, *47*(3), 331–347. doi:10.1108/IJRDM-11-2018-0251

De Mooij, M., & Hofstede, G. (2010). The Hofstede model: Applications to global branding and advertising strategy and research. *International Journal of Advertising*, *29*(1), 85–110. doi:10.2501/S026504870920104X

De Simone, S. (2015). Expectancy value theory: Motivating healthcare workers. *American International Journal of Contemporary Research*, *5*(2), 19–23.

Doraisamy, J. (2021). *18% of Australians aren't motivated at work*. Retrieved from https://www.wellnessdaily.com.au/culture/18-of-australians-arent-motivated-at-work

Erdman, K. (2018). *An analysis of Geert Hofstede's culture's consequences: Comparing values, behaviors, institutes and organizations across nations*. CRC Press.

Esther, P., Christian, S., & Jürgen, G. (2020). Understanding Employee Motivation for Work-to-Nonwork Integration Behavior: A Reasoned Action Approach. *Journal of Business and Psychology*, *35*(5), 683–696. doi:10.100710869-019-09648-5

Fornell, C., & Larcker, D. F. (1981). Structural equation models with unobservable variables and measurement error: Algebra and statistics. Sage Publications.

Franco, L. M., Bennett, S., Kanfer, R., & Stubblebine, P. (2004). Determinants and consequences of health worker motivation in hospitals in Jordan and Georgia. *Social Science & Medicine*, *58*(2), 343–355. doi:10.1016/S0277-9536(03)00203-X PMID:14604620

Gabor, M. R., Conţiu, L. C., & Oltean, F. D. (2012). A comparative analysis regarding European tourism competitiveness: Emerging versus developed markets. *Procedia Economics and Finance*, *3*, 361–366. doi:10.1016/S2212-5671(12)00165-7

Ghoddousi, P., Bahrami, N., Chileshe, N., & Hosseini, M. R. (2014a). Mapping site-based construction workers' motivation: Expectancy theory approach. *The Australasian Journal of Construction Economics and Building*, *14*(1), 60–77. doi:10.5130/AJCEB.v14i1.3712

Ghoddousi, P., Bahrami, N., Chileshe, N., & Hosseini, M. R. (2014b). Mapping site-based construction workers' motivation: Expectancy theory approach. *The Australasian Journal of Construction Economics and Building*, *14*(1), 60–77. doi:10.5130/AJCEB.v14i1.3712

Habanik, J., Martosova, A., Letkova, N., & Dubček, A. (2020). The Impact of Managerial Decision-Making on Employee Motivation in Manufacturing Companies. *Journal of Competitiveness, 12*(2), 38-50. doi:10.7441/joc.2020.02.03

Hair, J. F., Black, W. C., Babin, B. J., Anderson, R. E., & Tatham, R. (2006). *Multivariate data analysis.* Pearson Prentice Hall.

Hanaysha, J. R., & Majid, M. (2018). Employee motivation and its role in improving the productivity and organizational commitment at higher education institutions. *Journal of Entrepreneurship and Business*, *6*(1), 17–28. doi:10.17687/JEB.0601.02

Harman, H. H. (1976). *Modern factor analysis.* University of Chicago press.

Harris, K. J., Murphy, K. S., DiPietro, R. B., & Line, N. D. (2017). The antecedents and outcomes of food safety motivators for restaurant workers: An expectancy framework. *International Journal of Hospitality Management*, *63*, 53–62. doi:10.1016/j.ijhm.2017.02.004

HemaMalini, P. H., & Washington, A. (2014). Employees' Motivation and Valued Rewards as a Key to Effective QWL- from the Perspective of Expectancy Theory. *TSM Business Review, 2*(2), 45.

Hitka, M., Kozubíková, Ľ., & Potkány, M. (2018). Education and gender-based differences in employee motivation. *Journal of Business Economics and Management*, *19*(1), 80–95. doi:10.3846/16111699.2017.1413009

Hofstede, G. (1980). Culture and organizations. *International Studies of Management & Organization*, *10*(4), 15–41. doi:10.1080/00208825.1980.11656300

Hofstede, G. (2001). Culture's recent consequences: Using dimension scores in theory and research. *International Journal of Cross Cultural Management*, *1*(1), 11–17. doi:10.1177/147059580111002

Hofstede, G. (2011). Dimensionalizing cultures: The Hofstede model in context. *Online Readings in Psychology and Culture, 2*(1).

Islam, R., & Ismail, A. Z. H. (2008). Employee motivation: A Malaysian perspective. *International Journal of Commerce and Management.* Advance online publication. doi:10.1108/10569210810921960

Kuvaas, B., Buch, R., Weibel, A., Dysvik, A., & Nerstad, C. G. (2017). Do intrinsic and extrinsic motivation relate differently to employee outcomes? *Journal of Economic Psychology*, *61*, 244–258. doi:10.1016/j.joep.2017.05.004

Lee, H.-W. (2019). Moderators of the Motivational Effects of Performance Management: A Comprehensive Exploration Based on Expectancy Theory. *Public Personnel Management*, *48*(1), 27–55. doi:10.1177/0091026018783003

Lee, W.-N., & Choi, S. M. (2005). The role of horizontal and vertical individualism and collectivism in online consumers' responses toward persuasive communication on the web. *Journal of Computer-Mediated Communication*, *11*(1), 317–336. doi:10.1111/j.1083-6101.2006.tb00315.x

Litvin, S. W. (2019). Hofstede, cultural differences, and TripAdvisor hotel reviews. *International Journal of Tourism Research*, *21*(5), 712–717. doi:10.1002/jtr.2298

Ližbetinová, L., & Hitka, M. (2020). Gender Motivation Differences of Czech and Chinese Employees. *Periodica Polytechnica Social and Management Sciences*, *28*(1), 48–58. doi:10.3311/PPso.12867

Minkov, M., & Hofstede, G. (2011). The evolution of Hofstede's doctrine. *Cross Cultural Management*, *18*(1), 10–20. doi:10.1108/13527601111104269

Moorman, R. H., & Blakely, G. L. (1995). Individualism-collectivism as an individual difference predictor of organizational citizenship behavior. *Journal of Organizational Behavior*, *16*(2), 127–142. doi:10.1002/job.4030160204

Myers, R. H., & Myers, R. H. (1990). Classical and modern regression with applications (Vol. 2). Duxbury Press.

Nimri, M., Bdair, A., & Al Bitar, H. (2015). Applying the Expectancy Theory to Explain the Motivation of Public Sector Employees in Jordan. *Middle East Journal of Business, 10*(3), 70-82. doi:10.5742/MEJB.2015.92714

Nunnally, J. C. (1978). *Psychometric theory*. McGraw-Hill.

Nunnally, J. C., & Bernstein, I. H. (1994). *Psychometric Theory*. McGraw-Hill.

Parijat, P., & Bagga, S. (2014). Victor Vroom's expectancy theory of motivation–An evaluation. *International Research Journal of Business and Management*, *7*(9), 1–8.

Parker, S. L., Jimmieson, N. L., & Amiot, C. E. (2017). The motivational mechanisms underlying active and high-strain work: Consequences for mastery and performance. *Work and Stress*, *31*(3), 233–255. doi:10.1080/02678373.2017.1303551

Podsakoff, P. M., MacKenzie, S. B., Lee, J.-Y., & Podsakoff, N. P. (2003). Common method biases in behavioral research: A critical review of the literature and recommended remedies. *The Journal of Applied Psychology*, *88*(5), 879–903. doi:10.1037/0021-9010.88.5.879 PMID:14516251

Podsakoff, P. M., & Organ, D. W. (1986). Self-reports in organizational research: Problems and prospects. *Journal of Management*, *12*(4), 531–544. doi:10.1177/014920638601200408

Rhee, J., Zhao, X., Jun, I., & Kim, C. (2017). Effects of Collectivism on Chinese Organizational Citizenship Behavior: Guanxi As Moderator. *Social Behavior and Personality*, *45*(7), 1127–1142. doi:10.2224bp.6128

Ritz, A., Brewer, G. A., & Neumann, O. (2016). Public service motivation: A systematic literature review and outlook. *Public Administration Review*, *76*(3), 414–426. doi:10.1111/puar.12505

Roscoe, J. T. (1975). *Fundamental Research Statistics for the Behavioral Science*. Holt, Rinehart and Winston.

Sekaran, U., & Bougie, R. (2016). *Research methods for business: A skill building approach*. John Wiley & Sons.

Shahzadi, I., Javed, A., Pirzada, S. S., Nasreen, S., & Khanam, F. (2014). Impact of employee motivation on employee performance. *European Journal of Business and Management*, *6*(23), 159–166.

Singelis, T. M., Triandis, H. C., Bhawuk, D. P., & Gelfand, M. J. (1995). Horizontal and vertical dimensions of individualism and collectivism: A theoretical and measurement refinement. *Cross-Cultural Research, 29*(3), 240–275. doi:10.1177/106939719502900302

Sultana, S., Salman, Y., & Irfan, S. (2020). Exploring the relationship of HRM Practices on Employee motivation in public organizations: A systematic Literature review. *Global Management Journal for Academic & Corporate Studies, 10*(1), 143-163.

Taherdoost, H. (2016). Sampling methods in research methodology; how to choose a sampling technique for research. *How to Choose a Sampling Technique for Research.*

Triandis, H. C., & Gelfand, M. J. (1998). Converging measurement of horizontal and vertical individualism and collectivism. *Journal of Personality and Social Psychology, 74*(1), 118–128. doi:10.1037/0022-3514.74.1.118

Triandis, H. C., & Singelis, T. M. (1998). Training to recognize individual differences in collectivism and individualism within culture. *International Journal of Intercultural Relations, 22*(1), 35–47. doi:10.1016/S0147-1767(97)00034-5

van der Kolk, B., van Veen-Dirks, P. M., & ter Bogt, H. J. (2019). The impact of management control on employee motivation and performance in the public sector. *European Accounting Review, 28*(5), 901–928. doi:10.1080/09638180.2018.1553728

Van Dyne, L., Vandewalle, D., Kostova, T., Latham, M. E., & Cummings, L. (2000). Collectivism, propensity to trust and self-esteem as predictors of organizational citizenship in a non-work setting. *Journal of Organizational Behavior, 21*(1), 3–23. doi:10.1002/(SICI)1099-1379(200002)21:1<3::AID-JOB47>3.0.CO;2-6

Vroom, V. H. (1964). *Work and motivation*. Wiley.

Chapter 7
New Model to Promote Well-Being in Work Areas of an Aerospace Industry Facility in Mexicali:
Ergonomic Analysis

Carlos Raul Navarro Gonzalez
https://orcid.org/0000-0003-3873-3800
Autonomous University of Baja California, Mexico

Juan Ceballos-Corral
Autonomous University of Baja California, Mexico

Olivia Yessenia Vargas-Bernal
Autonomous University of Baja California, Mexico

Gustavo Lopez Badilla
UNEA University, Mexico

Judith M. Paz-Delgadillo
https://orcid.org/0000-0003-3468-5071
Autonomous University of Baja California, Mexico

ABSTRACT

This investigation was made to evaluate the health and well-being of workers who made activities in the manufacturing processes of an aerospace industry installed in the city of Mexicali and based on the evidence presented in certain stages of a production line. The cost-benefit of applying ergonomic methods was analyzed, developing a descriptive model, which involved important aspects. Said aspects analyzed were (1) work methods, (2) training of employees in the operational area, (3) evaluation of times and movements of industrial operations, and (4) working conditions as the relationship of workers with supervisors and managers.

DOI: 10.4018/978-1-7998-7396-9.ch007

INTRODUCTION

In Mexicali city, are located more than 35 industries with aerospace products (INDEX, 2020). According to the International Labor Organization (ILO), working life considers two very important factors, such as the health and well-being of workers, which includes the safety and quality of work activities, of employees in any operational area (Drury, 2010), to can develop their activities most comfortably. This concept has had a greater boom since the early 21st century, where working conditions have been constantly evaluated. On some occasions, in certain companies of various industrial activities, and especially the industries located in the city of Mexicali, where were presented in some industrial processes, with some unsuitable working conditions. These unsuitable conditions were by a lack of adequate tools, as well as repetitive and unnecessary movements and risky operations that can negatively affect the health of workers, mainly in manufacturing activities. At present, a greater number of industrial plants installed in this city, have been dedicated to improving the working conditions of employees in operational areas of industrial processes. In the manufacturing areas of industrial companies of this city, some programs of labor conditions have been developed that include actions to protect the integrity of workers to avoid occupational risks. This entailed generating health symptoms, being one of the important factor the postures, as is showed in next figure as a bad posture, within a short future can be damaged the back of worker, causing musculoskeletal disorders (Chandra A et al, 2009). The main benefits that helped to improve the working conditions of the employees in the manufacturing area were determined, evaluating internal and external variables of the manufacturing stages of a production line and that had an effect on the four aspects mentioned. Based on this evaluation, relevant improvements were developed to apply ergonomic interventions at each stage, to support workers who suffered from some health symptoms such as discomfort and pain in the arms, head, neck, back, shoulders, and hands. This was a concern, of managers and supervisor people, because was increased the percentage of workers that visited medical areas indoors of the industry analyzed, and in the Mexican Health Institutions (MHI) of public services, located outside of the industry where was made the investigation.

Figure 1. Bad posture of the worker in an industrial process of the aerospace industry

Working Conditions in the Industry

The industrial sector is a key element in the economy of each country, so each region of the world considers the development of industrial activities, where large personnel is required in all operational functions. The manufacturing areas are where the greatest amount of work risks are generated, so since the end of the last century efforts have been redoubled to maintain optimal working conditions, to have great comfort when they made its work activities and thus obtain the maximum operational yielding (Ahola K et al, 2013). The development of industrial operations is essentially divided into two types: simple and complex; wherein each one diverse functions are contemplated that require aptitudes and abilities that must be elaborated by the most suitable people, to avoid risks of work and obtain maximum efficiency of the industrial operations. In the global sphere and our country, since the beginning of the implementation of labor regulations, they have been preserved until today the optimal labor conditions, with some extraordinary situations that must be applied to achieve the goals proposed in each work period in the industrial companies. The great competitiveness in the industrial sector has led to the processes becoming increasingly complex and faster, which has been generated the development of industrial operations with more suitable personnel and with the need to develop a greater effort that causes work stress, and sometimes some acute and serious health symptoms. The personnel in charge of conserving and increasing the number of clients for an industry is the one that generates the production orders, in joint with the logistic, reception of materials, manufacturing, and quality departments. Based on this, the personnel from all areas of industrial companies are involved as managers, supervisors, engineers, technicians, and operators; of the areas of human resources, engineering, design, and manufacture of products, logistics, materials, and manufactured products, production, and quality. In each area, different work environments are generated, causing work stress and some acute or serious health symptoms, but it is mainly the personnel from manufacturing areas, who most suffer a great weight in the elaboration of their functions and especially when they not have the adequate working conditions, which is showed in Figure 2. This can cause the generation of accidents or serious diseases that provoke the temporal or definitive incapacity of the workers of the manufacturing areas (De Brito P et al, 2014).

Figure 2. Work stress in industrial activities

Occupational health

The concept of Occupational health comes from the middle of the last century, being promoted by the International Labor Organization and the World Health Organization (WHO), and being promoted as the pillar of the development of regulations of working conditions in any type of work activity, to take care of the integrity of the workers. At first, it was called work medicine or occupational medicine, to be reinforced the term as occupational health at the beginning of the 21st century (Harshal T, 2017). Since the beginning of the term of occupational health, it has focused on evaluating the generation of diseases and accidents caused by work activities in any company. This has been occurred, especially in the industrial sector, where there is a great diversity of occupational risks, and essentially, because the managers and supervisor personnel, which direct industrial operations, do not understand the need to analyze its relevant aspect. This factor encloses the concepts of occupational medicine, ergonomics, organizational psychology, industrial safety, and preventive medicine, which are related to the working conditions. In most of the world's industries, and specifically in those of the aerospace sector located in Mexicali, there has been an increase in visits to the doctor within industrial plants, in addition to medical consultations in public or private health institutions, external of industrial companies. This has caused an important factor in the economy of industrial companies, such as the risk premium, to increase due to fines from the health authorities of the governments where the industries are located. In this border city, the fines for this important factor have increased, being a concern for the management and administrative personnel, as well as the owners of the industrial plants located in this northwestern region of the Mexican Republic. In certain industrial companies of this city, Mexican health authorities have been elaborated visits, due to the high rate of visits by workers to public health institutions, external of the industrial plants, with symptoms ranging from work stress to serious injuries, where is necessary to develop surgical actions (Wilson J et al, 2009). Based on the above, it is of great relevance to promote the integrity of the workers and to constantly evaluate industrial operations, from the way they are made, times and movements, repetitive movements, and environmental comfort. The constant evaluation of these aspects has helped many industrial plants to improve their working conditions and obtain better performance from their workers, reduce the risk premium, achieving to decrease the percentage of accidents and diseases in workers, and increase the productivity and quality indexes. This has generated that every year workers receive economical bonus called profits, were in sometimes were very considerate to all people of any industrial company.

Musculoskeletal Disorders

They can present when there is an injury to muscles, tendons, blood vessels, ligaments, bones, nerves, and joints; and happens in the back, neck, head, waist, and upper and lower extremities. This can occur in any activity, and if it happens in work operations it is considered as an occupational accident or illness. This type of health symptom can be acute or serious and can occur mainly due to improper and uncomfortable postures, lifting heavy objects without the proper method or of great weight where a great effort is necessary, or by pulling on an object (Spinelli R et al, 2017). Sometimes musculoskeletal disorders (MSD) can start with minor discomfort and can become very painful in any upper and lower organ or limb. Sometimes management and supervisory personnel do not realize that a function of an industrial operation can cause from a minimum discomfort to something that requires surgical intervention and can cause a person to be unable to develop forever some type of activity. The inadequate imposition of goals between owners or representatives of owners, sales, managerial, specialized, and supervisory personnel of industrial companies, has caused maximum work demands and overloads on workers in manufacturing areas, causing specially job stress. This erroneous way of developing industrial operations has led to the operating personnel of the manufacturing areas, to suffer at least a discomfort in their physical integrity and even though the managerial, specialized, and supervisory personnel are aware of these situations; not takes any type of action to avoid work risks that cause MSD. Another important aspect is the inadequate planning of rest times for workers in the manufacturing areas, essentially those who made repetitive industrial operations, of great effort, with inappropriate and static postures and those who make activities with inadequate light, lack of comfort of climate and vibrations. This is due to the operation of industrial equipment and machinery (Aalmo G et al, 2016). In addition, the activities made at high speed, developed by the inadequate planning of the logistics area of the industrial plants, especially those located in the city of Mexicali of various industrial sectors, have caused labor accidents. This is because, at beginning industrial operations of high speed and without having the appropriate aptitudes, skills, and equipment, generating health symptoms in upper and lower organs and extremities, which cause the MSD. The generation of MSD is also originated by long hours of work such as certain industrial companies in Mexicali that work for four days in one week and three days in the next, and in weekly periods, for 12-hour periods in very complex activities that cause at least work stress, headaches or pain in some parts of the human body. This also occurs in the majorly of the industries located in this border city, due to poor organization in their industrial processes, which generate a large number of defective products. With this, it is necessary to request the operational personnel of the manufacturing areas to extend their work hours with overtime (Denbeigh K et al, 2013). This is promoted by managerial and supervisory personnel, telling workers that they will have an increase in their salary in their next pay week, but can cause overload on their body, thereby generating the MSD. The MSD can present various degrees of discomfort and in different parts of the human body, where pain can vary and lead to acute or serious health complications. It is necessary to attend to this type of annoyances because they can have serious consequences. Figure 3 shows various health symptoms in the lower and upper back areas, as well as the neck, shoulders, knee, and waist. Injured parts of the body are seen in red.

Figure 3. Musculoskeletal disorders presented in different parts of the human body

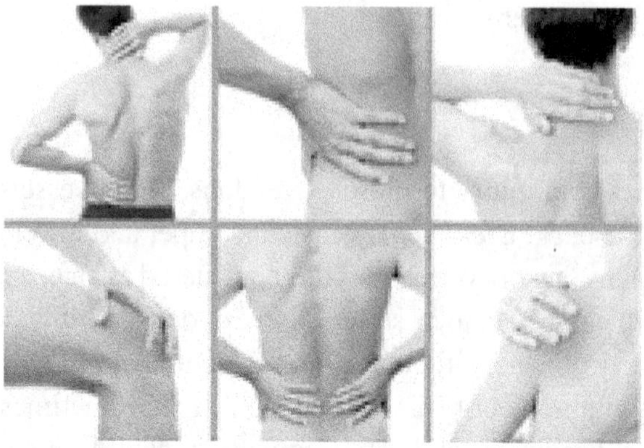

The MSD that occur most frequently according to the degree of discomfort and zone of the human body zone are mentioned below (Barbosa et al, 2014):

1. Carpal syndrome. It is a health symptom that can occur when the nerve that regulates sensitivity and movement of the wrist of either of the two hands is affected. This syndrome causes muscle damage that causes tingling, weakness, and low level of movement, and numbness.
2. Tendinitis. It can occur when overload is generated in joints that affect the tendons (fibrous cords that join the muscle of the bone), causing pain in parts outside the joint.
3. Muscle or tendon tension. It is also called myogelosis, and it occurs when the body is subjected to industrial overload operations, achieving extreme fatigue. The health symptoms are muscle aches and headaches.
4. Stretching of ligaments. It is known as an inadequate stretching of the ligaments, causing abnormalities in the fibrous tissue, and connect the bones through the joints. The most frequent area of this symptom is the ankle, which causes intense and uncomfortable pain.
5. Cervical tension syndrome. It is generated by a muscle contracture, whose pain is difficult to control and can occur for long periods, being the cervical area where this event occurs and can affect a muscle or group of muscles of any part of the human body.
6. Thoracic outlet compression syndrome. It generates health complications in the shoulders, arms, and neck, occurring when the nerves and blood vessels that are under the neck are very compressed, and feeling this effect in the muscles of the neck, shoulders, and the first rib attached to the clavicle.
7. Rotator cuff tendonitis. It occurs when tendons that are attached to the bones of the shoulder joint are irritated, and when a tear or injury is generated in one of the tendons that detach from the bone due to overloads of work in industrial operations
8. Epicondylitis or tennis elbow. It occurs when the elbow tendons become overloaded due to repetitive movements of the wrist and arm, which are very common in industrial activities.
9. Radial tunnel syndrome. This clinical picture develops when there is a compression in a section of the radial nerve of the forearm located at the elbow, and occurring due to inflammation of the muscles that are around this area of the arm.
10. Tendosynovitis or trigger finger. It occurs when the tendons of the fingers become inflamed, being able to be left with flexion in some finger of the hand, in a position to pull a trigger, by repetitive and rapid movements in the hands.
11. DeQuervain syndrome. It develops in the tendons of the wrist, due to repetitive movements, constantly turning the wrist or clenching the fist frequently.
12. Mechanical low back pain. It is a clinical picture presented in the lumbar part or lower part of the back, which is caused by muscle overload or trauma, and pain increases, while not at rest person.
13. Degenerative disc disease. It is generated when a disc causes lumbago (lumbar pain, which is in the lower part of the back, possibly being caused by genetic defects and overload by industrial operations.
14. Rupture or herniated disc. It is also called displacement or rupture of the intervertebral disc, originating in the lower part of the back, being a clinical picture of sciatica, causing pain in the legs.
15. According to the Secretaria de Trabajo y Prevision Social (STPS) (LFT, 2019) was presented an increase in complaints due to lack of training.

Engineering Models in the Industry

The evaluation of engineering models that are applied in industrial activities at any stage of manufacturing has been developed for a better understanding of the functions of each stage that is developed in industrial processes. In addition, how the operating personnel should be selected according to their qualities and abilities should be considered. Engineering models are structural representations, which include all the objects, parameters, and personnel required in each industrial activity, which are elaborated at the small-scale and evaluated by managers, specialized engineering personnel, continuous improvement, and supervision; to make each worker aware of the way of developing industrial activities (Harshal T, 2017).

METHODOLOGY

Materials and Methods

Analyzes of four aspects that are mentioned below were made to detect in greater detail the problematic situations that arose in various steps of manufacturing according to standard procedures as NOM 015 (2001), NOM 024 (2001), NOM 025 (2008), and OHSAS 18000 (2007), showing in next paragraphs:

1. Analysis of work methods. Analyzes were made of how to develop the functions of the workers of various industrial processes. At this stage, six actions were made, which are now indicated:
    a. In this investigation was selected the industrial activity to be evaluated, using continuous improvement tools, such as the Pareto diagram to define which are the most important to give a solution or the easiest to solve and develop improvement proposals so that problem situations are not generated again. In this action, managers, engineering personnel specialized in continuous improvement, supervisory personnel, and workers from the manufacturing stages analyzed have participated to brainstorm the possible optimal solutions quickly. Concerning working conditions, the manufacturing stages of greatest need to be evaluated in this investigation were determined, to avoid greater harm to workers who participated in industrial processes, while the scientific analysis was made.
    b. The second action consisted of determining the parameters to be analyzed to use verification sheets where was elaborated the annotations of numerical data and textual information and were obtained with automated systems with electronic devices connected to desktop or laptop computers. This has supported the specialized personnel of continuous improvement, to generate databases and be evaluated to corroborate the assumptions made when selecting the manufacturing stages to evaluate. In this part of the analysis, simple or rigorous evaluation processes were included, using control charts and histograms, where the behavior of the evaluated parameters is shown. The databases must be built simply, easy to organize the information, and be very understandable to quickly act to give the solution immediately and continue avoiding the generation of errors, defects, causing some discomfort to the operating workers and that cause greater economic losses. Regarding working conditions, this research has correlated the information on productivity, quality, and cases of operational personnel with some type of health symptom or suffering an accident at work.

c. Once, in this scientific study, the manufacturing stages to be evaluated were identified, considering mainly the subject of labor conditions, whether manual or automated, the processes for obtaining the information (numerical data and textual information) were determined. Based on that, we proceeded to establish the contributions of the group that evaluated the required activities, wherewith the brainstorming, the causes, and consequences were immediately detected. When evaluating this action, the Ishikawa diagram was used, obtaining very relevant information and applying statistical tools for continuous improvement such as the check sheet, control diagram, stratified sampling, scatter plot, and the Pareto diagram.

d. With the analysis of times and movements, the activities with the highest risk of generating accidents at work and the presence of diseases of some kind, organ, or upper and lower extremities were shown. Each movement of the workers in the manufacturing areas was analyzed, as well as the periods in which the activities were carried out, to detect unnecessary and inappropriate movements and occupational hazards. In this action, a manual movement counter and electronic period counters were used.

e. When the analysis was developed and the continuous improvement required at each stage of manufacturing was applied, to efficiently obtain the maximum operational performance of the industrial process workers, the operation of the new applied improvement was observed in detail, as a process implementation, allowing to have the right tools and equipment for workers, to increase the levels of productivity and quality of manufactured products. Innovative methods were applied in this action, with a simple automated system for 100 pesos with basic electronic devices, which is being evaluated as a utility model, and for this reason, can't be presented in this text, and found in various commercial centers for the sale of electronic components and located in the city of Mexicali.

f. The sixth and last action was the development of control activities to prevent the problem situations that caused health symptoms in workers in manufacturing areas from reappearing, and with it the generation of errors and defects when changing jobs. inexperienced personnel, or that the operating personnel of industrial processes sometimes worked in an injured way with some type of acute or serious discomfort.

2. Another aspect to be evaluated in great detail in this research was the job training procedure because according to experts on this topic from the city of Mexicali, they consider that a maximum of five out of ten industrial companies invests economic factors and specialized personnel in each industrial process work area. The other half considered before this scientific study, that it was not necessary and on the contrary, they elaborated hiring of trained workers in other industrial plants. Only it did not take into account that even having similar manufacturing areas, some parameters considered to be of a smaller scale in importance index, was an aspect in the negative effect, which was due to not having inadequate working conditions and with it the low indexes of operating performance, and thus decrease in the levels of productivity and quality of the products manufactured. In this stage, tools such as the verification sheet, Ishikawa diagram, and Pareto diagram were used to support the training processes of new personnel, in addition to workers who want to improve their professional development and receive an opportunity to improve their job. and salary compensation. In several industrial plants located in Mexicali, the human resources departments do not have an essential part among their functions. On occasions, the human resources personnel of industries in this city do not follow up on the personnel training procedures, considering that the workers, either from educational institutions in this region of the Mexican Republic, with studies

at a higher level. Professional level. They also receive in industrial companies in this region of the country, people who sometimes without having some type of experience or training obtained, are a risk factor especially for the generation of work activities and the generation of occupational accidents.

3. The detailed analysis of the times and movements was elaborated in this stage with the statistical tools of continuous improvement such as the Ishikawa diagram, verification sheet, control, and dispersion graph and, Pareto diagram. In addition, as already mentioned, in an action of stage 1, the movement counting equipment and special periods were used such as stopwatches with integer and decimal and centesimal values, to achieve greater accuracy of the activities made and thereby determine the most suitable solution actions in each analyzed manufacturing stage. At this stage, a detailed approach was taken of all the movements carried out by each operating personnel of industrial processes, and adapting their skills and qualities to each person. With this, the performance of each worker began to improve, considering the labor well-being of each person. The investigation allowed to show the inefficiency of certain specialized and supervisory engineering people, as well as certain managers, by an evaluation of 10 industries of the aerospace sector located in Mexicali, where their risk premium increased year after year without carrying out any type of investigation. In this scientific study elaborated in the industry that allowed the rigorous analysis, it was observed from the movements of the people of upper and lower extremities, as well as neck, back, and head positions. Also, the routes of each worker in their work areas were evaluated, being the number of steps, size of space between steps, left and right movements of hands, arms, and even fingers.
4. The development of the fourth stage was to evaluate everything that contemplated the working conditions, as well as the relationship of the workers with their superiors as supervisors and managers. As well as the previous stage involved detailed analysis of the times and movements, and with this the specialized engineering staff, elaborate the necessary improvements in developing the automated system's mechanisms that helped to improve the working conditions. This process was carried out by personnel from the evaluated industry and educational institutions in the research area on the subject of ergonomics and working conditions. The development of the improvements was with automated systems mechanisms, to provide comfort to the workers of industrial processes, observing in detail as in the previous stage, the times and movements; to implement the pertinent improvements in each manufacturing step. The continuous improvement processes considered the movements of the fingers, hands, arms, shoulders, legs, and feet; adapting the skills and qualities of each person to each step of manufacturing. With the implementation of the improvements, a better performance was observed on the part of the workers of the industrial processes, which led to an increase in the levels of productivity and quality of manufactured products. Also was made an evaluation of the environmental climate to determine the capacity to make the industrial operations and the comfort of workers and operative yielding of industrial equipment and machinery.

The analysis of the graphs and tables was made in Excel software.

RESULTS

The objective of the investigation made was to determine the industrial activities that required the implementation of continuous improvement with the use of new work methods, to achieve agreements that allowed each person in the manufacturing areas to make their functions adequately and with good cheer. The following sections show the results of the analyzes made, to obtain information that will show the process of industrial activities before and after the scientific study developed.

Experimental Process of Assembly Products

A was made of all the manufacturing steps of a production line called High Tech Assembly, where manufacturing functions of electronic boards used in the autopilot system were elaborated. The principal actions elaborated were the assembly of electronic components on electronic boards, as well as an evaluation of the location of the electronic components in their respective positions on the electronic boards. This action was developed at the beginning of the investigation visually by production operators and with a template connected to an electronic positioning detection system. In the initial process of the scientific study, a template in the form of a table and with four divisions was used as shown in Figure 4. As can be seen in the previous figure, the electronic components of a board were shown in a general way, where at the time of performing the function of evaluating with the template, the workers in periods of eight hours per shift, suffered from fatigue from work. sight, which caused a headache. In the section where the red circle is, there are electronic components damaged by a short circuit developed by electrical overload in an electronic board of industrial equipment. In addition, the operating personnel of these manufacturing areas was sitting on an inappropriate chair and table and with their head, and at the time they were with their head towards the floor, which caused neck and back discomfort. Due to this, workers with experience in this activity attended medical visits within the industrial company where the research was carried out, and sometimes to public or private health institutions outside the evaluated industry. This caused that these people were replaced by inexperienced workers, causing errors and with it defective products which caused the concern of the management and supervisory personnel. With this, an increase was observed in visits to the doctor by the industrial process personnel, both inside and outside the evaluated industrial plant, as well as an increase in defective products and a decrease in the productivity and quality of manufactured products. as shown in Table 1.

Figure 4. Template used in the initial process to detect damaged electronic components

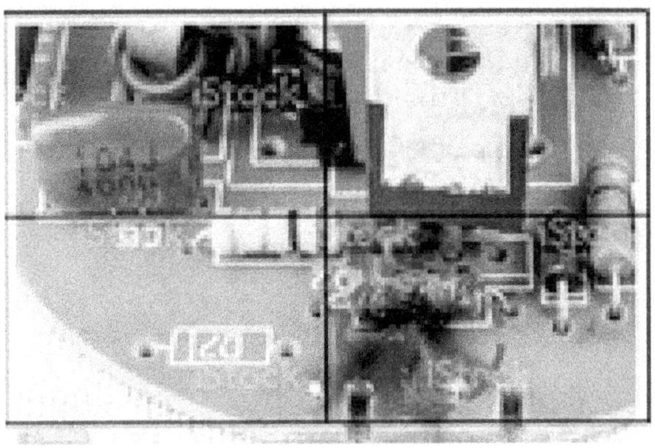

Table 1. Correlation of productive factors and principal health symptoms in the High-Tech Assembly line (2018)

Productive factors, levels	Productivity						Quality					
Health symptoms	L		M		H		L		M		H	
Headache	2	3	4	4	5	5	2	2	3	4	5	5
Arm pain	1	2	2	4	5	5	1	2	3	4	4	5
Back pain	2	2	3	4	4	5	2	2	3	3	4	5
Fingers pain	1	2	3	3	4	5	1	2	3	3	4	5
Hands pain	2	2	3	3	4	5	2	2	3	3	4	5
Neck pain	2	2	3	4	4	5	1	2	3	3	4	5
Shoulder pain	1	2	2	3	4	5	1	2	3	4	5	5
Waist pain		2	3	4	5	5	2	3	3	4	5	5

The table above shows the indices of work stress with the evaluation of productivity and quality parameters of manufactured products, where three levels are observed (low, medium, and high); with the respective pain levels, with 1 being the least discomfort, continuing with 2, 3, 4 and 5, according to color as represented by the pain levels; and as the value increases, the level of pain is more continuous and with greater intensity. In the eight health symptoms, they are observed by levels of pain, according to the types of colors in the three indices (low, medium, and high), which caused work stress in each evaluated manufacturing area. The productivity parameter is indicated that the presence of colors was observed with greater presence starting are blue with 13 occasions, followed by red with 11, orange with 10, yellow with 8, and green with 3. Regarding the evaluation of the quality, the parameter was observed with a greater presence than the yellow color with 12 occasions, followed by the blue and red colors with 11, later the orange color with 10, and the green with 4. The low, medium and high indices represented levels of demand that caused less or greater work stress and therefore less or greater generation of health symptoms in industrial process workers. This analysis showed that the greater the demand in industrial activities, without sometimes having adequate training, tools, equipment, and methods, the generation of health symptoms was greater and the faster they appeared in workers in manufacturing areas, both operating personnel as supervisory and managers. The productivity and quality indices, as well as the pain levels, were obtained from the numerical information obtained with verification sheets, in addition to the analysis with control charts, scatter, Pareto, and Ishikawa diagram. To obtain a solution to this situation problematic, an implementation of a template called GASE matrix was elaborated, as represented in Figure 5 with the evaluation of electronic components located on electronic boards of industrial equipment and manufactured products.

Figure 5. GASE matrix used to evaluate electronic components in electronic boards

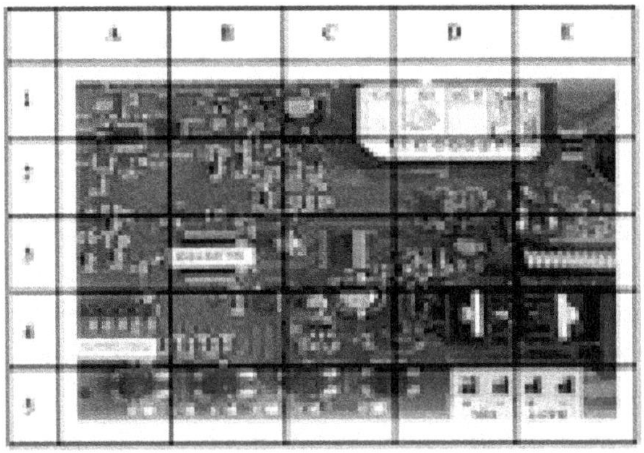

With this matrix, the evaluation of the electronic components located in the electronic boards was made more quickly and efficiently, and with a lesser effect on the health of the workers, without straining the eyes too much and with it the symptoms mentioned in Table 1 With this, a good mood, better performance and increases in 25% the productivity and quality levels of manufactured production the first month after concluded the investigation, and with this were presented fewer health symptoms in the workers of industrial processes.

Table 2. Correlation analysis of labor conditions in High Tech Assembly line (2018)

CONSEQUENCES CAUSES	HA	AP	BP	FP	HP	NP	SP	WP
Lack of training	0.81	0.78	0.83	0.75	0.80	0.84	0.82	0.79
Lack of motivation	0.77	0.83	0.74	0.76	0.80	0.82	0.76	0.78
Repetitive movements	0.79	0.88	0.80	0.74	0.80	0.82	0.84	0.78
Inexpert workers	0.84	0.89	0.77	0.71	0.82	0.79	0.86	0.75
Inadequate methods	0.79	0.85	0.79	0.78	0.77	0.75	0.82	0.83
Inadequate movements	0.87	0.90	0.83	0.83	0.73	0.72	0.79	0.81
Inadequate improvements	0.84	0.86	0.81	0.77	0.79	0.79	0.81	0.80
Inadequate tools and equipment	0.83	0.88	0.79	0.75	0.83	0.82	0.84	0.85
Bad relations with managers and supervision personnel	0.81	0.84	0.82	0.79	0.79	0.86	0.80	0.82

HA. Headache, AP. Arms pain, BP. Back pain, FP. Finger pain, HP. Hans pain,
NP. Neck pain, SP. Shoulder pain, WP. Wais pain

The table above shows the correlation of factors of working conditions, where levels with a range of 0.70 to 0.90 are observed, indicating that in most of the cases evaluated, the causes mentioned in Table 2 were those that generated the effects of illustrated health symptoms. This represents that in most of the cases before the investigation, acute and severe discomfort originated, in all the sections of the body analyzed, which caused a low operating performance and with it a decrease in the productivity and quality indexes of the products. manufactured products.

Analysis Using Continuous Improvement

To have a good understanding of the events that occurred, analyzes were carried out with the continuous improvement tools mentioned above, obtaining in each evaluation relevant information to determine the required improvements that should have been implemented, once it was observed how the activities are developed, showing the causes and consequences in the High-Tech Assembly line 1. To start the research analysis, the Ishikawa diagram was used with which, to determine the main causes and consequences and quickly consider the development of actions that will support the implementation of relevant improvements in each manufacturing area. Figure 6 represents a process mentioning the six factors that are linked to their respective causes in the form of a fish diagram, wherein the end of a problematic situation is indicated as part of one of several consequences of an industrial process. This is why each evaluation is in great detail to determine the greatest number of aspects involved that generate some type of anomaly and with it uncomfortable situations for workers such as those presented in this investigation regarding the working conditions of the industrial company evaluated.

Figure 6. Ishikawa diagram used in the analysis of labor conditions

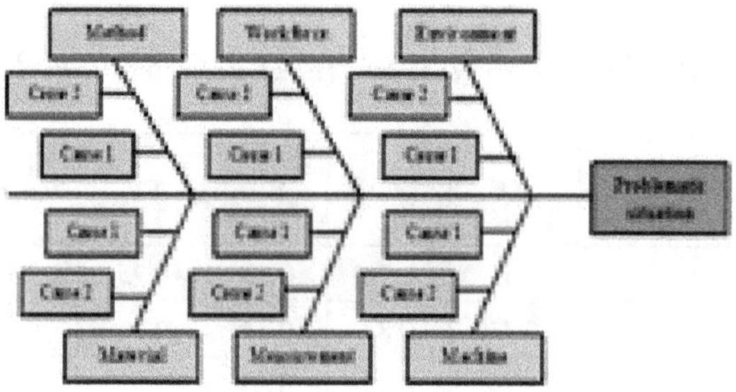

In a problematic situation like the one shown in the previous figure, more than two causes can be represented, and the most important ones considered, as well as analyzing any type of parameter through an evaluation with a histogram, as shown in Figure 9, illustrated in the form of bars with a line to follow the maximum levels of the indices represented by the bars. This generated the context in Figure 9, with which it was visualized that the quality indices were detected in percentage levels with the year 2018, observing that it increased as the investigation period began in January with the number 1 and so on. until the number 12 represented by December 2018 is illustrated. The histogram of Figure 7 shows the 58% as an initial value and begins to increase until reaching its maximum of 76%, and, from that value, generates a decrease to the value of 52%, forming with the linear tracking like a bell. The importance of using the Pareto chart in this research was to determine in which months, either separately or jointly between months, to find possible solutions immediately and efficiently. The same happened in Figure 8, only that the initial value of 69% being for January until reaching the maximum of 83% and from then on illustrating the decrease to 68%. These values are higher than those in graph 9, as they represent an evaluation of the year 2019, which was when the improvements that helped to increase both the operational performance of the workers and the productivity and quality indices were already implemented.

Figure 7. Quality analysis (2018) using a histogram in high tech assembly line

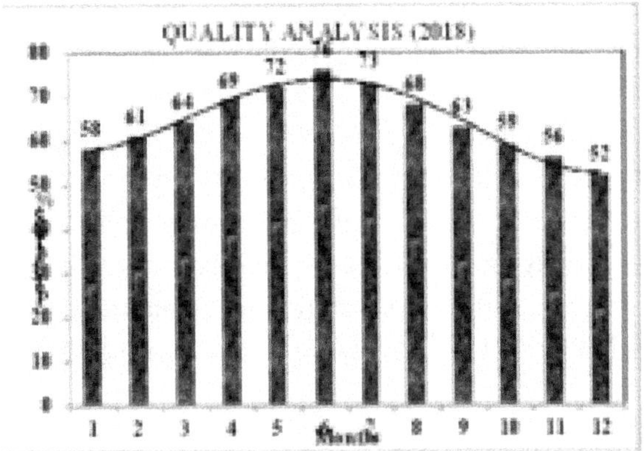

Figure 8. Quality analysis (2019) using a histogram in high tech assembly line

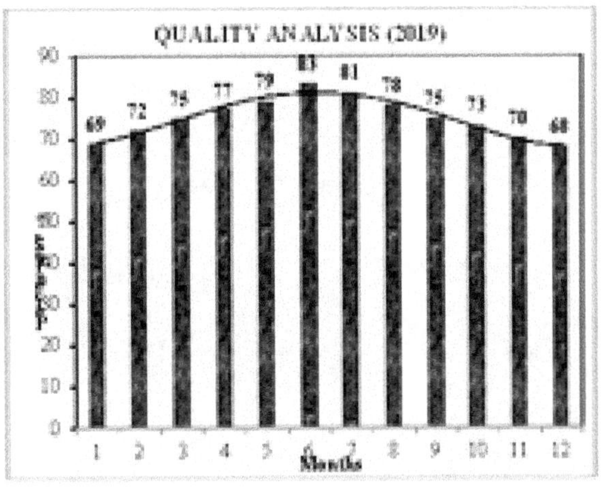

Once the quality analysis had been prepared with the statistical tool called a histogram, we proceeded to evaluate the monthly production levels of 2018 and 2019, being the monthly average of production established by the evaluated industrial company, according to human resources, equipment, and industrial machinery required in manufacturing areas. These are illustrated in Figures 9 (2018) and 10 (2019), where relevant information was observed that indicated a similar bell-shaped follow-up, such as graphs 9 and 10. In Figure 11, the trend that begins from the 15,500 manufactured products that are automated systems to the autopilot system, being a very essential part of an aircraft. Once the analysis process for January started, the subsequent months where it was detected that the maximum production was in August with 24,600, and from there begin to decrease until December with 17,300 products manufactured. This analysis process was with another statistical tool called the control chart. Figure 10, which represents the year 2019, indicates the same process as Figure 9, with which a greater amount of the production indices is observed, due to the improvements made in 2018. The amount of initial production in January 2019 was 18,800, continuing in monthly increases until reaching the maximum production of 28,400, which had a trend that exceeded 30,000 products manufactured in August 2020, where only comparative analyzes of production levels were made, quality, production, and working conditions for 2020, being better every year. Subsequently, production began to reduce until reaching 18,500 manufactured products in the month. This analysis was very useful to evaluate the possible causes presented that determined the indices of production, productivity, and quality of manufactured products. This control chart created at the beginning of the 20th century has been very useful to understand the monitoring of the aforementioned indices and to know the possible problematic situations that may arise in any industrial activity. The red line with black points represents the production level and the black with red points the number of defects, being around 7% in 2018 and 4% in 2019 for the improvements.

Figure 9. Evaluation with productivity control graph (2018)

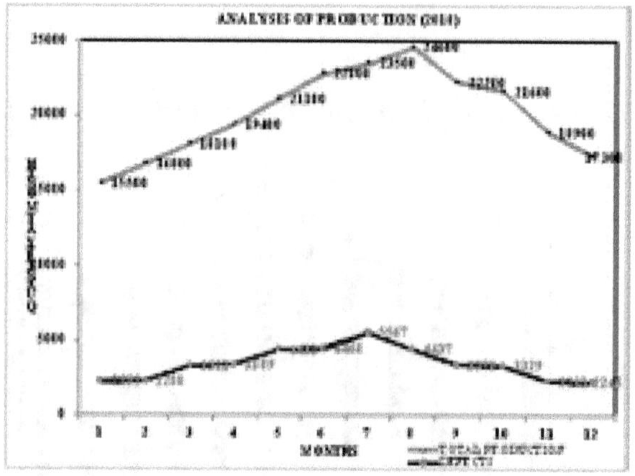

Figure 10. Evaluation with productivity control graph (2098)

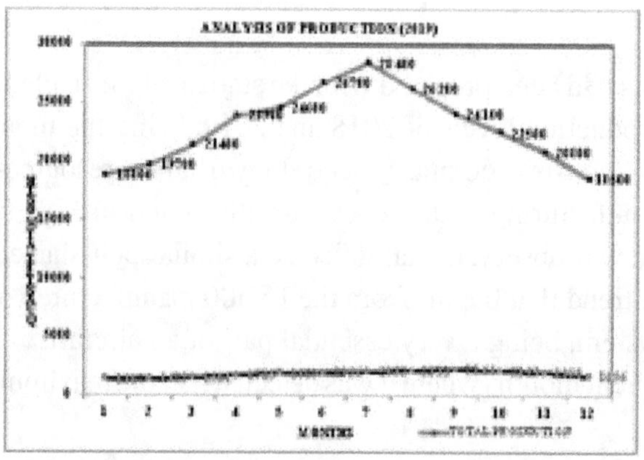

The elaboration of analysis with statistical tools was very useful in understanding the events of the evaluated industry, considering a fundamental aspect of the evaluation with the statistical tool of scatter diagram because based on this analysis information was obtained from the cases that were presented in the various steps of manufacturing. Also, was presented a trend of the cases evaluated and the obedience of a mathematical equation with which the production, productivity, and quality indices can be estimated in the short, medium, or long term, in addition, to be able to have the possibility of recovering numerical values that can be lost due to failures in programming systems or human errors. The analysis of the relationship of two variables shown in figures 11 shows a trend similar to the figure of a bell and in Figure 12 a trend of increase similar to a linear one was observed, with which in both graphs, the line was a trend and the mathematical equation based on a sixth-degree polynomial formula, being the one closest to the trend of the evaluated data of an industrial process of the High-Tech Assembly line 1. The evaluations indicated the productivity indices for the graphs analyzed, with percentage indices for each monthly period of the year 2018 in Figure 11, observing increases and decreases at the annual level, and 2019 in Figure 12 illustrated throughout the analysis of increases until reaching the last value of December 2019 and being higher than 2018, due to the implementation of the improvements developed in 2018. The estimation process served to consider the number of workers in the industrial process. trial evaluated and for other stages of the manufacturing areas, in addition to the fact that due to a human error of a supervisor some numerical data were lost that were recovered based on the mathematical equation obtained with this scatter diagram and said mathematical equation was improved obtaining the two mathematical equations as expressed below:

$y = 0.0275x^6 + 0.478x^5 - 0.8654x^4 + 6.578x^3 - 25.988x^2 + 49.677x + 22.344$

for 2018 and

$y = -0.00224x^6 + 0.08141x^5 - 1.07899x^4 + 8.23146x^3 - 29.14561x^2 + 38.67563x + 35.76893$

for 2019.

Figure 11. Analysis of productivity in High Tech Assembly 1 (2018)

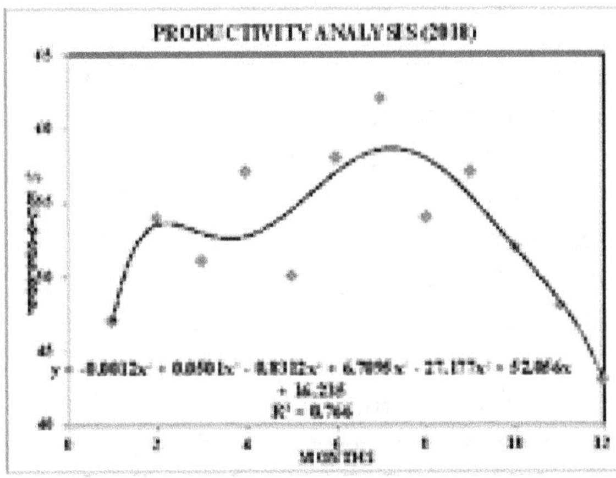

Figure 12. Analysis of productivity in High Tech Assembly 1 (2019)

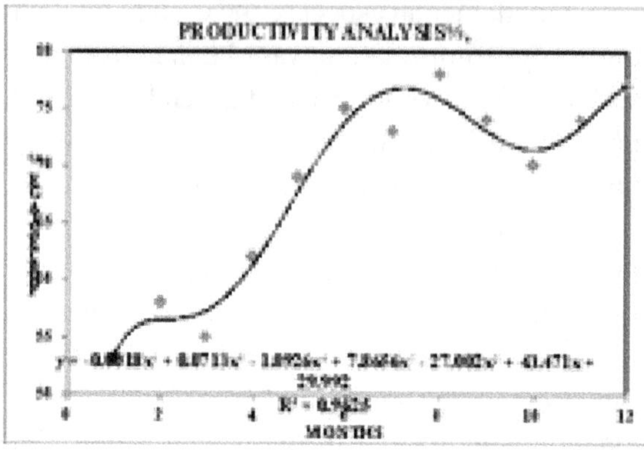

For the study of times and movements, each industrial activity was analyzed to have a better understanding of the functions, and thus evaluate each action of each required industrial operation. The industrial operations with the highest incidence in the generation of defective products and the highest occurrence of work accidents were evaluated. In each industrial operation where the activity was manual, how each movement was made by the workers and the periods in which each function was performed were observed in great detail. This helps to detect inappropriate and repetitive movements quickly and with greater precision, which caused discomfort no matter how minimal and sometimes severe damage. From this meticulous analysis, relevant information was obtained to detect major or minor anomalies that caused discomfort in the areas of the body mentioned above and that were affected by the functions of the industrial processes of the industrial company evaluated. The analyzes were made based on the fundamental movements called Therbligs defined by the Gilbreth family in joint with the philosophy of Frederick Winslow Taylor in the year 1950, which is shown in Table 3, evaluating the function of welding electronic components in various positions of electronic boards of a section of used equipment. in aircraft. The actions evaluated are shown below:

1. Movement 1. Place the electronic board with the right hand on a base to carry out the welding process in a standard period of 40 seconds.
2. Movement 2. Take the soldering iron with a temperature close to 100 ° C, with the right hand, with a standard period of 20 seconds.
3. Movement 3. Take the electronic component with the left hand and attach it to the base where the electronic board is placed, with a standard period of 30 seconds.
4. Movement 4. Was made the welding process with both hands, with a standard period of 30 seconds.

Table 3 shows an average of industrial operations in January 2018 with four different people in each stage of the week of the mentioned month, representing in the said table a total average.

Table 3. Analysis of times and activity movements stage 1 of High Tech Assembly 1 manufacturing (2018)

Movements / Period of time	Movement 1				Movement 2				Movement 3				Movement 4			
Calculation of standard time (CTE), seconds	40				20				30				30			
Real time calculation (CTR), seconds	**P1**	**P2**	**P3**	**P4**	**P1**	**P2**	**P3**	**P4**	**P1**	**P2**	**P3**	**P4**	**P1**	**P2**	**P3**	**P4**
	53	58	55	51	29	32	26	27	36	39	37	41	44	47	49	45
Difference of CTE and CTR	**P1**	**P2**	**P3**	**P4**	**P1**	**P2**	**P3**	**P4**	**P1**	**P2**	**P3**	**P4**	**P1**	**P2**	**P3**	**P4**
	-13	-18	-15	-11	-9	-12	-6	-7	-6	-9	-7	-11	-14	-17	-19	-15

P1. Person 1, P2. Person 2, P3. Person 3, P4. Person 4

The table above shows the evaluation of times and movements where both the standard times provided by specialized personnel of the industrial company evaluated were observed, as well as the times obtained from the experimentation events of the research developed, together with the difference of the periods times obtained from the four movements of the electronic component welding operation. This analysis was prepared in 2018, showing the differences between standard and real times, and by 2019, those periods of the four movements analyzed had already been improved.

Evaluation of Industrial Processes with Schematic Model

In this investigation, various types of schematic models were developed, where the parameters involved in each analysis were evaluated to detect the maximum amount of anomalies that would allow knowing in greater detail what happened at the beginning of the scientific study in 2018. One of the evaluations made, was the detection of the six main causes that caused occupational risks in the High Tech 1 line, as shown in Figure 13, the lack of motivation that caused distraction of operating personnel and low spirits were represented as the first cause. to perform their functions. The second cause detected was the use of the wrong or defective tool in industrial activity, causing discomfort in some areas of the human body, followed by the third cause with the use of the wrong method, causing inadequate functions that led to acute health symptoms and serious in workers. The fourth cause was having inexperienced personnel who were busy in situations when experienced workers suffered from some acute or serious discomfort and had to be disabled for some time. The fifth cause was generated by inappropriate and repetitive movements that caused discomfort and pain to the workers when they elaborated an overstrain of their functions and originated defective products. The sixth cause was due to the bad labor relationship that generated stress in the operating personnel of the manufacturing areas and with it, the distraction of the workers that caused inefficient operations and with it errors and defective products.

Figure 13. Analysis of six principal causes in labor risks (2018)

Table 4. Evaluation of six principal causes and relevant factors (2018)

CAUSES / FACTORS	LM	WDT	IM	IW	IRM	BLR
Inexpert manager and supervisor	X	X	X	X	X	X
Lack of training	X	X			X	X
Inadequate industrial processes	X		X		X	
Low salary	X					X
Inadequate production logistic	X	X	X		X	

LM. Lack of motivation, WDT. Wrong and defective tool, IM. Inadequate method, IW. Inexpert workers, IRM. Inadequate and repetitive movements, BLR. Bad labor relation.

Table 4 represents an evaluation of the six main causes and the five most relevant factors that caused the causes, observed with the letter X, as the relationship of the evaluated parameters. In the first relationship, it is indicated that the inexperience of the managerial and supervisory areas can cause a lack of motivation in the operational personnel of the manufacturing areas, as well as the use of wrong or defective tools, in addition to the inappropriate use of a method for the elaboration. of industrial activities. It was also observed that inexperienced management and supervisory personnel selected unsuitable workers for various jobs without evaluating their skills and qualities. In addition, it was detected that they were not interested in evaluating the inappropriate and repetitive movements that generated discomfort in industrial process workers and caused a bad relationship with their operating personnel.

New Model to Avoid Work Risks

Labor well-being is of great importance in any industrial activity, so it is relevant to evaluate all the parameters involved in working conditions. Various factors can alter working conditions, causing discomfort in workers in manufacturing areas, so their operational performance is not adequate. The aspect of the conduct of a person is a fundamental part of the development of industrial activities, labor relations, and support to the operating personnel of industrial processes. Sometimes some people have excellent training in professional institutions of the Mexican Republic or abroad, having a diversity of knowledge that applies to a great extent in the manufacturing processes in industrial companies, but they do not have the capacity for an excellent labor relationship. superior to their co-workers or even their bosses for feeling that they have more knowledge than they. What is very relevant for management, specialized, and supervisory personnel is to have an optimal awareness and excellent labor relations, which indicate an adequate coexistence, in addition to recognizing the aptitudes and abilities of their operational personnel, who is the one who supports them. in your results. These factors were observed in the evaluated industrial plant and according to specialists on the subject of Mexicali, who have prepared evaluations in other industries located in the city of Mexicali, confirm this aspect that has not been considered, leading to a decrease in the operating performance of the workers and the productivity and quality indices of the manufactured products or services provided. Based on this, once the investigation was carried out and certain situations of the aforementioned were observed, the pertinent improvements and the development of a new model to have efficient working conditions for optimal labor well-being were made. The model is represented in Figure 14, with six very relevant factors that are explained below:

a) Improvement in the organization. It is of great relevance to consider having an adequate organization in the manufacturing areas on which the industrial development of every industrial company depends, to develop the activities with the appropriate processes, as well as with the tools and an optimal work environment in the which is obtained the maximum operational performance of the workers.

b) Constant communication. The management, specialized and supervisory personnel must be constantly in contact to know the concerns of the workers in the manufacturing areas, as well as their discomforts, and take actions that support the rapid solution.

c) Promotion programs. Develop programs in which the operational personnel of industrial processes, constantly continue to carry out training that improves their skills and abilities and is promoted to new or other jobs with better salaries.

d) Professional development. It is of great importance to continue developing professionally the workers of industrial companies, to reinforce their knowledge by having a professional school program in the industries, with which the operating personnel of any work area, complete a professional career and also fulfill some dream that had been touched in a particular way.

e) Sentimental aspects. This factor should be considered so that the management, specialized and supervisory personnel are aware of the segmental situations that people go through, because when workers in manufacturing areas are considered in this way, they will feel that they are part of the Industrial company where they work and once their situation is solved they will have optimal performance.

f) Health habits. Every industrial company must have a program of health habits that includes both eating habits and personal hygiene, to avoid any health symptoms that lead to serious consequences in workers.

Figure 14. Improvements to well-being labor (2019)

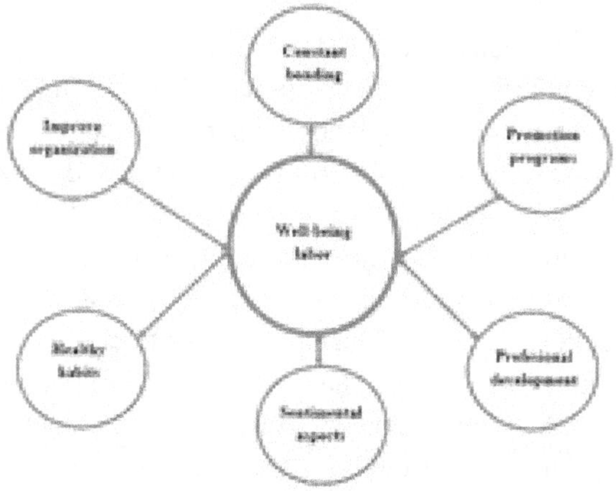

Evaluation of Environmental Climate

This factor was very important to evaluate the operative yielding of workers of manufacturing areas and industrial equipment and machinery, observing the functionality in percentage in Table 5.

Table 5. Evaluation of environmental climate (2018-2019)

CLIMATIC FACTORS	2018			2019		
EVENTS	T_1	T_2	T_3	RH_1	RH_2	RH_3
Discomfort to develop industrial activities	X			X		
Presenting low yielding of operability of industrial equipment and machinery	X			X		
Inconvenience and low level		X			X	
Presenting some electrical o mechanical failures in industrial equipment and machinery		X			X	
Headache and lack of elaboration of industrial activities			X			X
Some parts of industrial equipment and machinery not work			X			X
Need for medical assistance			X			X
Some industrial equipment and machinery does not work totally			X			X

T_1. Ranges of temperature from 0 °C to 15 °C, T_2. Ranges of temperature from 16 °C to 30 °C, T_3. Ranges of temperature from 31 °C to 45 °C

RH_1. Ranges of relative humidity from 30% to 45%, RH_2. Ranges of relative humidity from 46% to 60%, RH_3. Ranges of relative humidity from 61% to 75%.

In Table 5, it showed the evaluation of environmental climate that was relevant in the operative yielding of workers and industrial equipment and machinery. This table illustrates four steps of events presented in the industrial plant evaluated in Mexicali, representing in each step the consequences of the variations of climatic factors, being in step 3 a step 4 the major problematic situations, because was necessary to stop the industrial processes and generate low indexes of productivity and quality of manufactured products. In steps 1 and step 2, was presented the low level of problematic situations. With this can observe the causes of the lack of fulfillment of production goals

CONCLUSION

The evaluation of working conditions is of great importance to maintain the labor well-being of workers, especially in manufacturing areas, where the greatest amount of occupational hazards is generated. The elaboration of activities of industrial processes of the operative personnel has originated in the last ten an increase in the occurrence of work accidents, where the directive, management, and supervisory personnel. These personnel are constantly concerned because due, to this occurrence, the goals are not met and, in addition, large payments are made for risk premiums to Mexican health institutions. In the elaboration of the investigation made, relevant information was obtained that was used to achieve a good understanding of what was happening in each stage of the processes of the High-Tech Assembly 1 line, and develop the necessary improvements that helped improve working conditions. Having an optimal performance of the industrial operations of the evaluated company, generated an efficient operating performance, with which it was possible to meet the production goals and achieve increases in the productivity and quality indexes of the manufactured products. The use of various statistical tools to make the analysis contributed to evaluating all the manufacturing stages of the High-Tech Assembly 1 line, where the causes and consequences of what happened were observed in each industrial process and to develop the required actions quickly and efficiently. Very meticulous evaluations were made and information was obtained on each movement and period, obtaining from the specialized personnel who carried out experimental tests, the standard times. These temporary periods were provided to the supervisory personnel, to make each industrial process more efficient. In addition to the aforementioned on the part of the supervisory personnel, they adequately made a connection with the management and human resources of the industrial company evaluated, to have the necessary operational personnel in each stage of manufacturing, according to their skills and qualities. Another important aspect of supervisory personnel, supported largely by managers and continuous improvement specialists, was inspecting that each function of the industrial processes was made.

REFERENCES

Aalmo, G., Magagnotti, N., & Spinelli, R. (2016). Forest workers and steep terrain winching: The impact of environmental and anthropometric parameters on performance. *Croatian Journal of Forest Engineering*, *37*(1), 97–105.

Ahola, K., Salminen, S., Toppinen, S., Koskinen, A., & Vaananen, A. (2013). Occupational burnout and severe injuries: An eight-year prospective cohort study among finnish forest industry workers. *Journal of Occupational Health*, *55*(6), 450–457. doi:10.1539/joh.13-0021-OA PMID:24162145

Barbosa, R., Fiedler, N., Do Carmo, C., Minette, L., & Silva, E. (2014). Analysis of posture in semi-mechanized forest harvesting in steep areas. *Revista Arvore*, *38*(4), 733–738.

Chandra, A., Chandna, P., Deswal, S., & Kumar, R. (2009). Ergonomics in the Office Environment: A Review. *Proceedings of World Academy of Science: Engineering & Technology, 51*(1), 913-919.

De Britto, P., Da Silva, E., Lopes, E., De, E., & Fiedler, N. (2014). Biomechanical evaluation in workers of different statures at planting and fertilizing forest activities. *Forest Sciences*, *42*(102), 191–196.

Denbeigh, K., Slot, T., & Dumas, G. (2013). Wrist postures and forces in tree planters during three tree unloading conditions. *Ergonomics, 56*(10), 1599–1607.

Drury, C. (2010). Global quality: Linking ergonomics and production. *International Journal of Production Research*, *38*(2), 4007–4018.

Harshal, T. (2017). Historical Milestones of Ergonomics: From Ancient Human to Modern Human. *Journal of Economics*, *7*(4), 65–78.

INDEX-Mexicali. (2020). *Reporte de empresas de manufactura de Mexicali, 52*. Author.

Laschi, A., Marchi, E., Foderi, C., & Neri, F. (2016). *Identifying causes, dynamics and consequences of Ley Federal del Trabajo (LFT) (2019) "Diario Oficial de la Federación (DOF) de México. Regulaciones de condiciones laborales*. STPS-SSA.

Norma NOM-015-STPS-2001 (2001) "Condiciones térmicas elevadas o abatidas-Condiciones de seguridad e higiene".

Norma NOM-024-STPS-2001 (2001) "Vibraciones-Condiciones de seguridad e higiene en los centros de trabajo".

Norma NOM-025-STPS-2008 (2008) "Condiciones de iluminación en los centros de trabajo".

OHSAS 18000 (2007) "Gestión de la Seguridad y Salud Ocupacional".

Spinelli, R., Aminti, G., & De Francesco, F. (2017). Postural risk assessment of mechanized firewood processing. *Ergonomics*, *60*(3), 375–383. doi:10.1080/00140139.2016.1172738 PMID:27215281

Wilson, J., Ryan, B., Schock AFerreira, P., Smith, S., & Pitsopoulos, J. (2009). Understanding safety and production risks in rail engineering planning and protection. *Ergonomics Journal*, *52*(1), 774–790. doi:10.1080/00140130802642211 PMID:19562589

Chapter 8
Model for Determination of Musculoskeletal Disorder Cost/Benefit:
Base for Strategy for Implementation of a Preventive DME Program for a Company

Juan Alberto Castillo Martinez
Universidad del Rosario, Colombia

Andres Felipe Garcia S.
Universidad del Rosario, Colombia

ABSTRACT

It is generally considered that the costs related to musculoskeletal disorders (MSDs) stem from absenteeism, medical expenses, reduced productivity, and quality of life. To estimate the costs associated with MSDs in organizations and thus determine the benefits for a company of implementing an effective and sustainable prevention program, it is necessary to consider the need to know the current and future prevalence of MSDs as well as to understand whether these data vary according to the economic sector, geographic location, and demographic aspects. It is also necessary to understand whether there are comorbidities associated with MSDs as well as the direct and indirect impacts in terms of the productive and work capacity of organizations and individuals. In the development of this study, the authors wanted to generate an analysis tool to estimate the incidence of MSDs and their economic costs, which also serves as a baseline to evaluate the possible benefits derived from prevention programs for this type of work-related disease.

DOI: 10.4018/978-1-7998-7396-9.ch008

I. INTRODUCTION

Musculoskeletal disorders (MSDs) of the upper limb and back comprise a wide range of inflammatory, degenerative diseases and disorders that cause pain and functional impairment of the hand/wrist, elbow, shoulder, neck and back, which have a significant impact on the productivity of individuals and companies, while affecting social security systems, industrial development policies and career paths of labor-active individuals.

Musculoskeletal Disorders (MSD) is the term used to refer to the set of injuries in muscles, tendons or nerves that are related to the development of physical activities at work, such as problems in the locomotor system, muscles, tendons, ligaments, and nerves (WHO, 2004; Institute for Work & Health, 2005). The literature has shown that the development of this set of injuries and symptoms is related to the ergonomic characteristics of workstations, poor posture, fast work pace, repetitive movements, and exposure to vibration. MSDs are currently the largest category of work-related diseases, constituting just over one-third of all occupational diseases reported in the United States, the Nordic countries and Japan, and representing the most common cause of work absenteeism or work disability in the United States, Canada, Finland, Sweden, and England (Punnett and Wegman, 2004).

Estimating the overall economic burden and total costs associated with MSDs in companies requires the use of a variety of data sources. The analysis of the sources of information that can contribute to identify the internal burden in the company, the costs associated with the worker, the productivity losses for the worker and for the company, should be defined in an analysis model that is flexible enough to integrate the specific variables by economic sector, by geographic location and by characteristics and complexities of the tasks involved in the generation of MSDs.

The incidence and severity of these occupational disorders have a significant impact on the productivity of workers through a reduction in their production capacity and, in more serious cases, through absence from the workplace. Musculoskeletal disorders have high direct and indirect costs, as well as long-term effects on the quality of life of the people who suffer from them. Thus, this type of accident constitutes a risk factor that affects the cost structure of firms, which is reflected in an increase in economic compensation, loss of productivity, increase in medical risk insurance rates, high worker turnover, and even adverse effects on labor relations (Punnett, 2000).

Comparative studies of the incidence of MSDs in different regions have found that there is less exposure in more economically developed countries, where the implementation of occupational safety, prevention and health practices is stronger. In contrast, in developing countries there is lower reporting of occupational diseases and a higher presence of misdiagnosis or no diagnosis (Takala et. al., 2017).

For the estimation of the economic cost, international information sources such as the World Labor Organization (ILO) and the World Health Organization (WHO), local employment figures, occupational burden, reported accidents, accidents, disability, and death due to occupational diseases reported at work and surveys on self-reported occupational diseases and injuries are considered. The costs associated with this type of occupational disease are expressed not only in the productivity capacity of workers and costs that companies face, but also constitute a public health problem that can generate a significant burden on the social security system. There is evidence that in most countries in the world, the number of deaths caused by occupational diseases is ten times higher than the number of deaths caused by occupational accidents (Takala et. al., 2017), hence the importance of making a complete assessment of this type of diseases.

In the estimation of costs associated with DME, several works have been developed, among them, those of Asay GRB, Roy K, Lang JE, Payne RL, Howard DH. Absenteeism and Employer Costs Associated with Chronic Diseases and Health Risk Factors in the US Workforce. In this work, a method was presented that includes the study variables useful for estimating individual and organizational productivity loss costs.

Include the costs for presenteeism and absenteeism that make it possible to define the economic burden. It should also be considered that for the estimation of health-related costs and productivity losses, several data collection tools have been developed (HPQ-Select (IBI, 2014), Health and Work Performance Questionnaire; IBI's Absence Cost Estimator (ACE), among others).

Such tools have been created based on the identification of the following variables:

1. Absences due to sick days and wage replacements.
2. Workers' compensation medical payments, lost workdays, and wage replacements
3. Short-term disability (STD) with lost workdays and wage replacements
4. Long-term disability (LTI) with lost workdays and wage replacements
5. Non-concurrent absences due to family medical illness (FME) Medical and pharmaceutical claim costs
6. Presenteeism (decreased work performance due to injury or illness)
7. Productivity loss charges for lost productive time
8. Paid sick days
9. Unpaid sick days
10. Workers' compensation for lost workdays
11. Short-term disability and lost workdays
12. Long-term disability and lost workdays

Generally, these variables are included in the following 3 main methods of analysis:

1. salary conversion methods, which use survey responses and wage information to estimate productivity loss; the simple version is "the human capital approach (HCA)".
2. Introspective methods, which use survey responses as the basis for thought experiments to give firms an idea of the magnitude of their productivity loss; and
3. Firm-level methods that attempt to monetize productivity losses based on the cost of countermeasures used to address absenteeism and presenteeism.

From a statistical perspective, it is proposed in this study to perform a series of estimations based on regression analysis to make forecasts associated with the costs of DME. First, we estimate the effect of each risk factor approximated from socioeconomic variables of workers, region, and sector on the costs of DME. In turn, this allows adjusting the costs associated with absenteeism as the factors that determine the risk profile of occurrence of this type of incident are agreed upon.

The risk profile of workers is determined to a large degree by the economic sector in which they work. For example, according to Punnet and Wegman (2004), workers at higher risk of MSDs are employed in sectors related to air transport, mining, food processing, leather tanning, medical centers (nursing), and heavy and light industry (vehicles, furniture, household appliances, electrical and electronic products, textiles, clothing, and footwear).

Other labor-intensive activities such as office work, janitorial work, and industrial inspection are more associated with upper extremity MSDs, while back and lower extremity disorders occur more in truck drivers, airplane baggage handlers, warehouse workers, construction workers, nurses, and other occupations involving patient care, crane operators, and large vehicles. Estimating the economic cost of MSDs is a complex task that involves significant statistical challenges. First, there is underreporting of cases for which no diagnoses exist, so both direct and indirect costs tend to be underestimated. A study by IWH (1997) estimates that only 29% of workers who said they had experienced MSD-related symptoms such as neck or arm pain related to their work activities had consulted a professional, and most of those who had these conditions had not mentioned it to their employer or company for various reasons.

Secondly, a small proportion of health professionals still do not recognize MSDs as a real health problem, which increases under-reporting, and consequently, under-formulation and under-treatment. On the other hand, it is possible to say that there is a lack of information about SMD. There is currently a lack of research on the subject, which means that the estimation of the costs associated with these disorders is still unclear and leads to erroneous prescribing and a lack of a common language to refer to these diseases (divergence between names and classifications for this group of disorders).

All this makes it more difficult to approximate the real number of conditions and therefore their cost (Institute for Work & Health, 2005). In this context, Amell and Kumar (2002) argue that in addition to the problem of under-reporting, it is observed that not all reported cases are compensated, e.g., in Canada only 41% of reported cases received some form of compensation. In a simplified cost analysis model, MSDs can be considered to have both direct and indirect economic costs. Direct costs include those associated with the care of the disease, such as hospital care costs, medication costs and payment of health professionals and other care providers; while indirect costs refer to the loss of productivity, the value of economic output lost due to the disease or disability, and the secondary effects on the quality of life of workers.

In this context, a study developed by Health Institute of Canada estimates the economic burden of illness, disability, and premature death due to these types of diseases, finding that the annual direct and indirect costs total around 17.8 billion (Canadian dollars), only lower than costs in addition, this study argues that an important part of the costs associated with MSDs are due to the long-term disability that it can cause.

Unfortunately, these types of studies are rare in developing countries, particularly in the case of Colombia. Even the evidence exists for developing countries cannot be directly extrapolated to other countries consequently in the difference between legal criteria and the compensation of the same disease; specifically, there is a high divergence of the diseases that are considered as work-related in each country, in general, the number of diseases recognized as work-related depend on the development of the country, the political commitment and the financial capacity of the same (Takala et. al., 2017).

These factors make it interesting to deepen the knowledge of this type of diseases at work for the case of Colombia. In addition, the high degree of labor informality in the country, plays an important role since many of the informal workers do not have access to health services and the informality in the contractual work relationships also represents a barrier in the recognition of work-related diseases. According to Valbuena (2017), MSDs are the main work-related diseases presented by workers in Colombia, as in other countries in the world, which has important consequences on economic development and productivity. Given these two situations, statistical information on MSDs is only available for a small fraction of the population: formal workers.

In a more specific exercise, Quintana and Pawlowitz (1999) study direct medical costs, which they model through a Poisson-type model specification with incident frequency as the reference variable based on information from a used clothing sorting company for the period 1989-1997. The construction of the cost variable considers shoulder diseases or disorders such as rotator cuff tendinitis, bicipital tendinitis, tendon tears, bursitis, prolonged shoulder muscle pain, and nerve-related disorders, in addition to specific forearm tendon and tendon sheath disorders, along with carpal tunnel syndrome. As a result, this study identifies that MSDs are associated with risk factors such as repetition, duration, recovery, strength, and awkward limb postures.

For his part, Ahlberg (2014) studies the economic costs of DME for the case of Sweden, considering both direct and indirect costs. The calculation of direct costs is based on the prevalence approach, estimating the economic burden of the health condition for the year 2012. For its part, the calculation of indirect costs is based on the incidence approach, according to which it is costs are calculated from the year of retirement and thereafter are discounted until the occurrence of death. For the valuation of resources, the "top-down" approach is used, considering the average value of the variables included.

For the estimation of direct costs, resources related to outpatient care, inpatient care and associated drugs were considered. In the first case, costs were calculated based on statistics from the Skåne Region together with published data from the Swedish Association of Local Authorities and Regions (SKL). In the second case, published statistics from NBHW and SKL's cost per patient (KPP) database were used. And for associated drugs, published data from the NBHW report on pharmaceutical costs for 2012 are considered.

As for indirect costs, reduced work capacity (or lost productivity) as well as costs associated with premature death were considered. In the first case, taking into consideration that the health condition is the main cause of sick leave or absence due to illness, sick compensation, and activity (SA), data from the Swedish Social Insurance Agency (SSIA) were used. And for the second case, productivity costs up to retirement age (65 years) and mortality and life table data for 2012 were used. The value of lost working years was calculated using data from the Labor Force Survey (AKU, equivalent to household surveys).

Punnett (2000) studied the costs of MSDs in the case of the automotive manufacturing industry in the United States. This industry is particularly sensitive to this type of work-related diseases as the inadequate application of ergonomic principles in the design of workstations significantly increases risk factors and has adverse consequences for the health and safety of workers. This research differentiates between financial and non-financial costs.

As regards the first financial costs, the uncompensated medical costs are: loss of working time, loss of future income (opportunity costs), loss of job security, and professional performance. Non-financial costs include the economic valuation of factors such as pain, family relationships, social relationships, and recreational activities, among others. This study considered data from 5 companies for a period of 10 years, where the MSDs reported by the medical units of the companies are observed, from which an underreporting of 60% of the cases is estimated.

Davis et. al. (2007) conducted an industry-wide study for Ohio (United States) in which age was a crucial risk factor. In this analysis, the authors used data from claims submitted to The Ohio Bureau of Workers' Compensation (OBWC) for the period 1999-2004. Cost calculations considered sectoral disaggregation and age, and included medical costs, treatment costs, indemnity payments, number of days lost, and percentage of high-cost medical procedures. Regarding the risk profile, it was found that 55% of MSD claims appear in the age range 25-44 years and the number of claims for different types of these injuries follow an inverse U-shaped behavior during the life cycle.

Were found between industries, which evidences the existence of industry-specific risk factors; in particular, the warehousing services sector shows the highest increase in DME costs. Mirelman (2016) conducted a cost-effectiveness analysis for a selection of successful public policy cases. The results obtained, show that great advances in health have been achieved through programs that represent good value for money. However, it is not always possible to perform this type of exercise since interventions, e.g., at the sectoral level, that include access to care or that provide resources directly (e.g., cash transfers), present difficulties in estimating standard measures of cost-effectiveness. Therefore, estimation of efficiency losses and representation of scale is only possible through modeling based on assumptions that are not always realistic. In practice, it is usual to take as a reference the income level (GDP per capita) of the countries, a benchmark for comparing magnitudes.

Amell and Kumar (2002) review studies on the design of strategies for the prevention of MSDs. In this review, they find that at the plant or company level, the evidence suggests that prevention attempts have been especially due to a lack of knowledge of the problem. To carry out these strategies, the authors suggest that a multidisciplinary group including engineers, psychologists and specialists in ergonomics should oversee designing an appropriate and healthy workspace. For which, three different levels of Prevention and/or Treatment should be considered:

1. prevention of injuries before their manifestation or existence.
2. Early detection and treatment of the disease, mainly based on
    1. mainly based on surveillance and control.
    2. Prevention of the consequences of MSD, as well as prevention of disease recurrence.
    3. recurrence of the disease.

In a specific study on prevention of low back disorders, Lahiri et al. (2005) developed a model at the level of a company with the objective of carrying out an economic evaluation of an intervention aimed at reducing this type of illness at work. Applying a simple but transparent method, they estimate net economic costs of investments in ergonomic items to reduce morbidity. This estimation is done through an accounting model where net costs are defined as the cost of the intervention (or program implementation) plus work costs minus reduction in health costs, injury costs and productivity losses; all costs are calculated for annual periods. Data are obtained through surveys. The results of this study reveal that these types of interventions can generate substantial savings for companies.

II. METHODOLOGICAL ASPECTS

With the objective of quantifying the economic cost associated with the occurrence of DME, following the literature previously described, in this strategy a methodological approach is implemented that allows estimating costs in a wide perspective, including both direct costs (e.g., medical costs) and indirect costs (other economic costs and opportunity costs).

For this purpose, the information available in the administrative records on work-related disease associated with MSDs for the period January 2009 to December 2016 is used, where information on MSDs, information on the company and basic characteristics of the workers is collected, as well as the direct costs associated with the occurrence of the claims. Additionally, there is secondary information that allows an economic valuation of the indirect costs related to absenteeism and worker replacement costs, which is a crucial component of the cost assumed by the companies.

To contextualize the economic impact of DME, the costs are estimated from the social point of view, i.e., medical costs, costs associated with the system and the loss assumed by the companies are considered. In addition, to provide a microeconomic perspective with emphasis on human resource management and cost optimization, which are crucial variables in the decisions from the point of view of the company's performance, the estimation of the employer's costs is considered. This exercise provides further evidence for the case of Colombia and provides a decision-making tool to assess the impact of this type of diseases and to motivate the discussion on the relevance of prevention and early warning programs for MSDs. In this way, this exercise constitutes an important input to study the impact and effects of the implementation of programs for the prevention of MSDs.

To have a complete view of the costs associated with MSDs, the results of the study by Weerd et. al. (2014) is followed, in which a careful review is made of 29 studies dedicated to quantifying the cost of occupational illnesses and injuries, from which the costs are classified into 5 major categories that summarize the entire cost structure or chain. These are:

1. productive costs (associated with the loss of human capital, the drop-in productivity and labor costs).
2. Medical costs.
3. Costs associated with the loss of quality of life (intangible cost of suffering the illness or injury).
4. Administrative or logistical costs (opportunity cost of time spent on managing the activities associated with an illness or injury).
5. Insurance costs (insurance premium).

As shown in Table 1, from the perspective of social cost or productivity cost, understood as indirect costs associated with MSDs, the study concentrates on quantifying the productive costs, which are associated with the loss of production derived from the absence of workers or the decrease in their productivity. This requires information on the incidence and prevalence of MSDs for different levels of aggregation (e.g., industry, region, occupation), which can be approximated through the "attributable risk" method, in other words, by measuring the fraction of the employed population in a study population that is potentially affected by MSDs.

To get a monetary valuation of this cost, the methodology proposed by the International Labor Organization is followed (Takala et. al., 2017), in which a valuation is made of the loss of productivity through the value lost by workers during the period in which they are affected by an occupational disease. This component can be estimated from the years of life with disability (YLD for its acronym in English) or based on the productivity of workers (value of production per worker) approximated through their wage level. The above-mentioned studies consider different levels of YLD depending on the degree of severity of the disease, and even consider costs associated with loss of life.

These approaches will be adopted depending on the availability of information. In this case, a cost perspective of lost productivity is proposed, which has as its basic cost the salary received by the workers. Thus, to capture the different risk profiles in the implementation of the "attributable risk" method, and to incorporate the ethereal and demographic structure of the population at risk in the case of Colombia, it is made specific to economic sectors, gender, age, and region. The estimation of this component has as input the average salary reported by workers in the Large Integrated Household Survey, 2016 for different risk and income profiles defined by the previously mentioned variables.

To calculate this cost, the methodology used in HSE (2011) and Russell (2016) is followed, where the incidence of MSDs is estimated based on the predicted occurrence of this type of disease as a function of the socioeconomic and demographic characteristics of workers, as well as the characteristics of the occupation and the sector in which they work. The result of this exercise serves as an alert model for companies, to recognize the part of the population of workers most sensitive to suffer MSDs. As for the estimation of the effective cost, using information on the average duration of absences from work due to DME (estimated by studies for other countries, e.g., Rusell, 2016) and wage remuneration (specific to the sector), the valuation of the productive cost assumed by the employer is made.

Table 1. Economic cost of work-related accidents and diseases, by perspective and type

Type of cost/ Affected ↓	Productivity costs	Health care costs	Quality of life losses	Administration costs	Insurance costs
Workers and families	Loss of present and future income (net of taxes)	Direct and indirect medical costs and rehabilitation costs	Physical pain and suffering Emotional pain and suffering	Cost of time spent claiming benefits, waiting for treatment, etc.	Compensation payments
Employers	Treatment payments Production losses Production disruptions Damage to equipment Damage to company image (All the above damages are net of taxes)			Administrative and legal costs Costs of reinstatement and retraining of workers (disabled)	Impact on insurance premiums
Government	Payment for treatment Government benefits and social programs (disability or early retirement) Tax revenue losses	Direct and indirect medical costs and rehabilitation costs		Administrative and legal costs	
Society (over and above all)	Loss of production (Due to deaths disability/early retirement)				

Source: Adapted from Weerd et. al. (2014)

To approximate the medical costs associated with MSDs, which is a key variable for the cost-benefit analysis of interventions to reduce the incidence or prevent the incidence of these occupational diseases, the behavior of the total cost of the accident is studied. For this purpose, a regression analysis is performed in which a function of this cost is estimated as a function of different risk factors such as gender, age, and sector, from which statistical inference can be made on the relevance of each factor and forecasts can be made of the expected cost of the accident as a function of these factors. The results of this exercise serve as a decision-making tool for companies and governmental entities with the objective of implementing prevention policies to identify the main determinants of the increase in the cost of claims associated with MSDs. Thus, the estimation of total costs will follow the following model:

Total cost = Indirect cost + Direct cost.

In this estimation, indirect costs are calculated taking as a reference the opportunity cost associated with suffering from MSDs, which is approximated from the loss of productivity, i.e., indirect costs are given by:

$$Costo\,indirecto = \sum_{j=i}^{J} YLD_j PT_j \tag{1}$$

Where YLD is a proxy for years of life with disability or some measure associated with the severity of the occupational disease and PT is work productivity. In this case, the first variable is related to the severity of MSDs, the second refers to the cost in terms of salaries. Therefore, to standardize the direct and indirect costs, the associated cost in terms of labor cost is taken as the unit of analysis, leaving as a parameter to be assigned the absence from work as a measure of severity. In other words, the model provides a basic cost by estimating an adjusted factor that depends on the salary received, multiplied by the absence from work. This adjustment factor is determined from a total labor cost of 1.6 with respect to the expected salary and multiplied by a factor of 2 that determines the adjustment costs of the workforce in the absence of one of them.

Thus, the indirect cost constitutes the part of the total costs that a company must assume to compensate a worker suffering from an occupational disease associated with MSDs and considers potential replacement costs and administrative costs. Subindex j refers to the risk group to which the workers belong, which is defined by the intersection between the characteristics of gender, sector, and region.

As for the direct costs, the information from the accident costs is exploited. To analyze the relationship between risk factors and this cost, a model of the following form is estimated:

Direct cost=Cost of loss= m (X, β)

Where X is the set of risk factors, β is the set of parameters that relate these variables to the direct cost of a claim associated with MSDs, and m(.) is a specified functional form that describes this relationship. Since the objective of this model is to forecast the cost given a set of worker characteristics, models are estimated for different functions m(.), for example log-linear models, and different transformations of the exogenous variables, and their performance is compared using the mean square error as a comparison criterion to determine the model that best forecasts the claim cost. This model is trained (or estimated) for a proportion of the sample and tested with the remaining part, where such sub-samples are chosen randomly. Thus, taking a particular worker profile, characterized by gender, age, region, sector and type of diagnosis, the cost associated with MSDs is estimated using the incidence rate of these diseases, and applying the above models to the population at risk.

III. DATA DESCRIPTION

Having as reference the information available in the administrative records, an exploratory analysis of the socioeconomic characteristics that may constitute risk factors that may explain the incidence of MSDs and therefore be key input in the estimation of costs is performed. These analyses are derived from the study of 10248 cases registered between 2009 and 2016 and the differences in registered cases at the level of sex, age, sector, and geographical area are studied.

Figure 1 presents the distribution of MSDs cases by gender and shows a higher incidence of cases among women, with 60% of cases. It is worth noting that this indicator allows us to determine that gender is a determining factor in the incidence of this type of occupational disease, since in the population of affiliates registered by Insurance company the proportion is the reverse of this, i.e., 60% of affiliates are male.

Regarding the distribution of the incidence of work-related disease by age group, younger workers have, on average, lower incidence rates, but this indicator has an inverse U-shape, like that recorded in the work of Davis et al. (2007). Workers between 19 and 25 years of age presented only 18 cases (0.2% of the total number of cases, while workers between 25 and 35 years of age had a total of around 2,500 cases. On the other hand, it is observed that the highest frequency of cases occurs for people between 46 and 55 years of age, with a total of 4320 (42.2%) cases.

Figure 1. Distribution of the incidence of MSDs by sex
Source: Authors' own calculations

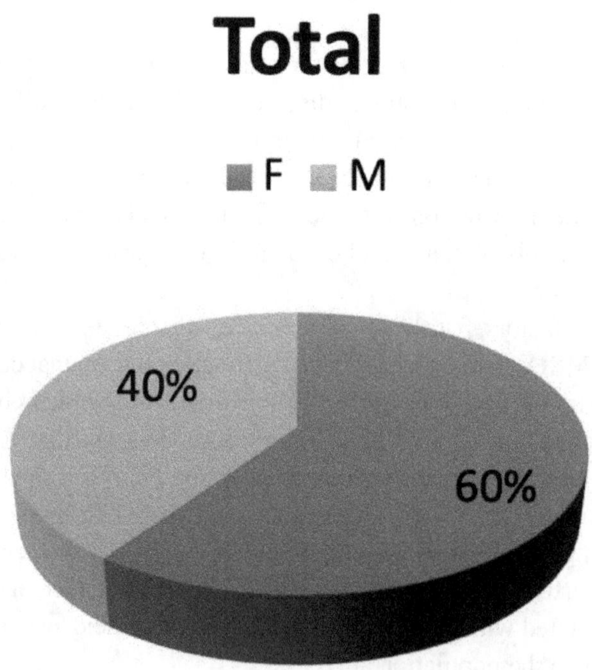

The distribution from a sectoral point of view shows a significant level of asymmetry. As can be seen in Table 2, the sectors with the highest number of cases were Commerce, Electricity, gas and water supply and Manufacturing, with a total of 1366, 1614 and 6599 cases, respectively. It is highlighted that the sector with the highest incidence of MSDs is the manufacturing sector with more than half of the 6599 cases (64.4%), while the sectors with the lowest incidence are Mining and Construction with only 3 and 30 cases, respectively.

A key variable that can determine the incidence of MSDs is the number of workers in the companies. It can be thought that larger companies tend to have higher levels of protection in terms of occupational diseases that would reduce the risk, but at the same time they may operate under higher levels of productivity, which is closely related to higher levels of effort, and therefore a higher incidence of MSDs. Table 3 shows that the number of cases of MSDs decreases as a function of company size; however, considering the distribution of companies (i.e., the productive structure in Colombia is characterized by MSMEs), it is expected that the number of workers has a positive effect on risk.

Figure 2. Distribution of the incidence of MSDs by age group
Source: Authors' own calculations

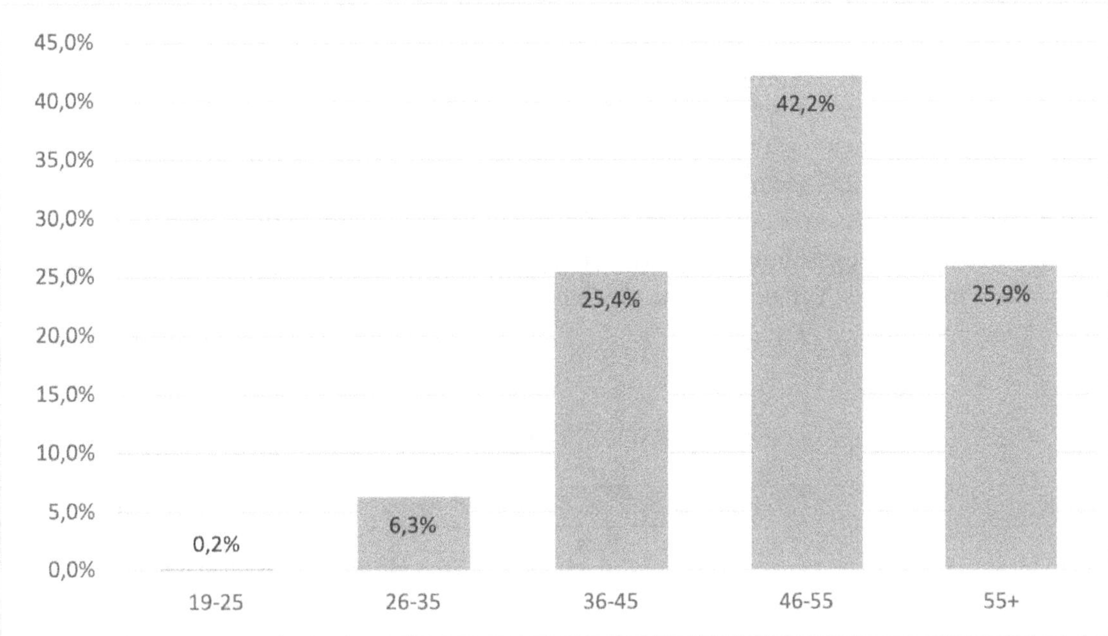

The geographical distribution of MSDs cases also provides evidence in favor of this factor being a determinant of its incidence. Cundinamarca (including Bogota) presents a total of 4528 cases (44% of the total), but the level of affiliation to the insurance company of this population is 31%.

This is like the case of Antioquia, where about 16% of the cases were registered, but the proportion of affiliates from this region is 5%. This implies that each affiliate from these regions has a higher risk, on average, than an affiliate from any other region. Other departments with a significant number of reported cases are Norte de Santander, Santander, and Cauca (See Figure 3).

Table 2. Distribution of the incidence of MSDs by sector

Sector	FA	FR
Agriculture and livestock	27	0.003
Commerce	1366	0.133
Construction	30	0.003
Manufacturing	6599	0.644
Mining	3	0.000
Electricity, gas, and water supply	1614	0.157
Transportation and communication	609	0.059

Source: Authors' own calculations

Finally, to estimate the cost structure, the distribution of total claim costs is analyzed, which are calculated from the direct costs associated with the treatment of this type of disease. This variable presents a high level of heterogeneity, which may be associated with the different levels of severity with which MSDs may occur, as well as the heterogeneity of the treatments.

After performing an exercise of exclusion of extreme values (2% of outliers both on the right and left), and considering a logarithmic transformation, it is observed (see Figure 4) that a wide variability persists in this indicator, which needs to be validated through the relationship that this has with the different risk factors proposed here.

Table 3. Distribution of the incidence of MSDs by sector

Workers	FA
1-400	1339
401-1000	835
1001-3000	832
3001-5000	613
5001-10000	306
10000+	245

Source: Authors' own calculations

Figure 3. Distribution of the incidence of MSDs by department
Source: Authors' own calculations

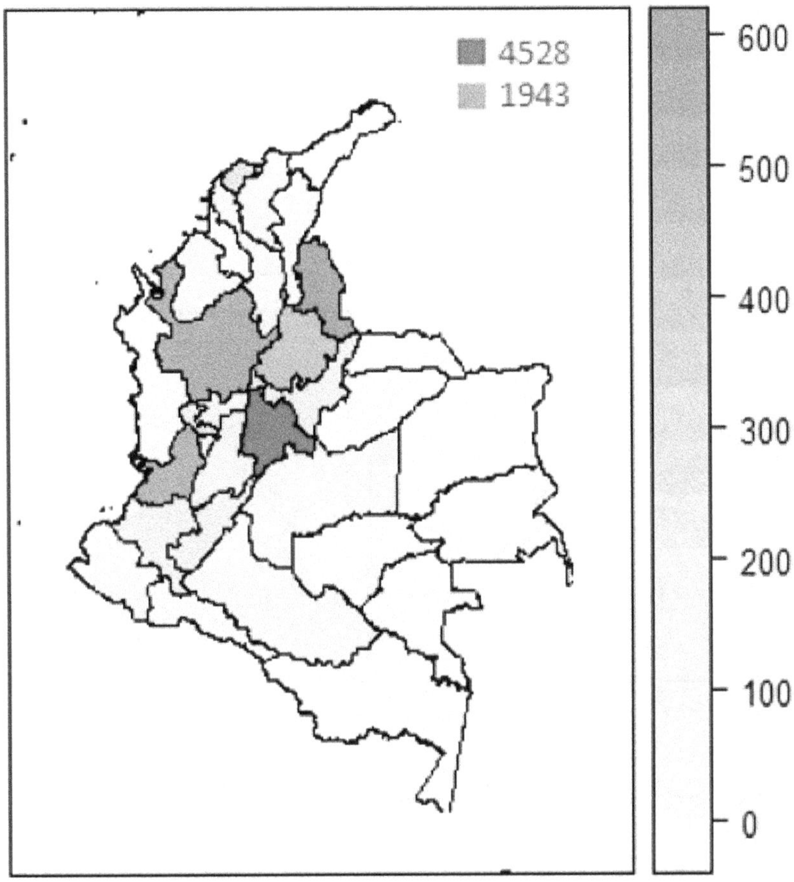

This exploratory analysis allows us to conclude that the incidence (or rate) of MSDs occurring among the population affiliated with This insurance company. is related to key characteristics of the worker population such as gender, age, sector, and region. It is worth noting that a better understanding of this phenomenon requires a more specific study of these characteristics, including, for example, the occupation of the workers and more detail on the severity through diagnosis or days of absence from work.

Figure 4. Number of claims cost distribution
Source: Authors' own calculations

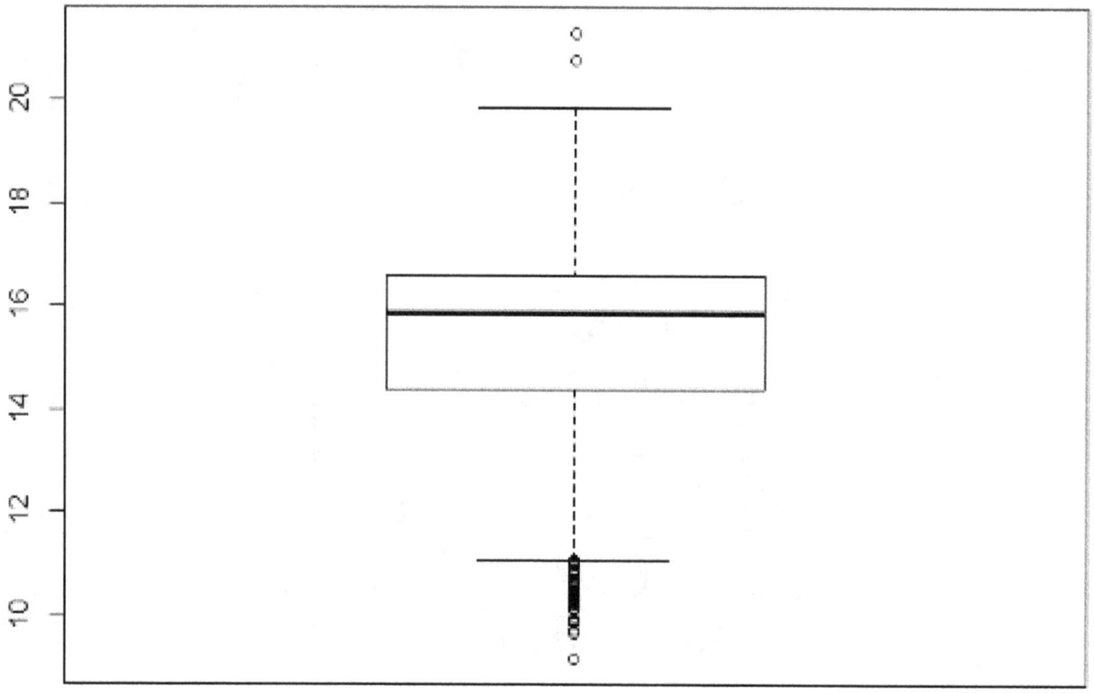

IV. METHODOLOGICAL IMPLEMENTATION AND RESULTS

4.1 Indirect Cost Estimation

With the objective of estimating the indirect costs associated with the opportunity costs that a company has to face, that is, the labor costs associated with the loss of productivity of a worker and his subsequent replacement, a source of secondary information is explored that allows a valuation of these costs by taking advantage of a set of data with high heterogeneity from which an approximation of workers' wages is obtained for a combination of sex, sector and region, i.e., for example, it is possible to obtain an estimate of the income of a male worker in the construction sector in the department of Antioquia.

This source of heterogeneity of workers' wages according to their characteristics is important in that it allows us to capture the structural differences in wage costs particular to these characteristics. For this purpose, the 2016 Great Integrated Household Survey (GEIH), which is a measurement instrument through which the DANE comprehensively collects information on workers from all sectors of the economy in all territories of the country, is considered as a secondary information base. To obtain the estimation of labor costs, the average wage was estimated for all sex-region-sector combinations among full-time salaried workers (40 hours or more). This results in 336 worker combinations or profiles.

This analysis results in a battery of labor costs with a high level of heterogeneity, which corresponds to the risk and differential cost structure that a company may face. For example, it is found that the lowest salary is received by women in the agricultural sector residing in the department of Sucre, which amounts to a little less than 200,000 CP (53,02 US Dollar, Approx.) per month. In contrast, the mining sector presents the highest overall labor costs, particularly for men in Bogota, whose average salary is 6,792,383 CP (1800.74 US Dollar, Approx.).

Although age is a key factor in the risk of suffering DME, and can also increase costs significantly, it was not considered in this component of the estimation since excessive detail can affect the significance of the results obtained.

In fact, in the estimations it is observed that some of the sex-region-sector combinations do not record observations, and for this reason an imputation method was used consisting of the average value between the regions maintaining the sex and sector of the worker, i.e., the missing wages were estimated as the average wage for the same sex and sector among the other regions. These combinations were: Male-Caquetá-Mining, Female-Choco-Agriculture, and Female-Mining for the regions of Caquetá, Cauca, Cordoba, Choco and Quindío.

Based on these estimates, the indirect cost is constructed based on a set of parameters that must be specified in the model. The first of these parameters refers to the benefit burden, which is an amplifying factor of the cost. According to the parameters usually used in this type of exercise, a factor corresponding to 1.6 is usually associated, indicating a benefit cost corresponding to 60% of the salary. This value is usual in this type of exercise. Thus, the cost for each day of absence from work is calculated as the wage cost of one day of work multiplied by 2, the latter indicating that the absence from work also entails a replacement cost.

This estimate may be conservative in the sense that it does not consider other costs associated with training and short-term productivity loss, e.g., the cost of workers' apprenticeship. However, it is a first approximation to the valuation of indirect costs. A crucial input to obtain accurate results in this estimation of indirect costs is the severity factor, which in this model is likened to a longer absence from the job. In this sense, the model is flexible as it allows assigning this parameter to obtain a cost estimate in different scenarios

4.2 Direct cost Estimation

To estimate the direct cost, a strategy like that for indirect costs is followed in terms of the grouping of risk factors; however, forecasting techniques are used on the cost of claims recorded in the administrative data. In addition to considering sex, region and sector as key variables, age and a simplified form of diagnosis are added as determinants of direct costs. Log-linear models are estimated using different specifications or groupings of diagnoses.

In particular, the model is considered:

$$\ln work\,place\,damage = \beta_0 + \beta_1 age + \beta_2 Age2 + \beta_3 Female + \sum^{I} \lambda_i R_i + \sum^{S} \theta_i C_i + \sum^{E} \vartheta_i D_i + \epsilon \tag{2}$$

Where Woman is a dummy variable that takes the value of 1 if the reference individual is a woman, and 0 otherwise. R_i and C_i correspond to a set of categorical dummy variables of region and sector with sizes, where I and S represent the number of categories. Finally, D_i is a set of dummy variables, with number of categories E, related to the type of diagnosis according to the international code of diseases ICD-10. For the latter, 3 different specifications (groupings) are carried out with respect to the recorded diagnosis:

1. groups according to the Chapter of the international code of diseases ICD-10 (or identification letter of the chapter),
2. it takes as a reference 3 major categories type M diagnoses that refer directly to MSD, G560 which is a high incidence diagnosis in the database that refers to carpal tunnel syndrome, and the rest of the diagnoses are grouped in the third category.
3. and makes an aggregation with the objective of reducing dimension considering as individual categories those with more than 50 registered cases, and all the others are grouped in a single category. From this model, it is possible to forecast the medical cost of a typical or average worker, given a set of characteristics that describe him/her.

The accident rate variable, which in this case is the dependent variable of the model, i.e., the variable to be explained and predicted, requires a prior exploratory analysis to obtain statistically more reliable results. This analysis consists of studying its variability and the possible presence of outliers.

Based on descriptive data and a graphical analysis, it is observed that the accident rate shows a significant accumulation of null values and significantly large values in the right tail of the distribution, for which reason a truncation.

Figure 5. Claims Cost Density
Source: Authors' own calculations

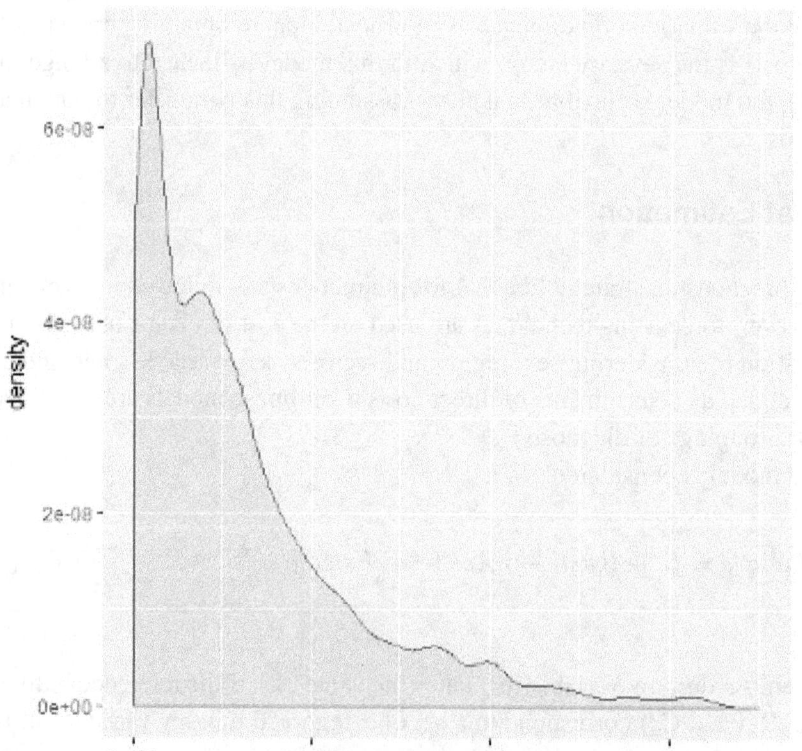

In purpose of choosing the model with the best prognostic goodness of fit, 3 models are estimated in which the way in which the diagnoses are introduced varies as described above. These models are estimated for 2/3 of the randomly chosen sample, and the mean square error of the forecast error for the remaining 1/3 of the sample is compared

V. CONCLUSION

This type of out-of-sample prediction exercise is a widely validated strategy in statistics, and currently key in the implementation of statistical learning models. From this exercise, it turns out that the best forecasting model corresponds to the one comprising 3 diagnostic categories (M, G560 and rest), which are classified as M, G and R, respectively. The results of this model are presented in Table 4. Age is a factor that significantly increases the claims cost over the entire life cycle. In particular, the quadratic form introduced in the model shows that the effect of age on the direct cost is convex implying that the additional cost for each additional year of a worker is increasing.

Additionally, for the profile defined by sex-region-sector-diagnosis, differential patterns can be observed. In terms of sector, workers in the transportation sector have relatively higher costs than the rest of the sectors. 41.5% higher than the commerce sector, which serves as a reference, and this difference is statistically and economically significant. In the case of the regions, significant heterogeneity is observed. Taking Antioquia as a reference, regions such as Guainía, San Andrés or Casanare show significantly lower accident costs, while in Norte de Santander these tend to be higher. For gender, no differential factor is observed in terms of accident rates. Finally, in the proposed aggregation of diagnoses, taking carpal tunnel syndrome as a reference, both MSDs in Chapter M and the other diagnoses show 23% and 33% higher costs, respectively.

This model makes it possible to establish the worker profile that may result in higher accident costs; in this case, it corresponds to an elderly worker who works in the transportation sector in the Norte de Santander region. From these parameters, it is possible to estimate the accident cost, or direct cost, associated with a set of worker characteristics. For example, following the previous exercise, it is possible to estimate the accident cost of a man located in Antioquia who works in the construction sector and is 30 years old and suffers from an MSDs belonging to the diagnostic chapter M. The results of this exercise are presented in Figure 7. The value 8,219,056, which implies that the cost of an occupational disease event that implies absence from the workplace for 30 days (1 month) for a worker with this profile has a total cost of approximately 11,900,263. This tool gives an idea of the magnitude of the problem of this type of occupational diseases, considering the heterogeneity that they generate in costs through different characteristics of the population and workers and the sector in which they operate.

From the point of view of company decisions, the calculation model presented is an important starting point for thinking about the relevance of MSD prevention programs. The model described above does not consider the size of the company in terms of workers as a determinant of the cost of MSDs. If this variable affects the incidence, it consequently impacts the severity in which the accidents occur and therefore the associated direct and indirect costs, which is why it is necessary to estimate an additional model that considers the number of workers in the company as a control variable.

Table 4. Log-linear model for claims cost forecasting

Variables		Coefficient	p-value
Intercept		15.946	0.000
Age		-0.012	0.008
Age (Square)		0.00010	0.001
Sector	**Construction**	-0.242	0.354
	Manufacturing	0.000	0.992
	Mining	-0.159	0.542
	Electricity, gas and water supply	0.015	0.799
	Transportation and communication	0.415	0.000
Sex (Female)		-0.006	0.853
Department	**Arauca**	-0.960	0.002
	Atlántico	-0.064	0.549
	Bogotá, D.C.	-0.122	0.062
	Bolívar	-0.632	0.000
	Boyacá	0.115	0.310
	Caldas	-0.460	0.004
	Caquetá	-0.721	0.002
	Casanare	-1.061	0.001
	Cauca	-0.152	0.192
	Cesar	-0.112	0.509
	Chocó	0.259	0.788
	Córdoba	-0.780	0.000
	Cundinamarca	-0.293	0.001
	Guainía	-2.265	0.019
	Guaviare	-0.149	0.913
	Huila	-0.158	0.166
	La Guajira	-0.210	0.406
	Magdalena	-0.522	0.000
	Meta	-0.137	0.373
	Nariño	-0.498	0.007
	Norte de Santander	0.293	0.001
	Putumayo	0.218	0.699
	Quindío	-0.482	0.003
	Risaralda	-0.559	0.000
	San Andres	-1.518	0.000
	Santander	-0.222	0.014
	Sucre	0.343	0.188
	Tolima	0.021	0.866
	Valle del Cauca	-0.457	0.000

Continued on following page

Table 4. Continued

Variables		Coefficient	p-value
Diagnoses	M	0.229	0.000
	Rest	0.327	0.000

Source: Authors' own calculations

Table 5. Estimated direct costs

Characteristics	Profile
Gender	Male
Region	Antioquia
Sector	Construction
Age	30
Type of diagnosis	M
Direct medical costs	$ 8.219.056 [COP]
Costs associated with 1 month of absence by MSD	$ 11.900.263 [COP]

Source: Authors' own calculations

REFERENCES

Ahlberg, I. (2014). *The economic costs of musculoskeletal disorders-A cost-of-illness study in Sweden for 2012*. Academic Press.

Amell, T., & Kumar, S. (2001). Work-related musculoskeletal disorders: Design as a prevention strategy. A review. *Journal of Occupational Rehabilitation*, *11*(4), 255–26. doi:10.1023/A:1013344508217 PMID:11826726

Asay, G. R. B., Roy, K., Lang, J. E., Payne, R. L., & Howard, D. H. (2016). Absenteeism and Employer Costs Associated with Chronic Diseases and Health Risk Factors in the US Workforce. *Preventing Chronic Disease*, *13*, 150503. doi:10.5888/pcd13.150503 PMID:27710764

Coyte, P. C., Asche, C. V., Croxford, R., & Chan, B. (1998). The economic cost of musculoskeletal disorders in Canada. *Arthritis & Rheumatology (Hoboken, N.J.)*, *11*(5), 315–325. doi:10.1002/art.1790110503 PMID:9830876

Davis, K., Dunning, K., Jewell, G., & Lockey, J. (2014). Cost and disability trends of work-related musculoskeletal disorders in Ohio. *Occupational Medicine*, *64*(8), 608–615. doi:10.1093/occmed/kqu126 PMID:25298392

HSE (Health and Safety Executive). (2011). *Cost to Britain of workplace injuries and work-related ill health: 2010/11*. Available at: https://www.hse.gov.uk/statistics/pdf/cost-to-britain.pdf

Institute for Work & Health. (2005). *The Burden of Work-related Musculoskeletal Disorders (MSDs)*. Author.

Lahiri, S., Gold, J., & Levenstein, C. (2005). Estimation of net-costs for prevention of occupational low back pain: Three case studies from the US. *American Journal of Industrial Medicine*, *48*(6), 530–541. doi:10.1002/ajim.20184 PMID:16299707

Mirelman, A., Glassman, A. L., & Temin, M. (2016). Estimating the Avertable Disease Burden and Cost-Effectiveness in Millions Saved (3rd ed.). Academic Press.

OIT. (2013). *La prevención de las enfermedades profesionales*. OIT.

OMS. (2004). *Prevención de trastornos músculo esqueléticos en los lugares de trabajo*. OMS.

Piedrahita, H. (2006). Costs of work-related musculoskeletal disorders (MSDs) in developing countries: Colombia case. *International Journal of Occupational Safety and Ergonomics*, *12*(4), 379–386. doi:10.1080/10803548.2006.11076696 PMID:17156613

Punnett, L. (2000). The costs of work-related musculoskeletal disorders in automotive manufacturing. *New Solutions*, *9*(4), 403–426. doi:10.2190/Y93Q-DEAQ-FEU2-8B26 PMID:17208891

Punnett, L., & Wegman, D. H. (2004). Work-related musculoskeletal disorders: the epidemiologic evidence and the debate. *Journal of Electromyography and Kinesiology, 14*(1), 13-23.

Quintana, R., & Pawlowitz, I. (1999). A Poisson model for work-related musculoskeletal disorder cost estimation. *Safety Science*, *32*(1), 19–31. doi:10.1016/S0925-7535(99)00008-9

Russell, H., Maitre, B., & Watson, D. (2016). *Work-related Musculoskeletal Disorders and Stress, Anxiety and Depression in Ireland: Evidence from the QNHS 2002–2013. Economic and Social Research Institute (ESRI)* Research Series.

Takala, J., Hämäläinen, P., Nenonen, N., Takahashi, K., Chimed-Ochir, O., & Rantanen, J. (2017). Comparative analysis of the burden of injury and illness at work in selected countries and regions. *Cent. Eur. J. Occup. Environ. Med*, *23*, 6–31.

Takala, J., Hämäläinen, P., Saarela, K. L., Yun, L. Y., Manickam, K., Jin, T. W., & Lin, G. S. (2014). Global estimates of the burden of injury and illness at work in 2012. *Journal of Occupational and Environmental Hygiene*, *11*(5), 326–337. doi:10.1080/15459624.2013.863131 PMID:24219404

Valbuena. (2017). *OVA Programa de Gestión para la prevención de los Desórdenes Músculo Esquelético*. Author.

Weerd, M. D., Tierney, R., Duuren-Stuurman, B. V., & Bertranou, E. (2014). *Estimating the cost of accidents and ill-health at work: a review of methodologies*. Academic Press.

Chapter 9
Comparison of Six Passive Exoskeletons for Upper Limbs Using the TOPSIS Method

Pablo Antonio Muñoz Gutierrez
Autonomous University of Ciudad Juarez, Mexico

Juan Luis Hernández-Arellano
https://orcid.org/0000-0002-8612-5132
Autonomous University of Ciudad Juarez, Mexico

Juan Alberto Castillo Martinez
Universidad del Rosario, Colombia

Aide Aracely Maldonado-Macias
https://orcid.org/0000-0002-4959-161X
Autonomous University of Ciudad Juarez, Mexico

ABSTRACT

The use of exoskeletons in occupational tasks has increased significantly in the last five years. However, few comparative studies have been conducted to understand the advantages and disadvantages of existing exoskeletons. This chapter presents the comparison of six exoskeletons using the TOPSIS method. Using databases of patents and commercial products, a total of six that were chosen to be compared by experts in the design and/or use of exoskeletons. The criteria evaluated were exoskeleton weight, load capacity, anthropometric adjusts, maintenance, and installation on the user. The Shoulder-X exoskeleton was selected as the best, serving as a reference for the acquisition of characteristics for recommendations for the development of new models for use in occupational tasks.

DOI: 10.4018/978-1-7998-7396-9.ch009

INTRODUCTION

As a new and rapidly emerging technology, the use of exoskeletons in different occupational applications is likely to raise new and challenging questions and concerns (Nussbaum et al., 2019). The exoskeleton is defined as a portable device that increases, enables, helps, or improves movement, posture, or physical activity (Lowe et al., 2019), to prevent injuries or treat them, exoskeletons have been a tool for the prevention of musculoskeletal disorders and may represent a relevant solution to reduce pain in workers and prevent musculoskeletal disorders (MSD) (Sylla et al., 2014).

The first device to be registered as an exoskeleton is found under US Patent Registration #3,449,769. Called "Man Amplifier," the design featured human-matched joints as well as one or two servo motors per joint, however. In 1990 the first occupational exoskeleton research records emerged (DiFonzo & Bordia, 1998) and it is until the beginning of the year 2000 that a record of exoskeletons began to be generated, each with different technologies and approaches, these first documents laid the foundations for future efforts in two areas. First, the technological utility to address the wide range of demands of occupational tasks. Second, various evaluation approaches with potential impacts (Nussbaum et al., 2019).

Currently, the number of commercial exoskeletons with an occupational focus is increasing, the following being the most common: CDYS (Crimson Dynamics, 2020) The Paxeo (Paexo, 2019), The Laevo (Laevo V2, 2020), EskoEVO (EskoEVO, 2018). These exoskeletons, all lower limbs, have a focus on the occupational area, are for sale, and are used by brands such as AUDI (Hensel & Keil, 2019), Toyota (Selko, 2019), BMW (Hetzner, 2016), and FORD (Haridy, 2018). The utility of exoskeletons in their production lines is increasingly accepted in markets such as Ford Motor Company (Krok, 2017), BMW (Hetzner, 2016), Hyundai Motor Group (Kim, 2018), and Toyota (Selko, 2019), their applications have also been studied in the construction industry by Kim et al (2019), and in agriculture by Upasani et al., (2019)

However, each brand of exoskeletons claims to do their job to the best of their ability. Therefore, the exoskeletons found will be listed through a technological review that covers both commercial exoskeletons and registered patents to know their main characteristics and functions. This chapter aims to compare the attributes of six different exoskeletons to later classify them by groups and functions.

BACKGROUND

Musculoskeletal disorders (MSD) are today a public health problem both globally and nationally. Due to its high incidence in recent years, DME has become one of the leading causes of absenteeism and loss of productivity, significantly affecting the individual's ability to carry out their usual activities (Rodríguez Buitrago Sandra Paola, 2020). In Mexico, DME represented 650 shoulder injuries, an increase of 30% compared to the previous year (IMSS, 2017). Despite the automation of industrial processes, exposure to heavy work has not decreased in recent years (de Vries et al., 2019). A new strategy to reduce the risk of MSD in heavy work could be the use of exoskeletons in the workplace.

Exoskeletons are devices used in the body that help reduce mechanical loads on body structures and contribute to the generation of joint moments that are necessary for specific postures or movements (de Looze et al., 2016). According to Alabdulkarim & Nussbaum (2019), exoskeletons are classified as passive or active. The former generates forces and torsional moments in response to deformation, using non-motorized mechanisms that include springs or spring-like elements. The latter generate forces with the help of motors. At present, passive exoskeletons are predominant in the commercial market and the literature in the occupational field (Nussbaum et al., 2019).

With the use of exoskeletons, positive effects have been reported in the reduction of the activation of the muscles, however, the usability of exoskeletons in real-life work contemplates situations that are still considered a great challenge (Nussbaum et al., 2019). Exoskeletons are often evaluated in postures in which they are expected to be effective, while many works in practice show wider posture movements (de Vries et al., 2019). This chapter has three main objectives: 1) to carry out an extensive technological review of the patented exoskeletons and those already marketed both in intellectual property offices and on official sales pages, 2) to develop a comparative study between upper limb exoskeletons, and 3) list the mechanical, physical and aesthetic characteristics of each exoskeleton to describe their main characteristics and generate applicable knowledge to facilitate future research and development of exoskeletons.

METHODOLOGY

For the comparative study, the methodology of Aguilar-Duque et al. (2018) was followed, where he proposes the generation of 3 stages that are applied to define the relevance of exoskeletons. In the first stage, the search criteria are explained, the second stage describes the main characteristics and functionality of the selected devices, in the third stage, a comparative matrix table is developed using the TOPSIS method based on the opinion of six exoskeletons experts. The stages will be described in detail below.

Stage 1

For the selection and analysis, an exhaustive search was generated using PatBase and Google Patent to identify the patented exoskeletons. In the same way, a search was made for commercial exoskeletons already for sale on their sale WEB pages. The words used to feed the search engine were used the following words: exoskeleton, passive exoskeleton, passive exoskeleton upper limbs. To locate the exoskeletons of the upper limbs, a search was carried out in scientific articles where they are evaluated

The device list was filtered according to the following three phases

-Phase 1. The results are filtered considering its method of mechanisms (Active-Passive) obtaining a preliminary list that contains the title of each exoskeleton located.

The exoskeletons that meet these requirements are shown in the first column of Appendix 1.1.

-Phase 2. The results of phase 1 are filtered considering the exoskeletons destined for the upper limb. Generating a list with the information on exoskeletons, with their name and origin of obtaining either patent or commercial exoskeleton, the exoskeletons that meet these requirements are shown in the second column of Appendix 1.1

-Phase 3. The formal and functional characteristics of exoskeletons are reviewed and analyzed. Commercial exoskeletons are located on web pages. The exoskeletons that meet all the criteria and parameters are shown in column 3 of Appendix 1.1

Stage 2

Using the list obtained from exoskeletons, the characteristics and functionality of one's selected were described, specifying the title, patent number to be obtained, manufacturer, date, and country of origin.

This information makes it possible to form the comparative matrix of characteristics of the exoskeleton devices.

Stage 3

According to Kim et al. (2019), Kim & Nussbaum (2019), and Nussbaum et al. (2019), the relevant criteria when evaluating an exoskeleton are weight, load capacity, anthropometric adjustments, installation, and maintenance. Considering this, Table 1 shows the interpretation of the criteria.

Table 1. Criteria and their interpretation

Criterion	Interpretation
Weight	Total weight of the exoskeleton
Load capacity	Load capacity provided by the exoskeleton to the user
Anthropometric adjusts	Anthropometric adjusts for different users
Installation	Ease of installation
Maintenance	Ease of maintenance

The exoskeletons selected for phase 3 were entered in a comparative matrix seeking to demonstrate the advantages, disadvantages, main characteristics, and mechanisms to demonstrate the advantages and disadvantages of the six exoskeletons evaluated.

The TOPSIS method, developed by Hwang and Yoon (1981), is a ranking in conception and application. The TOPSIS method tries to choose alternatives that simultaneously have the shortest distance from the ideal solution positive and the distance furthest from the negative ideal solution. he positive is known as the ideal solution which maximizes profit criteria and minimizes cost, while the counterpart is known as the ideal solution negative in which the cost is maximized and the profit criteria are minimized (Behzadian et al, 2012).

Both solutions, the ideal and the anti-ideal, are fictitious. The ideal solution is a solution for which all the attribute values correspond to the optimal values of each attribute contained in the alternatives; the anti-ideal solution is the solution for which all attribute values correspond to the values minus desired values of each attribute contained in the alternatives. In this way, TOPSIS provides a solution that does not it is only the closest to a hypothetically better solution, but also the furthest from the hypothetically worst (Realyvazquez & Maldonado Macias, 2011).

For the application of the technique, it should be noted that the values must be numerical and must be well understood identified the objectives and attributes to evaluate.

Data were obtained by four experts selected based not only on their knowledge about the topic (exoskeletons) but also on their knowledge of ergonomics, human factors, and product design. Additionally, the experts have collaborated on several studies related with the design, construction, and validation tests of similar products. Based on these criteria, an online survey was developed and delivered to the experts where the information, images, and videos of the selected exoskeletons were analyzed by the experts to apply the TOPSIS method.

RESULTS

Stage 1

After documentation of patents and commercial exoskeletons, 36 exoskeletons were analyzed and underwent the 3 phases of filtering and analysis, they were reduced by 21, 12, and 6 exoskeletons per phase, respectively. Table 2 shows the exoskeletons found and the three applied filters. Table 3 shows the six exoskeletons in addition to their brand and Country of origin.

Table 2. List of exoskeletons

Exoskeleton Name	Filter 1	Filter 2	Filter 3
Airframe	X	X	
Armor-man2	X	X	
Besk	X	X	
Cdys	X	X	X
Evo	X	X	
Exhauss	X	X	
Exy one	X	X	X
Light	X	X	
Mate-mx	X	X	X
Shoulder-x	X	X	X
Paxeo	X		X
Cdys	X	X	X
X-rise	X		
X-arm	X		
Fortis	X		
Exo-haver	X		
Aldak	X		
Carry suit	X		
Flx ergoskeleton	X		
Plum	X	X	
Wieldy exoskeleton	X		

Table 3. The final list of exoskeletons

Name	Brand	Origin country
MATE-XT	EMATE EXOSKELETON	Italy
CDYS	Crison Dynamics	China
Plumb	HMT	France
Shoulder X	Suit X	EUA
Exy one	Exy	France
Paexo Shoulder	Ottobock	Germany

Stage 2

The six devices selected in the previous stage are presented below. The first to be shown is the CDYS Industrial Exoskeleton.

Product name: CDYS industrial Exoskeleton

Manufacturer: Crimson Dynamics

Country: China

CDYS is an exoskeleton for arm support, designed for repetitive tasks the CDYS can balance the weight of the arms giving dynamic assistance reducing shoulder fatigue and the risks of suffering from a musculoskeletal disorder, using the CDYS does not affect movements user naturals whether walking, sitting, or running. It will only begin to assist when the arm is raised to a certain angle. CDYS is a passive system and requires no power supply, only initial settings are required for users of different body sizes.

The exoskeleton worked in carbon fiber is based on the movements of the scapula to provide a natural movement and stable assistance, through the combination of suspension type bracelet and the support is transferred through soft textiles, and no tightening is required for support stable, with an adjustment of 7 levels adjustable to the requirements of different users, using the CDYS does not affect the natural movement of the user whether running, walking or sitting, with a weight of 2.4 kg resulting from a carbon fiber manufacturing (see Figure 1).

Figure 1. CDYS (PRODUCT | Crimson Dynamics431, 2020)

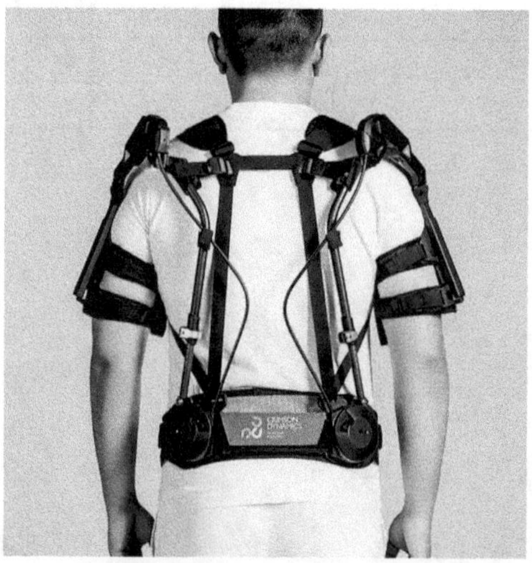

Product name: MATE-XT
Manufacturer: EMATE EXOSKELETON
Country: Italia

It is reinforced for indoor and outdoor use. This Exo for work and industry is made to handle water, dust, UV light, and wider temperature ranges than its predecessor. In addition, the MATE-XT has been redesigned with a thinner and lighter carbon fiber structure that is also more breathable (See Figure 2).

Technical specifications:

- Passive spring-based mechanism
- Addition of breathable fabrics
- 8 levels of assistance
- Redesigned lock / unlock mechanism for easy donning and doffing
- The light carbon fiber structure
- Expected height of users: 1.6 m (5.2 ft) to 1.9 m 6.2 ft)

Figure 2. MATE-XT (Comau Mate – Fit for Workers, 2020)

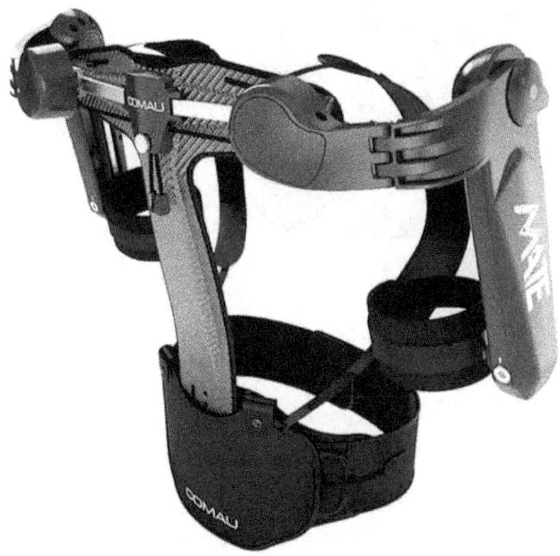

Product name: ShoulderX
Manufacturer: SUIT X
Country: EUA

ShoulderX allows you to perform tasks from chest to ceiling for longer or with less effort. The device supports the user's shoulder joint by transferring the load from the user's elevated arm and tool, beyond the shoulder complex, directly to the user's hips for movement, the anthropomorphic design follows the user's body to accommodate tight spaces and changing environments, shoulder X weighs 7 pounds (3.17 kg), allows user to use the device for extended periods without worrying about charging and maintaining batteries, minimal inhibition of arm and torso range of motion. Designed for all-day wear, shoulderX is legX and backX compatible, modules can be combined to make 7 different exoskeletons to provide a custom solution for each task, can be worn with tool belts, allowing workers to maintain normal equipment functionality installed on the user takes less than 1 minute to put on or take off, designed for use in harsh environments such as construction sites, manufacturing plants, and shipbuilding facilities.

Figure 3. Shoulder X (ShoulderX | Suitx, 2020)

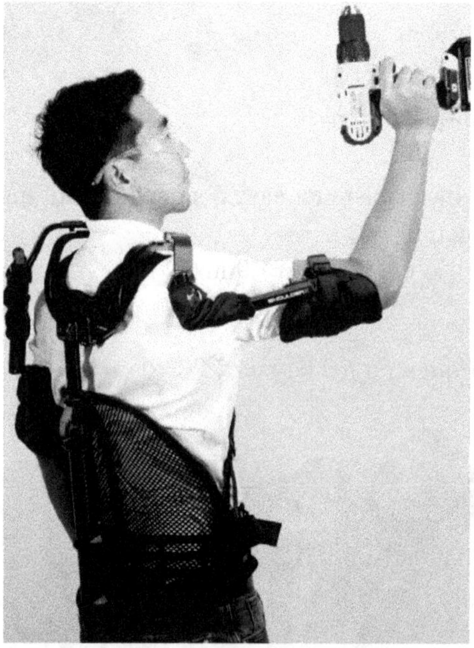

Product name: Plumb
Manufacturer: HMT
Country: Francia

Plum is an exoskeleton designed to alleviate awkward postures caused by high arm work and to reduce shoulder pain. Our patented technology can be tailored according to the context, needs, and morphology of the user for all jobs where the frequency of passing the arms above the level of the heart is sufficient for the operator to require assistance, with as little as 1, 6 kg, it is also the lightest in the world in the category “Exoskeleton for working with arms at height”, each of the devices designed and manufactured by HMT can be used by different collaborators.

The adjustment ranges allow it to fit approximately 90% of body types, the textile parts are removable and washable, the visible mechanical structure can be cleaned with a slightly damp cloth. You will find the cleaning instructions in the user manual of the device, assistance: from 1 to 6 kg per arm, it can be activated and deactivated in a single gesture.

Figure 4. PLUMB (HMT France - Accueil, 2020)

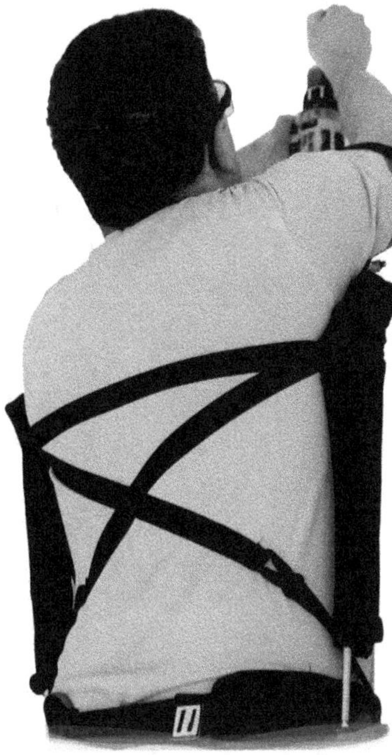

Product name: Exy One
Manufacturer: Exy
Country: Brazil

The Exy ONE increases the power of its user, reducing the forces necessary to perform activities, acting on the complex of shoulders, arms, and back, substantially reducing the risk of shoulder injuries and increasing productivity in the workplace. It is important to say that the equipment does not allow the worker to carry/manipulate loads greater than the weight limit that Ergonomics stipulates in their studies (23 kg), it allows the worker to save time to dress, adjust and remove the equipment in an intuitive and fast. There is no need for another person to help you with adjustments or wardrobe - the time to put on or take off the equipment takes an average of about 30 seconds, and even less as the user becomes accustomed to the equipment.

-Weight: from 3.55 kg
-Reduction of effort up to 8 kg per arm
-Lifting force adjustable in 4 levels
-Freedom of movement of shoulders and arms.
-Connected version (IoT) to monitor the use and maintenance of equipment and monitor user data (arm angle, hours of use per user, equipment hours counter).

Figure 5. Exy One (Linha Industrial | Exy Innovation Company, 2020)

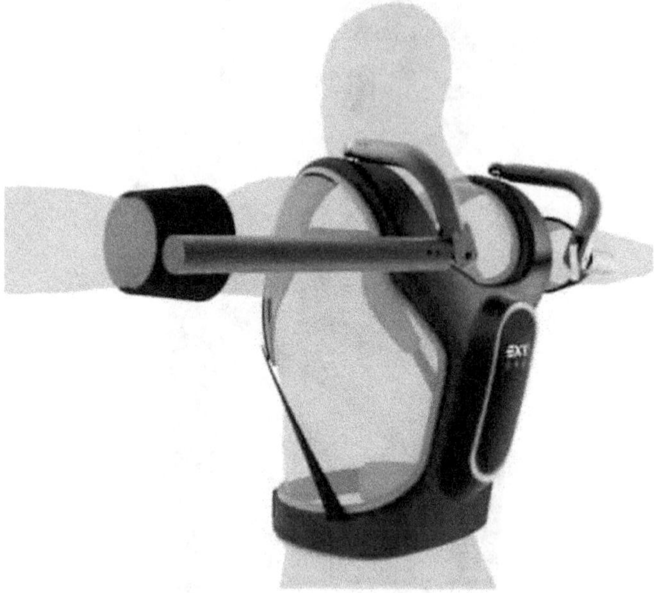

Product name: Paxeo
Manufacturer: Ottobok
Country: Alemania

Product design is based on natural human movements. Users can walk, sit, and also pick up objects with the exoskeleton. It can be worn comfortably for more than eight hours while providing noticeable relief to the shoulders and arms during overhead work. The Paexo Shoulder is the lightest exoskeleton of its kind weighing less than two kilograms. It can be worn comfortably for more than eight hours while providing noticeable relief to the shoulders and arms during overhead work. Thanks to the biomechanical design, Paexo Shoulder is friendly to the body and follows your every movement at work. You can walk and sit comfortably with the exoskeleton, and pick up objects, after a familiarization phase, it takes less than 20 seconds to put on and take off the Paexo Shoulder. Thanks to quick and easy handling, the exoskeleton can be removed between uses, for example during breaks or when rotating workstations. Its weight is only 1.9 kg.

Figure 6. Paxeo (Ottobock Industrials, 2021)

Stage 3. TOPSIS Method Application

After the analysis of the six exoskeletons, it is observed that all of them comply with their shape with the functions to be evaluated in addition to keeping the user safe and generating a reduction of loads on the body allowing to manipulate of heavy objects above the head without problems as well as continuous use, in its mechanisms is the main difference of using either using springs or ratchets, in addition, its placement, as well as its contact areas with the body, are different, each of the manufacturers looking for the best point of support in the body distributing the weight of the exoskeleton as well as the arms at different points.

Experts completed the online survey, and three tables were developed for this chapter. Table 4 shows the weighted weight of each exoskeleton obtained by the experts. Table 5 shows the individual decision index (IDI) obtained by every expert for the six exoskeletons. Table 6 shows final decision matrix developed with the average values from the IDI, being the highest rated exoskeleton by experts the Shoulder X. On the contrary, the exoskeleton with the lowest rating was the Plum.

Table 4. Weighted weights

Weight	Load capacity	Anthropometric adjusts	Maintenance	Installation
22%	19%	19%	18%	19%

Table 5. Individual decision index

Exoskeleton	Expert 1		Expert 2		Expert 3		Expert 14	
	IDI	Rank	IDI	Rank	IDI	Rank	IDI	Rank
Shouled X	0.5736	1	0.572	1	0.6329	1	0.6329	1
MATE.XT	0.5617	2	0.5675	2	0.5291	2	0.5291	2
Exoy one	0.4619	3	0.4483	3	0.4544	3	0.4544	3
CDYS	0.3351	6	0.3695	5	0.4077	4	0.4077	4
Paxeo	0.3518	5	0.4221	4	0.3726	5	0.3726	5
Plum	0.3586	4	0.3188	6	0.2963	6	0.2963	6

IDI: individual decision index

Table 6. Decision matrix

Exoskeleton	Decision index	Rank
Shoulder X	0.6029	1
MATE.XT	0.5468	2
Exoy one	0.4547	3
CDYS	0.3800	4
Paxeo	0.3798	5
Plum	0.3175	6

The exoskeleton selected as the best is the one that has the least areas of support in the body in addition to having Rest areas for the arms that cover the entire lower face of the arm, generating better support in addition to having a support mesh of posture for which the lower fixing area has ventilation systems that allow the passage of air thus avoiding the generation of heat and sweat, its adjustment areas are simple so it allows adjusting to different ways dynamically, as an extra The SuirX company that manufactures it handles a series of attachments to provide support to the lower limbs and back, these being compatible with each other, the second has the same qualities in addition to being made of carbon fiber and providing static and non-dynamic mechanical supports so the arms can rest in a position without the need to make effort to maintain it and it has an extra adjustment system for the Back width this because the suspension mechanism is in contact with the man and is less dynamic than that of the Shoulder-X.

The importance matrix allows us to see that the most important parameter is the weight of the exoskeleton as it allows a more comfortable continuous use in addition to processing less weight to the lower limbs generating a good response in support of forces without being generated by problems in lower limbs due to the weight of the same, the weight supported is the second best evaluated by the capacity of reduction of force necessary to keep the arms in tares above the head also, the third place of the matrix was the anthropometric adjustments the fourth the ease of placement on the user and the last maintenance

CONCLUSION

This chapter presented the identification and comparison of six different upper limb exoskeleton designs using the TOPSIS method. Through the support of 5 experts in the design, evaluation, and validation of exoskeletons, the weighting and final decision matrices were integrated. Additionally, very specific characteristics of the six designs included in the chapter were shown that are helpful for the selection of these teams.

The exoskeleton that was the winner, the shoulder-x, is a sample of how to conform an exoskeleton, always looking for a weight reduction, this without sacrificing the load capacity, in addition to achieving that the points of contact with the body are the least possible, thus reducing problems of breathability this without sacrificing a reliable and comfortable support system for the user achieved by the mesh support technology used at the same time as an optimizing posture corrector. The function of its parts is an achievement that should serve as an example for future developments, as it is chosen in all the applications as the best exoskeleton, it turns out to be a source of analysis for developers, without detracting from the other exoskeletons analyzed which managed to go through the three phases being reliable for their application and analysis because each one of them has redeemable elements for their application and analysis.

CHAPTER LIMITATIONS

The main limitation for this analysis is the lack of data obtained from each of the exoskeletons, which is strange since they all work with simple mechanical technologies which briefly show their function mechanisms and other characteristics, this factor reduced a possible evaluation list from 19 exoskeletons to only 6. In addition to this, the method sought to be as objective as possible using evaluation criteria that are used by other researchers on the subject.

FUTURE RESEARCH DIRECTIONS

Exoskeletons are a rapidly growing technology, therefore, constant research on the subject has to be maintained investigating the effects on workers in different environments and applications. Following this research, we offer several possible topics for future research:

1. Establish what type of exoskeleton is recommended to use based on the task to be performed and not the type of technology, to establish what mechanisms could be better for each task (dynamic, static, or repetitive).
2. Evaluate the cognitive demand that the exoskeleton presents to the worker to better calculate the necessary time of use that takes from learning to daily use of it.
3. Perform quick adjustment modes that facilitate use between users and between different tasks.
4. Limit contact areas without sacrificing a good restraint system to facilitate continuous use and better adaptation to less controlled work environments.
5. Seek that the elements that make up the exoskeleton achieve more than one function, for example: structural and support, to reduce the number of components.

6. Look for applications of exoskeletons outside of companies or production lines, since musculoskeletal disorders are generated in any task that leads us to place our arms above the head in a dynamic, static, or repetitive way.
7. Analyze the exoskeleton as a set of mechanisms that work in synchrony to avoid musculoskeletal disorders. However, these can be used independently in tasks that require it either due to the characteristics of the environment or the needs of the job.
8. Investigate applications of different mechanisms and materials with the aim of a more economic development that benefits a broader sector of companies.

REFERENCES

Aguilar-Duque, J. I., Amaya, G., & Juarez, V. M. (2018). Anthropometry devices: a comparative study. Handbook of Research on Ergonomics and Product Design, 153–171. doi:10.4018/978-1-5225-5234-5.ch010

Alabdulkarim, S., & Nussbaum, M. A. (2019). Influences of different exoskeleton designs and tool mass on physical demands and performance in a simulated overhead drilling task. *Applied Ergonomics*, *74*(August), 55–66. doi:10.1016/j.apergo.2018.08.004

Behzadian, M., Otaghsara, S. K., Yazdani, M., & Ignatius, J. (2012). A state-of the-art survey of TOPSIS applications. *Expert Systems with Applications*, *39*(17), 13051–13069. doi:10.1016/j.eswa.2012.05.056

Comau Mate – Fit for workers. (2020). https://mate.comau.com/?

de Looze, M. P., Bosch, T., Krause, F., Stadler, K. S., & O'Sullivan, L. W. (2016). Exoskeletons for industrial application and their potential effects on physical workload. *Ergonomics*, *59*(5), 671–681. doi:10.1080/00140139.2015.1081988 PMID:26444053

de Vries, A., Murphy, M., Könemann, R., Kingma, I., & de Looze, M. (2019). The Amount of Support Provided by a Passive Arm Support Exoskeleton in a Range of Elevated Arm Postures. *IISE Transactions on Occupational Ergonomics and Human Factors*, *7*(3–4), 311–321. doi:10.1080/24725838.2019.1669736

DiFonzo, N., & Bordia, P. (1998). Reproduced with permission of the copyright owner. *The Journal of Allergy and Clinical Immunology*, *130*(2), 556. doi:10.1016/j.jaci.2012.05.050

DynamicsC. (2020). https://www.c-dyn.com/product?

EskoEVO. (2018). https://eksobionics.com/ekso-evo/

Haridy. (2018). *Ford makes EksoVest exoskeletons available to employees worldwide after successful US trials*. https://newatlas.com/eksovest-exoskeleton-rolled-out-worldwide-ford/55804/

Hensel, R., & Keil, M. (2019). Subjective Evaluation of a Passive Industrial Exoskeleton for Lower-back Support: A Field Study in the Automotive Sector. *IISE Transactions on Occupational Ergonomics and Human Factors*, *7*(3–4), 213–221. doi:10.1080/24725838.2019.1573770

Hetzner. (2016). *BMW workers don "Iron Man" suit.* https://www.autonews.com/article/20160626/OEM01/306279965/bmw-workers-don-iron-man-suit

HMT France - Accueil. (2020). https://www.hmt-france.com/

Hwang y Yoon. (1981). *Multiple attribute decision making: methods and applications: a state-of-the-art survey.* Springer-Verlag.

IMSS. (2017). *Acercando el IMSS al Ciudadano.* Retrieved from: http://www.imss.gob.mx/conoce-al-imss/memoria-estadistica-2018

Industrials, O. (2021). Retrieved September 9, 2021, Retrieved from https://paexo.com/paexo-shoulder/?lang=en

Kim, S., Moore, A., Srinivasan, D., Akanmu, A., Barr, A., Harris-Adamson, C., Rempel, D. M., & Nussbaum, M. A. (2019). Potential of Exoskeleton Technologies to Enhance Safety, Health, and Performance in Construction: Industry Perspectives and Future Research Directions. *IISE Transactions on Occupational Ergonomics and Human Factors, 7*(3–4), 185–191. doi:10.1080/24725838.2018.1561557

Kim. (2018). *Hyundai brings wearable robotics to factories.* https://koreajoongangdaily.joins.com/news/article/article.aspx?aid=3054561&cloc=joongangdaily%7Chome%7Cnewslist1

Krok. (2017). *Ford's exoskeleton could help factory workers in a big way - Roadshow.* https://www.cnet.com/roadshow/news/fords-exoskeleton-could-help-factory-workers-in-a-big-way/

Linha Industrial. (2020). *Exy Innovation Company.* https://www.exy9br.com/produtos?

Lowe, B. D., Billotte, W. G., & Peterson, D. R. (2019). ASTM F48 Formation and Standards for Industrial Exoskeletons and Exosuits. *IISE Transactions on Occupational Ergonomics and Human Factors, 7.* doi:10.1080/24725838.2019.1579769

Nussbaum, M. A., Lowe, B. D., de Looze, M., Harris-Adamson, C., & Smets, M. (2019). An Introduction to the Special Issue on Occupational Exoskeletons. *IISE Transactions on Occupational Ergonomics and Human Factors, 7*(3–4), 153–162. doi:10.1080/24725838.2019.1709695

PRODUCT | Crimson Dynamics431. (2020). https://www.c-dyn.com/product?

Realyvazquez, A., & Maldonado Macias, A. A. (2011). Selección de fresadoras con topsis usando ponderaciones de ahp. *CULCYT, 8*(45), 95–102.

Selko. (2019). SLC: 2019 Toyota's Finding Success with Exoskeletons. *EHS Today.* https://www.ehstoday.com/safety-leadership-conference/article/21920474/slc-2019-toyotas-finding-success-with-exoskeletons

Sylla, N., Bonnet, V., Colledani, F., & Fraisse, P. (2014). Ergonomic contribution of ABLE exoskeleton in automotive industry. *International Journal of Industrial Ergonomics, 44*(4), 475–481. doi:10.1016/j.ergon.2014.03.008

Upasani, S., Franco, R., Niewolny, K., & Srinivasan, D. (2019). The Potential for Exoskeletons to Improve Health and Safety in Agriculture—Perspectives from Service Providers. *IISE Transactions on Occupational Ergonomics and Human Factors, 7*(3–4), 222–229. doi:10.1080/24725838.2019.1575930

Chapter 10

Factorial Solution for Determination of Critical Success Factors (CSF) in Deployment of Six Sigma and Its Relation to Sustainability: Case Study – Baja California Aerospace Industry

Aida López Guerrero
https://orcid.org/0000-0002-8856-0779
Autonomous University of Baja California, Mexico

Jesús Andrés Hernández Gómez
https://orcid.org/0000-0003-2325-2051
Autonomous University of Ciudad Juarez, Mexico

Karla Isabel Velázquez Victorica
https://orcid.org/0000-0002-8073-6119
Autonomous University of Baja California, Mexico

Mydory Oyuky Nakasima López
Autonomous University of Baja California, Mexico

Luz del Consuelo Olivares Fong
https://orcid.org/0000-0003-3790-6810
Autonomous University of Baja California, Mexico

ABSTRACT

Recently, the interest in being part of more competitive companies has increased. For this, organizations apply various strategies of continuous improvement that allow them to maintain high standards of competitiveness. In this sense, organizations make use of various techniques, tools, and methodologies that support the achievement of objectives. This research presents an approach towards the Six Sigma (SS) strategy, one of the main continuous improvement strategies used to achieve competitiveness. On

DOI: 10.4018/978-1-7998-7396-9.ch010

the other hand, organizations currently seek that during manufacture of their products, caring for the environment is naturally part of their objectives, seeking to achieve benefits with a sustainable impact. Therefore, this research seeks to define the CSF for implementation of SS through a factor analysis that allows identifying the relationship between SS and obtaining sustainable benefits (SB) through its implementation.

INTRODUCTION

There is enough evidence that shows that large organizations seek continuous improvement within their processes, products and services as well as remain in range of the most competitive companies in the field in which they develop. To achieve these objectives, the administrators of organizations always search to implement continuous improvement strategies that support them to stay within the most competitive. Among the continuous improvement strategies, there is Six Sigma (SS), in order to reduce defects in such a way that organizations become more competitive, reduce their costs and improve the quality of their processes, products and services.

In addition to this, organizations are currently seeking to be sustainable in two ways in internal manufacturing processes and in products they provide to their final customers, in order to reduce damage to the environment. That is, organizations seek to be competitive at the same time they achieve continuous improvement, plus responsible with care of environment, so their priority is no longer just focus on productivity, but being productive, having a good quality and being sustainable.

Considering that SS strategy is commonly used for continuous improvement in organizations, it is important to mention that the critical factors must be considered to achieve a successful implementation. In this sense, and for companies to achieve a correct deployment of the SS strategy, it is important that Critical Success Factors (CSF) are considered during the implementation process. That is why this research is focused on identification of CSF through a factorial solution, managing to identify which are the most substantial CSF for the achievement of operational objectives and achievement of competitiveness in organizations.

According to literature review and considering that with a successful implementation, sustainable benefits and care for the environment can be achieved, Alhuraish, Robledo, and Kobi (2017) mention that a competitive advantage is achieved when organizations develop linked practices with sustainable development strategies, and thereby control waste and the implementation of practices that are environmentally and socially responsible.

The relation between SS and sustainability, give the impression that SS can have a positive influence on sustainability (Chugani, Kumar, Garza-Reyes, Rocha-Lona and Upadhyay, 2017), this through application of tools that make up to SS, seeking to obtain benefits in caring for the environment.

Based on the above, a measurement instrument was developed in this research to identify the CSF that have been considered by the organizations that have implemented SS, likewise, through the same instrument, it seeks to verify the relationship between a correct implementation of SS and sustainability.

For development of the instrument it was necessary to perform an extensive literature review, identifying those articles that will show the results obtained with implementation of SS and those that will present sustainable results from its implementation.

As a result of the literature review, it was possible to develop a measurement instrument initially composed of 39 questions, which were distributed in five constructs, where four of them allow identifying the CSF and one the relationship with sustainability. In this way, the instrument has been developed with three main objectives, the identification of CSF, verifying the relation between SS and sustainability, and knowing to what extent sustainable benefits are achieved with a successful SS implementation.

Prior to application phase of the instrument, it is important to mention that it was subjected to the pertinent statistical validations recommended by existing literature; these validations have been presented in another book chapter.

In particular, this chapter presents the results of a factorial solution for determination of CSF in deployment of SS and its relationship with sustainability in the aerospace industry.

BACKGROUND LITERATURE REVIEW

Relation of SS with Other Strategies

In order to contextualize the relation of SS with other strategies, it is important to mention its origins. Vinod, Devadasan, Sunil, and Thilak (2015) state that, since the mid-1980s, the concept of SS emerged at Motorola. Because the implementation of SS made it easier for companies to achieve profitability, it was subsequently implemented around of the world. SS is implemented by most companies through the application of phases, DMAIC (define, measure, analyze, improve and control).

Vinod, Devadasan, Sunil, and Thilak (2015) refer to Karthi, who states that SS fully emerged on January 15, 1987 at Motorola and that it was developed by Bill Smith. Mehrabi (2012) agrees that SS was developed in 1987.

Contrarily, and according to the literature review, SS has been defined from various perspectives. Several points of view from authors it is defined below.

In general terms, Arturo Garza-Reyes, Flint, Kumar, Antony, and Soriano-Meier (2014) consider SS as one of the most important developments for quality management and process improvement in the last two decades. Moreover, Arturo Garza-Reyes et al, Sagnak and Kazancoglu (2016), Acharya and Mathur (2016), Linderman, Schroeder, Zaheer and Choo (2003), and Al-agha and Al-agha (2015) state that SS has three meanings, first, that is a statistical measure of variation that when achieved, a process would produce 3.4 defects per million opportunities, second, that is a management philosophy and strategy that allows organizations to obtain lower costs, ensuring operations competitive, and third, that is a problem-solving and improvement methodology that can be applied through an all-round process to eliminate the root cause of defects.

SS is also defined as a business strategy that focuses on improving understanding of customer requirements, business systems, productivity, and financial performance (Mehrabi, 2012).

For their part, Thakore, Dave, Parsana, and Solanki (2014) expand this definition, considering it as a quality initiative that reduces variations in a process and helps reduce the cost of the product and process.

Given many areas of application of this methodology, specific interpretations can be considered; for example, Tjahjono et al., (2010) propose four interpretations for SS definition. The first one is defined as a set of statistical tools, the second as an operational management philosophy, the third one as a business culture and analysis methodology that uses scientific methods.

On the other hand, there are different practices associated with implementation of SS, and in that sense Zu, Fredendall, y Douglas (2008) identify three practices that are critically associated with implementation. These practices are the SS role structure, SS structured improvement procedure and SS focus on metrics, further mentioning that SS use a group of improvement specialists, generally called Green Belt, Black Belt, Master Black Belt. Those specialists receive intensive differentiated training that is tailored to their ranks and is designed to enhance their knowledge and skills in statistical methods, project management, process design, problem-solving techniques, leadership skills, and other management skills. Shafer and Moeller (2012), for their part, support this role structure and specify that SS has well-defined specialized process improvement functions and they are compatible with extensive training, with understanding that their role will be 100% dedicated to deployment of SS activities (Raisinghani, Ette, Pierce, Cannon, and Daripaly, 2005).

According the role and commitment of company's management represents is a fundamental part for deployment of SS, having the main support the groups of specialists, already mentioned, as well as work teams focused on implementation of the strategy.

With this in mind, the main objective of SS is to reduce the variation in processes and costs in manufacturing and services, as well as increase customer satisfaction, measure defects, increase product quality and reduce defects to 3.4 parts per million opportunities (DPMO) in an organization, where a defect opportunity represents a critical process failure for customer (Mehrabi, 2012); (Roadmap, 2015); (Mason, Nicolay and Darzi, 2015).

In this way, Weiner (2004) mentions that the main objective of SS is to achieve a percentage of non-defective production of 99.999998%. Due to this and the benefits obtained in many applications, SS has become the most popular business strategy for development of continuous improvement in manufacturing, service and public sectors (Erdoğan and Canatan, 2015); (Albliwi, Antony and Lim, 2015).

Once the strategy is described, practices associated with it and their main objectives are presented. A description according to different ways of managing and developing are performed, based on specific contexts and organizations needs.

In this sense, SS established several uses, as statistical tool, competitive strategy, as a part of a strategic plan, manufacturing strategy, among others.

With the objective to know all SS uses, descriptions are presented below.

SS as a Statistical Tool

Echeveste, Rozenfeld, and Sonego (2016) define SS in statistical terms, as a program that appeared as an improvement process based on dissemination of statistical knowledge, conceived to reduce the variability of product specification around an objective value, originating the name "Six Sigma". Echeveste et al, mention that SS ensures that the probability of producing products with specification outside the limits is practically null.

At the distance of six deviations (6σ) between the data distribution of a given characteristic that follows a normal distribution in relation to specification limits. Under this approach, Nedeliaková, Štefancová, and Kudláč (2017) define SS as a set of statistical techniques and tools, for example the histogram, flowchart, Pareto chart control chart, and the Ishikawa fish diagram. For their part, Felizzola Jiménez and Luna Amaya (2014) define SS as a progress of classical theories of quality and continuous improvement, such as Design of Experiments and Total Quality Management, which have as a purpose to increase the capacity in processes and in this way to minimize errors or failures in the product.

Finally, SS is defined as a tool that systematizes and organizes the improvement of processes as well as development of new products and services, which is based on scientific and statistical methods, with the purpose of significantly reducing the quantity of defects that are defined by clients (Calia, Guerrini and de Castro, 2009); (Linderman, Schroeder, Zaheer, and Choo, 2003).

SS as a Competitive Strategy

Literature reports that for various authors SS is a strategy that provides guidance to organizations to achieve competitiveness. In this way, Mintzberg (1994) declares that strategy is a word defined differently from how make it in practice for many. The definition of strategy is "a plan", although in reality the strategy appears as a pattern that combines the anticipated responses with responses that emerge from the changing environment. The influence and importance of strategy increases when compared to the fact that less than ten percent of planned strategies are successfully implemented.

SS is considered a strategy with a critical focus on quality, customer satisfaction and that results of the implementation are expressed in financial terms such as cycle time, product quality and delivery, inventory, production floor area, productivity measurement, suppliers, profitability, market share and hierarchical levels in positive terms, SS is considered also a strategy that significantly favors the competitiveness of organizations (Ismyrlis and Moschidis, 2013). That is why Alhuraish, Robledo, and Kobi (2017) argue that SS is an essential methodology to ensure that the company/organization acquires and maintains a competitive advantage, in addition to not requiring participation of the entire organization, since only one select group of professionals trained for implementation.

Antony and Desai (2009) state that SS has been defined as a strategic business improvement initiative, systematic, highly disciplined, customer-focused and profit-oriented, based on a rigorous methodology focused on processes and data, driving customer satisfaction. Differently, due to development and deployment of the SS strategy, final results obtained in organizations through systematic reduction of the variation in processes and customer satisfaction, has led them to promote SS as a competitive strategy that favors the increase of competitiveness in organizations.

For Weiner (2004), SS is used as a set of improvement techniques in any part of its business, not only focusing on product quality, but also considered as a strategic corporate initiative to enhaising profitability, increase market share and improve customer satisfaction through statistical tools and techniques that can lead to great advances in quality, provides business leaders and executives with the strategy, methods, tools and techniques to change the culture of organizations (Antony and Desai, 2009).

On the other hand, a strategy by itself is defined as the creation of a unique and valuable position, which involves a different set of activities, requires that concessions be made to compete, to choose what not to do and implies creating adjustment between the activities of a company (Development and Execution, 2008).

A competitive strategy, then, provides tools to capture the wealth and heterogeneity of industries and firms, while also providing a disciplined structure to examine them (Competitiva, 2013).

As has been observed in the literature, organizations have different approaches, for example, the quality of their products, customer satisfaction and maximizing their profits, but above all, achieving competitiveness in the environment in which they develop. To achieve this, they are immersed in making strategic decisions with long-term repercussions, where there is a probability of not being able to foresee all commercial possibilities in short term, it is in these activities that organizations seek to support themselves with various quality and improvement continuous tools that allow them to achieve competitiveness. This opens the field for deployment of SS as an organizational strategy, since it brings benefits in relation to making resources efficient, client satisfaction and maximizing profits, mainly, thus advancing on the path of competitiveness.

Through this conceptualization, the conclusion is reached that SS is considered a manufacturing strategy derived from competitive strategy, and should be part of the strategic planning developed in organizations, which gives the guideline for SS to be part of organizational strategies providing a valuable guide to achieve the objectives that the organization seeks to achieve in long term. Then SS provides a guide to improve manufacturing and business processes, through reduction of defects and customer satisfaction.

SS as part of Strategic Planning

Strategic project planning involves the development of methodologies, reference models, and processes while organizing project management offices in perspective of optimizing the use of available resources in the organization. It is here where the gap opens to take SS as a project management strategy, which has the objective of improving processes, which provides an approach for the organization to optimize its resources (Amorim, de-Siqueira and Martínez-Sáez, 2012). It this context, Kantardjieva (2015) shows how strategic management symbolizes the perception of how to make use of organization's resources as efficiently as possible, understanding that environment variable is taken as a reference. In the strategic decision-making process, many factors have their impact, including complexity of the environment, the value system, and motivation. Strategic decisions lead to improvement of the strategic position and the action decided in present.

Cusumano, Kahl, and Suarez (2008) mention that strategic planning increases flexibility in some contexts by making the company respond better through efficiencies created in related processes. Companies use strategic planning to focus activities and increase efficiency; such planning prioritizes investment of resources and optimizes the use of resources, that is why it has been widely accepted as an important task of drawing a long-term direction for a company, it is here where existing relationship between planning, strategic and SS is found, since SS has been defined in various ways. The definition of SS can be highlighted by Zu et al, (2010), who defines SS as a tool that systematizes and organizes the improvement of processes as well as the development of new products and services, which is based on scientific and statistics methods in order to significantly reduce the number of defects that are defined by customers.

Acharya and Mathur (2016), concluded that objectives of SS include the development of a world-class culture, development of leaders and support of long-term objectives, as well as strategic planning. In addition, they expose SS as a business system with many statistical aspects, and naturally it adapts to commercial systems of most companies, it is an improvement unit that has the ability to introduce a common measure of quality perceived by customer, which should be applicable to any size and type of organization. Ultimately, they define SS as a business strategy that focuses on improving understanding of customer requirements, business systems, productivity, and financial performance.

SS is an organized and parallel structure to reduce variation in organizational processes through use of improvement specialists, a structured method and performance metrics in order to achieve strategic objectives (Cherrafi, Elfezazi, Chiarini, Mokhlis and Benhida, 2016). Therefore, organization's portfolio of improvement projects must be aligned with general business strategy (Easton y Rosenzweig, 2012), that is, the SS strategy must be aligned and be part of company strategic planning.

When comparing SS benefits from several sources, it is clear that the introduction of this methodology offers better performance for companies, increases productivity, increases productivity and competitiveness and market growth shares. In addition, it helps to maintain regular customers and attract new ones, reducing cost of production through the reduction of repariring and disposing cost of non-conforming products, designing new products, and ultimately increasing qualification and employees' professional level (Simanová, 2015). SS is a comprehensive and flexible system solution to achieve, maintain and maximize business success, it is based exclusively on deep understanding of consumer requirements, orderly use of actions, data and statistical analysis, and proper reinvention care, management and improvement of processes (Ertürk, Tuerdi, Maimaitiaili,Tuerdi, and Wujiabudula, 2016).

SS as a Manufacturing Strategy

Taking as a precedent that SS is a competitive strategy and it is aligned with the objectives developed in organizations within their strategic planning frameworks; SS is introduced as a manufacturing strategy. This is due to the conceptualization that literature reports, for example, Thun (2008) refers to Hayes and Wheelwright who define manufacturing strategy as "a strategy that consists of a sequence of decisions that, over time, allows a commercial unit to achieve a specific manufacturing structure, infrastructure, and set of capabilities". And to Lewis, who defines manufacturing strategy as total pattern of decisions that shape the long-term capabilities of any type of operation and their contribution to overall strategy. Therefore, the relation between SS as a competitive and manufacturing strategy is strengthened, and is an important part of strategic planning processes of organizations.

Reinforcing the relation between SS as a competitive strategy and a manufacturing strategy, there is evidence that companies are based on the ability to create strategic alignment between market and manufacturing opportunities, while a manufacturing strategy can achieve competitive advantages, therefore which is described as a tool for effective use of manufacture of strengths as a competitive weapon for the achievement of commercial and corporate objectives (Hallgren and Olhager, 2006).

In this sense, manufacturing strategy must coincide with the organization's resources, such as financial, manufacturing, marketing, technology and labor, to its changing environment and its markets in the pursuit of its objectives. Therefore, achieving a link between strategy formulation and implementation represents a challenge for companies today, as mentioned by Pun, Chin, White, and Gill (2004). In such a way that process in which the strategy is implemented plays an important role in manufacturing (Amoako-Gyampah and Acquaah, 2008).

For his part, Skinner (2007) defines a manufacturing strategy as a set of manufacturing policies designed to maximize performance between compensations of different success criteria, to fulfill the manufacturing task determined by a competitive strategy. Dangayach and Deshmukh (2006) stablished that that manufacturing strategy should act in support of company strategic directions and provide competitive advantages. Due to this, companies recognize the manufacturing strategy as a potential source to gain a competitive advantage, and be able to differentiate themselves from competitors (MacHuca, Ortega Jiménez, Garrido-Vega, and De Los Ríos, 2011).

Then it would appear that authors agree that the manufacturing strategy should support corporate objectives, provide manufacturing objectives, cost, quality, reliability and flexibility, offering a competitive advantage and focusing on a consistent pattern for making decision within manufacturing and resources that are key to its development (Kim and Lee, 1993). In relation to manufacturing processes, SS combines management, financial and methodological elements to improve the process and manufacturing products at the same time (Antony and Desai, 2009).

From this conceptualization, it is possible to reinforce the theory related to SS as a competitive and manufacturing strategy, which is invariably immersed in strategic planning processes that organizations develop. In such a way, that the main objective to advance in field of competitiveness, can be achieved. In this sense, Gutiérrez and De la Vara (2013) describe that SS is mainly a managerial program that implies changes in the way of operating and making decisions. For this, strategy must be understood and supported from the highest levels of organization management. However, given that many of projects do not meet client's expectations or do not reach the productivity goals, SS strategy relies in a special way on ideas and methodologies linked to what is known as the lean process. Therefore, with this integration, SS belongs to a broader operational strategy known as Lean Six Sigma (LSS), allowing deepening the importance of waste, process flow and cycling time concepts.

RELATION OF SS TO SUSTAINABILITY

Sustainability has become a crucial element around the world, allowing generation of profits and at the same time, citizens living in a healthy environment. For Zhang and Iru (2012) sustainable manufacturing is the creation of manufactured products through economically viable processes that minimize negative environmental impacts, conserving energy and natural resources simultaneously, improving the safety of employees, community and products. Likewise, the objective of SS strategy pursues to obtain products and processes that meet high quality standards, developing economic processes, seeking to reduce waste and decrease the use of energy, bringing valuable repercussions in the reduction of environmental impacts.

On the other hand, the interpretation of sustainability remains a debatable issue, considering two main perspectives, suggested by Palmeros Parada, Osseweijer and Posada Duque (2017): (1) the fact that the environmental and economic aspects are quantitative, and (2) social sustainability is often measured in qualitative terms, as a result of flexibility sustainability concept, which is often reduced to subjective interpretations derived from norms and values of people trying to implement sustainable practices.

According to Faulkner and Badurdeen (2014), sustainable manufacturing implies not only the manufacture of sustainable products, but also use of more production sustainable processes for those products. To achieve the sustainable manufacturing objective, deployment of SS allows the reduction of costs and profitability (poor quality cost), customer satisfaction (risk management) and the market increase. In addition SS presents a structured framework for problems and organizational leadership resolution, and enables managers and leaders to use new ways of understanding and solving their sustainability problems, it focuses on defect reduction to improve product quality, helping to reduce environmental waste (i.e. material, water and energy consumption, and waste generation) and focuses attention on reducing conditions that cause accidents, leading to safer and healthier working conditions for operators.

Höfer and Bigorra (2008) mention that sustainability trend is driven by changing values in society, with consumers demanding that the industry act more responsibly and governments around the world introducing increasingly stringent legislation to ensure that it is. Bogue (2014), for his part, adopts the term sustainable manufacturing and cites Sustainable Manufacturing Initiative of the US Department of Commerce, who defines it as "The generation of manufactured products that use processes that tend to reduce negative environmental impacts, they preserve energy and natural resources, they are safe for employees, communities and customers, as well as being economically healthier". He also mentions that sustainable manufacturing also encompasses aspects of product design, such as ease of disassembly for renovation, reuse or recycling, and minimizing or eliminating the use of hazardous or scarce materials.

SS, for its part, focuses on defects and waste elimination, which is why it is considered a strategy that can achieve significant improvements in sustainable terms, since by eliminating defects in manufacturing processes it has a direct impact on waste elimination generated in manufacture of products, caused by lack of renewal, reuse and recycling, positively supporting the organization's sustainable goals.

Wong and Wong (2014) mention that a sustainable process is one that reduces the ecological impact and is capable of eliminating waste from sub-assembled components and raw material used to manufacture products. They also affirm that without elimination and reduction waste, processes and operations are less likely to be sustainable, as resources are increasingly scarce. In relation to reduction of waste and environmental pollution, multinational companies have implemented SS in order to know if the implementation can improve pollution prevention programs, obtaining positive results, so it is considered necessary to carry out research with a quantitative approach to explain how the SS methodology has a positive impact on programs that prevent pollution (Calia et al., 2009).

In research of Fliedner (2008), some examples are reported about environmental benefits observed through the deployment of SS:

- Fewer defects that reduce energy and resource needs; avoid waste.
- Focuses attention on reducing conditions that cause accidents, spills, and malfunctions, thereby reducing solid and hazardous waste.
- Improving durability and reliability of product can increase its useful life and consequently reduce environmental impacts.

Finally, and from literature review, it has been possible to observe the impact of SS on environment caring. Chugani et al., (2017), Chiarini (2014), De Freitas and Costa (2017), Sagnak y Kazancoglu (2015) have positively related the impact of SS on energy issues, global warming, pollution and use of resources, they conducted research to determine if lean manufacturing tools reduce environmental impacts, obtaining positive results and recommending further investigation and increased sustainable processes within organizations. Therefore, it is observed that when implementing SS projects, favorable results are obtained in sustainable terms, and for that reason it is that SS can achieve positive results on innovation and organizational sustainability.

As a consequence of literature, there is evidence of a possible relation between the SS strategy, that is, with the contributions and benefits obtained with its implementation, positive effects are achieved in environment caring, considered as sustainable benefits. In this research, the main contribution is sought to verify the incidence of SS with sustainable benefits, as well as the extent to which a successful implementation leads to sustainable benefits. However, literature is not conclusive, on the contrary, it barely provides the first findings in relation of SS and sustainable benefits, which is why it is considered an opportunity area to deepen and develop research in a field that has not been explored in its entirety.

IDENTIFICATION OF CSF

O´Sullivan (2009) defines critical success factors as variables that, once they have been managed and identified by the organization, will lead to success and effective attention to planned goals. He also identifies that the critical factors term was initially considered by Thus (1961), however, they were initially defined by Rockhart in 70's - 80's, who provided several definitions:

- They are key areas of activity in which favorable results are absolutely necessary to achieve business objectives.
- Factors those are critical to the organization.
- Key areas of activities that should receive constant and careful attention.
- A relatively small number of truly important issues on which a manager should focus her attention.

For Suárez Amaya and Díaz Barrios (2013), the critical success factors are a concept related to capabilities, resources and competitive advantages for an organization, representing those areas of interest for those who lead the organization, a guide for making of decisions in any type of activity. For Zambrano (2006), cited by Suárez Amaya and Díaz Barrios (2013), CSF are internal qualitative and quantitative elements that determine management results, they refer to internal capacities and skills over which the person who directs the organization has control. As a consequence, to contemplate CSF in organizations, literature reports some benefits:

- Process helps the manager to determine the factors on which he or she should focus. It also helps ensure that those significant factors will receive careful and ongoing management scrutiny.
- The process forces the manager to develop good measures for those factors and investigate reports on each measure.
- CSF identification allows a clear definition of information amount that must be collected by organization and limits the costly collection of more data than is necessary.
- CSF identification removes an organization from the trap of building its reporting and information system primarily around data that is "easy to collect". Rather, it focuses on data that could not otherwise be collected, but is important to success of particular management level involved.
- The process recognizes that some factors are temporary and which CSF must be specifically managed.

The literature has reported that for the SS deployment, there are factors that influence the projects execution. Those that have been considered most relevant according to Júnior and Lima (2011) are the lack of alignment of SS project with the company's objectives, the quality of projects did not meet the expectations of senior management leaders little participation and project development at inappropriate times for company. For Alhuraish, Robledo, and Kobi (2017) for example, critical success factors include communication, culture change, and senior management commitment. However, various authors consider numerous critical factors for SS projects development in organizations, of which a general consensus has not been identified. In this sense, CSF identified in literature by different authors are presented, which were classified into five main constructs described in the following paragraphs:

The first of identified constructs in literature is related to support and commitment of senior management. To define it, Tlapa, Limon, García-Alcaraz, Baez and Sánchez (2016) mention that to manage a good project, one must begin with participation and commitment of senior management, since they are the ones who promote an adequate project selection and who provides the means for education and training. In this sense, Tlapa et al, cite previous studies by Lee (2002); Hahn (2005); Kwak y Anbari (2006); Brady and Allen (2006), who mention that participation and commitment of senior management is one of the most important factors in SS implementation. Table 1 shows the CSF classified within this construct.

Table 1. Factors related to senior management support

In relation to senior management support:	Authors
Company managers provide support and are committed to SS projects.	(Tlapa, Limon, García-Alcaraz, Baez and Sánchez, 2016); (Zu, Robbins and Fredendall, 2010); (Ho, Chang and Wang, 2008); (Dileep and Rau, 2009); (Banuelas Coronado and Antony, 2002)
Top management assigns a mentor/supervisor and necessary tools for SS projects.	
Company supervisors support SS projects.	
SS Projects are aligned to the company strategic vision.	
Projects meet the management objectives and goals.	
Communication between managers and workers is considered appropriate during the SS project execution.	
The organization managers provide an environment of cooperation and trust for the SS projects development.	

Table 2 summarizes the CSF related to customers and suppliers. Accordingly, Ho et al. (2008), relate the strategy to clients demands, for which they cite various authors, for example, Pande et al. (2000), observing that 16 British companies concluded that for an SS program to be successful, a company must connect it two ways with its commercial strategy and with its customers. Harry and Schroeder discuss the importance of benchmarking to ensure that an organization understands what its clients need, while Dedeke (2002) suggests that an auditing process should be established to ensure that projects satisfy their clients. Likewise, Dileep and Rau (2009) consider that a well-implemented customer management system is essential for the SS success.

In relation to suppliers, Zu et al., (2010) mention they are re involved in development of products and quality improvement projects, which must be evaluated based on quality. The organization must provide training and technical assistance to suppliers, in this sense Dileep and Rau (2009) indicate that a well-developed supplier management system, where the main criteria for selecting suppliers is based on quality aspects has an impact positive in SS success, and that processes should be built to monitor the suppliers quality performance levels.

Table 2. Factors related to customers and suppliers

In relation to customers and suppliers	Authors
Organization members seek to know the customers opinion (needs) to determine quality and delivery requirements.	(Zu et al., 2010); (Ho, Chang, and Wang 2008); (Dileep and Rau, 2009); (Zu et al., 2006); (Banuelas Coronado and Antony, 2002)
The company has an efficient customer management system (which includes: response time, delivery time, database, customer service, administration, customer organization, etc.).	
SS projects are related to customer demands and satisfaction.	
Organization members maintain efficient communication with suppliers.	
An effective supplier management system is in place.	
Suppliers are evaluated based on quality, delivery performance, and price.	
Specialized service providers meet all quality specifications.	
Suppliers actively collaborate in product design/redesign process through of their materials or services improvement.	

Table 3 summarizes the CSFs related to education and training. In this sense, continuous training and education for management and employees help companies to develop the knowledge and skills of their employees for effective quality improvement Breyfogle et al., (2001) and Gale, (2003) cited by Zu, Fredendall and Robbins (2006). In short, Wang, Yeh, and Chu (2016) mention that to obtain the effectiveness of an SS project, the high levels of company must commit to investing resources to start, promote, update and support the program. Specifically, providing employees with training, resources, knowledge, and authority to solve problems.

Table 3. Factors related to education and training

<table>
<tr><th>In relation to education and training:</th><th>Authors</th></tr>
<tr><td>Organization provides ongoing training in fundamentals of SS, quality, problem solving skills, teamwork.</td><td rowspan="3">(Tlapa et al., 2016); (Ho, Chang, and Wang, 2008), (Dileep and Rau, 2009), (Banuelas Coronado and Antony, 2002); (Szeto and Tsang, 2005); (Henderson and Evans, 2000)</td></tr>
<tr><td>Organization provides differentiated training so that employees who have different roles gain knowledge and skills to fulfill their assigned responsibilities.</td></tr>
<tr><td>Quality-related training is provided to plant managers and supervisors.</td></tr>
</table>

Table 4 shows the CSF that are related to the strategy implementation. In this part, senior management must consider a series of attributes elements to achieve a correct deployment that allows the objectives achievement set by the organization. Whit this in mind, literature reports scattered factors that must be considered and encourage an adequate environment for development and implementation of SS projects, considering mainly that it must have the support and contribution of a collaborative team that promotes a successful SS implementation. With respect to this, support and collaboration can be defined as degree to which people in a group actively and mutually support each other in their work. From this perspective, the collaborative team is characterized by members who know and fully understand the SS methodology, techniques and tools, in addition, there is appropriate leadership, effective communication and team participation, Hurley and Hult (1998) cited by Tlapa et al (2016). With respect to this, it is convenient to consider team communication and participation, in addition to promoting a supportive environment to encourage participation in continuous improvement teams.

Within the strategy implementation, it is important to mention that product design, organizational culture, improvement procedures, focus on metrics; aligned organization objectives and communication are a fundamental part for successful results to be obtained.

Table 4. Factors related to the strategy implementation

In relation to the SS strategy implementation:	Authors
SS projects are related to the organization strategic objectives.	(Goldstein, 2001); (Zu, Robbins and Fredendall, 2010); (Flynn et al., 1995); (Breyfogle et al., 2001); (Ho, Chang and Wang, 2008); (Dileep and Rau, 2009). (Banuelas Coronado y Antony, 2002); (Aviation Week,1998); (Hurley and Hult,1998)
The expected financial benefits of an SS project are identified during its planning.	
Those involved in the project understand SS methods, techniques, practices and tools.	
A structured plan and/or procedure is followed for SS implementation.	
Los miembros de la organización tienen experiencia en proyectos de SS.	
There is a person responsible for managing and documenting the steps to be developed for and during SS implementation.	
During SS implementation project, a program of regular audits is in place and their progress is reported.	
During SS implementation project, a program of regular audits is in place and their progress is reported.	
There is an organizational structure to plan and implement SS projects.	
Members of SS team continually participate in SS projects.	
SS team members meet regularly to communicate and discuss effectively.	
There is a willingness to collaborate through multidisciplinary teams within the organization.	
SS team members have their roles and responsibilities specifically identified.	
A previous selection of the collaboration team is made, trying to make it multidisciplinary.	
A Black Belt is in place to analyze problems and provide advice during SS implementation.	

In table 5, the CSF that refer to sustainable benefits are summarized as part of specification. It was necessary to develop a construct that allows measuring the research objective, so this section was constructed with the objective of identify and/or verify that there is a relation between a successful implementation of SS with sustainable benefits.

Table 5. Factors related to sustainable benefits

Regarding sustainable benefits:	Authors
SS practices integration has a positive influence and benefits the company in a sustainable way.	(Zhang and Iru, 2012); (Cherrafi et al., 2016); (Faulkner and Badurdeen, 2014).
With SS implementation, the level of sustainability of a company can be measured.	
SS adoption by company can be the first stage to become a sustainable company.	
The efforts of SS team and employees collaborate in improving the environment.	
SS strategy implementation prevents pollution and reduces negative impact on the environment.	
The SS strategy introduces sustainable reasoning.	

METHODOLOGY

Given the importance of continuous improvement in companies dedicated to aerospace manufacturing and because they are frequent users of the SS methodology, the target population is profiles with knowledge and experience in SS deployment that work in aerospace industry in Baja California. The people who were considered to answer the instrument, were those with positions that included general managers, area managers, supervisors, engineers, planners, mainly. The instrument was sent to the contact managers of each company, as well as to the users who work in aerospace industry of Baja California.

The methodology was divided into three stages, described in the following sections.

STAGE ONE: SURVEY DESIGN

To identify CSFs related to a successful SS implementation, the procedures described by Hernández et al (1998) and Levy and Varela (2003), cited by (Gómez et al. 2015), were taken considered.

As a result of factors identification shown in tables 1, 2, 3, 4 and 5, five constructs and variables that measure them were proposed a priori, which are adjusted to factor analysis shown in the following sections.

Consequently, a questionnaire made up of five sections was constructed, where each one is related to a construct and is composed of items (variables) that are measured on a 5-point Likert scale. So that, participants select their perception in relation to its experience lived in the company, within the evaluation in scale of 1 considered the opinion totally in disagreement, while the score of 5 represented totally agree.

The section corresponding to senior management construct was designed considering seven indicators. In order to identify to extent senior management represents one of the most important factors for SS deployment. The section that represents customers and suppliers construct was integrated with eight indicators, which sought importance of being considered to achieve the successful SS implementation. The training and skill development section was integrated by three indicators with which it is sought to observe to extent it is necessary for those involved in the implementation of SS to receive both training and skill development appropriated. To develop the section that represents the strategy implementation construct, 15 indicators were considered, in which it is mainly sought to observe the importance that methods, plans and procedures are followed within the implementation of SS, that responsible person exist in charge of the project administration and documentation, that periodic follow-up meetings are held and that the participants have the experience required to collaborate in the project. Finally, in the section that represents the construct of sustainable benefits, it was integrated by 6 indicators, with them we seek to determine an index that indicates the relationship between SS and Sustainable Benefits (SB), as well as to verify that with the integration of SS practices will have a direct and positive influence with sustainable benefits, and even that SS can be the first stage for a company to become sustainable.

To check the validity of questionnaire content, Escobar and Cuervo (2008) were taken into consideration, the opinion of 5 experts on the SS implementation topic was consulted, in order to determine if each item is related with the construct that intend to measure. To verify the reliability of the instrument, the Cronbach's Alpha index was calculated in a preliminary sample of 30 questionnaires, taking as a reference point of acceptance 0.70 proposed by George and Mallery (2003).

SECOND PHASE: APPLICATION OF THE QUESTIONNAIRE APPLICATIONS

The measurement instrument was sent to 43 companies located in Tijuana, 34 in Mexicali, 5 in Ensenada and Tecate and 1 in Rosarito, the positions profile included managers, supervisors and personnel with experience in SS projects deployment, to determine the sample size, the criteria established by Jackson (2003) and Henson and Robert (2006) were considered, who suggest that the sample size be 200 and that there be at least 5 subjects surveyed for each item that be integrated to the instrument. In various studies with samples of at least 200 applied questionnaires, high communalities have been presented, offering good factorial solutions. From this process, 273 surveys were collected, and answered in their entirety. With this counting of surveys, the suggestion about indicated sample size was satisfied.

THIRD PHASE: IDENTIFICATION OF CRITICAL FACTORS SIGNIFICANT (CSF)

In this phase, the information was analyzed with the SPSS 22 computer package. Initial data pre-treatment was started, which included extreme values tests (atypical), to identify errors in collection data. In order to verify the adequacy of the sample size for the factor analysis, the Kaiser-Meyer-Olkin and Barlett's sphericity tests were applied, described by Lévy and Varela (2003), in order to identify the significant values, the principal component factor method was chosen, taking as extraction criteria the components with eigenvalues greater than unity, contained in the correlation matrix of the analyzed variables. In order to improve the interpretation of the correlation matrix, the varimax rotation method described by Lévy and Varela (2003) was applied.

RESULTS

The obtained results are described in the following sections, starting with sample demographic description, followed by the results of the initial data pre-treatment and the statistical validation of the instrument's reliability, finally the factor analysis carried out for the identification of the CSF is included.

SAMPLE DEMOGRAPHIC DESCRIPTION

273 questionnaires were collected from employees with knowledge and experience in the SS strategy and sustainable benefits; the information from the interviewed profiles is presented in Figure 1.

Figure 1. People surveyed profile
Source: Own elaboration, based on the questionnaire results.

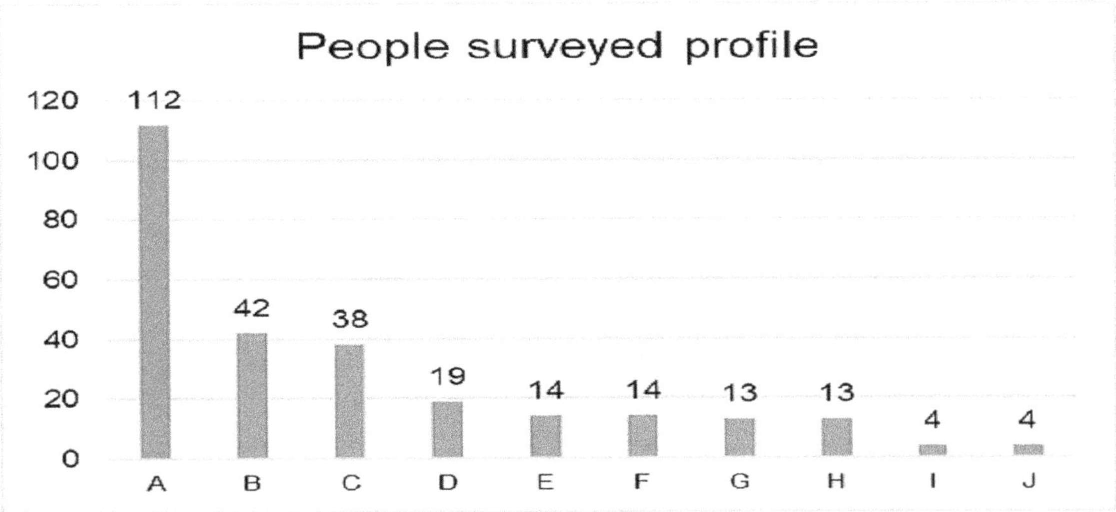

For a higher quality of information, the respondent's profiles are identified with the codes described in Table 6.

Table 6. Codes description presented in Figure 1

Profile code	Description
A	Continuous improvement engineer
B	Manufacturing engineer
C	Supervisor
D	Quality engineer
E	Industrial Engineer
F	Project leader
G	Area manager
H	Various
I	General manager
J	Production planner

Source: Own elaboration, based on the questionnaire results

As can be seen in figure 1, the highest percentage of those interviewed held positions related to continuous improvement, followed by manufacturing engineers and supervisors, for which reason the information obtained is considered relevant for the research.

Regarding the seniority in the company in figure 2, it is shown that most of them have been in the company between three and seven years, which allows having adequate knowledge about the company and therefore being able to answer some questions contained in the questionnaire.

Figure 2. Seniority in company
Source: Own elaboration, based on the questionnaire results.

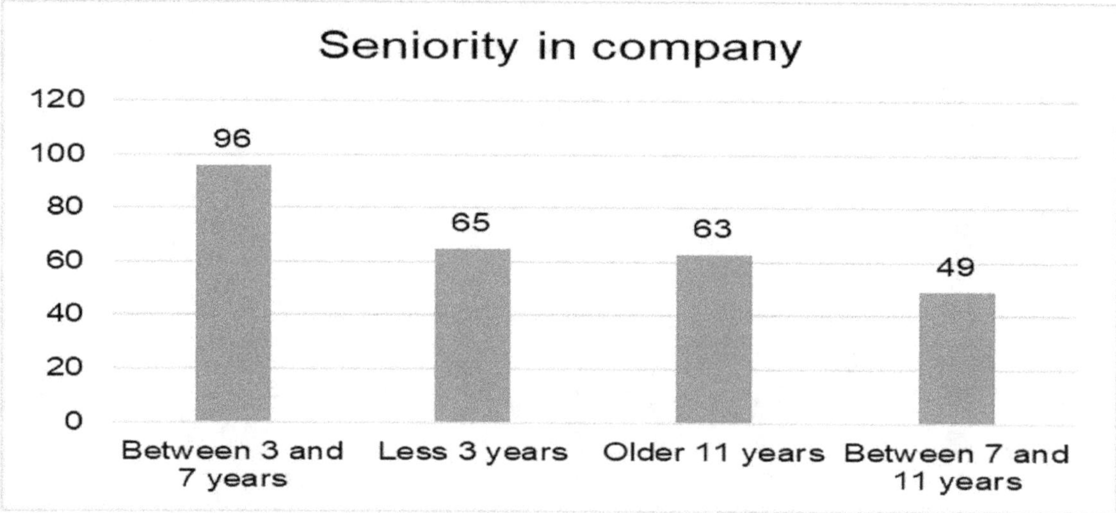

INSTRUMENT RELIABILITY VALIDATION

The validation of internal consistency of each of the constructs identified in literature is shown in Table 7.

Table 7. Internal consistency validation of latent variables

Construct to evaluate	Cronbach Alfa (D)
Senior management support	0.880
Strategy implementation	0.943
Relationship with customers and suppliers	0.845
Training and skill development	0.798
Sustainable benefits	0.896
Complete instrument	0.959

Source: Own elaboration, based on the questionnaire results

The Cronbach's alpha values show, in all the constructs, a high reliability of the instrument, since they all exceed the minimum value recommended by Levy and Varela (2003) cited by Gómez et al., (2015).

KISER-MEYER-OLKIN (KMO) TEST

To check the adequacy of the sample required to perform a factor analysis, the KMO test was performed, and the Bartlett sphericity test, the results are shown in Table 8.

Table 8. KMO and BARLETT tests

Kaiser-Meyer-Olkin measure to sampling adequacy		**0.956**
Bartlett's sphericity test	Approx. Chi squared	7000.892
	gl	741
	Sig.	**0.000**

Source: Own elaboration, based on the questionnaire results

The value obtained in the KMO test is .956, higher than the minimum recommended by Levy and Varela (2003) cited by Gómez et al. (2015), which means that the partial correlations are small, this indicates that they are measuring highly the same common factor. In relation to the Bartlett sphericity test, a value of 7000.892 and a significance of .000 are obtained, for that reason, the hypothesis of that the correlation matrix is an identity matrix is rejected, that is, it is verified that a high proportion in the correlations between the variables shown in the sample, which favors the grouping in principal components.

FACTORIAL ANALYSIS

This section presents the results obtained from the application of the Factor Analysis of the data collected to adjust the CSF identified in the literature review, reducing variables number that measure each of these factors.

The significant factors were extracted with the principal component factoring method, and the Kaiser criterion was applied to determine the number of factors to retain, based on the correlation matrix. In the same way, the Varimax rotation method was applied to improve the interpretation of the factorial solution, taking as retention criterion saturations greater than 0.5 in the factors extracted by the analyzed variables, the results are shown in table 9, where it can be appreciated that there are five components that explain approximately 70% of the variance.

Table 9. Variance explained by factors

Number	Initial eigenvalues		
	Total	**% variance**	**% accumulated**
1	19.588	50.226	50.226
2	2.013	5.162	55.388
3	1.805	4.628	60.015
4	1.399	3.586	63.601
5	1.310	3.359	66.960

Source: Own elaboration, based on the questionnaire results

ROTATED MATRIX

Rotated matrix results are shown in table 10, in which the item (variable) and the associated factor load are illustrated.

The Varimax rotation with Kaiser normalization, showed five components in the factorial structure of the model, obtaining an explained variance of 67%, in that sense, in the rotated matrix, shown in Table 10, also were observed the 39 items considered in the first version of the instrument with its associated load, as a result of the rotation, seven items with crossed loads were identified (AG6, AG7, IE8, IE9, IE12, CP1 and CP3), which indicates that they were measuring more than one construct, for that reason, the decision was made to eliminate them from the consecutive tests, thus avoiding later difficulties in the modeling stages. This adjustment was made by reviewing in detail the factor loadings of each item, as well as the correlations between the constructs.

As seen in Table 10, the variables contained in the Senior Management (SM) construct, mostly coincide with those that were identified a priori, being these from AG1 to AG5, which in turn it was detected that AG6 and AG7 present overlap with the Strategy Implementation (SI) construct. In relation to the Strategy Implementation construct, shows in IE1, IE3-IE7, IE10, IE11, IE13, IE14, IE15 indicators coincide with the previous identification carried out in the construction of this construct, however, an overlap is detected among the following indicators IE2, IE8, IE9, IE12. Regarding to Clients and Suppliers (CS), it is observed that all the indicators grouped to measure this construct coincide with the prior identification, except for the CP1 and CP3 indicators that overlap with the Strategy Implementation construct. With respect to the constructs Training and Skill Development (TSD) and Sustainable Benefits (SB), it can be seen that in both cases they coincide 100% with the identification carried out a priori to this analysis.

The overlapping items identified suggest that in addition to measuring more than one construct, one item implied another, that is to say which when one occurred by consequence the other occurred, so the elimination of these indicators did not affect the conceptual definition of the constructs that make up the structural model to be tested. As a result of this procedure, the final model is made up of 30 variables, reducing the initial proposed model by 9 observable variables.

To conclude with the analysis of the results, the non-redundant residuals between the observed and reproduced correlation matrices were inspected, checking the quality of the factorial solution proposed in this research

Table 10. Rotated matrix results

ITEM	COMPONENT				
	AG	CP	CE	IE	BS
AG1	.559				
AG2	.612				
AG3	.538				
AG4	.736				
AG5	.662				
AG6	***.478***			***.487***	
AG7	***.509***			***.425***	
IE1	.764				
IE2	***.663***				
IE3				.524	
IE4				.691	
IE5				.609	
IE6				.627	
IE7				.711	
IE8	***.487***			***.423***	
IE9	***.435***			***.550***	
IE10				.687	
IE11				.748	
IE12	***.468***			***.517***	
IE13				.723	
IE14				***.616***	
IE15				.567	
CP1	***.416***	***.532***			
CP2		.608			
CP3	***.495***	***.538***			
CP4		.642			
CP5		.761			
CP6		.785			
CP7		.774			
CP8		.589			
CE1			.798		
CE2			.779		
CE3			.734		
BS1					.627
BS2					.706
BS3					.813
BS4					.788
BS5					.714
BS6					.587

Source: Own elaboration, based on the questionnaire results

CONCLUSIONS

Literature review, related 39 factors related to the successful implementation of SS and their relationship with sustainable benefits, that works to design the initial questionnaire and discriminate them by their impact on the aerospace industry in Baja California. With the application of factor analysis, five constructs were identified, four of them represent the CSF of the SS implementation and one to measure the sustainable benefits. The identified CSFs initially included 33 key indicators, while the sustainable benefits construct was built with six indicators. As a consequence of the factor analysis, the CSF were summarized in 21 observable variables and 6 for sustainable benefits. For that matter, the observable variables were grouped into the latent variables described below:

Support and commitment from Senior Management. The importance of this variable for the implementation of the strategy begins with the commitment and involvement that leaders of the organization show regarding the deployment of SS, this should reinforce a correct selection of the project, aligned with the strategic vision of the organization, and provide all the necessary for a correct implementation, senior management favors having a strategy for the deployment of projects.

Relationship with Clients and Suppliers. If the implementation of SS the relationship with customers and suppliers is considered, it will be possible in first instance to know their needs, which should be considered for the manufacture of products or services, thus during the deployment of the strategy, the requirements presented by the client will be will be consider in relation to the quality of the product and delivery dates, in another sense it is consider utmost importance to develop close relationships with the suppliers of the inputs required for production, since theirs is who mainly supplies the raw material required for the manufacture of the products.

Training and Skill development. If senior management provides the means for its employees to be trained and skill developed prior to the implementation of the strategy, several advantages will be achieved during the process, for example, achieving a reduction in implementation time, this will allow the organization to obtain savings in terms of costs, the main objective of the education and training is to provide knowledge and skills for those who will actively participate in the implementation of SS, as well as, to provide the knowledge, tools and techniques necessary for the development of SS projects, for example DMAIC. In that regard, it should be considered that the personnel involved, including the leaders, have training that allows them to carry out analysis and improve processes, considering the above if the organization has certified personnel in techniques and tools that make up SS, the chances of achieving a successful strategy implementation are increased.

Strategy implementation. During the development of SS projects, there must be a strategy for its implementation, which will consider the participation and importance that the collaborative team has within this since this means that the team members have knowledge about SS and that they understand the methodology, techniques and tools used for its correct implementation. In this sense, it is recommended that the work teams be interdisciplinary and consider skills, knowledge and experience, since this will have greater possibilities of improving processes.

Sustainable Benefits. The construct of sustainable benefits was built from the first findings identified in the literature, this, in relation to the incidence that a successful implementation of SS has with sustainable benefits, in that sense the variables considered to measure the construct were identified, these were evaluated and validated in the statistical tests carried out in the measurement and structural model, which made it possible to determine the variables that most strongly measure the construct, thus verifying that the SS strategy introduces sustainable thinking which allows organizations have closer possibilities of achieving a sustainable manufacturing that consequently benefits the care of the environment.

On the other hand, the determined CSFs and their joint influence on the sustainable activities shown in this chapter constitute the main contribution of this research, otherwise, the results provide evidence that the support of senior management, relationship with customers and providers and training, lead to a successful implementation of SS. In addition to achieving the strategic objectives set by the organization, benefits are consequently on the subject of sustainability, in this sense first findings in this regard that sustainable benefits were obtained without having them as part of the objectives of the SS projects, for which a detailed research is carried out, managing to identify various studies that mention having developed SS with the intention of minimizing the negative effects on the environment, giving way to obtaining sustainable benefits.

The identified CSFs constitute the main contribution of this research to the theory of the field of management, although coincidences were found with some of the critical factors mentioned in the literature, there were others that were discarded as CSF, which do not seem to be critical for a successful implementation of SS. In addition to this, the research results constitute evidence that the successful deployment of SS is part of a manufacturing strategy focused on the continuous improvement of the processes and services developed in an organization and that with a correct implementation sustainable benefits can be obtained. Likewise, it is considered that the factors presented here constitute a frame of reference that can allow company managers to manage the key predictive activities of the implementation of the SS strategy. It is recommended to replicate this type of research to strengthen and increase the evidence, as well as to test the generality of the CSF proposed here.

REFERENCES

Acharya & Mathur. (2016). A Study on Green Cloud Computing and Technologies. *International Journal of Advance Research in Engineering, Science & Technology, 2444*(6), 13–17.

Al-agha, O. I., & Al-agha, M. I. (2015). *Implementing Six Sigma Methodology in Industrial Control Systems*. Academic Press.

Albliwi, S. A., Antony, J., & Lim, S. A. (2015). A Systematic Review of Lean Six Sigma for the Manufacturing Industry. *Business Process Management Journal, 21*(3), 665–691. doi:10.1108/BPMJ-03-2014-0019

Alhuraish, I., Robledo, C., & Kobi, A. (2017). A Comparative Exploration of Lean Manufacturing and Six Sigma in Terms of Their Critical Success Factors. *Journal of Cleaner Production, 164*, 325–337. doi:10.1016/j.jclepro.2017.06.146

Amoako-Gyampah, K., & Acquaah, M. (2008). Manufacturing Strategy, Competitive Strategy and Firm Performance: An Empirical Study in a Developing Economy Environment. *International Journal of Production Economics, 111*(2), 575–592. doi:10.1016/j.ijpe.2007.02.030

Amorim, J. A., de-Siqueira, J. M., & Martínez-Sáez, A. (2012). Large Scale Multimedia Production Management: From Strategic Planning to Six Sigma. *Procedia: Social and Behavioral Sciences, 46*, 1430–1434. doi:10.1016/j.sbspro.2012.05.315

Antony, J., & Desai, D. A. (2009). Assessing the Status of Six Sigma Implementation in the Indian Industry. *Management Research News*, *32*(5), 413–423. doi:10.1108/01409170910952921

Banuelas Coronado, R., & Antony, J. (2002). Critical Success Factors for the Successful Implementation of Six Sigma Projects in Organisations. *The TQM Magazine*, *14*(2), 92–99. doi:10.1108/09544780210416702

Bogue, R. (2014). Sustainable Manufacturing: A Critical Discipline for the Twenty-First Century. *Assembly Automation*, *34*(2), 117–122. doi:10.1108/AA-01-2014-012

Calia, R. C., Guerrini, F. M., & de Castro, M. (2009). The Impact of Six Sigma in the Performance of a Pollution Prevention Program. *Journal of Cleaner Production*, *17*(15), 1303–1310. doi:10.1016/j.jclepro.2009.05.001

Cherrafi, A., Elfezazi, S., Chiarini, A., Mokhlis, A., & Benhida, K. (2016). The Integration of Lean Manufacturing, Six Sigma and Sustainability: A Literature Review and Future Research Directions for Developing a Specific Model. *Journal of Cleaner Production*, *139*, 828–846. doi:10.1016/j.jclepro.2016.08.101

Chiarini, A. (2014). Sustainable Manufacturing-Greening Processes Using Specific Lean Production Tools: An Empirical Observation from European Motorcycle Component Manufacturers. *Journal of Cleaner Production*, *85*, 226–233. doi:10.1016/j.jclepro.2014.07.080

Chugani, N., Kumar, V., Garza-Reyes, J. A., Rocha-Lona, L., & Upadhyay, A. (2017). International Journal of Lean Six Sigma Investigating the Green Impact of Lean, Six Sigma, and Lean Six Sigma: A Systematic Literature Review Investigating the Green Impact of Lean, Six Sigma, and Lean Six Sigma: A Systematic Literature Review. *International Journal of Lean Six Sigma*, *8*(8), 7–32. Advance online publication. doi:10.1108/IJLSS-11-2015-0043

Competitiva, H. (2013). *C Ompetitive a Bility*. Academic Press.

Cusumano, Kahl, & Suarez. (2008). Services, Industry Evolution, and the Copetitive Strategies of Product Firms. *Academy of Management Journal*, *51*(2), 315–334. doi:10.1002mj

Dangayach, G. S., & Deshmukh, S. G. (2006). An Exploratory Study of Manufacturing Strategy Practices of Machinery Manufacturing Companies in India. *Omega*, *34*(3), 254–273. doi:10.1016/j.omega.2004.10.009

Development, S., & Execution, S. (2008). HBR's Must-Reads on Strategy What Is Strategy? *Strategy*, *86*(12), 143. doi:10.1111/j.0955-6419.2005.00347.x

Dileep, G., & Rau, S. S. (2009). Applying Six-Sigma in Health Service: A Study of Critical Success Factors, Critical To Quality Characteristics and Key Performance Indicators in Medium Scale Hospitals. *Information Sciences & Computing*, *3*(1), 25–31. doi:10.18000/ijisac.50037

Easton, G. S., & Rosenzweig, E. D. (2012). The Role of Experience in Six Sigma Project Success: An Empirical Analysis of Improvement Projects. *Journal of Operations Management*, *30*(7–8), 481–493. doi:10.1016/j.jom.2012.08.002

Echeveste, M. E., Rozenfeld, H., & Sonego, M. (2016). Potential Application of Six Sigma Tool in the Integrated Product Development Process. *Journal of the Brazilian Society of Mechanical Sciences and Engineering*, *38*(8), 2499–2511. doi:10.100740430-016-0503-0

Erdoğan, A., & Canatan, H. (2015). Literature Search Consisting of the Areas of Six Sigma's Usage. *Procedia: Social and Behavioral Sciences*, *195*(0212), 695–704. doi:10.1016/j.sbspro.2015.06.160

Ertürk, Tuerdi, & Wujiabudula. (2016). The Effects of Six Sigma Approach on Business Performance: A Study of White Goods (Home Appliances) Sector in Turkey. *Procedia: Social and Behavioral Sciences*, *229*, 444–452. doi:10.1016/j.sbspro.2016.07.154

Escobar-Pérez, J., & Cuervo-Martínez, Á. (2008). Validez De Contenido Y Juicio De Expertos: Una Aproximación a Su Utilización. *Avances En Medición*, *6*, 27–36.

Faulkner, W., & Badurdeen, F. (2014). Sustainable Value Stream Mapping (Sus-VSM): Methodology to Visualize and Assess Manufacturing Sustainability Performance. *Journal of Cleaner Production*, *85*, 8–18. doi:10.1016/j.jclepro.2014.05.042

Felizzola Jiménez, H., & Luna Amaya, C. (2014). Lean Six Sigma En Pequeñas y Medianas Empresas: Un Enfoque Metodológico. *Ingeniare. Revista Chilena de Ingeniería*, *22*(2), 263–277. doi:10.4067/S0718-33052014000200012

Fliedner, G. (2008). Sustainability : A New Lean Principle."*Proceedings of the 39th Annual Meeting of the Decision Sciences Institute*, 3321–26.

Freitas, J. G. D., & Costa, H. G. (2017). Impacts of Lean Six Sigma over Organizational Sustainability. *International Journal of Lean Six Sigma*, *8*(1), 89–108. doi:10.1108/IJLSS-10-2015-0039

Garza-Reyes, A., Jose, A. F., Kumar, V., Antony, J., & Soriano-Meier, H. (2014). A DMAIRC Approach to Lead Time Reduction in an Aerospace Engine Assembly Process. *Journal of Manufacturing Technology Management*, *25*(1), 27–48. Advance online publication. doi:10.1108/JMTM-05-2012-0058

Gómez, A. H., Escobar Toledo, C., Larios Prado, J. M., & Noriega Morales, S. (2015). Factores Críticos de Éxito Para El Despliegue Del Mantenimiento Productivo Total En Plantas de La Industria Maquiladora Para La Exportación En Ciudad Juárez: Una Solución Factorial. *Contaduría y Administración*, *60*, 82–106. doi:10.1016/j.cya.2015.08.005

Hallgren, M., & Olhager, J. (2006). Quantification in Manufacturing Strategy: A Methodology and Illustration. *International Journal of Production Economics*, *104*(1), 113–124. doi:10.1016/j.ijpe.2005.09.004

Ho, Y. C., Ou, C. C., & Wen, B. W. (2008). An Empirical Study of Key Success Factors for Six Sigma Green Belt Projects at an Asian MRO Company. *Journal of Air Transport Management*, *14*(5), 263–269. doi:10.1016/j.jairtraman.2008.05.002

Höfer, R., & Bigorra, J. (2008). Biomass-Based Green Chemistry: Sustainable Solutions for Modern Economies. *Green Chemistry Letters and Reviews*, *1*(2), 79–97. doi:10.1080/17518250802342519

Ismyrlis, V., & Moschidis, O. (2013). Six Sigma's Critical Success Factors and Toolbox. *International Journal of Lean Six Sigma*, *4*(2), 108–117. doi:10.1108/20401461311319310

Júnior, C. H. M., & Lima, E. (2011). Descontinuidade de Programas Seis Sigma: Um Estudo Comparativo de Casos. *Revista de Gestão*, *18*(4), 639–658. doi:10.5700/rege445

Kantardjieva, M. (2015). The Relationship between Total Quality Management (TQM) and Strategic Management. *Journal of Economics, Business and Management, 3*(5), 537–541. doi:10.7763/JOEBM.2015.V3.242

Kim, Y., & Lee, J. (1993). Manufacturing Strategy and Production Systems: An Integrated Framework. *Journal of Operations Management, 11*(1), 3–15. doi:10.1016/0272-6963(93)90029-O

Linderman, K., Schroeder, R. G., Zaheer, S., & Choo, A. S. (2003). Six Sigma: A Goal-Theoretic Perspective. *Journal of Operations Management, 21*(2), 193–203. doi:10.1016/S0272-6963(02)00087-6

MacHuca, J. A. D., Ortega Jiménez, C. H., Garrido-Vega, P., & Luis Pérez Diez De Los Ríos, J. (2011). Do Technology and Manufacturing Strategy Links Enhance Operational Performance? Empirical Research in the Auto Supplier Sector. *International Journal of Production Economics, 133*(2), 541–550. doi:10.1016/j.ijpe.2010.12.010

Mason, S. E., Nicolay, C. R., & Darzi, A. (2015). The Use of Lean and Six Sigma Methodologies in Surgery: A Systematic Review. *The Surgeon, 13*(2), 91–100. doi:10.1016/j.surge.2014.08.002 PMID:25189692

Mehrabi, J. (2012). Application of Six-Sigma in Educational Quality Management. *Procedia: Social and Behavioral Sciences, 47*, 1358–1362. doi:10.1016/j.sbspro.2012.06.826

Mintzberg, H. (1994). The Rise and Fall of Strategic Planning: Reconceiving Roles for Planning, Plans, Planners. *Harvard Business Review, 72*, 458. doi:10.1016/0737-6782(96)85711-0

Nedeliaková, E., Štefancová, V., & Kudláč, Š. (2017). Six Sigma and Dynamic Models Application as an Important Quality Management Tool in Railway Companies. *Procedia Engineering, 187*, 242–248. doi:10.1016/j.proeng.2017.04.371

O´Sullivan, C. (2009). *A Study of Critical Success Factors for Regional*. Academic Press.

Parada, P., Mar, P. O., & Posada Duque, J. A. (2017). Sustainable Biorefineries, an Analysis of Practices for Incorporating Sustainability in Biorefinery Design. *Industrial Crops and Products, 106*, 105–123. doi:10.1016/j.indcrop.2016.08.052

Pun, K. F., Chin, K. S., White, A. S., & Gill, R. (2004). Determinants of Manufacturing Strategy Formulation: A Longitudinal Study in Hong Kong. *Technovation, 24*(2), 121–137. doi:10.1016/S0166-4972(02)00050-0

Raisinghani, M. S., Ette, H., Pierce, R., Cannon, G., & Daripaly, P. (2005). Six Sigma: Concepts, Tools, and Applications. *Industrial Management & Data Systems, 105*(4), 491–505. doi:10.1108/02635570510592389

Roadmap. (2015). We Bring Good Things to Life Impact. *Quality*.

Sagnak, M., & Kazancoglu, Y. (2015). Integration of Green Lean Approach with Six Sigma: An Application for Flue Gas Emissions. *Journal of Cleaner Production, 127*, 112–118. doi:10.1016/j.jclepro.2016.04.016

Shafer, S. M., & Moeller, S. B. (2012). The Effects of Six Sigma on Corporate Performance: An Empirical Investigation. *Journal of Operations Management, 30*(7–8), 521–532. doi:10.1016/j.jom.2012.10.002

Simanová, Ľ. (2015). Specific Proposal of the Application and Implementation Six Sigma in Selected Processes of the Furniture Manufacturing. *Procedia Economics and Finance*, *34*(15), 268–275. doi:10.1016/S2212-5671(15)01629-9

Skinner, W. (2007). Manufacturing Strategy: The Story of Its Evolution. *Journal of Operations Management*, *25*(2), 328–335. doi:10.1016/j.jom.2006.10.008

Suárez Amaya & Díaz Barrios. (2013). *Factores Criticos de Èxito En La Investigacion Universitaria Venezolana.* Academic Press.

Thakore, R., Dave, R., Parsana, T., & Solanki, A. (2014). OPEN ACCESS A Review : Six Sigma Implementation Practice in Manufacturing Industries. *International Journal of Engineering Research and Applications*, *4*(11), 63–69.

Thun, J. H. (2008). Empirical Analysis of Manufacturing Strategy Implementation. *International Journal of Production Economics*, *113*(1), 370–382. doi:10.1016/j.ijpe.2007.09.005

Tjahjono, B., Ball, P., Vitanov, V. I., Scorzafave, C., Nogueira, J., Calleja, J., Minguet, M., Narasimha, L., Rivas, A., Srivastava, A., Srivastava, S., & Yadav, A. (2010). Six Sigma: A Literature Review. *International Journal of Lean Six Sigma*, *1*(3), 216–233. doi:10.1108/20401461011075017

Tlapa, D., Limon, J., García-Alcaraz, J. L., Baez, Y., & Sánchez, C. (2016). Industrial Management & Data Systems Six Sigma Enablers in Mexican Manufacturing Companies: A Proposed Model"Six Sigma Enablers in Mexican Manufacturing Companies: A Proposed Model. *Industrial Management & Data Systems*, *116*(5), 926–959. doi:10.1108/IMDS-06-2015-0265

Vinod, M., Devadasan, S. R., Sunil, D. T., & Thilak, V. M. M. (2015). Six Sigma through Poka-Yoke: A Navigation through Literature Arena. *International Journal of Advanced Manufacturing Technology*, *81*(1–4), 315–327. doi:10.100700170-015-7217-9

Wang, F.-K., Yeh, C.-T., & Chu, T.-P. (2016). Using the Design for Six Sigma Approach with TRIZ for New Product Development. *Computers & Industrial Engineering*, *98*, 522–530. doi:10.1016/j.cie.2016.06.014

Weiner, M. (2004). Six Sigma. *Communication World*, *21*(1), 26–29.

Wong, W. P., & Wong, K. Y. (2014). Synergizing an Ecosphere of Lean for Sustainable Operations. *Journal of Cleaner Production*, *85*, 51–66. doi:10.1016/j.jclepro.2014.05.093

Zhang, M., & Iru, A. A. (2012). *Using Six Sigma To Achieve Sustianble Manufacturing*. Advance online publication. doi:10.1109/IDAM.2014.6912713

Zu, X., Fredendall, L. D., & Douglas, T. J. (2008). The Evolving Theory of Quality Management: The Role of Six Sigma. *Journal of Operations Management*, *26*(5), 630–650. doi:10.1016/j.jom.2008.02.001

Zu, X., Fredendall, L. D., & Robbins, T. L. (2006). Organizational Culture and Quality Practices in Six Sigma. *The 2006 Annual Meeting of the Academy of Management*, 1–40. 10.5465/ambpp.2006.27175447

Zu, X., Robbins, T. L., & Fredendall, L. D. (2010). Mapping the Critical Links between Organizational Culture and TQM/Six Sigma Practices. *International Journal of Production Economics*, *123*(1), 86–106. doi:10.1016/j.ijpe.2009.07.009

Chapter 11
Gradual Technology Development for Ethnic Groups: Ergonomics, Processes, and Education

Eusebio Jimenez Lopez
Universidad La Salle Noroeste, Mexico

Victor Manuel Martinez Molina
Citi Hall of Cajeme, Mexico

Victoria Moroyoqui Galaviz
Casa Etchohuaquila, Mexico

Lilia Zulema Gaytán Martínez
Universidad Tecnológica del Sur de Sonora, Mexico

José Manuel Luna Nemecio
Centro Universitario CIFE, Mexico

Aldo Augusto Lopez Martínez
Centro de Ingeniería y Diseño Industrial (CIDESI), Mexico

ABSTRACT

This chapter presents the application of the concept of gradual technology to improve and increase the productivity of a workshop for the manufacture of handcrafted furniture owned by a cooperative formed by members of the Guarijía ethnic group, located in San Bernardo, Alamos, Sonora. The production process of the rustic furniture called "stool" was systematized and equipment was designed taking into account basic ergonomic aspects. Production sub-processes of the workshop and equipment were improved, including machinery design, purchase of basic technology, adaptation of electric current, water, and air conditioning systems. The basic inputs for manufacturing the furniture, such as wood and cowhide, were studied to determine whether the production of the stool affected the environment. The operating personnel in charge of the cooperative were trained in the use of the equipment and in the visualization of the improved processes.

DOI: 10.4018/978-1-7998-7396-9.ch011

INTRODUCTION

According to the World Bank (WB, 2017), indigenous peoples represent 8% of the population of Latin America and constitute, approximately, 14% of people in poverty and 17% of those in extreme poverty. Currently in Mexico, at least 25 million people are recognized as indigenous, and of which only 7 million 382 thousand are speakers of one of the 68 indigenous languages spoken (Instituto Nacional de Lenguas Indígenas en México, 2019). According to Miguel, Torres, and Hernandez (2015), the National Commission for the Development of Indigenous Peoples in Mexico, in conjunction with INEGI, prepared the "Catalog of Indigenous Localities", which shows that in Mexico there are a total of 64 172 localities of indigenous peoples, so it is important, and necessary to create public policies that improve the living conditions of this segment of society. For various reasons, and especially because of their customs and traditions, indigenous groups have been marginalized and their economic development has been slow and unequal. An important fact to highlight is the poverty rate among indigenous communities in Mexico, which is around 70% (Coneval, 2016).

The problem of inequality in indigenous communities is long-standing, starting with the conquest. According to Haro, Lara, Salido and Salazar (1996), in Mexico, this indigenous question alludes to the existing tension between the destiny of indigenous peoples and their role in society. The central argument of the debate is that five hundred years after the initial Spanish invasion, a large part of the country's indigenous population has preserved its distinctive language and culture under very different historical and territorial situations, and that this population remains, in spite of the different programs and policies implemented by the Mexican government, in conditions of extreme poverty and marginality, largely dependent on the governmental welfare model. Undoubtedly, ethnic minorities and indigenous communities in Mexico have been affected by the systematic abandonment not only by governments, but also by the private sector, which has meant that the quality of life of these communities is undignified and on the margins of a healthy and growing economy, depriving many of their young people of transformative education and dignified social growth.

In order to promote the economic development of indigenous communities, it is necessary to propose effective programs and projects that help transform their means of production and improve their living conditions. The indigenous or ethnic economy is not a simple concept to define. For Weber (2008), an ethnic group is a collective whose members share a belief in a common past due to physical similarities or customs, or both, or due to memories of colonization and migration. The members of an ethnic group do not necessarily have to share the same blood origin. On the other hand, ethnicity is a type of social group with an agenda of interests and is the result of the absence of clear class divisions. According to (Alba, 1990), ethnicity can serve as a principle of social allocation and as a form of social solidarity. Traditionally, the ethnic economy has been defined as: "that employment created by a minority for itself, which implies co-ethnic relations within the labor market" (Bonacich, 1973). For Light and Karageorgis (1994), the ethnic economy is any enterprise owned, supervised or staffed by members of a racial or ethnic minority group, regardless of size, type, and spatial concentration.

The central element identified as characteristic of the indigenous economy is based on the power to give and receive, within the cultural norms of reciprocal exchange (Inter-American Institute of Human Rights [IIDH], 2007). It is an economy based on personal appreciation, as a source of reciprocal obligation. Just as for the market economy the organizing axis or logical principle is accumulation, for the indigenous economy the organizing axis is distribution. The gift is the central instrument by means of which alliances are established that make it possible to glimpse relationships in order to form a solid social fabric. The development of this economy based on generosity, in turn, brings prestige and respect, a social benefit derived precisely from giving. The basic rule is that every "gift" must be returned. Therefore, the obligation to receive the gift is fundamental. In this way, the aim is the generation of a perpetual cycle of exchanges and reciprocity, and ultimately, cultural creation. In the indigenous case, one should not assume an automatic relationship between production and income on the one hand and the level of consumption on the other without understanding the role of reciprocity and redistribution.

According to the Inter-American Institute of Human Rights (IIDH, 2007), there are some key aspects regarding the relationship between the indigenous economy and the market:

1. The impoverishment of the environmental setting and quality of life necessarily means and implies the restriction of options, of satisfiers; therefore, the preservation of ecological and cultural diversity is a requirement of coexistence to expand the recovery of the culture of sustainability.
2. Greater diversity and distribution associated with the search for self-sufficiency and resilience capacities is the best advantage for minimizing environmental and social vulnerability.
3. The weight and value of social capital, the family, communal and social fabrics that collectively share reciprocities, which include market and cooperation networks, explain the "successful" positioning of communities and indigenous peoples in the market.
4. Economic institutions are culturally determined, i.e., norms and rules regulate internal and external economic relations.

In order to support the development of indigenous peoples, it is necessary for the public and private sectors to invest resources in programs and projects that trigger the economy, and at the same time, it is necessary to design practical mechanisms to improve the conditions for a dignified life in ethnic communities.

According to Vázquez, (2019), one of the mechanisms that have shown the greatest potential to improve the quality of life of rural communities is social entrepreneurship. The idea of enterprises having a social objective, creating economic, social, and environmental value while using market mechanisms to finance their operation, has generated multiple attempts from the public and private spheres to promote these organizations. However, there are few cases of social enterprises that have managed to be sustainable and achieve their mission, mainly in contexts of widespread marginalization and poverty. Many of these enterprises continue to depend on an external source of financing, fail to develop a successful product, or fail to solve social problems due to a lack of understanding of the context of the enterprise's beneficiaries. One of the most common mistakes is to manage these entities as if they were a commercial enterprise, under a logic of control and value appropriation, privileging profit maximization to the detriment of value creation mechanisms. This generally leads to a loss of legitimacy with different interest groups within the community, which ends up compromising the continuity of the company. However, there are successful cases of organizations that have generated certain processes of social innovation to achieve the development of their community and region.

On the other hand, indigenous people represent the social group with the greatest backwardness and vulnerability in Mexico and in Sonora. They currently live in small rural communities, generally far from large cities, with roads in poor condition; they have the greatest backwardness in the social development indicators: their level of schooling, illiteracy, sources of income (mostly low-paying salaried jobs), housing conditions, goods, and health services, among others. Although they have usable natural resources, they lack production assets or the means to exploit them. To this social backwardness is added the insertion of a globalized way of life, altering traditions, festivities and ways of eating, causing economic dependence and consumerism, and disrupting and modifying the ways of reproducing culture and language, thereby threatening the existence of ethnic groups (Zarate, 2016).

In order to contribute to the development and economy of indigenous groups in Sonora, it is necessary to leave aside the discrimination they are subject to today, and to consider these communities as social groups that deserve respect and recognize them with pride and national dignity, making them participants in government public policies and including them in decision making. Similarly, technological development must be proposed that is aligned with sustainable use and customs. It is necessary to apply visions, theories, or systematic methods that have already been elaborated, in order to invite as many actors as possible to the design, planning and execution of social programs in support of indigenous groups, such as, for example, universities, government, entrepreneurs and civil society. A conceptual vision that can be used for the development of comprehensive projects that impact the quality of life of indigenous groups is Inclusive Economic Development (GPCEE, 2014). The Inclusive Economic Development (DEI) project seeks to enhance the productive capacities of the population living in poverty and vulnerability and to expand their opportunities in terms of employment and income generation, so that they can autonomously exercise their rights as citizens and improve their quality of life sustainably (PDEI, 2011).

In this sense, this chapter presents the development of a project developed for a cooperative formed by members of the Guarijío ethnic group. This project consisted of technologically updating a rustic furniture factory and improving the operating conditions of the workers who belong to the ethnic group. The concept of gradual technology and the basic principles of ergonomics were applied to improve the workshop and increase production.

THE GUARIJÍO/MAKURAWE COMMUNITY OF SONORA

Sonora has nine indigenous groups, seven of which are indigenous: Guarijíos, Mayos, Yaquis, Pimas, Seris, Papagos, and Cucapás. The Kikapú and other ethnic groups in the country are considered transit groups and migrate temporarily in search of work or are on their way to the United States (Zárate, 2016). According to Bañuelos and Salido (2020), the Guarijío/Makurawe of Sonora represent one of the most forgotten indigenous peoples in northwestern Mexico. The conditions of poverty and marginalization that prevail in the Guarijío territory are even more difficult than those faced in the rest of the municipalities where they are located. In addition, the rugged geography of the territory, the dispersion of the population, the presence of poor soils, together with scarce rainfall, etc., limit not only the activities traditionally carried out there but also the possibilities of biological and cultural reproduction. The regional indices of marginalization are multiplying, due to the insufficient network of regular drinking water services, electrification, adequate road and telephone communication, etc., aspects linked to the problems of education, food, and health.

At present, the two main groups of Guarijío -self-named "guarijó" (/wareehó/) in Chihuahua and "guarijío" (/makurawe/) in Sonora- inhabit a region in the rugged foothills of the western Sierra Madre, near the border between Chihuahua and Sonora, federative entities that separated the political, administrative and social life of the Guarijío territory (Vélez and Harris, 2004). INEGI estimated a total of 2,136 Guarijío speakers over the age of 5 in the country, distributed in the aforementioned states. They reside mainly in the municipalities of Álamos and El Quiriego, towards the south of the state (see Figure

1). The population is distributed in a very dispersed manner in 22 localities that make up 3 ejidos. The towns of Mesa Colorada, Los Bajíos and Guajaray are the most populated (Bañuelos and Salido, 2020).

Figure 1. Geographic region of the Guarijío/Makurawe
Source: Bañuelos and Salido 2020

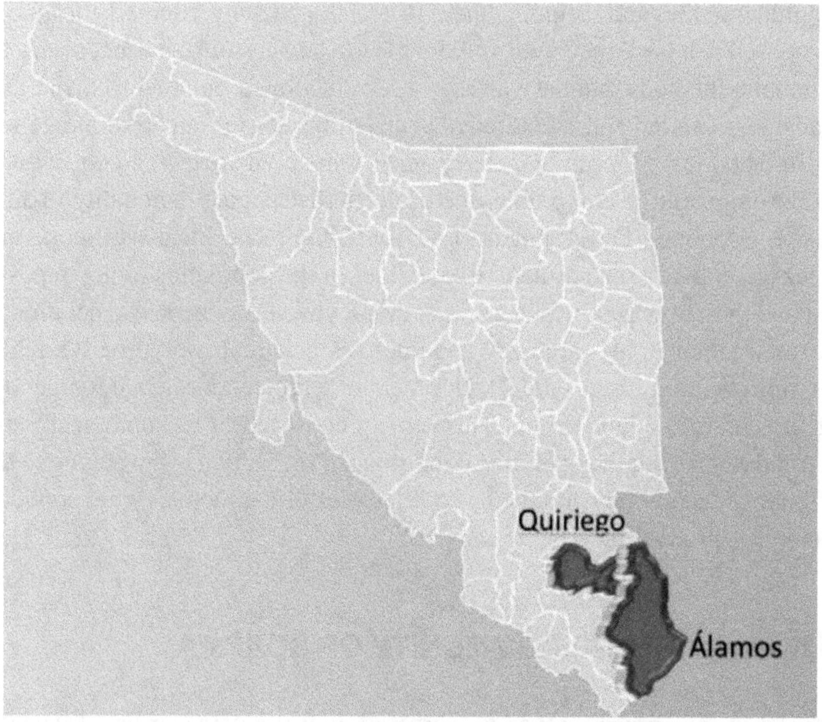

The territory occupied by the Guarijío of Sonora includes the northern part of Álamos and the northwestern part of El Quiriego, with an area of 24,318 ha. To the south, it borders the town of San Bernardo; to the north, the municipality of Urauchic; to the east, the municipality of Chínipas; and to the west, El Quiriego. In San Bernardo, there are two Guarijío colonies, Colonia Makurague and Los Jacales, which are made up of Guarijíos who used to live in Mesa Colorada.

THE CASE OF THE RUSTIC FURNITURE WORKSHOP

The community of San Bernardo is in southern Sonora, in the municipality of Alamos. This community is home to the Hermanos Saila Cooperative, whose business activity is the manufacture of rustic furniture using raw materials provided by the environment. This organization is made up of members of the Guarijío ethnic group and six workers who carry out all the operations and processes necessary to manufacture handcrafted furniture. The high demand for a particular stool which they make, led the cooperative to plan to improve its production systems to increase production from 300 to 450 pieces of furniture per month. In order to achieve this production, an investment project was developed and guided by the Universidad Tecnológica del Sur de Sonora through its intermediary technology incubator. The Project was financed by SAGARPA (Secretaría de Agricultura y Desarrollo Rural) and a spin-off company located in Cd. Obregón, Sonora (Amavizca, García, Jiménez, Duarte and Vázquez, 2014), was hired for the technical development. Subsequently, the company in charge of the project made a social service agreement with Universidad La Salle Noroeste for the accompaniment and development of human resources.

Characteristics of the Original Workshop

For the development of the project, several visits were made to the cooperative's facilities. The first was to learn about the state of the equipment, the operating conditions, and the characteristics of the stool. Figure 2 shows the workshop building.

Figure 2. Stool Factory Building

The workshop operated in a building that was previously used for school activities and had limited electrical service, water pumping systems in poor condition and no air conditioning systems. It had smooth floors, two rooms, and a large interior room, as well as a bathroom, and a large patio. The rustic furniture manufactured in this workshop is shown in Figure 3.

Figure 3. Rustic furniture called stool

The product shown in Figure 3 was developed mainly from wood and cattle hide. The operations were all manual and the cuts were made with basic tools such as knives and machetes. The preliminary field study revealed the following ten important considerations:

1. The stool manufacturing process was manual.
2. The working woods were guácima and mauto, and they are produced wild in the nearby region. In order to obtain these raw materials, the aforementioned trees were pruned.
3. The leather was from cattle.
4. The factory facilities were not equipped with industrial equipment.
5. The working environment was not cooled.
6. The stool factory used the facilities of what was formerly an elementary school.
7. The factory produced various types of rustic furniture.
8. It produced 300 stools per month, using the manual process.
9. There were six workers.
10. The standard manufacturing (assembly) time for the stool was 30 minutes.

Once the processes and other requirements of the workshop workers were known, the following needs were included in the project:

- The need for tools or a machine with a fixed or semi-industrial base to drill the hoops (see Figure 3).
- The need for a tool or machine to make lateral grooves (incisions) in the rods (see Figure 3).
- The need for a machine to mold the hoops since manual forming and fastening with nails and hammer is very tiring (see Figure 3).
- The need for a suitable place to assemble the stools, since this process was carried out on the floor.
- The need to reduce the cost of materials.
- The conditioning of the work area, since the weather conditions in the area make it difficult to work in some seasons of the year.
- The water supply system needed to be put into operation.
- Safety equipment was needed for the use of the machines.
- A machine was needed to cut the leather into strips and circumferences.

Characteristics of the Original Process

An extensive second visit to the workshop was carried out to learn the main technical operations involved in the manufacturing of the furniture. The main parts of the stool are identified in Figure 4.

Figure 4. Parts that make up a stool

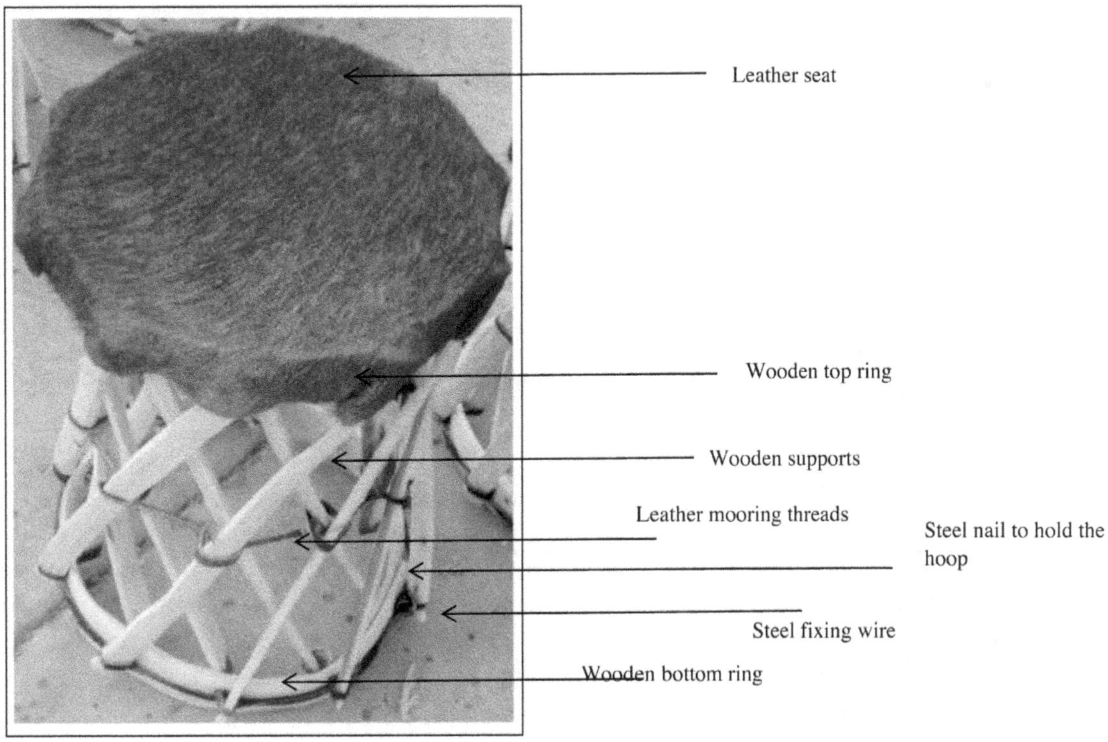

According to the explanation of the workshop workers, the rods and hoops shown in Figure 4 were obtained from wooden logs. From each 6-feet log of up to 6 inches in diameter approximately, either of mauto or elm, only two rods of approximately 1/8inches X 1/4 inches X 12 inches were obtained. This waste in the wood was due to the shape and finish of the pieces, for which knives and machetes were used. This part of the process was the most tiring for the worker and required constant maintenance of the tools used. The main operations used to develop the stool are described in Table 1 (Martínez *et al.* 2012).

Table 1. Main operations for the manufacture of the stool

PART NUMBER	GRAPHIC DESCRIPTION	PHYSICAL DESCRIPTION	DESCRIPTION OF RAW MATERIAL	ORIGIN OF RAW MATERIAL	SUSTAINABILITY
1	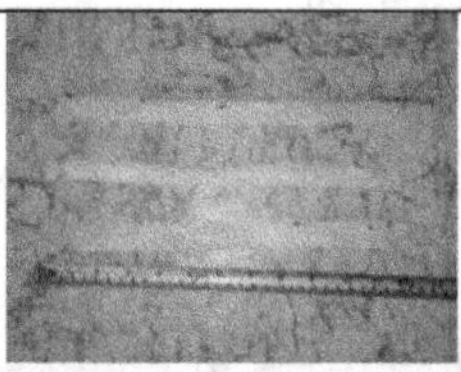	Brackets	Mauto (*Lysiloma divaricatum*, Fabaceae) 20 sticks/rods The height varies depending on the model.	Nature	The pruning does not endanger the environment of the region (it recovers naturally)
2	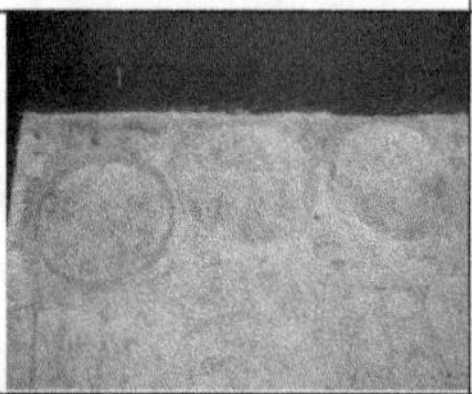	Lower ring	West Indian elm (Guazuma ulmifolia) 1 piece	Nature	The pruning does not endanger the environment of the region (it recovers naturally)
3	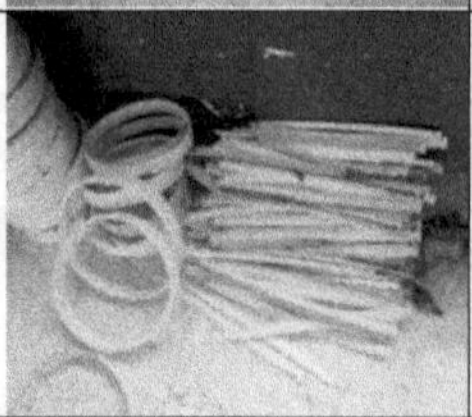	Top ring	West Indian elm (Guazuma ulmifolia) 1 piece	Nature	The pruning does not endanger the environment of the region (it recovers naturally)
4	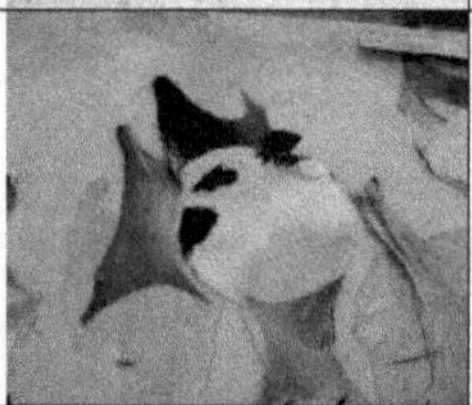	Seat	Bovine leather 1 round piece of 15.748 inches of diameter.	Beef Cattle	Cattle are raised in the region and the use of leather does not endanger the cattle herd.
5	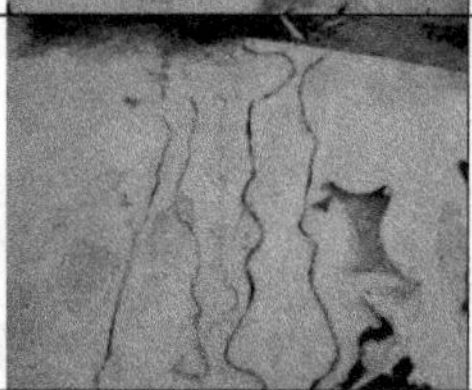	Mooring threads	Bovine leather 2 straps of 3.937 inches in length by 0.039 inches wide	Beef Cattle	Cattle are raised in the region and the use of leather does not endanger the cattle herd.
6		Nail to hold the hoop	Steel 4 2-inch nails	Factory	Carbon footprint

Continued on following page

Table 1. Continued

7	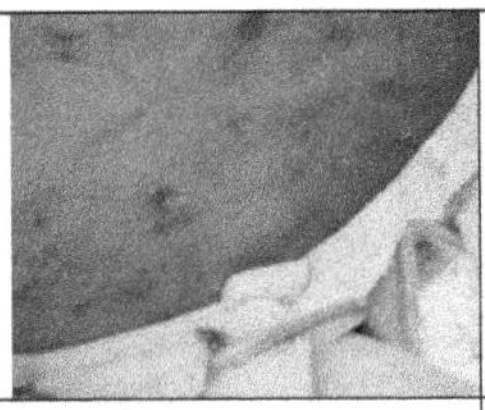	Fixing wire	Steel. 47.244 inches of 20-gauge steel wire	Factory	Carbon footprint
8	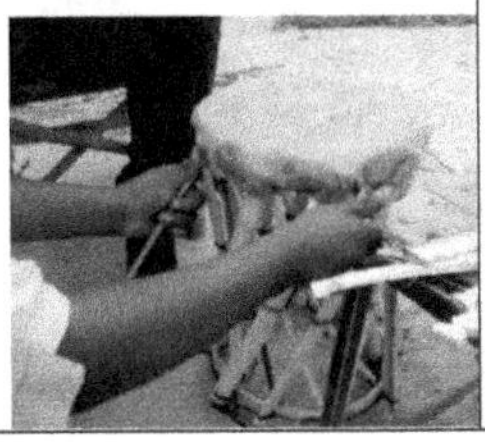	General assembly	Fastening of all components of the stool	Does not apply	Does not generate pollution

Origin and Procurement of Materials

The raw materials used to manufacture the stool are taken from the environment surrounding the community of San Bernardo. The main wood materials are obtained from mauto and West Indian elm trees. The process of obtaining the wood is by "pruning" and harvesting by hand. Table 2 shows complete information on the raw materials needed to manufacture the stool.

Original Working Tools

The following tools were used in the original manufacture of the stool:

- Drill: to drill the hoops.
- 3/8 inches paddle bit: to drill the holes for the upper hoops.
- 1/2 inches paddle bit: to drill the holes for the lower hoops.
- Steel ring mold: to make the rings.
- Tongs: to make the hoops.
- Machete: to make the incision of the wood strips.
- Hammer: to nail the hoops.

Table 2. Raw materials

PART NUMBER	GRAPHIC DESCRIPTION	NAME	DESCRIPTION	LOCATION
1		Mauto	The mauto (Lysiloma divaricatum (Jacq.) is a thornless, arborescent legume plant that is abundant in tropical deciduous forests of northwestern Mexico (Breceda, Ortiz and Scrosati, 2005). It is about 98.42 ft high.	Bajíos Estrado, Chorijoa, Mesachi, San Bernardo, Sawananto, Wajaray in the Sonoran region.
2		West Indian Elm	It is a medium tree or deciduous shrub, 6.56 ft to 49.21 ft (up to 82.02 ft) tall, with a diameter at chest height of 11.82 in to 15.74 in (up to 31.49 in), usually smaller in size (26.34 ft). Sterculiaceae (1789). It has a fairly straight log, frequently branched low with long, very spreading, horizontal or slightly hanging branches.	Very common in Cuba, in barren and cultivated lands, foothills and forests in low and medium elevation lands, in the state of Sonora.
3	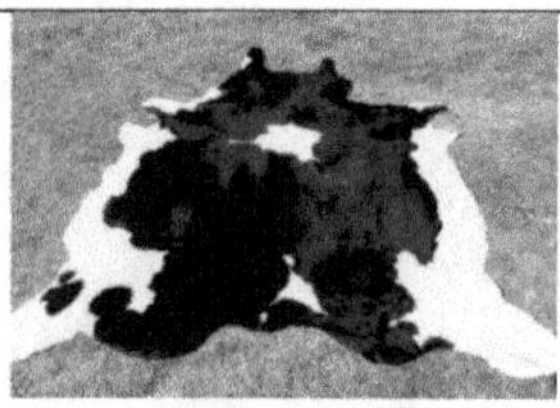	Cattle hide	The hide undergoes a cleaning and drying process, leaving the animal's fur as an important part of the presentation of the final product. It is used for the upper cover of the stool and the strips that adorn it.	It is bought from the farmers of the San Bernando region and surrounding region
4		Nails	One-inch long industrial steel nails	Hardware stores in Álamos, Sonora.
5		Wire	20-gauge steel wire	Hardware stores in Álamos, Sonora.

- Compass: to trace the holes.

This information was important to consider because it is the basis for the manufacturing operations and the working conditions of the operators.

Stool Workshop Conditions

In order to study in detail, the working conditions of the furniture workshop of the Saila Brothers Co-operative, a tour of the facilities was made. Table 3 shows a summary of the conditions of the electrical and water pumping systems in the workshop.

Table 3. Original operating conditions of the workshop

KIND	GRAPHIC DESCRIPTION	NAME	GENERAL DESCRIPTION	OPERATING CONDITIONS
1		Craft workshop	Steel rod and concrete slab building (previously used as a rural school).	The building was well preserved and had all the services, i.e., electricity, piped water and sanitary drainage.
2		Pumping system	Motor pump with a 120 VAC 1/2 inches hp motor to draw water from the cistern to the water tank on top of the building.	System had motor connected in 120 VAC circuit and level control electrodes for automatic ON/OFF.
3		Electrical system: 120 / 220 VAC	Single-phase system network for wall contacts and lighting distributed overhead	The system had a direct connection to the wall with contacts for 120 VAC equipment and a 220 VAC circuit for 24 inches diameter circular saw.

PROPOSED SOLUTIONS

The improvements or technologies proposed for the development of the indigenous economy should be designed taking into account cultural and traditional considerations. Thus, the concept of gradual technology is oriented towards the design, reconversion or updating of productive systems and towards the improvement of services, products and processes for the communities; this improvement takes into account their ancestral, cultural and environmental knowledge, that it does not substitute or displace workers through automation, and that the quality of the products obtained be equivalent to those obtained by the original production.

The concept of gradual technology implies that the designs be developed with great care, ignoring traditional criteria of industrial design. The proposed technology must coexist with the workers and aspects of sustainability must be considered when it comes to increasing productivity, since care for the environment is part of the nature and culture of indigenous groups. In general, in the productive systems of indigenous groups, there are several operations where workers operate under postures that are not adequate for their health, so anthropomorphic aspects need to be applied (Del Prado, 2007) as well as basic ergonomic criteria (Fan et al. 2019) to design or reconvert equipment and help the welfare of the people who operate it.

After analyzing the problem of the stool workshop remodeling in depth through visits and survey data and additional requests, the following considerations were reached:

1. The product to be manufactured (stool) was complex to automate while maintaining the craftsmanship and authenticity of the product.
2. The personnel that would operate the production system did not have the technical knowledge to handle sophisticated machinery.
3. The change from manual processes to automatic processes could detract commercially speaking from the handmade product.
4. The technological solution offered to a rural ethnic community should be in accordance with its traditions and marketing methods and consider the possibility of gradually entering other sectors and products.
5. The personnel that would operate the factory should feel close to the technology and not displaced.
6. The production of stools should be self-sustainable, as well as environmentally and culturally sustainable.
7. Adequate technical and administrative training had to be given to the beneficiaries.

The main idea that guided the updating of the stool workshop can be summarized as follows:

"To develop design methods (Jimenez et al. 2019), processes, machines and devices for the manufacture of a stool, using gradual technological reconversion, that aid in an improvement of the furniture manufacturing process and an increase in productivity".

This main idea gave rise to the following systematization or actions:

1. Design or reconvert machinery and provide administrative training.
2. Condition facilities so that they are safe, and operable.
3. Design equipment for ergonomics, functionality and safety.

In addition, the following considerations were proposed:

1. The production lines had to be designed considering:
    a. Purchasing industrial equipment.
    b. Reconverting existing equipment.
    c. Designing special devices.
    d. Systematizing the plant layout

e. Generating the specific process flow diagram.

2. The conditioning of the facilities includes:
    a. Running the electrical system.
    b. Running the water pump.
3. The design of comfort equipment includes:
    a. Air conditioning.
    b. Ergonomic equipment design.

ERGONOMICS, SUSTAINABILITY, AND GREENHOUSE GASES (GHG)

As is well known, indigenous peoples, due to their traditions and customs, take care of their environment and live from nature, taking from it what they need without putting their environment at risk. Three basic raw materials were required to make stools: 1) mauto wood, 2) elm wood and 3) cattle hides. The wood was obtained by harvesting and pruning, so there was no risk of deforestation. The distance from the workshop to the trees was 4.34 miles, so transportation was on foot and sometimes the wood was brought from land 31.6 miles away using transportation to haul it. As a result, the harvesting and pruning of timber can be considered sustainable operations.

In the case of cowhide, which was used for the seats and lashing straps, it was purchased from cattle ranchers in the region. Each hide measured approximately 6.56 ft X 5.24 ft and yielded 17 to 20 seat covers for the standard stool size. For the purpose of evaluating sustainability, it can be stated that the

Figure 5. Cutting of wood and cowhide with knife

number of hides does not considerably affect the cattle herd or the flora of the region, since the cattle were raised on local ranches that took advantage of the grasses and herbs that exist in nature. Granted, and as is well known, cattle contribute to the generation of greenhouse gases; an adult cow can generate up to 132.08 Gallon of methane per day, an amount that depends on the animal's diet. Methane of enteric origin is produced naturally as part of the digestive process of cattle, being a by-product of the microbial decomposition of food that occurs mainly in the rumen. Nevertheless, the acquisition of locally produced cowhide for the production of these stools was not deemed to be detrimental to the environment.

Another aspect to be considered for the GHG assessment is the carbon footprint (IHOBE, 2009) that would originate from the electrical consumption of the workshop machines. Wood cutting using machinery required robust motors, since mauto and elm are hard and the cut depended on the size of the logs harvested and the humidity, so the energy consumption for this type of motor had to be analyzed.

On the other hand, the production of stools in the traditional way required many operations that generated fatigue, such as cutting the wood with knives and machetes and assembling the furniture, whose forced postures caused health problems. These operations produce ergonomic risks – in particular overexertion, causing musculoskeletal disorders or injuries (MSD) in workers; for example, pain and inflammatory or degenerative injuries generally in the back and upper extremities. Working conditions that require the adoption of forced postures, repeated movements, manual handling of loads, etc., carry a high probability of producing MSDs. If unfavorable environmental conditions and deficient characteristics in the work environment are added to these risk situations, the overall ergonomic risk level of the workplace will increase considerably (ISTAS, 2015). Risk factors are those working conditions or demands during the performance of repetitive work that increase the probability of developing a pathology and, therefore, increase the level of risk (Psicoprevent, 2018). To improve the working conditions in the workshop, basic ergonomic principles were (Alsaffar and Ketan, 2018), used to size the machines

Figure 6. Assembly and finishing process of the furniture

and devices in the workshop according to the basic anthropomorphic measurements of the personnel operating them. Figures 5 and 6 show some uncomfortable and forced postures in stool manufacturing.

As shown in Figures 5 and 6, the traditional operations for the manufacture of furniture involved uncomfortable postures that resulted in fatigue and ailments in the joints and back mainly (information obtained from the workers). Therefore, the redesign of the workshop considered the need to design devices that would affect the health of the workers as little as possible, since the increase in production would bring more work and activities. In order to obtain the design information, it was necessary to take anthropomorphic measurements of people and identify those operations that involved harmful postures.

PROCESS DIAGRAM

In order to systematize the operations and flows of raw materials, a diagram of operations and processes was generated based on three fundamental raw materials: 1) mauto, 2) elm, and 3) cowhide, so that their process flows would coincide with the assembly of the stool. The diagram starts with the collection of the wood and the purchase and collection of the cowhide and follows through to the assembly of the stool. Figure 7 shows the redesigned process flow diagram for the workshop.

DEVELOPMENT OF DEVICES AND MACHINERY

Once the various considerations on the characteristics of the process and the nature of the furniture production were analyzed and studied, the design and manufacture of the devices and the purchase of the necessary technology were undertaken. The proposed design of the workshop considered that:

1. The final design proposal was not to go outside the limits of the initial.
2. The solutions to be proposed should be practical and facilitate the handling of the proposed equipment, accompanied by the necessary information: maintenance and operation manuals.
3. Cultural and traditional aspects of the Guarijío ethnic group should be considered in the design of the process and the proposed devices and machines.
4. The product should not lose its quality and originality.
5. The final proposal should consider the improvement of electrical, water, and comfort services.

Figure 7. Diagram of stool workshop processes

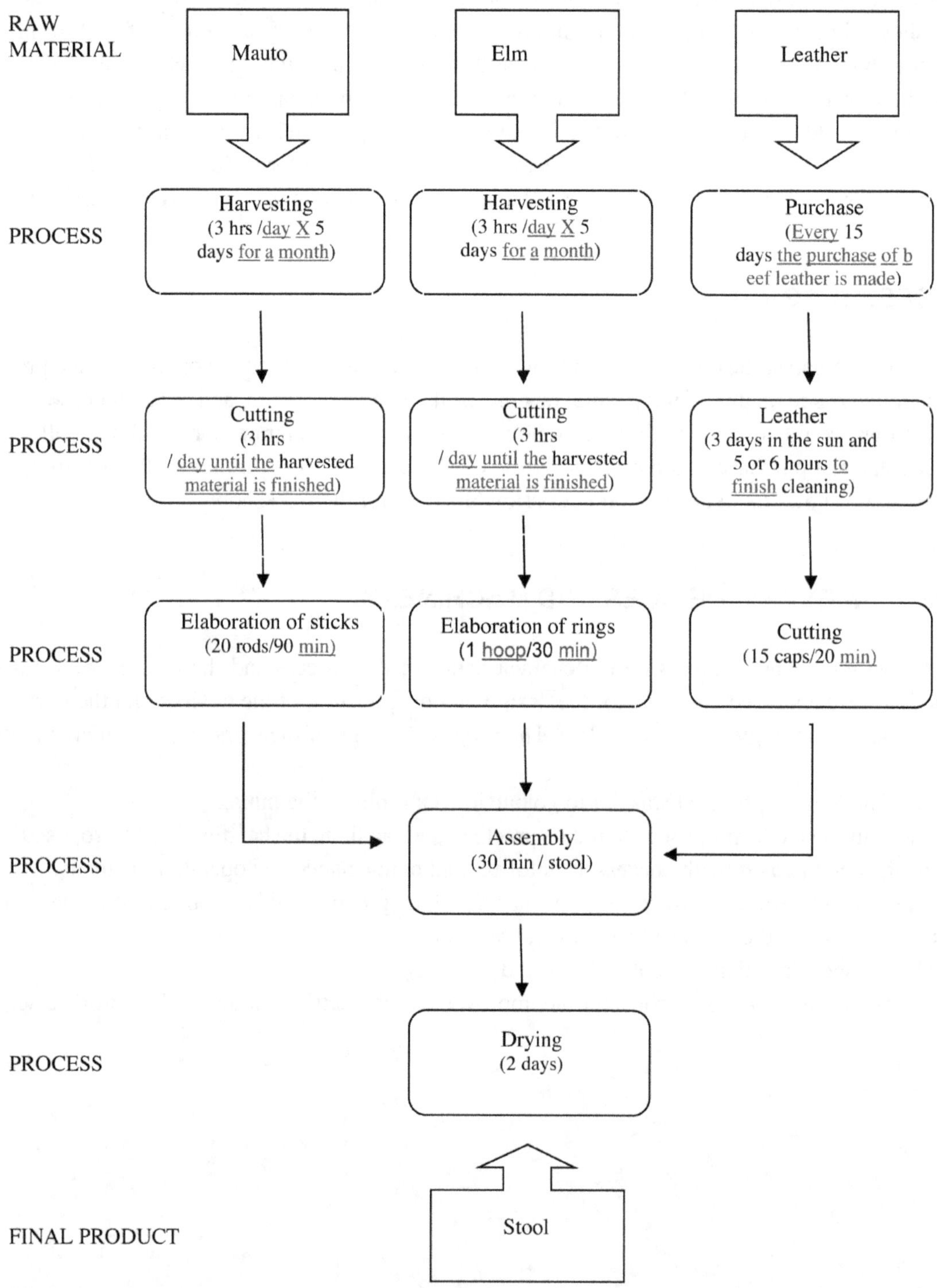

Table 4. Machines and devices for the upgraded workshop

NUMBER	GRAPHICAL DESCRIPTION	OPERATION	MACHINE DESCRIPTION	IMPROVEMENT OVER TRADITIONAL OPERATION	APPROXIMATE ENERGY CONSUMPTION
1	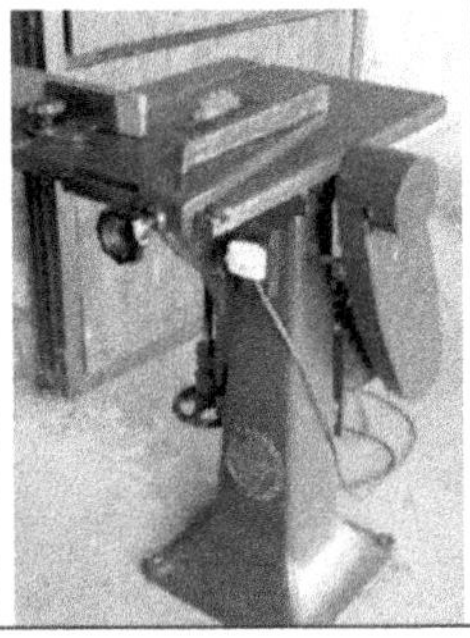	Wood cutting. It cuts wood of different types, but particularly small logs of mauto and elm with a maximum diameter of 2 inches.	Circular saw with 6 inches diameter, single-phase 220 VAC, 3200 rpm motor.	Reduces the diameter of the tree log to more manageable dimensions (slabs or boards and/or rectangular shapes).	6.0 kw/h
2		Leather cutting. It only cuts the circle for the seats, as the tie straps are cut with a knife	The motor drives a vertical knife that follows the contour of the line marked on the leather. Several skins (3 maximum) are placed to take advantage of the cut. Its operation is manual and depends on the operator's skill. It works at 120 VAC and with a 1/2 HP motor.	The previous operation was done with a knife and there was a high risk of cutting one's hands. This device cuts three pieces at the same time and the operator has no contact with the blade during the cut.	2.0 kw/h
3		Wood bending. There is no standard time for this operation, and it depends on the wood's humidity (It makes it more flexible and more manageable, 2 minutes on average)	It has stop and initial position insurance; it is held fastened as the arm rotates around the ring carrying the wet piece of wood in the middle, until it reaches the other end and is joined by placing a metal clamp. Previously, nails were used, which made the process slow and dangerous	The process was sped up and the dimensions were improved, which implied that the size of the rings was more uniform, which facilitates the assembly.	Not applicable

Continued on following page

Table 4. Continued

			for the operator.		
4		Wood cutting. This circular saw can cut larger wood (elm and mauto), logs with diameters of 4 to 5 inches, and with much more moisture inside, without breaking the blade.	It has a 24 inches diameter disc and a 5 hp, 220 VAC, single-phase electric motor at 3200 rpm.	It takes advantage of larger wood (the previous cutting process was slow and complicated), reducing waste considerably.	20 kw/h
5		Assembly of the stool. The wooden hoop is mounted on the rotating base and the table is used to hold the hoop and place the rods (wood cut as a thin strip that makes the supports of the stool, placing them crossed and tying them in the middle) at the end the upper hoop is placed and then in leather or skin that is stapled while it remains wet (facilitates handling) then it is tied with thread or leather strap to hold it when drying and stretching, and avoiding deforming.	Table for assembly of the stool; its seat allows the operator to rest and work avoiding damage to the lower back. On the top and sides of the table is placed material for assembly (rods, hoops, and leather for the seat, pneumatic stapler and other accessories) so the operator need not go for the material every time he finishes a stool. The worker would have enough material to assemble 4 to 5 stools per hour.	Previously the assembly was done on the floor and caused excessive exhaustion, lowering production; no assembly material was advanced and therefore the process became very slow because each operator had to enable their own material and assemble the stool; for the younger ones it was not inconvenient but for older people (men and women) the working position was extremely tiring and caused bodily harm.	Not applicable

Continued on following page

Table 4. Continued

6	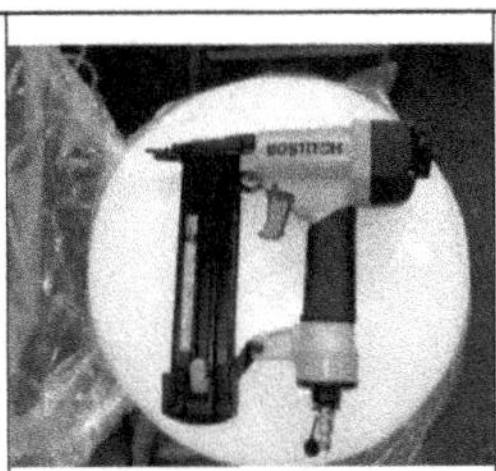 	Stapler Used to place the staples at the time of joining the wooden rings and at the end when the leather or skin for the seat was placed.	Device that places the staple semi-automatically using compressed air at 100 psi as energy source. 2 HP compressor, single phase at 120/220 VAC, at 1750 rpm.	Avoids driving nails that protrude into the wood and then have to be cut. The staples are purchased at the right size. This device facilitates the work and avoids risks for the operator; it eliminates the need to have an assistant hold the furniture while nailing; and the operation gives a better appearance and preserve the rustic and handmade appearance.	8.0 kw/h
7		Structure for drying leather.	The table stretches the cowhide allowing the removal of fat and drying as stretched as possible.	Previously, the leather was placed on the floor and to keep it stretched, some rocks and heavy objects were placed on it to prevent it from closing. It was complicated to remove the grease and it was not completely stretched.	Not applicable
8	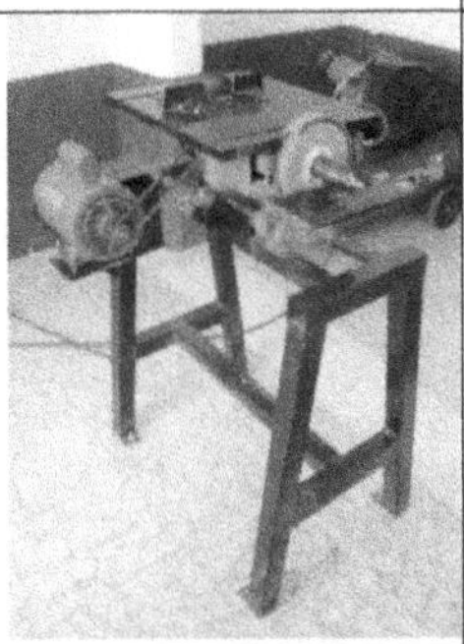	Three-operation machine	Three-operation machine equipped with disc saw, grinding stone and drill. Motor 1 HP at 120 VAC	Previously many operations such as machete and knife sharpening and drilling were done manually and separately. This machine helps to perform basic operations especially on work tools.	8.0 kw/h
9		Storage of parts	Rack for placing wooden rings and sticks, as well as cowhide circles.	In the original process, the parts and components were in several places, which required people to move around and which consumed time.	Not applicable

Continued on following page

Table 4. Continued

10		Motor pump	Device for pumping water to the workshop	Previously this device was not working properly	1/2 HP 120 VAC 8.0 kw/h, approximately
11		Air conditioner	Device that generates humid air Motor 1 HP at 120 1 120 VAC	Previously this device did not exist, so workers suffered from heat.	8.0 kw/h,

Table 4 shows the devices and machinery that were developed and purchased to upgrade the stool workshop.

According to the table above, the devices designed, and the machinery purchased, as well as the systematization of the processes, made it possible to meet three important objectives:

1. Increase production from 30-60 to 200 - 300 stools per month.
2. The proposed devices helped to improve various awkward postures of people and reduce various time-consuming and tiring sub-operations.
3. The machines and devices did not displace any workers.

In general, the wood cutting machinery and the assembly table concentrated many operations, which considerably reduced production times. The process improvements described in Table 4 are substantial despite the fact that many components and devices do not have a complex design.
With respect to improving working conditions, the following tasks were performed:

1. Cooling (humid air) was placed to lower heat to a comfortable temperature for workers.
2. The damaged water pump was fixed and the cistern was cleaned.
3. The electrical system was upgraded and now provides power to machinery and devices.

Figure 8 shows the work done for air conditioning.

Figure 8. Conditioning of the work center

On the other hand, once the electrical consumptions of each machine were known (see Table 4), we proceeded to perform a carbon footprint calculation (IHOBE, 2009) using the ISO 14064-1 standard (Bastianoni, Marchi, Caro, Casprini and Maria, 2014) and the following formula:

$FkWh$

$TonCO2e = kW_h*$

$1000kg/ton$

Where $TonCO2e$ indicates the tons of carbon dioxide equivalent; kWh indicates Kilowatt-hours of electrical energy consumed; $FkWh$ indicates the emission factor of the National Electric System (0.505 Tco2e/ MWh, data provided for each year); and $1000kg/ton$ factors from kilograms to tons.

For the calculation of electrical energy consumption, an average percentage of 30% of the maximum monthly consumption was taken into account, since it is difficult to quantify the punctual expenditure of the machines in operation because the workers do not follow a standardized production.

Figure 9. Ergonomic table of the stool assembly

With respect to ergonomic issues, the heights of the machines were designed according to the anthropomorphic measurements of the personnel working in the workshop. Since there are only six workers, the average measurements were taken. One of the devices whose ergonomic design greatly helped to eliminate awkward postures was the assembly table shown in Figure 9.

The table shown in Figure 8, is ideal to avoid postures that damage the back of the workers. It has extensions on which various parts are placed and the worker can perform many operations without having to move. The rotating plate in the center of the table allows the stool to be rotated, which facilitates its assembly. The table is connected to a shelf where the main parts and finished products are stored. This makes the supply of materials a simple and time-saving task. Similarly, the leather cutting machine proved to be very useful for the workers since it facilitated operations and reduced the risk of accidents.

It is worth mentioning that all the devices have heights that adjust to the average anthropomorphic measurements of the workers, which helps them to perform the operations under non-harmful postures.

EDUCATION AND TRAINING

The SAGARPA-funded furniture workshop upgrade project also included training the members of the Zaila Brothers Cooperative in project management so that they could systematically manage their business and grow if the market demanded it. In the case of equipment management, the following aspects were taken into account:

1. Most of the equipment is semi-industrial, which means that the machines have the potential to cause serious accidents to personnel if they are not operated properly.

2. An operating manual for each piece of equipment needed to be generated.
3. A maintenance manual needed to be developed.
4. Both manuals should be explained in detail to the workshop personnel.

Training on industrial equipment must consider certain fundamental knowledge for its understanding, operation and maintenance. This project's training was given as clearly as possible with the objective being the workers' full involvement, including continuous practice which would result in the workers obtaining experience in safety measures. Figure 10 presents images of the technical training given to the workshop personnel.

Figure 10. Training in the operation of workshop equipment

Training involved putting each machine into operation, explaining its mode of operation in detail, and showing proper maintenance. Finally, Figure 11 shows the finished products and their display for sale.

RESULTS AND DISCUSSION

The results obtained from the furniture workshop project are summarized in the following points:

1. It was possible to transform the artisan workshop that used very basic tools for the manufacture of stools into a production system made up of machines and semi-industrial devices whose operation

made it possible to increase production from 30 - 60 to 200 - 300 pieces of furniture per month, thus meeting the technical and commercial goal setting.

2. The financial resources provided by SAGARPA made it possible to purchase the equipment needed to update the workshop and to finance the technological supplier, making it possible to deliver the turnkey project to the beneficiaries.
3. The stool manufacturing process does not put the environment of the region where the workshop is located at risk, since raw materials such as wood are collected by pruning and cowhides are collected and purchased from cattle ranchers in the region, so production can be considered sustainable.
4. Under the philosophy of gradual technological development, it was possible to design and select equipment for furniture production whose operation did not displace the workers and under consideration of their customs and traditions.
5. By using very basic principles of ergonomics, it was possible to design and select equipment whose operation minimized the risks of accidents to workers and improved their health since it was possible to transform the operations that involved harmful postures into conditions where work was easier and with less risk of suffering health problems in the medium and long term.
6. By improving working conditions in the workshop with the installation of humid air and improvements to the facilities, workers were able to operate with the comfort necessary for the required production.
7. Training the workshop personnel on the operation and maintenance of the equipment allowed them to learn about the potential capabilities of each machine and device, as well as the procedures for keeping the equipment in the best-operating conditions.

Figure 11. Finished products and display for sale

8. The carbon footprint calculated from electrical consumption is not significantly high, emitting few greenhouse gases.

The update of the stool workshop provided information on the characteristics and considerations that must be accounted for in the development of projects that have an impact on the economies of indigenous peoples and the importance of the advice of universities and spin-off companies in the management of resources and technical guidance that make it possible to achieve favorable results for the beneficiaries. The path followed by this project from the management of resources, the injection of funds by government programs and the execution and implementation of the workshop, can be taken as an example for the implementation of more ambitious programs that help to spark the economy of ethnic groups.

CONCLUSION

This paper presented the experience of updating a rustic furniture workshop, owned by a cooperative made up of members of the Guarigío ethnic group. The main conclusions obtained are summarized below:

With the updating of the furniture workshop it was possible to increase production from 60 stools to a maximum of 300 per month. This was possible because the semi-industrial machinery can perform various operations quickly and because the design of the devices made it possible to eliminate unnecessary trips by the workers, saving time and effort. The machinery and devices were selected and adapted to eliminate various harmful postures that were present in the original process, thus helping to improve the health of workers. The basic principles of ergonomics were useful to design the work elements according to the anthropometric measurements of the employees. The increase in stool production does not have a significant impact on the environment in the area surrounding the workshop, since the wood is obtained by pruning and there is a large area in the San Bernardo region where there are enough mauto and elm trees. Cowhide is purchased from local cattle ranchers, so the impact on the environment is not significant and the process can be considered sustainable. The operation of the workshop does not generate a significant volume of greenhouse gases, since the carbon footprint calculated from electricity consumption was not significant. The implementation of technology in the production processes of ethnic groups must necessarily take into account their uses and customs and ensure that workers are not displaced by machinery. Technology or social assistance projects aimed at indigenous peoples are not easy or simple to develop, and not every supplier understands the characteristics of the uses and customs that must be taken into account to deliver a complete project in accordance with real needs and growth.

The projects of indigenous communities must be developed in the cultural context and traditions they practice. The economy of these communities cannot be developed under objectives or public policies that are applied in the cities because their development does not follow the same dynamics, and the social systems of each entity are different. On the other hand, the traditional production processes of indigenous groups are generally not ergonomic, which implies that the health of workers is compromised in the medium and long term. It is important to design a social ergonomics program that can be applied to solve the postural problems of indigenous groups. Finally, the participation of universities, companies and the government in social development projects for indigenous communities is necessary to achieve positive social objectives and impacts on vulnerable groups.

REFERENCES

Alba, R. D. (1990). *Ethnic Identity: The transformation of White America*. Yale University Press.

Alsaffar, I., & Ketan, H. (2018). Reviewing the Effects of Integrated Lean Six Sigma Methodologies with Ergonomics Principles in an Industrial Workstation, 2nd International Conference on Engineering Sciences IOP Conf. Series. *Materials Science and Engineering*, *433*, 012060. doi:10.1088/1757-899X/433/1/012060

Amavizca, L. O., García, A. C., Jiménez, E., Duarte, G. L., & Vázquez, J. C. (2014). Aplicación de la metodología semi-ágil ICONIX para el desarrollo de software: implementación y publicación de un sitio WEB para una empresa SPIN - OFF en el Sur de Sonora, México. *Twelfth LACCEI Latin American and Caribbean Conference for Engineering and Technology (LACCEI'2014) "Excellence in Engineering To Enhance a Country's Productivity"*.

Bañuelos, N., & Salido, P.L. (2020). Enredados con la sierra. Las plantas en las estrategias sostenibles de sobrevivencia del grupo indígena Guarijío/Makurawe de Sonora, México. *Tecnología en Marcha, 33*(1), 178-192.

Bastianoni, S., Marchi, M., Caro, D., Casprini, P., & Maria, F. (2014). The connection between 2006 IPCC GHG inventory methodology and ISO 14064-1 certification standard – A reference point for the environmental policies at sub-national scale. *Environmental Science & Policy*, *44*, 97–107. doi:10.1016/j.envsci.2014.07.015

Bonacich, E. (1973). A theory of middleman minorities. *American Sociological Review*, *38*(5), 583–594. doi:10.2307/2094409

Breceda, A., Ortiz, V., & Scrosati, R. (2005). Mauto (Lysiloma divaricatum, Fabaceae) Allometry as an Indicator of Cattle Grazing Pressure in a Tropical Dry Forestin Northwestern Mexico. *Rangeland Ecology and Management*, *58*(1), 85–88. doi:10.2111/1551-5028(2005)58<85:MLDFAA>2.0.CO;2

Coneval. (2016). *Evaluación de la política de desarrollo social 2016*. Coneval.

Del Prado, J. L. (2007). Anthropometric measurement of Filipino manufacturing workers. *International Journal of Industrial Ergonomics*, *37*(6), 497–503. doi:10.1016/j.ergon.2007.02.004

Fan, H., Yu, S., Chu, J., Wang, M., Chen, D., Zhang, S., Wang, W., Wu, T., & Wan, N. (2019). Anthropometric characteristics and product categorization of Chinese auricles for ergonomic design. *International Journal of Industrial Ergonomics*, *69*, 118–141. doi:10.1016/j.ergon.2018.11.002

GPCEE. (2014). *Guía Práctica Centros de Empleo y Emprendimiento ventanillas únicas de atención para grupos en pobreza y exclusión. Programa de las Naciones Unidas para el Desarrollo*. PNUD.

Haro, A., Lara, B., Salido, P., & Salazar, V. (1996). El Sistema local de salud en la región Guarijio/Makuraque de Sonora: Retos y perspectivas. Región y Sociedad, Julio-diciembre. *VII*, *NO*(12), 47–106.

IHOBE. (2009). *Análisis del ciclo de vida y huella del carbono: dos maneras de medir el impacto ambiental de un producto*. Primera Edición. Sociedad Pública de Gestión Ambiental.

IIDH. (2007). Instituto Interamericano de Derechos Humanos. Economía indígena y mercado.

Instituto Nacional de Lenguas Indígenas en México. (2019). *En el país, 25 millones de personas se reconocen como indígenas*. Recuperado el 19 de Mayo de 2019, de Instituto Nacional de Lenguas Indígenas en México: https://www.inali.gob.mx/es/comunicados/701-2019-02-08-15-22-50.html

ISTAS. (2015). Factores de riesgo ergonómico y causas de exposición. Herramientas de prevención de riesgos laborales para pymes, Madrid, España.

Jiménez, E., Acosta, M., Luna, G., Lucero, B., Delfín, J., & Velásquez, L. A. (2019). Reverse Engineering and Straightforward Design as Tools to Improve the Teaching of Mechanical Engineering. In M. Abdulwahed, A. Bouras, & L. Veillard (Eds.), *Industry Integrated Engineering and Computing Education* (pp. 93–188). Springer.

Light, I., & Karageorgis, S. (1994). The ethnic economy. In N. Smelser & R. Swedberg (Eds.), *The handbook of economic sociology* (pp. 646–671). Russell Sage Foundation.

Martínez, V. M., Jiménez, E., Arellano, L., Uzeta, C. R., Sotelo, R., & Reyes, L. A. (2012). Desarrollo de equipos para la manufactura de muebles rústicos de la etnia guarijía: un ejemplo de transferencia tecnológica. *XII International Conference on Engineering and Technology Education*, 190-194.

Miguel, A. E., Torres, J. C., & Hernández, B. R. (2015). El turismo y las redes territoriales en ciudades de pueblos originarios. El caso de Oaxaca, México. *Revista Turydes: Turismo y Desarrollo, 19*. Recuperado el 10 de diciembre de 2016, de: https://www.eumed.net/rev/turydes/19/pueblos.html

PDEI. (2011). *Proyecto Desarrollo Económico Incluyente*. Programa de las Naciones Unidas para el Desarrollo (PNUD). Recuperado el 9 de septiembre de 2018 de:http://www.desarrolloeconomico.gov.co/sites/default/files/marcolegal/Proyecto-Desarrollo-Economico- Incluyente.pdf

Psicopreven. (2018). *ISO 11228-1:2013*. Recuperado el 19 de Diciembre de 2020, de https://ergosoft.nextprevencion.com/bat/ajax.funciones.php

Sterculiaceae. (1789). Guazuma ulmifolia Lam. *Encyclopédie Méthodique, 3*, 52.

Vázquez, M. (2019). *El desarrollo sostenible a través de empresas sociales en comunidades indígenas de América Latina, Estudios Sociales*. Revista de Alimentación Contemporánea y Desarrollo Regional.

W.B. (2017). *Latinoamérica indígena en el siglo XXI. Banco Mundial*. Recuperado de: https://www.bancomundial.org/es/region/lac/brief/indigenous-latin-america-in-the-twenty-first-century-brief-report-page

Weber, M. (2008). *Economía y sociedad*. Fondo de Cultura Económica.

Zárate, J. L. (2016). *Grupos étnicos de Sonora: territorios y condiciones actuales de vida y rezago Región y Sociedad*. Academic Press.

Compilation of References

Aalmo, G., Magagnotti, N., & Spinelli, R. (2016). Forest workers and steep terrain winching: The impact of environmental and anthropometric parameters on performance. *Croatian Journal of Forest Engineering*, *37*(1), 97–105.

Abadi, F. E., Jalilvand, M. R., Sharif, M., Salimi, G. A., & Khanzadeh, S. A. (2011). A study of influential factors on employees' motivation for participating in the in-service training courses based on modified expectancy theory. *International Business Management*, *2*(1), 157–169.

Abate, D. (2021, February 26). *Hong kong's covid-19 vaccination program: Considerations for employers*. Society for Human Resource Management (SHRM). https://www.shrm.org/resourcesandtools/hr-topics/global-hr/pages/coronavirus-hong-kong-vaccination-program.aspx

Abbe, O. O., Harvey, C. M., Ikuma, L. H., & Aghazadeh, F. (2011). Modeling the relationship between occupational stressors, psychosocial/physical symptoms, and injuries in the construction industry. *International Journal of Industrial Ergonomics*, *41*(2), 106–117. doi:10.1016/j.ergon.2010.12.002

Acevedo, G., Farias, M., Sanchez, J. & Astegiano, C. (2012). *Condiciones de trabajo del equipo de salud en centros de atención primaria desde la perspectiva del trabajo decente*. Academic Press.

Acharya & Mathur. (2016). A Study on Green Cloud Computing and Technologies. *International Journal of Advance Research in Engineering, Science & Technology, 2444*(6), 13–17.

Aguilar-Duque, J. I., Amaya, G., & Juarez, V. M. (2018). Anthropometry devices: a comparative study. Handbook of Research on Ergonomics and Product Design, 153–171. doi:10.4018/978-1-5225-5234-5.ch010

Ahlberg, I. (2014). *The economic costs of musculoskeletal disorders-A cost-of-illness study in Sweden for 2012*. Academic Press.

Ahola, K., & Hakanen, J. J. (2008). Job strain, burnout, and depressive symptoms: A prospective study among dentists. *Journal of Affective Disorders*, *104*(1-3), 103–110. doi:10.1016/j.jad.2007.03.004 PMID:17448543

Ahola, K., & Hakanen, J. J. (2014). Burnout and health. In *Burnout at work: A psychological perspective* (pp. 10–31). Psychology Press.

Ahola, K., Hakanen, J. J., Perhoniemi, R., & Mutanen, P. (2014). Relationship between burnout and depressive symptoms: A study using the person-centred approach. *Burnout Research*, *1*(1), 29–37. doi:10.1016/j.burn.2014.03.003

Ahola, K., Salminen, S., Toppinen, S., Koskinen, A., & Vaananen, A. (2013). Occupational burnout and severe injuries: An eight-year prospective cohort study among finnish forest industry workers. *Journal of Occupational Health*, *55*(6), 450–457. doi:10.1539/joh.13-0021-OA PMID:24162145

AHRAE. (1999). *Handbook, Heating, Ventilating and Ari-Conditioning; applications*. American Society of Heating, Refrigerating, and Air-Conditioning Engineers Inc.

Ahram, T., & Jang, R. (2014). Advances in Physical Ergonomics and human factors. *Proceedings of the AHFE Conference*, 403.

Akdem, ir, E. (2020). The Determination of Teachers' Motivation Based on Herzberg's Motivation Theory. *The Turkish Online Journal of Educational Technology*, *19*(4).

Alabdulkarim, S., & Nussbaum, M. A. (2019). Influences of different exoskeleton designs and tool mass on physical demands and performance in a simulated overhead drilling task. *Applied Ergonomics*, *74*(August), 55–66. doi:10.1016/j.apergo.2018.08.004

Al-agha, O. I., & Al-agha, M. I. (2015). *Implementing Six Sigma Methodology in Industrial Control Systems*. Academic Press.

Alarcon, G. M. (2011). A meta-analysis of burnout with job demands, resources, and attitudes. *Journal of Vocational Behavior*, *79*(2), 549–562. doi:10.1016/j.jvb.2011.03.007

Alarcon, G. M., Eschleman, K. J., & Bowling, N. A. (2009). Relationships between personality variables and burnout: A meta-analysis. *Work and Stress*, *23*(3), 244–263. doi:10.1080/02678370903282600

Alavi, H. S., Churchill, E. F., Wiberg, M., Lalanne, D., Dalsgaard, P., Schieck, A. F. G., & Rogers, Y. (2019). Introduction to human-building interaction (HBI): Interfacing HCI with architecture and urban design. *ACM Transactions on Computer-Human Interaction, 26*(2), 6:1-6:10.

Alavinia, S. M., Molenaar, D., & Burdorf, A. (2008). Productivity Loss in the Workforce: Associations with Health, Work Demands, and Individual Characteristics. *American Journal of Industrial Medicine*. PMID:18942667

Alba, R. D. (1990). *Ethnic Identity: The transformation of White America*. Yale University Press.

Albliwi, S. A., Antony, J., & Lim, S. A. (2015). A Systematic Review of Lean Six Sigma for the Manufacturing Industry. *Business Process Management Journal*, *21*(3), 665–691. doi:10.1108/BPMJ-03-2014-0019

Alhuraish, I., Robledo, C., & Kobi, A. (2017). A Comparative Exploration of Lean Manufacturing and Six Sigma in Terms of Their Critical Success Factors. *Journal of Cleaner Production*, *164*, 325–337. doi:10.1016/j.jclepro.2017.06.146

Alker, J. (2014, September 25). Office buildings are key to workers' health, wellbeing and productivity. *The Guardian*. https://www.theguardian.com/sustainable-business/2014/sep/24/office-building-design-worker-health-wellbeing-productivity

Allen, J. G. (2020, March 4). Your building can make you sick or keep you well. *The New York Times*. https://www.nytimes.com/2020/03/04/opinion/coronavirus-buildings.html

Allen, J. G., & Macomber, J. D. (2020a). Healthy buildings: How indoor spaces drive performance and productivity (3rd ed.). Harvard University Press.

Allen, J. G., & Macomber, J. D. (2020b, June 8). Tenants and investors will be looking for healthy buildings. *Urban Land Magazine*. https://urbanland.uli.org/sustainability/tenants-and-investors-will-be-looking-for-healthy-buildings/

Allen, J. G., Bernstein, A., Cao, X., Eitland, E. S., Flanigan, S., Gokhale, M., Goodman, J., Klager, S., Klingensmith, L., Laurent, J. G. C., Lockley, S. W., MacNaughton, P., Pakpour, S., Spengler, J., Vallarino, J., Williams, A., Young, A., & Yin, J. (2017). *The 9 foundations of a healthy building* (No. 1). Harvard University. https://forhealth.org/9_Foundations_of_a_Healthy_Building.February_2017.pdf

Allen, T. (2018, November 18). Layoffs on the horizon? How to lead through a reduction in force. *Forbes*. https://www.forbes.com/sites/terinaallen/2018/11/28/do-all-of-this-before-you-lay-me-off-how-gm-and-others-can-get-this-right/

Alsaffar, I., & Ketan, H. (2018). Reviewing the Effects of Integrated Lean Six Sigma Methodologies with Ergonomics Principles in an Industrial Workstation, 2nd International Conference on Engineering Sciences IOP Conf. Series. *Materials Science and Engineering*, *433*, 012060. doi:10.1088/1757-899X/433/1/012060

Altaf, A., & Awan, M. A. (2011). Moderating Affect of Workplace Spirituality on the Relationship of Job Overload and Job Satisfaction. *Journal of Business Ethics*, *104*(1), 93–99. doi:10.100710551-011-0891-0

Al-Tkhayneh, K., Kot, S., & Shestak, V. (2019). Motivation and demotivation factors affecting productivity in public sector. *Administratie si Management Public*, *1*(33), 77–102. doi:10.24818/amp/2019.33-05.

Amavizca, L. O., García, A. C., Jiménez, E., Duarte, G. L., & Vázquez, J. C. (2014). Aplicación de la metodología semi-ágil ICONIX para el desarrollo de software: implementación y publicación de un sitio WEB para una empresa SPIN - OFF en el Sur de Sonora, México. *Twelfth LACCEI Latin American and Caribbean Conference for Engineering and Technology (LACCEI'2014) "Excellence in Engineering To Enhance a Country's Productivity"*.

Amell, T., & Kumar, S. (2001). Work-related musculoskeletal disorders: Design as a prevention strategy. A review. *Journal of Occupational Rehabilitation*, *11*(4), 255–26. doi:10.1023/A:1013344508217 PMID:11826726

American Psychological Association. (2018). *Treating Depression, Anxiety, and Stress in Ethnic and Racial Groups: Cognitive Behavioral Approaches*. The American Psychological Association. doi:https://www.apa.org/topics/depression/

Amoako-Gyampah, K., & Acquaah, M. (2008). Manufacturing Strategy, Competitive Strategy and Firm Performance: An Empirical Study in a Developing Economy Environment. *International Journal of Production Economics*, *111*(2), 575–592. doi:10.1016/j.ijpe.2007.02.030

Amor, A. (2014). *La violencia laboral*. Defensoría Del Pueblo.

Amorim, J. A., de-Siqueira, J. M., & Martínez-Sáez, A. (2012). Large Scale Multimedia Production Management: From Strategic Planning to Six Sigma. *Procedia: Social and Behavioral Sciences*, *46*, 1430–1434. doi:10.1016/j.sbspro.2012.05.315

Ann, S., & Blum, S. C. (2020). Motivating senior employees in the hospitality industry. *International Journal of Contemporary Hospitality Management*, *32*(1), 324–346. doi:10.1108/IJCHM-08-2018-0685

Antony, J., & Desai, D. A. (2009). Assessing the Status of Six Sigma Implementation in the Indian Industry. *Management Research News*, *32*(5), 413–423. doi:10.1108/01409170910952921

Antosz, P., Rembiasz, T., & Verhagen, H. (2020). Employee shirking and overworking: Modelling the unintended consequences of work organisation. *Ergonomics*, *63*(8), 997–1009. doi:10.1080/00140139.2020.1744710 PMID:32188339

Aranda, C., López, J., & Barraza, J. (2013). Factores psicosociales y síndrome de burnout en trabajadores de la industria de la transformación de la masa, Tepic, México. *Revista Colombiana de Psiquiatría*, *42*(2), 167–172. doi:10.1016/S0034-7450(13)70003-9 PMID:26572811

Armon, G., Melamed, S., Shirom, A., & Shapira, I. (2010). Elevated Burnout Predicts the Onset of Musculoskeletal Pain Among Apparently Healthy Employees. *Journal of Occupational Health Psychology*, *15*(4), 399–408. doi:10.1037/a0020726 PMID:21058854

Arruda, W. (2018, April 7). 10 employee wellness ideas that will help you attract top talent. *Forbes*. https://www.forbes.com/sites/williamarruda/2018/04/08/10-employee-wellness-ideas-that-will-help-you-attract-top-talent/

Artacoz, L., & Molinero, E. (2004). Evaluación de los factores de riesgo psicosocial, combinando metodología cuantitativa y cualitativa. *Archivos de Prevencion de Riesgos Laborales, 7*(4), 134–142.

Arunesh, C., Surinder, D., Pankaj, Ch., & Randejer, K. (2009). Ergonomics in the Office Environment: A Review. *Int. Conf. on Energy and Environment,* 43-56.

Asay, G. R. B., Roy, K., Lang, J. E., Payne, R. L., & Howard, D. H. (2016). Absenteeism and Employer Costs Associated with Chronic Diseases and Health Risk Factors in the US Workforce. *Preventing Chronic Disease, 13,* 150503. doi:10.5888/pcd13.150503 PMID:27710764

Asensio-Cuesta, S., Diego-Mas, J. A., Cremades-Oliver, L. V., & González-Cruz, M. C. (2012). A method to design job rotation schedules to prevent work-related musculoskeletal disorders in repetitive work. *International Journal of Production Research, 50*(24), 7467–7478. https://doi.org/10.1080/00207543.2011.653452

Ashworth, M., & Martinuzzi, E. (2020, November 9). *Wfh is old news: The 'near home' office is the next big thing.* https://www.bloomberg.com/opinion/articles/2020-11-09/stanchart-wants-to-go-way-beyond-wfh

Asia Society. (2020). *Jati: The Caste System in India.* Author.

Associated Press (AP). (2020, December 2). *EU pushes for "right to disconnect" from work at home.* AP News. https://apnews.com/article/europe-europe-coronavirus-pandemic-f6f56884206c921a379ae5a060511571

Astudillo, P. (2003). *Factores psicosociales en el trabajo: ¿Cómo comprender las tensiones psicosociales para regularlas?* Departamento de Salud Ocupacional Instituto de Salud Pública de Chile.

Aven, T. (2015). Risk assessment and risk management: Review of recent advances on their foundation. *European Journal of Operational Research, 253*(1), 1–13.

Aven, T., & Zio, E. (2013). Model output uncertainty in risk assessment. *International Journal of Performability Engineering, 9*(5), 475–486.

Awang, M., Dollard, M., Coward, J., & Dormann, C. (2012). Psychosocial safety climate: Conceptual distinctiveness and effect on job demands and worker psychological health. *Safety Science, 50,* 19–28.

Baciu, L. E. (2018). Expectancy Theory Explaining Civil Servants' work Motivation. Evidence from A Romanian City Hall. *The USV Annals of Economics and Public Administration, 17*(2 (26)), 146–160.

Baker, M. (2020, July 14). *Gartner survey reveals 82% of company leaders plan to allow employees to work remotely some of the time.* Gartner. https://www.gartner.com/en/newsroom/press-releases/2020-07-14-gartner-survey-reveals-82-percent-of-company-leaders-plan-to-allow-employees-to-work-remotely-some-of-the-time

Baker, M. (2021, January 4). *9 tips for managing remote employees.* Smarter with Gartner. www.gartner.com/smarterwithgartner/9-tips-for-managing-remote-employees/

Bakker, A. B., & Demerouti, E. (2014). Job demands-resources theory. In *Work and wellbeing: A Complete Reference Guide* (Vol. 3, pp. 37–64). Wiley-Blackwell. doi:10.1002/9781118539415.wbwell019

Bakker, A. B., & Demerouti, E. (2017). Job demands–resources theory: Taking stock and looking forward. *Journal of Occupational Health Psychology, 22*(3), 273–285. doi:10.1037/ocp0000056 PMID:27732008

Bakker, A. B., & Demerouti, E. (2018). *Multiple levels in job demands-resources theory: Implications for employee well-being and performance.* DEF Publishers.

Bakker, A. B., Demerouti, E., & Euwema, M. C. (2005). Job Resources Buffer the Impact of Job Demands on Burnout. *Journal of Occupational Health Psychology, 10*(2), 170–180. doi:10.1037/1076-8998.10.2.170 PMID:15826226

Bakker, A. B., ten Brummelhuis, L. L., Prins, J. T., & der Heijden, F. M. M. A. (2011). Applying the job demands–resources model to the work–home interface: A study among medical residents and their partners. *Journal of Vocational Behavior*, *79*(1), 170–180. doi:10.1016/j.jvb.2010.12.004

Bani-Melhem, S., Zeffane, R., & Albaity, M. (2018). Determinants of employees' innovative behavior. *International Journal of Contemporary Hospitality Management*, *30*(3), 1601–1620. doi:10.1108/IJCHM-02-2017-0079

Banuelas Coronado, R., & Antony, J. (2002). Critical Success Factors for the Successful Implementation of Six Sigma Projects in Organisations. *The TQM Magazine*, *14*(2), 92–99. doi:10.1108/09544780210416702

Bañuelos, N., & Salido, P.L. (2020). Enredados con la sierra. Las plantas en las estrategias sostenibles de sobrevivencia del grupo indígena Guarijío/Makurawe de Sonora, México. *Tecnología en Marcha*, *33*(1), 178-192.

Barbosa, R., Fiedler, N., Do Carmo, C., Minette, L., & Silva, E. (2014). Analysis of posture in semi-mechanized forest harvesting in steep areas. *Revista Arvore*, *38*(4), 733–738.

Barki, H., & Hartwick, J. (2004). Conceptualizing The Construct of Interpersonal Conflict. *International Journal of Conflict Management*, *15*(3), 216–244. doi:10.1108/eb022913

Barrios & Illada. (2013). Valoración del desgaste laboral como riesgo psicosocial. *Revista ingeniería industrial.*

Barton, S. (2019, November 20). Why designing for dementia means designing for everyone. *Work in Mind.* https://workinmind.org/2019/11/20/designing-for-dementia/

Bastianoni, S., Marchi, M., Caro, D., Casprini, P., & Maria, F. (2014). The connection between 2006 IPCC GHG inventory methodology and ISO 14064-1 certification standard – A reference point for the environmental policies at sub-national scale. *Environmental Science & Policy*, *44*, 97–107. doi:10.1016/j.envsci.2014.07.015

BBC News. (2019). *What is India's caste system?* BBC News.

Beatley, T. (2018). Biophilic flourishing: The role of nature in creating healthy cities. In T. Beatley, C. Jones, & R. Rainey (Eds.), *Healthy Environments, Healing Spaces* (pp. 81–106). University of Virginia Press. doi:10.2307/j.ctv8d5sgp.8

Beebe, R. S. (2007). Predicting Burnout, Conflict Management Style, and Turnover Among Clergy. *Journal of Career Assessment*, *15*(2), 257–275. doi:10.1177/1069072706298157

Behzadian, M., Otaghsara, S. K., Yazdani, M., & Ignatius, J. (2012). A state-of the-art survey of TOPSIS applications. *Expert Systems with Applications*, *39*(17), 13051–13069. doi:10.1016/j.eswa.2012.05.056

Bergh, L. I. V., Leka, S., & Zwetsloot, G. I. J. M. (2018). Tailoring Psychosocial Risk Assessment in the Oil and Gas Industry by Exploring Specific and Common Psychosocial Risks. *Safety and Health at Work*, *9*(1), 63–70. doi:10.1016/j.shaw.2017.05.001 PMID:30363066

Bevan, S. (2015). Impacto económico de los trastornos musculoesqueléticos (TME) en el trabajo en Europa. *Best Practice & Research Clinical Rheumatology Journal*, *29*(3), 356–373. doi:10.1016/j.berh.2015.08.002

Bianchi, R., Schonfeld, I., & Laurent, E. (2014). Is burnout a depressive disorder? A reexamination with special focus on atypical depression. *International Journal of Stress Management, 21*, 307-324. doi:10.1037/a0037906

Bianchi, R., Schonfeld, I., & Laurent, E. (2015). Burnout-depression overlap: A review. *Clinical Psychology Review, 36*, 28-41. doi:10.1016/j.cpr.2015.01.004

Bickerton, G. R., Miner, M. H., Dowson, M., & Griffin, B. (2014). Spiritual resources and work engagement among religous workers: A three - wave longitudinal study. *Journal of Occupational Psychology*, *87*(2), 370–391. doi:10.1111/joop.12052

Bickerton, G. R., Miner, M. H., Dowson, M., & Griffin, B. (2015). Incremental validity of spiritual resources in the job demands-resources model. *Psychology of Religion and Spirituality*, *7*(2), 162–172. doi:10.1037/rel0000012

Blanch, J., Sahagún, M., & Cervantes, G. (2010). Estructura factorial del cuestionario de condiciones de trabajo. *Revista de Psicología del Trabajo y de las Organizaciones*, *26*(3), 175–189.

Blom, V., Sverke, M., Bodin, L., Bergström, G., Lindfors, P., & Svedberg, P. (2014). Work–home interference and burnout: A study based on swedish twins. *Journal of Occupational and Environmental Medicine*, *56*(4), 361–366. doi:10.1097/JOM.0000000000000128 PMID:24709761

Bogue, R. (2014). Sustainable Manufacturing: A Critical Discipline for the Twenty-First Century. *Assembly Automation*, *34*(2), 117–122. doi:10.1108/AA-01-2014-012

Boland, B., de Smet, A., Palter, R., & Sanghvi, A. (2020, June 8). *Reimagining the office and work life after COVID-19*. https://view.ceros.com/mckinsey/coronavirus-promo-video-desktop

Bolt, L. (2019, May 28). The science behind smart office design. *Ideas*. https://www.wework.com/ideas/office-design-space/the-science-behind-smart-office-design

Bonacich, E. (1973). A theory of middleman minorities. *American Sociological Review*, *38*(5), 583–594. doi:10.2307/2094409

Borg, W. R., Gall, M. D., & Gall, J. P. (2007). Educational Research: An Introduction (8th ed.). New York: Longman.

Borritz, M., Rugulies, R., Bjorner, J. B., Villadsen, E., Mikkelsen, O. A., & Kristensen, T. S. (2006). Burnout among employees in human service work: Design and baseline findings of the PUMA study. *Scandinavian Journal of Public Health*, *34*(1), 49–58. doi:10.1080/14034940510032275 PMID:16449044

Boubekri, M., Cheung, I. N., Reid, K. J., Wang, C.-H., & Zee, P. C. (2014). Impact of windows and daylight exposure on overall health and sleep quality of office workers: A case-control pilot study. *Journal of Clinical Sleep Medicine*, *10*(6), 603–611. doi:10.5664/jcsm.3780 PMID:24932139

Breceda, A., Ortiz, V., & Scrosati, R. (2005). Mauto (Lysiloma divaricatum, Fabaceae) Allometry as an Indicator of Cattle Grazing Pressure in a Tropical Dry Forestin Northwestern Mexico. *Rangeland Ecology and Management*, *58*(1), 85–88. doi:10.2111/1551-5028(2005)58<85:MLDFAA>2.0.CO;2

British Council of Offices (BCO). (2018). *Wellness matters: British Council for Offices completes major research study into health and wellbeing in offices*. https://www.bco.org.uk/News/News34396.aspx

Brown, D. (2020, November 17). *Coronavirus: How to be happier while working from home*. BBC. https://www.bbc.com/news/uk-54886125

Brummelhuis, T., Lieke, L., & Bakker, A. B. (2012). A resource perspective on the work–home interface: The work–home resources model. *American Psychologist*, *67*(7), 545-556. doi:10.1037/a0027974

Brunborg, G. (2008). Core Self-Evaluations: A Predictor Variable for Job Stress. *European Psychologist*, *13*(2), 96–102. doi:10.1027/1016-9040.13.2.96

Bruzzonne, A., Anghinoli, D., Paolucci, M., & Tonelli, F. (2012). Energy-aware scheduling for improving manufacturing process sustainability: A mathematical model for flexible flow shops. *CIRP Annals Journal*, *61*(1), 459–462. doi:10.1016/j.cirp.2012.03.084

Buettner, D. (2011). Thrive: Finding happiness the blue zones way (Illustrated ed). National Geographic.

Burton, J. (2010). Who healthy workplace framework and model: Background and supporting literature and practices (No. 1). World Health Organization.

Busciantella-Ricci, D., & Scataglini, S. (2019). A co-model for research through co-design. Academic Press.

Byron, K., & Laurence, G. A. (2015). Diplomas, photos, and tchotchkes as symbolic self-representations: Understanding employees' individual use of symbols. *Academy of Management Journal, 58*(1), 298–323. doi:10.5465/amj.2012.0932

Calia, R. C., Guerrini, F. M., & de Castro, M. (2009). The Impact of Six Sigma in the Performance of a Pollution Prevention Program. *Journal of Cleaner Production, 17*(15), 1303–1310. doi:10.1016/j.jclepro.2009.05.001

Campbell, L. (2017, October 19). We've broken down your entire life into years spent doing tasks. *Huffington Post.* https://www.huffingtonpost.com.au/2017/10/18/weve-broken-down-your-entire-life-into-years-spent-doing-tasks_a_23248153/

Caramela, S. (2018, February 21). 4 ways to create a healthier workplace for your employees. *Business News Daily.* https://www.businessnewsdaily.com/10065-create-healthy-workplace.html

Carlos, R. N. G., González, Y. V., Pedro, A. E. Z., Ana, L. S. C., Robledo, V. A., Mildrend, I. M. R., Moreno, E. M., Margarita, G. S. R., & Olivia, Y. V. B. (2020, July-September). Analysis of Ergonomic Methods used to Prevent Negative Effect in the Health of Workers in a Metallic Industry in Mexicali, Mexico. *Mediterranean Journal of Basic and Applied Sciences, 4*(3), 33–41. doi:10.46382/MJBAS.2020.4304

Carrasco Martínez, A. C. (2010). *Estudio ergonómico en la estación de trabajo PT0780 de la empresa S-Mex, S.A de C.V. León. México.* Tesis de Ingeniería Industrial. Universidad Tecnológica de la Mixteca. Huajuapan de Leóm.

Carter, L. (2016). *Presenteeism costs economy $34 billion a year through lost productivity, report shows.* Retrieved from https://www.abc.net.au/news/2016-04-12/presenteeism-costing-the-economy-billions/7318832

Center for Active Design (CfAD). (2021, February). *About Fitwel.* https://fitwel.org/

Centers for Disease Control and Prevention (CDC). (2020, July 24). *Communities, schools, workplaces, and events.* https://www.cdc.gov/coronavirus/2019-ncov/community/index.html

Cerasoli, C. P., Nicklin, J. M., & Ford, M. T. (2014). Intrinsic motivation and extrinsic incentives jointly predict performance: A 40-year meta-analysis. *Psychological Bulletin, 140*(4), 980–1008. doi:10.1037/a0035661 PMID:24491020

Chadda, R. K., & Deb, K. S. (2013). Indian family systems, collectivistic society and psychotherapy. *Indian Journal of Psychiatry, 55*(6, Suppl 2), S299–S309. doi:10.4103/0019-5545.105555 PMID:23858272

Chandra, A., Chandna, P., Deswal, S., & Kumar, R. (2009). Ergonomics in the Office Environment: A Review. *Proceedings of World Academy of Science: Engineering & Technology,* 51(1), 913-919.

Channon, B. (2019). *Happy by design: A guide to architecture and mental wellbeing.* RIBA Publishing. doi:10.4324/9780367814625

Chappell, D., & Di Martino, V. (1998). *Violence at work.* Organización Internacional del Trabajo.

Charria, V., Sarsosa, K., & Arenas, F. (2011). Factores de riesgo psicosocial laboral: Métodos e instrumentos de evaluación. *RevistaFacultad Nacional SaludPública, 29*(4), 380–391.

Chartered Institute of Personnel and Development (CIPD). (2020). *Health and well-being at work.* https://www.cipd.co.uk/Images/health-and-well-being-2020-report_tcm18-73967.pdf

Chen, B., Vansteenkiste, M., Beyers, W., Boone, L., Deci, E. L., Van der Kaap-Deeder, J., Duriez, B., Lens, W., Matos, L., Mouratidis, A., Ryan, R. M., Sheldon, K. M., Soenens, B., Van Petegem, S., & Verstuyf, J. (2015). Basic psychological need satisfaction, need frustration, and need strength across four cultures. *Motivation and Emotion, 39*(2), 216–236. doi:10.100711031-014-9450-1

Chen, C. C., Meindl, J. R., & Hunt, R. G. (1997). Testing the effects of vertical and horizontal collectivism: A study of reward allocation preferences in China. *Journal of Cross-Cultural Psychology*, *28*(1), 44–70. doi:10.1177/0022022197281003

Chen, Y., & Lou, H. (2002). Toward an understanding of the behavioral intention to use a groupware application. *Journal of Organizational and End User Computing*, *14*(4), 1–16. doi:10.4018/joeuc.2002100101

Cherrafi, A., Elfezazi, S., Chiarini, A., Mokhlis, A., & Benhida, K. (2016). The Integration of Lean Manufacturing, Six Sigma and Sustainability: A Literature Review and Future Research Directions for Developing a Specific Model. *Journal of Cleaner Production*, *139*, 828–846. doi:10.1016/j.jclepro.2016.08.101

Chiang, C.-F., & Jang, S. (2008). An expectancy theory model for hotel employee motivation. *International Journal of Hospitality Management*, *27*(2), 313–322. doi:10.1016/j.ijhm.2007.07.017

Chiang, C.-F., Jang, S., Canter, D., & Prince, B. (2008). An expectancy theory model for hotel employee motivation: Examining the moderating role of communication satisfaction. *International Journal of Hospitality & Tourism Administration*, *9*(4), 327–351. doi:10.1080/15256480802427263

Chiarini, A. (2014). Sustainable Manufacturing-Greening Processes Using Specific Lean Production Tools: An Empirical Observation from European Motorcycle Component Manufacturers. *Journal of Cleaner Production*, *85*, 226–233. doi:10.1016/j.jclepro.2014.07.080

Chirkov, V., Ryan, R. M., Kim, Y., & Kaplan, U. (2003). Differentiating autonomy from individualism and independence: A self-determination theory perspective on internalization of cultural orientations and well-being. *Journal of Personality and Social Psychology*, *84*(1), 97–110. doi:10.1037/0022-3514.84.1.97 PMID:12518973

Chopra, K. (2019). Indian shopper motivation to use artificial intelligence: Generating Vroom's expectancy theory of motivation using grounded theory approach. *International Journal of Retail & Distribution Management*, *47*(3), 331–347. doi:10.1108/IJRDM-11-2018-0251

Chugani, N., Kumar, V., Garza-Reyes, J. A., Rocha-Lona, L., & Upadhyay, A. (2017). International Journal of Lean Six Sigma Investigating the Green Impact of Lean, Six Sigma, and Lean Six Sigma: A Systematic Literature Review Investigating the Green Impact of Lean, Six Sigma, and Lean Six Sigma: A Systematic Literature Review. *International Journal of Lean Six Sigma*, *8*(8), 7–32. Advance online publication. doi:10.1108/IJLSS-11-2015-0043

Cohen, A., Hoskins, D., Shick, R., & Taylor, L. (2021). *Design forecast 2021: Reconnect* (Design Strategies for a Post-COVID World). Gensler.

Cole, A. H. (2014). Anxiety. In Encyclopedia of Psychology and Religion. Boston, MA: Springer. doi:10.1007/978-1-4614-6086-2_38

Comau Mate – Fit for workers. (2020). https://mate.comau.com/?

Competitiva, H. (2013). *C Ompetitive a Bility*. Academic Press.

Coneval. (2016). *Evaluación de la política de desarrollo social 2016*. Coneval.

Cox, T. (2000). Work-related stress, risk management, and management standards. *Work and Stress*, *18*(3), 89–90.

Coyte, P. C., Asche, C. V., Croxford, R., & Chan, B. (1998). The economic cost of musculoskeletal disorders in Canada. *Arthritis & Rheumatology (Hoboken, N.J.)*, *11*(5), 315–325. doi:10.1002/art.1790110503 PMID:9830876

Cruz, M., López, E., Cruz, R., & Llanillo, M. E. (2016). *El estrés laboral en México. La Micro y Pequeña Empresa: Un Análisis Desde La Perspectiva Economico-Administrativa*. Retrieved from https://www.ecorfan.org/actas/A_1/32.pdf

Csikszentmihalyi, M. (2008). *Flow: The psychology of optimal experience* (1st ed.). Harper Perennial.

Csikszentmihalyi, M. (2014). *Flow and the foundations of positive psychology the collected works of Mihaly Csikszentmihalyi* (1st ed.). Springer.

Cusumano, Kahl, & Suarez. (2008). Services, Industry Evolution, and the Copetitive Strategies of Product Firms. *Academy of Management Journal*, *51*(2), 315–334. doi:10.1002mj

D'Souza, R., Strazdins, L., Broom, D., Rodgers, B., & Berry, H. (2006). Work demands, job insecurity, and sickness absence from work. How productive is the new, flexible labour force? *Australian and New Zealand Journal of Public Health*, *30*(3), 205–212.

Da Silva, S. L. C., & Amaral, F. G. (2019, August 1). Critical factors of success and barriers to the implementation of occupational health and safety management systems: A systematic review of literature. In *Safety Science*. Elsevier B.V. doi:10.1016/j.ssci.2019.03.026

da Silva, J. M. N., da Silva, L. B., & Gontijo, L. A. (2017). Relationship between psychosocial factors and musculoskeletal disorders in footwear industry workers. *Production*, *27*(0), 1–13. doi:10.1590/0103-6513.231516

Dai, D., Prussin, A. J. II, Marr, L. C., Vikesland, P. J., Edwards, M. A., & Pruden, A. (2017). Factors shaping the human exposome in the built environment: Opportunities for engineering control. *Environmental Science & Technology*, *51*(14), 7759–7774. doi:10.1021/acs.est.7b01097 PMID:28677960

Dangayach, G. S., & Deshmukh, S. G. (2006). An Exploratory Study of Manufacturing Strategy Practices of Machinery Manufacturing Companies in India. *Omega*, *34*(3), 254–273. doi:10.1016/j.omega.2004.10.009

Danna, K., & Griffin, R. W. (1999). Health and Well-Being in the Workplace: A Review and Synthesis of the Literature. *Journal of Management*, *25*(3), 357–384. doi:10.1177/014920639902500305

Daum, K. (2017, January 20). *25 ways you can make your life healthier in the office*. Inc.Com. https://www.inc.com/kevin-daum/25-ways-you-can-make-your-life-healthier-in-the-office.html

Davis, D. (2020, November). *The workplace beyond 2020*. Hassell. https://www.hassellstudio.com/conversation/the-workplace-beyond-2020

Davis, K., Dunning, K., Jewell, G., & Lockey, J. (2014). Cost and disability trends of work-related musculoskeletal disorders in Ohio. *Occupational Medicine*, *64*(8), 608–615. doi:10.1093/occmed/kqu126 PMID:25298392

de Beer, L. T., Pienaar, J., & Rothmann, S. Jr. (2016). Work overload, burnout, and psychological ill-health symptoms: A three-wave mediation model of the employee health impairment process. *Anxiety, Stress, and Coping*, *29*(4), 387–399. doi:10.1080/10615806.2015.1061123 PMID:26079200

de Botton, A. (2007). *The architecture of happiness*. Penguin.

De Britto, P., Da Silva, E., Lopes, E., De, E., & Fiedler, N. (2014). Biomechanical evaluation in workers of different statures at planting and fertilizing forest activities. *Forest Sciences*, *42*(102), 191–196.

De Dreu, C., van Dierendonck, D., & Dijkstra, M. (2004). Conflict at work and individual well-being. *International Journal of Conflict Management*, *15*(1), 6–26. doi:10.1108/eb022905

de Lange, M. (2013). The smart city you love to hate: Exploring the role of affect in hybrid urbanism. *ResearchGate*, 8.

de Looze, M. P., Bosch, T., Krause, F., Stadler, K. S., & O'Sullivan, L. W. (2016). Exoskeletons for industrial application and their potential effects on physical workload. *Ergonomics*, *59*(5), 671–681. doi:10.1080/00140139.2015.1081988 PMID:26444053

De Mooij, M., & Hofstede, G. (2010). The Hofstede model: Applications to global branding and advertising strategy and research. *International Journal of Advertising*, *29*(1), 85–110. doi:10.2501/S026504870920104X

De Simone, S. (2015). Expectancy value theory: Motivating healthcare workers. *American International Journal of Contemporary Research*, *5*(2), 19–23.

de Vries, A., Murphy, M., Könemann, R., Kingma, I., & de Looze, M. (2019). The Amount of Support Provided by a Passive Arm Support Exoskeleton in a Range of Elevated Arm Postures. *IISE Transactions on Occupational Ergonomics and Human Factors*, *7*(3–4), 311–321. doi:10.1080/24725838.2019.1669736

Deci, E. L., & Ryan, R. M. (2008). Hedonia, eudaimonia, and well-being: An introduction. *Journal of Happiness Studies*, *9*(1), 1–11. doi:10.100710902-006-9018-1

Del Prado, J. L. (2007). Anthropometric measurement of Filipino manufacturing workers. *International Journal of Industrial Ergonomics*, *37*(6), 497–503. doi:10.1016/j.ergon.2007.02.004

Deloitte. (2021, February 17). JLL: Human-centric tech will recast the workplace. *The Wall Street Journal*. https://deloitte.wsj.com/cio/2021/02/17/jll-human-centric-tech-will-recast-the-workplace/

Demerouti, E., Bakker, A. B., Nachreiner, F., & Schaufeli, W. B. (2001). The job demands-resources model of burnout. *Journal of Applied Psychology, 86*(3), 499-512. http://dx.doi.org.excelsia.idm.oclc.org/10.1037/0021-9010.86.3.499

Denbeigh, K., Slot, T., & Dumas, G. (2013). Wrist postures and forces in tree planters during three tree unloading conditions. *Ergonomics, 56*(10), 1599–1607.

Detwiler, J. (2020, October 23). *You are your workspace*. Medium. https://forge.medium.com/you-are-your-workspace-eede562b36fb

Development, S., & Execution, S. (2008). HBR's Must-Reads on Strategy What Is Strategy? *Strategy*, *86*(12), 143. doi:10.1111/j.0955-6419.2005.00347.x

Díaz, J. M. C. (2007). *Técnicas de prevención de riesgos laborales*. TÉBAR.

DiFonzo, N., & Bordia, P. (1998). Reproduced with permission of the copyright owner. *The Journal of Allergy and Clinical Immunology*, *130*(2), 556. doi:10.1016/j.jaci.2012.05.050

Dileep, G., & Rau, S. S. (2009). Applying Six-Sigma in Health Service: A Study of Critical Success Factors, Critical To Quality Characteristics and Key Performance Indicators in Medium Scale Hospitals. *Information Sciences & Computing*, *3*(1), 25–31. doi:10.18000/ijisac.50037

Doraisamy, J. (2021). *18% of Australians aren't motivated at work.* Retrieved from https://www.wellnessdaily.com.au/culture/18-of-australians-arent-motivated-at-work

Drury, C. (2010). Global quality: Linking ergonomics and production. *International Journal of Production Research*, *38*(2), 4007–4018.

DynamicsC. (2020). https://www.c-dyn.com/product?

Easton, G. S., & Rosenzweig, E. D. (2012). The Role of Experience in Six Sigma Project Success: An Empirical Analysis of Improvement Projects. *Journal of Operations Management*, *30*(7–8), 481–493. doi:10.1016/j.jom.2012.08.002

Ebbers, J. J., & Wijnberg, N. M. (2017). Betwixt and between: Role conflict, role ambiguity and role definition in project-based dual-leadership structures. *Human Relations*, *70*(11), 001872671769285. doi:10.1177/0018726717692852 PMID:29081536

Echeveste, M. E., Rozenfeld, H., & Sonego, M. (2016). Potential Application of Six Sigma Tool in the Integrated Product Development Process. *Journal of the Brazilian Society of Mechanical Sciences and Engineering, 38*(8), 2499–2511. doi:10.100740430-016-0503-0

Enriquez Diaz, J. A., Kotzab, D., Sytch, A., & Frieling, E. (2012). Impact of increasing productivity on work content and psychosocial work characteristics in Chaku-Chaku assembly lines – A follow-up study in a German automotive manufacturing company. *Work (Reading, Mass.), 41*(Suppl.1), 5121–5128. https://doi.org/10.3233/WOR-2012-0803-5121

Erdman, K. (2018). *An analysis of Geert Hofstede's culture's consequences: Comparing values, behaviors, institutes and organizations across nations.* CRC Press.

Erdoğan, A., & Canatan, H. (2015). Literature Search Consisting of the Areas of Six Sigma's Usage. *Procedia: Social and Behavioral Sciences, 195*(0212), 695–704. doi:10.1016/j.sbspro.2015.06.160

Erica, L., & Barak, M. M. (2015). *Job burnout and affective wellbeing: A longitudinal study of burnout and job satisfaction among public child welfare workers.* doi:10.1016/j.childyouth.2015.05.005

Ertürk, Tuerdi, & Wujiabudula. (2016). The Effects of Six Sigma Approach on Business Performance: A Study of White Goods (Home Appliances) Sector in Turkey. *Procedia: Social and Behavioral Sciences, 229*, 444–452. doi:10.1016/j.sbspro.2016.07.154

Escobar-Pérez, J., & Cuervo-Martínez, Á. (2008). Validez De Contenido Y Juicio De Expertos: Una Aproximación a Su Utilización. *Avances En Medición, 6*, 27–36.

EskoEVO. (2018). https://eksobionics.com/ekso-evo/

Esther, P., Christian, S., & Jürgen, G. (2020). Understanding Employee Motivation for Work-to-Nonwork Integration Behavior: A Reasoned Action Approach. *Journal of Business and Psychology, 35*(5), 683–696. doi:10.100710869-019-09648-5

Estrada, J., & Romero, N. (2014). Factores psicosociales del trabajador en la industria manufacturera en México. *Trabajo Y Sociedad, 20*, 119–129. www.unse.edu.ar/trabajoysociedad/20SALAZARROMEROtrabajadormanufactura mexico.pdf

Fan, H., Yu, S., Chu, J., Wang, M., Chen, D., Zhang, S., Wang, W., Wu, T., & Wan, N. (2019). Anthropometric characteristics and product categorization of Chinese auricles for ergonomic design. *International Journal of Industrial Ergonomics, 69*, 118–141. doi:10.1016/j.ergon.2018.11.002

Farnacio, Y., Pratt, M. E., Marshall, E. G., & Graber, J. M. (2017). Are Workplace Psychosocial Factors Associated With Work-Related Injury in the US Workforce? *Journal of Occupational and Environmental Medicine, 59*(10), e164–e171. https://doi.org/10.1097/JOM.0000000000001143

Faulkner, W., & Badurdeen, F. (2014). Sustainable Value Stream Mapping (Sus-VSM): Methodology to Visualize and Assess Manufacturing Sustainability Performance. *Journal of Cleaner Production, 85*, 8–18. doi:10.1016/j.jclepro.2014.05.042

Felizzola Jiménez, H., & Luna Amaya, C. (2014). Lean Six Sigma En Pequeñas y Medianas Empresas: Un Enfoque Metodológico. *Ingeniare. Revista Chilena de Ingeniería, 22*(2), 263–277. doi:10.4067/S0718-33052014000200012

Fernet, C., Torrès, O., Austin, S., & St-Pierre, J. (2016). The psychological costs of owning and managing an SME: Linking job stressors, occupational loneliness, entrepreneurial orientation, and burnout. *Burnout Research, 3*(2), 45–53. doi:10.1016/j.burn.2016.03.002

Fliedner, G. (2008). Sustainability : A New Lean Principle."*Proceedings of the 39th Annual Meeting of the Decision Sciences Institute*, 3321–26.

Flood, S. M., & Genadek, K. R. (2016). Time for Each Other: Work and Family Constraints Among Couples. *Journal of Marriage and Family*, *78*(1), 142–164. doi:10.1111/jomf.12255 PMID:26778856

Fornell, C., & Larcker, D. F. (1981). Structural equation models with unobservable variables and measurement error: Algebra and statistics. Sage Publications.

Franco, L. M., Bennett, S., Kanfer, R., & Stubblebine, P. (2004). Determinants and consequences of health worker motivation in hospitals in Jordan and Georgia. *Social Science & Medicine*, *58*(2), 343–355. doi:10.1016/S0277-9536(03)00203-X PMID:14604620

Franklin, N. (2021, March 1). *Zoom fatigue is real and has four basic causes*. Workplace Insight. https://workplaceinsight.net/zoom-fatigue-is-real-and-has-four-basic-causes/

Freitas, J. G. D., & Costa, H. G. (2017). Impacts of Lean Six Sigma over Organizational Sustainability. *International Journal of Lean Six Sigma*, *8*(1), 89–108. doi:10.1108/IJLSS-10-2015-0039

Fujiwara, K., Tsukishima, E., Tsutsumi, A., Kawakami, N., & Kishi, R. (2003). Interpersonal conflict, social support, and burnout among home care workers in Japan. *Journal of Occupational Health*, *45*(5), 313–320. doi:10.1539/joh.45.313 PMID:14646273

Gabor, M. R., Conţiu, L. C., & Oltean, F. D. (2012). A comparative analysis regarding European tourism competitiveness: Emerging versus developed markets. *Procedia Economics and Finance*, *3*, 361–366. doi:10.1016/S2212-5671(12)00165-7

Garza-Reyes, A., Jose, A. F., Kumar, V., Antony, J., & Soriano-Meier, H. (2014). A DMAIRC Approach to Lead Time Reduction in an Aerospace Engine Assembly Process. *Journal of Manufacturing Technology Management*, *25*(1), 27–48. Advance online publication. doi:10.1108/JMTM-05-2012-0058

Gensler Research Institute. (2021). *Workplace surveys: Research and insight*. Gensler. https://www.gensler.com/research-insight/workplace-surveys

Gensler. (2021). *Design forecast 2021: Places and spaces in a post-covid world*. https://www.gensler.com/research-insight/publications/design-forecast/reconnect?utm_source=gensler-home-dsk

Gerdman, D. (2020, March 16). *How the coronavirus is already rewriting the future of business*. HBS Working Knowledge. https://hbswk.hbs.edu/item/how-the-coronavirus-is-already-rewriting-the-future-of-business

Gershon, L. (2017, September 12). *Does a job need to be meaningful?* The Orange Dot. https://www.headspace.com/blog/2017/09/12/meaningful-job/

Ghoddousi, P., Bahrami, N., Chileshe, N., & Hosseini, M. R. (2014a). Mapping site-based construction workers' motivation: Expectancy theory approach. *The Australasian Journal of Construction Economics and Building*, *14*(1), 60–77. doi:10.5130/AJCEB.v14i1.3712

Giebels, E., & Janssen, O. (2004). Conflict Stress and Reduced Wellbeing at Work: The Buffering Effect of Third-Party Help. *European Journal of Work and Organizational Psychology*, *14*. Advance online publication. doi:10.2139srn.602063

Gil-Monte, P. R. (2002). Influencia del género sobre el proceso de desarrollo del síndrome de quemarse por el trabajo (Burnout) en profesionales de enfermería. *Psicologia em Estudo*, *7*(1), 3–10. https://doi.org/10.1590/S1413-73722002000100003

Global Wellness Institute (GWI). (2018). *Build well to live well: Wellness lifestyle real estate & communities*. https://globalwellnessinstitute.org/industry-research/wellness-real-estate-communities-research/

Goldberg, D., & Williams, P. (1988). *A User's Guide to the General health Questionnaire*. NFER-Nelson.

Goldhagen, S. W. (2017). *Welcome to your world: How the built environment shapes our lives* (1st ed.). Harper.

Gomes Carrana, P. (2015). *Evaluación de riesgos psicosociales en los trabajadores de la industria de la limpieza.* Academic Press.

Gómez, A. H., Escobar Toledo, C., Larios Prado, J. M., & Noriega Morales, S. (2015). Factores Críticos de Éxito Para El Despliegue Del Mantenimiento Productivo Total En Plantas de La Industria Maquiladora Para La Exportación En Ciudad Juárez: Una Solución Factorial. *Contaduría y Administración*, *60*, 82–106. doi:10.1016/j.cya.2015.08.005

Gondim, S., Mazzieri, S., & Torres, A. (2016). *Percepción de innovación en las organizaciones. Percepción de innovación en organizaciones de España y Latinoamérica.* Academic Press.

Gourarie, C. (2021, February 12). Spotify will allow its staff to work from anywhere permanently. *Commercial Observer*. https://commercialobserver.com/2021/02/spotify-will-allow-its-staff-to-work-from-anywhere-permanently/

GPCEE. (2014). *Guía Práctica Centros de Empleo y Emprendimiento ventanillas únicas de atención para grupos en pobreza y exclusión. Programa de las Naciones Unidas para el Desarrollo*. PNUD.

Griffiths, K., & Clarence-Smith, L. (2021, February 24). HSBC to cut office space by 40 per cent. *The Times*. https://www.thetimes.co.uk/article/hsbc-to-cut-office-space-by-40-per-cent-xgg3dxq3w

Grosse, E., Christoph, H., Glock, M., Mohamed, J., & Patrick, N. (2015). Incorporating human factors in order picking planning models: Framework and research opportunities. *International Journal of Production Research*, *3*(3), 695–717. doi:10.1080/00207543.2014.919424

Güntert, S. (2014). The impact of work design, autonomy support, and strategy on employee outcomes: A differentiated perspective on self-determination at work. *Motivation and Emotion*, *39*(1), 74–87. doi:10.100711031-014-9412-7

GWI. (2020). *Statistics and facts*. https://globalwellnessinstitute.org/press-room/statistics-and-facts/

Habanik, J., Martosova, A., Letkova, N., & Dubček, A. (2020). The Impact of Managerial Decision-Making on Employee Motivation in Manufacturing Companies. *Journal of Competitiveness, 12*(2), 38-50. doi:10.7441/joc.2020.02.03

Hair, J. F., Black, W. C., Babin, B. J., Anderson, R. E., & Tatham, R. (2006). *Multivariate data analysis.* Pearson Prentice Hall.

Hallgren, M., & Olhager, J. (2006). Quantification in Manufacturing Strategy: A Methodology and Illustration. *International Journal of Production Economics*, *104*(1), 113–124. doi:10.1016/j.ijpe.2005.09.004

Hanaysha, J. R., & Majid, M. (2018). Employee motivation and its role in improving the productivity and organizational commitment at higher education institutions. *Journal of Entrepreneurship and Business*, *6*(1), 17–28. doi:10.17687/JEB.0601.02

Hancock, K., Polites, G., & Fitzgibbon, C. (1985). *Report of Committee of Review into Australian Industrial Relations Law and Systems*. Commonwealth Government Printer.

Haridy. (2018). *Ford makes EksoVest exoskeletons available to employees worldwide after successful US trials*. https://newatlas.com/eksovest-exoskeleton-rolled-out-worldwide-ford/55804/

Harman, H. H. (1976). *Modern factor analysis*. University of Chicago press.

Haro, A., Lara, B., Salido, P., & Salazar, V. (1996). El Sistema local de salud en la región Guarijio/Makuraque de Sonora: Retos y perspectivas. Región y Sociedad, Julio-diciembre. *VII*, *N0*(12), 47–106.

Harris, K. J., Murphy, K. S., DiPietro, R. B., & Line, N. D. (2017). The antecedents and outcomes of food safety motivators for restaurant workers: An expectancy framework. *International Journal of Hospitality Management*, *63*, 53–62. doi:10.1016/j.ijhm.2017.02.004

Harshal, T. (2017). Historical Milestones of Ergonomics: From Ancient Human to Modern Human. *Journal of Economics, 7*(4), 65–78.

Harvard, T. H. C. (2021). *9 Foundations of a Healthy Building*. 9 Foundations. https://9foundations.forhealth.org/

Hatcher, J. (2018, November 1). Smart building controls are delivering a way to wellness. *Smart Buildings Magazine*. https://smartbuildingsmagazine.com/features/smart-building-controls-are-delivering-a-way-to-wellness

HemaMalini, P. H., & Washington, A. (2014). Employees' Motivation and Valued Rewards as a Key to Effective QWL-from the Perspective of Expectancy Theory. *TSM Business Review, 2*(2), 45.

Hensel, R., & Keil, M. (2019). Subjective Evaluation of a Passive Industrial Exoskeleton for Lower-back Support: A Field Study in the Automotive Sector. *IISE Transactions on Occupational Ergonomics and Human Factors, 7*(3–4), 213–221. doi:10.1080/24725838.2019.1573770

Hetzner. (2016). *BMW workers don "Iron Man" suit*. https://www.autonews.com/article/20160626/OEM01/306279965/bmw-workers-don-iron-man-suit

Higgins, D., & Bianzino, N. M. (2020, October 12). Tech should enable change, not drive it. *Harvard Business Review*, 6.

Hillhouse, J., Adler, C., & Walters, D. (2000). A simple model of stress, burnout and symptomatology in medical residents: A longitudinal study. *Psychology Health and Medicine, 5*(1), 63–73. doi:10.1080/135485000106016

Hitka, M., Kozubíková, Ľ., & Potkány, M. (2018). Education and gender-based differences in employee motivation. *Journal of Business Economics and Management, 19*(1), 80–95. doi:10.3846/16111699.2017.1413009

HMT France - Accueil. (2020). https://www.hmt-france.com/

Höfer, R., & Bigorra, J. (2008). Biomass-Based Green Chemistry: Sustainable Solutions for Modern Economies. *Green Chemistry Letters and Reviews, 1*(2), 79–97. doi:10.1080/17518250802342519

Hofstede, G. (2011). Dimensionalizing cultures: The Hofstede model in context. *Online Readings in Psychology and Culture, 2*(1).

Hofstede, G. (1980). Culture and organizations. *International Studies of Management & Organization, 10*(4), 15–41. doi:10.1080/00208825.1980.11656300

Hofstede, G. (2001). Culture's recent consequences: Using dimension scores in theory and research. *International Journal of Cross Cultural Management, 1*(1), 11–17. doi:10.1177/147059580111002

Hohnen, P., & Hasle, P. (2018). Third party audits of the psychosocial work environment in occupational health and safety management systems. *Safety Science, 109*, 76–85. doi:10.1016/j.ssci.2018.04.028

Ho, Y. C., Ou, C. C., & Wen, B. W. (2008). An Empirical Study of Key Success Factors for Six Sigma Green Belt Projects at an Asian MRO Company. *Journal of Air Transport Management, 14*(5), 263–269. doi:10.1016/j.jairtraman.2008.05.002

HSE (Health and Safety Executive). (2011). *Cost to Britain of workplace injuries and work-related ill health: 2010/11*. Available at: https://www.hse.gov.uk/statistics/pdf/cost-to-britain.pdf

Huang, X., Ribeiro, J. D., Musacchio, K. M., & Franklin, J. C. (2017). Demographics as predictors of suicidal thoughts and behaviors: A meta-analysis. *PLoS ONE, 12*(7). doi:10.1371/journal.pone.0180793

Hubert, S., & Aujoulat, I. (2018). Parental Burnout: When Exhausted Mothers Open Up. *Frontiers in Psychology, 9*, 1021–1021. doi:10.3389/fpsyg.2018.01021 PMID:29997543

Hui, C. H., & Triandis, C. H. (1986). Indivitualism -Collectivism- A study of cross cultural researchers. *A Study of Cross Cultural Psychology, 17*(2), 225-248.

Hulin, C., Netemeyer, R., & Cudeck, R. (2001). Can a Reliability Coefficient Be Too High? *Journal of Consumer Psychology, 10*, 55–58. doi:10.1207/S15327663JCP1001&2_05

Hwang y Yoon. (1981). *Multiple attribute decision making: methods and applications: a state-of-the-art survey*. Springer-Verlag.

IHOBE. (2009). *Análisis del ciclo de vida y huella del carbono: dos maneras de medir el impacto ambiental de un producto*. Primera Edición. Sociedad Pública de Gestión Ambiental.

IIDH. (2007). Instituto Interamericano de Derechos Humanos. Economía indígena y mercado.

Ilies, R., Huth, M., Ryan, A. M., & Dimotakis, N. E. (2015). Explaining the links between workload, distress, and wor‹ family conflict among school employees: Physical, cognitive, and emotional fatigue. *Journal of Educational Psychology, 107*(4), 1136–1149. doi:10.1037/edu0000029

IMSS. (2017). *Acercando el IMSS al Ciudadano*. Retrieved from: http://www.imss.gob.mx/conoce-al-imss/memoria-estadistica-2018

INDEX-Mexicali. (2020). *Reporte de empresas de manufactura de Mexicali, 45*. Author.

INDEX-Mexicali. (2020). *Reporte de empresas de manufactura de Mexicali, 52*. Author.

Industrials, O. (2021). Retrieved September 9, 2021, Retrieved from https://paexo.com/paexo-shoulder/?lang=en

Institute for the Future (IFTF). (2020). *After the pandemic: Writing the stories of the future*. Writing the Stories of the Future. https://www.iftf.org/our-work/health-self/whathappensnext/writing-the-stories-of-the-future/

Institute for Work & Health. (2005). *The Burden of Work-related Musculoskeletal Disorders (MSDs)*. Author.

Instituto Nacional de Lenguas Indígenas en México. (2019). *En el país, 25 millones de personas se reconocen como indígenas*. Recuperado el 19 de Mayo de 2019, de Instituto Nacional de Lenguas Indígenas en México: https://www.inali.gob.mx/es/comunicados/701-2019-02-08-15-22-50.html

Instituto Nacional de Seguridad e Higiene en el Trabajo. (2011). *Vii encuesta nacional de condiciones de trabajo 2011*. Ministerio De Empleo Y Seguridad Social.

International Labour Organization (ILO). (2008). *Seoul declaration on safety and health at work*. https://www.ilo.org/safework/info/promo/WCMS_151736/lang--en/index.htm

International WELL Building Institute (IWBI). (2021). *WELL v2 standard*. https://v2.wellcertified.com/wellv2/en/overview

Iqbal, M. (2020, October 30). *Zoom revenue and usage statistics*. Business of Apps. https://www.businessofapps.com/data/zoom-statistics/

Islam, R., & Ismail, A. Z. H. (2008). Employee motivation: A Malaysian perspective. *International Journal of Commerce and Management*. Advance online publication. doi:10.1108/10569210810921960

Ismyrlis, V., & Moschidis, O. (2013). Six Sigma's Critical Success Factors and Toolbox. *International Journal of Lean Six Sigma, 4*(2), 108–117. doi:10.1108/20401461311319310

ISTAS. (2015). Factores de riesgo ergonómico y causas de exposición. Herramientas de prevención de riesgos laborales para pymes, Madrid, España.

Ivancevich, J. M., & Matteson, M. T. (1980). Optimizing Human Resources: A Case for Preventive Health and Stress Management. *Organizational Dynamics*, *9*(2), 5–25. doi:10.1016/0090-2616(80)90037-6 PMID:10249451

Izquierdo, F. M. (2012). *Manual de Riesgos Psicosociales en el trabajo: Teoría y Práctica*. Editorial Académica Española.

Jespersen, A. H., Hohnen, P., & Hasle, P. (2016). Internal audits of psychosocial risks at workplaces with certified OHS management systems. *Safety Science*, *84*, 201–209. doi:10.1016/j.ssci.2015.12.013

Jiménez, B. (2011). Factores y riesgos laborales psicosociales: Conceptualización, historia y cambios actuales. Academic Press.

Jiménez, E., Acosta, M., Luna, G., Lucero, B., Delfín, J., & Velásquez, L. A. (2019). Reverse Engineering and Straightforward Design as Tools to Improve the Teaching of Mechanical Engineering. In M. Abdulwahed, A. Bouras, & L. Veillard (Eds.), *Industry Integrated Engineering and Computing Education* (pp. 93–188). Springer.

Jones, M., Rice, L., Meraz, F., & ProQuest. (2019). *Designing for health & wellbeing: Home, city, society*. Vernon Press.

Júnior, C. H. M., & Lima, E. (2011). Descontinuidade de Programas Seis Sigma: Um Estudo Comparativo de Casos. *Revista de Gestão*, *18*(4), 639–658. doi:10.5700/rege445

Kalpakjian, S. (2014). Manufacturing engineering and technology. Prentice Hall.

Kantardjieva, M. (2015). The Relationship between Total Quality Management (TQM) and Strategic Management. *Journal of Economics, Business and Management*, *3*(5), 537–541. doi:10.7763/JOEBM.2015.V3.242

Karasek, R. A. (1979). Job demands, job decision latitude, and mental strain: Implications for job redesign. *Administrative Science Quarterly*, *24*, 285–308.

Karasek, R. A., Theorell, T., Schwartz, J., Schnall, P., Pieper, C., & Michela, J. (1988). Job characteristics in relation to the prevalence of myocardial infarction in the U.S. HES and HANES. *American Journal of Public Health*, *78*, 910–918.

Kashima, E. S., Halloran, M., Yuki, M., & Kashima, Y. (2004). The effects of personal and collective mortality salience on individualism: Comparing Australians and Japanese with higher and lower self-esteem. *Journal of Experimental Social Psychology*, *40*(3), 384–392. doi:10.1016/j.jesp.2003.07.007

Kehrt, S. (2020, December 15). The 'healthy building' surge will outlast the pandemic. *Wired*. https://www.wired.com/story/healthy-building-outlast-pandemic/

Khazan, O. (2020, May 4). Work from home is here to stay. *The Atlantic*. https://www.theatlantic.com/health/archive/2020/05/work-from-home-pandemic/611098/

Kim. (2018). *Hyundai brings wearable robotics to factories*. https://koreajoongangdaily.joins.com/news/article/article.aspx?aid=3054561&cloc=joongangdaily%7Chome%7Cnewslist1

Kim, J., & de Dear, R. (2013). Workspace satisfaction: The privacy-communication trade-off in open-plan offices. *Journal of Environmental Psychology*, *36*, 18–26. doi:10.1016/j.jenvp.2013.06.007

Kim, S., Moore, A., Srinivasan, D., Akanmu, A., Barr, A., Harris-Adamson, C., Rempel, D. M., & Nussbaum, M. A. (2019). Potential of Exoskeleton Technologies to Enhance Safety, Health, and Performance in Construction: Industry Perspectives and Future Research Directions. *IISE Transactions on Occupational Ergonomics and Human Factors*, *7*(3–4), 185–191. doi:10.1080/24725838.2018.1561557

Kim, Y., & Lee, J. (1993). Manufacturing Strategy and Production Systems: An Integrated Framework. *Journal of Operations Management*, *11*(1), 3–15. doi:10.1016/0272-6963(93)90029-O

Kinnunen, U., & Mauno, S. (1998). Antecedents and outcomes of work-family conflict among employed women and men in Finland. *Human Relations, 51*(2), 157–177. doi:10.1177/001872679805100203

Klepeis, N. E., Nelson, W. C., Ott, W. R., Robinson, J. P., Tsang, A. M., Switzer, P., Behar, J. V., Hern, S. C., & Engelmann, W. H. (2001). The National Human Activity Pattern Survey (NHAPS): A resource for assessing exposure to environmental pollutants. *Journal of Exposure Science & Environmental Epidemiology, 11*(3), 231–252. doi:10.1038j.jea.7500165 PMID:11477521

Knight, C., & Haslam, S. A. (2010). The relative merits of lean, enriched, and empowered offices: An experimental examination of the impact of workspace management strategies on well-being and productivity. *Journal of Experimental Psychology. Applied, 16*(2), 158–172. doi:10.1037/a0019292 PMID:20565201

Kondō, M., & Sonenshein, S. (2020). *Joy at work: Organizing your professional life*. Little, Brown Spark.

Krok. (2017). *Ford's exoskeleton could help factory workers in a big way - Roadshow*. https://www.cnet.com/roadshow/news/fords-exoskeleton-could-help-factory-workers-in-a-big-way/

Kuhlang, P., Edtmayr, T., & Sihn, W. (2011). Methodical approach to increase productivity and reduce lead time in assembly and production-logistic processes. *CIRP Journal of Manufacturing Science and Technology, 4*(1), 24–32. doi:10.1016/j.cirpj.2011.02.001

Kuvaas, B., Buch, R., Weibel, A., Dysvik, A., & Nerstad, C. G. (2017). Do intrinsic and extrinsic motivation relate differently to employee outcomes? *Journal of Economic Psychology, 61*, 244–258. doi:10.1016/j.joep.2017.05.004

Kyaw-Myint, S. M., Strazdins, L., Clements, M., Butterworth, P., & Gallagher, L. (2017). A method of identifying health-based benchmarks for psychosocial risks at work: A tool for risk assessment. *Safety Science, 93*, 143–151. doi:10.1016/j.ssci.2016.11.016

Lahiri, S., Gold, J., & Levenstein, C. (2005). Estimation of net-costs for prevention of occupational low back pain: Three case studies from the US. *American Journal of Industrial Medicine, 48*(6), 530–541. doi:10.1002/ajim.20184 PMID:16299707

Laschi, A., Marchi, E., Foderi, C., & Neri, F. (2016). *Identifying causes, dynamics and consequences of Ley Federal del Trabajo (LFT) (2019) "Diario Oficial de la Federación (DOF) de México. Regulaciones de condiciones laborales*. STPS-SSA.

Lass, H. (2018). Developing intra-personal skills as a proactive way to personal sustainability. In O. Parodi & K. Tamm (Eds.), *Personal Sustainability: Exploring the Far Side of Sustainable Development* (1st ed., pp. 21–21). Routledge. doi:10.4324/9781315159997-7

Law, R., Dollard, M., Tuckey, M., & Dormann, C. (2011). Psychosocial safety climate as a lead indicator of workplace bullying and harassment, job resources, psychological health, and employee engagement. *Accident; Analysis and Prevention, 43*, 1782–1793.

Layard, P. R. G. (2005). *Happiness: Lessons from a new science*. Penguin Press.

Lee, & Ashforth, B. (1996). A meta-analytic examination of the correlates of the three dimensions of job burnout. *J. Appl. Psychol., 81*(2), 123-133. doi:10.1037/0021-9010.81.2.123

Lee, H.-W. (2019). Moderators of the Motivational Effects of Performance Management: A Comprehensive Exploration Based on Expectancy Theory. *Public Personnel Management, 48*(1), 27–55. doi:10.1177/0091026018783003

Lee, W.-N., & Choi, S. M. (2005). The role of horizontal and vertical individualism and collectivism in online consumers' responses toward persuasive communication on the web. *Journal of Computer-Mediated Communication, 11*(1), 317–336. doi:10.1111/j.1083-6101.2006.tb00315.x

Leinonen, T. (2020, December 28). Wellbeing of a university community and its members during remote working. *Teemu Leinonen.* https://teemuleinonen.fi/2020/12/28/wellbeing-of-a-university-community-and-its-members-during-remote-working/

Leiter, M. P., & Maslach, C. (2009). Nurse turnover: The mediating role of burnout. *Journal of Nursing Management, 17*, 331–339. doi:10.1111/j.1365-2834.2009.01004.x

Leka, S., Jain, A., Cox, T., & Kortum, E. (2011). The development of the European framework for psychosocial risk management: PRIMA-EF. *Journal of Occupational Health, 53.* doi:10.1539/joh.O10010

Leka, S., Jain, A., Iavicoli, S., Vartia, M., & Ertel, M. (2011). The role of policy for the management of psychosocial risks at the workplace in the European Union. *Safety Science, 49*(4), 558–564. doi:10.1016/j.ssci.2010.02.002

Lepine, J. A., Podsakoff, N. P., & Lepine, M. A. (2005). A meta-analytic test of the challenge stressor-hindrance stressor framework: An explanation for inconsistent relationships among stressors and performance. *Academy of Management Journal, 48*(5), 764–775. doi:10.5465/amj.2005.18803921

Ley Federal del Trabajo-Diario Oficial de la Federación (DOF) de México. (2019). *Regulaciones de condiciones laborales.* STPS-SSA.

Light, I., & Karageorgis, S. (1994). The ethnic economy. In N. Smelser & R. Swedberg (Eds.), *The handbook of economic sociology* (pp. 646–671). Russell Sage Foundation.

Linderman, K., Schroeder, R. G., Zaheer, S., & Choo, A. S. (2003). Six Sigma: A Goal-Theoretic Perspective. *Journal of Operations Management, 21*(2), 193–203. doi:10.1016/S0272-6963(02)00087-6

Linha Industrial. (2020). *Exy Innovation Company.* https://www.exy9br.com/produtos?

Litvin, S. W. (2019). Hofstede, cultural differences, and TripAdvisor hotel reviews. *International Journal of Tourism Research, 21*(5), 712–717. doi:10.1002/jtr.2298

Liu, J. (2020, May 27). *So your company has said you can work from home forever—Now what?* CNBC. https://www.cnbc.com/2020/05/27/so-your-company-has-said-you-can-work-from-home-forevernow-what.html

Ližbetinová, L., & Hitka, M. (2020). Gender Motivation Differences of Czech and Chinese Employees. *Periodica Polytechnica Social and Management Sciences, 28*(1), 48–58. doi:10.3311/PPso.12867

Llorens, C., Navarro, A., Salas, S., Utzet, M., & Moncada, S. (2019). For better or for worse? Psychosocial work environment and direct participation practices. *Safety Science, 116*, 78–85. doi:10.1016/j.ssci.2019.02.028

Loos, M., Merino, E., & Taboada, C. (2016). Mapping the state of the art of ergonomics within logistics. *Scientometrics Journal, 109*(1), 85–101. doi:10.100711192-016-1960-z

López, G. (2008). Caracterización de la corrosión en materiales metálicos de la industria electrónica en Mexicali, BC (Tesis de doctorado). UABC, Instituto de Ingeniería, Mexicali.

López, V., Marín, E., & Cornejo, R. (2011). Riesgos de Trabajo en Una Planta Maquiladora: Un Análisis Longitudinal. *Revista International Administración & Finanzas., 3*(2), 103–115.

Lowe, B. D., Billotte, W. G., & Peterson, D. R. (2019). ASTM F48 Formation and Standards for Industrial Exoskeletons and Exosuits. *IISE Transactions on Occupational Ergonomics and Human Factors, 7.* doi:10.1080/24725838.2019.1579769

Lucchesi, E. L. B. (2019, January 3). The unbearable heaviness of clutter. *The New York Times*. https://www.nytimes.com/2019/01/03/well/mind/clutter-stress-procrastination-psychology.html

Lucchini, R. G., & London, L. (2014, July 1). Global occupational health: Current challenges and the need for urgent action. *Annals of Global Health*. doi:10.1016/j.aogh.2014.09.006

Luchman, J. N., & González-Morales, M. G. (2013). Demands, control, and support: A meta-analytic review of work characteristics interrelationships. *Journal of Occupational Health Psychology, 19*(3), 376–384. doi:10.1037/a0030541

MacHuca, J. A. D., Ortega Jiménez, C. H., Garrido-Vega, P., & Luis Pérez Diez De Los Ríos, J. (2011). Do Technology and Manufacturing Strategy Links Enhance Operational Performance? Empirical Research in the Auto Supplier Sector. *International Journal of Production Economics, 133*(2), 541–550. doi:10.1016/j.ijpe.2010.12.010

Magrab, E., Azarm, S., Balachandran, B., Duncan, J., Herold, K., & Walsh, G. (2011). An Engineer's Guide to MATLAB: with Applications from Mechanical, Aerospace, Electrical, and Civil Engineering. Prentice Hall.

Mañas, M. A., Díaz-Fúnez, P., Pecino, V., López-Liria, R., Padilla, D., & Aguilar-Parra, J. M. (2018). Consequences of Team Job Demands: Role Ambiguity Climate, Affective Engagement, and Extra-Role Performance. *Frontiers in Psychology, 8*(2292). Advance online publication. doi:10.3389/fpsyg.2017.02292292 PMID:29375424

Mark, G., & Smith, A. P. (2012). Occupational stress, job characteristics, coping, and the mental health of nurses. *British Journal of Health Psychology, 17*(3), 505–521. doi:10.1111/j.2044-8287.2011.02051.x PMID:22107162

Martela, F., & Riekki, T. J. J. (2018). Autonomy, competence, relatedness, and beneficence: A multicultural comparison of the four pathways to meaningful work. *Frontiers in Psychology, 9*, 1157. doi:10.3389/fpsyg.2018.01157 PMID:30042710

Martínez, V. M., Jiménez, E., Arellano, L., Uzeta, C. R., Sotelo, R., & Reyes, L. A. (2012). Desarrollo de equipos para la manufactura de muebles rústicos de la etnia guarijía: un ejemplo de transferencia tecnológica. *XII International Conference on Engineering and Technology Education*, 190-194.

Maslach, C., & Leiter, M. P. (2016). Understanding the burnout experience: Recent research and its implications for psychiatry. *World Psychiatry; Official Journal of the World Psychiatric Association (WPA), 15*(2), 103–111. doi:10.1002/wps.20311 PMID:27265691

Maslach, C., Schaufeli, W. B., & Leiter, M. P. (2001). Job burnout. *Annual Review of Psychology, 52*(1), 397–422. doi:10.1146/annurev.psych.52.1.397 PMID:11148311

Mason, S. E., Nicolay, C. R., & Darzi, A. (2015). The Use of Lean and Six Sigma Methodologies in Surgery: A Systematic Review. *The Surgeon, 13*(2), 91–100. doi:10.1016/j.surge.2014.08.002 PMID:25189692

Mathisen, G. E., Brønnick, K., Arntzen, K. J., & Bergh, L. I. V. (2016). Identifying and managing psychosocial risks during organizational restructuring: It's what you do and how you do it. *Safety Science, 100*, 20–29. https://doi.org/10.1016/j.ssci.2016.12.007

Matthew, M. F. M. (2020). *The Radical Individualism Raging Throughout America*. Academic Press.

McLaurin, J. P. (2021). *5 trends driving the new post-pandemic workplace*. Gensler. https://www.gensler.com/research-insight/blog/5-trends-driving-the-new-post-pandemic-workplace

McLaurin, J. P., & Barber, C. (2020, December 8). *Surprising truths about the new hybrid workplace*. Gensler. https://www.gensler.com/research-insight/blog/surprising-truths-about-the-new-hybrid-workplace

Medina, S. (2019, May 7). *How the "happiness industry" is changing architecture*. Metropolis. https://www.metropolismag.com/architecture/cca-happy-life-architecture-exhibition/

Meerding, W. J., Ijzelenberg, W., Koopmanschap, M. A., Severens, J. L., & Burdorf, A. (2005). Health problems lead to considerable productivity loss at work among workers with high physical load jobs. *JournalofClinicalEpidemiology, 58*, 517–523.

Mehrabi, J. (2012). Application of Six-Sigma in Educational Quality Management. *Procedia: Social and Behavioral Sciences, 47*, 1358–1362. doi:10.1016/j.sbspro.2012.06.826

Melamed, S., Shirom, A., Toker, S., Berliner, S., & Shapira, I. (2006). Burnout and Risk of Cardiovascular Disease: Evidence, Possible Causal Paths, and Promising Research Directions. *Psychological Bulletin, 132*(3), 327–353. doi:10.1037/0033-2909.132.3.327 PMID:16719565

Meliá, J. (2006). *¿Cómo evaluar los riesgos psicosociales en la empresa? Metodologías, oportunidades y tendencias.* Ponencia presentada en el IV Congreso Internacional de Prevención y Riesgos Laborales, Sevilla, España. Recuperado de: http://www.acosomoral.org/ pdf/sevilla06/0303.pdf

Memish, K., Martin, A., Bartlett, L., Dawkins, S., & Sanderson, K. (2017, August 1). Workplace mental health: An international review of guidelines. In *Preventive Medicine.* Academic Press Inc. doi:10.1016/j.ypmed.2017.03.017

Memoori. (2020). *Occupancy analytics and in-building location based services research: Commercial office space 2019 to 2024.* https://memoori.com/portfolio/occupancy-analytics-in-building-location-based-services/

Meunier, S., Roberge, C., Coulombe, S., & Houle, J. (2019). Feeling better at work! Mental health self-management strategies for workers with depressive and anxiety symptoms. *Journal of Affective Disorders, 254*, 7–14. doi:10.1016/j.jad.2019.05.011 PMID:31082629

Miguel, A. E., Torres, J. C., & Hernández, B. R. (2015). El turismo y las redes territoriales en ciudades de pueblos originarios. El caso de Oaxaca, México. *Revista Turydes: Turismo y Desarrollo, 19.* Recuperado el 10 de diciembre de 2016, de: https://www.eumed.net/rev/turydes/19/pueblos.html

Miner, M. H., Bickerton, G. R., Dowson, M., & Sterland, S. (2015). Spirituality and work engagement among church leaders. *Mental Health, Religion & Culture, 18*(1), 57–71. doi:10.1080/13674676.2014.1003168

Minkov, M., & Hofstede, G. (2011). The evolution of Hofstede's doctrine. *Cross Cultural Management, 18*(1), 10–20. doi:10.1108/13527601111104269

Mintzberg, H. (1994). The Rise and Fall of Strategic Planning: Reconceiving Roles for Planning, Plans, Planners. *Harvard Business Review, 72*, 458. doi:10.1016/0737-6782(96)85711-0

Mirelman, A., Glassman, A. L., & Temin, M. (2016). Estimating the Avertable Disease Burden and Cost-Effectiveness in Millions Saved (3rd ed.). Academic Press.

Mohren, D., Swaen, G., Kant, I., Amelsvoort, L., Borm, P., & Galama, J. (2003). Common infections and the role of burnout in a Dutch working population. *Journal of Psychosomatic Research, 55*(3), 201–208. doi:10.1016/S0022-3999(02)00517-2 PMID:12932792

Moorman, R. H., & Blakely, G. L. (1995). Individualism-collectivism as an individual difference predictor of organizational citizenship behavior. *Journal of Organizational Behavior, 16*(2), 127–142. doi:10.1002/job.4030160204

Moreno-Jiménez, B., & Báez León, C. (2011). Factores y riesgos psicosociales, formas, consecuencias, medidas y buenas prácticas. *Instituto Nacional de Seguridad E Higiene En El Trabajo*, 4–144. doi:10.1016/0277-9536(85)90255-2

Moreno, M. P. (2014). *De Diversos Giros Laborales Reliability and Validity of an Identification Guide on Psychosocial.* Academic Press.

Moss, J. (2019, December 11). Burnout is about your workplace, not your people. *Harvard Business Review*. https://hbr.org/2019/12/burnout-is-about-your-workplace-not-your-people

Moss, J. (2021, February 10). Beyond Burned Out. *Harvard Business Review*. https://hbr.org/2021/02/beyond-burned-out

Mudditt, J. (2020, May). *How offices will change after coronavirus*. BBC. https://www.bbc.com/worklife/article/20200514-how-the-post-pandemic-office-will-change

Muñoz, R. D., Nataly, O., & Hernández, P. H. (2018). *Riesgo psicosocial: tendencias y nuevas orientaciones laborales*. Psicogente.

Munroe, R. L., & Munroe, R. H. (1972). Obedience Among Children in an East African Society. *Journal of Cross-Cultural Psychology*, *3*(4), 395–399. doi:10.1177/002202217200300408

Murray, B. (2020, November 17). *Tomorrow's office to be a mix of work styles, workspaces: JLL*. Commercial Property Executive. https://www.cpexecutive.com/post/tomorrows-office-to-be-a-mix-of-work-styles-workspaces-jll/

Myers, R. H., & Myers, R. H. (1990). Classical and modern regression with applications (Vol. 2). Duxbury Press.

Navinés, R., Martín-Santos, R., Olivé, V., & Valdés, M. (2016). Estrés laboral: Implicaciones para la salud física y mental. *Medicina Clínica*, *146*(8), 359–366. doi:10.1016/j.medcli.2015.11.023 PMID:26806767

Ncube, F., & Kanda, A. (2018, December 1). Current Status and the Future of Occupational Safety and Health Legislation in Low- and Middle-Income Countries. In *Safety and Health at Work*. Elsevier Science B.V. doi:10.1016/j.shaw.2018.01.007

Nedeliaková, E., Štefancová, V., & Kudláč, Š. (2017). Six Sigma and Dynamic Models Application as an Important Quality Management Tool in Railway Companies. *Procedia Engineering*, *187*, 242–248. doi:10.1016/j.proeng.2017.04.371

Neffa, J. C. (2002). *Cómo evaluar los riesgos psicosociales en el trabajo?Prevención*. Recuperado de.

Netemeyer, R. G., Boles, J. S., & McMurrian, R. (1996). Development and validation of work–family conflict and family–work conflict scales. *The Journal of Applied Psychology*, *81*(4), 400–410. doi:10.1037/0021-9010.81.4.400

Neumann, W., & Medbo, L. (2010). Ergonomic and technical aspects in the redesign of material supply systems: Big boxes vs. narrow bins. *International Journal of Industrial.*

Ngo, H.-Y., Foley, S., & Loi, R. (2005). Work role stressors and turnover intentions: A study of professional clergy in Hong Kong. *International Journal of Human Resource Management*, *16*(11), 2133–2146. doi:10.1080/09585190500315141

Nieuwenhuis, M., Knight, C., Postmes, T., & Haslam, S. A. (2014). The relative benefits of green versus lean office space: Three field experiments. *Journal of Experimental Psychology. Applied*, *20*(3), 199–214. doi:10.1037/xap0000024 PMID:25068481

Nimri, M., Bdair, A., & Al Bitar, H. (2015). Applying the Expectancy Theory to Explain the Motivation of Public Sector Employees in Jordan. *Middle East Journal of Business, 10*(3), 70-82. doi:10.5742/MEJB.2015.92714

Nixon, A., Mazzola, J., Bauer, J., Krueger, J., & Spector, P. (2011). Can Work Make You Sick? A Meta-Analysis of the Relationships Between Job Stressors and Physical Symptoms. *Work and Stress*, *25*(1), 1–22. doi:10.1080/02678373.2011.569175

NOM-035. (2018). *NORMA Oficial Mexicana NOM-035-STPS-2018, Factores de riesgo psicosocial en el trabajo-Identificación, análisis y prevención*. Secretaría de Gobernación.

Nordlöf, H., Wiitavaara, B., Högberg, H., & Westerling, R. (2017). A cross-sectional study of factors influencing occupational health and safety management practices in companies. *Safety Science*, *95*, 92–103. doi:10.1016/j.ssci.2017.02.008

Norma NOM-011-STPS-2001 (2001) Condiciones de seguridad e higiene en los centros de trabajo donde se genere ruido

Norma NOM-015-STPS-2001 (2001) "Condiciones térmicas elevadas o abatidas-Condiciones de seguridad e higiene".

Norma NOM-015-STPS-2001 (2001) Condiciones térmicas elevadas o abatidas-Condiciones de seguridad e higiene

Norma NOM-024-STPS-2001 (2001) "Vibraciones-Condiciones de seguridad e higiene en los centros de trabajo".

Norma NOM-024-STPS-2001 (2001) Vibraciones-Condiciones de seguridad e higiene en los centros de trabajo

Norma NOM-025-STPS-2008 (2008) "Condiciones de iluminación en los centros de trabajo".

Norma NOM-025-STPS-2008 (2008) Condiciones de iluminación en los centros de trabajo.

Norma NOM-172-SEMARNAT-2019 (2019) Lineamientos para la obtención y comunicación del Índice de Calidad del Aire y Riesgos a la Salud

Novet, J. (2020, August 7). *Atlassian tells employees they can work from home indefinitely*. CNBC. https://www.cnbc.com/2020/08/07/atlassian-tells-employees-they-can-work-from-home-indefinitely.html

NSW. (2021). *Workplace Policies and Procedures Checklist.* doi:https://www.industrialrelations.nsw.gov.au/employers/nsw-employer-best-practice/workplace-policies-and-procedures-checklist/

Nunnally, J. C. (1978). *Psychometric theory*. McGraw-Hill.

Nunnally, J. C., & Bernstein, I. H. (1994). *Psychometric Theory*. McGraw-Hill.

Nussbaum, M. A., Lowe, B. D., de Looze, M., Harris-Adamson, C., & Smets, M. (2019). An Introduction to the Special Issue on Occupational Exoskeletons. *IISE Transactions on Occupational Ergonomics and Human Factors*, *7*(3–4), 153–162. doi:10.1080/24725838.2019.1709695

O´Sullivan, C. (2009). *A Study of Critical Success Factors for Regional*. Academic Press.

Oakman, J., Macdonald, W., Bartram, T., Keegel, T., & Kinsman, N. (2018). Workplace risk management practices to prevent musculoskeletal and mental health disorders: What are the gaps? *Safety Science*, *101*, 220–230. doi:10.1016/j.ssci.2017.09.004

Ocampo, R., Juárez, A., Arias, L., & Hindrichs, I. (2015). Factores psicosociales asociados al engagement en empleados de un restaurante de Morelos, México. *Revista Liberabit, 21*|(2), 207–219.

OHSAS 18:000 (OHSAS 18:000-2007) Gestión de la Seguridad y Salud Ocupacional.

OHSAS 18000 (2007) "Gestión de la Seguridad y Salud Ocupacional".

OIT. (2013). *La prevención de las enfermedades profesionales*. OIT.

OMS. (2004). *Prevención de trastornos músculo esqueléticos en los lugares de trabajo*. OMS.

Organización Internacional del Trabajo (OIT). (2016). *Estrés en el trabajo*. Retrieved from www.ilo.org/safeday

Orsini, C., & Rodrigues, V. (2020). Supporting motivation in teams working remotely: The role of basic psychological needs. *Medical Teacher*, *42*(7), 828–829. doi:10.1080/0142159X.2020.1758305 PMID:32366152

Ortiz, F., & Jaramillo, V. (2013). Factores de riesgo psicosocial en una industria alimenticia de la ciudad de Cali. *Pensamiento Psicológico*, *11*(1), 99–113.

Panari, C., Caricati, L., Pelosi, A., & Rossi, C. (2019). Emotional exhaustion among healthcare professionals: The effects of role ambiguity, work engagement and professional commitment. *Acta bio-medica. Atenei Parmensis, 90*(6-S), 60–67. doi:10.23750/abm.v90i6-S.8481 PMID:31292416

Pando, M., Aranda, C., Parra, L., & Ruiz, D. (2013). *Eugenesia Laboral: Salud Mental Positiva en el Trabajo*. Editorial Universidad Libre Seccional.

Paola Espeleta, C. (2015). Los riesgos psicosociales: causas, consecuencias y posibles soluciones. *Facultad de Ciencias Empresariales Y Del Trabajo*, 77.

Parada, P., Mar, P. O., & Posada Duque, J. A. (2017). Sustainable Biorefineries, an Analysis of Practices for Incorporating Sustainability in Biorefinery Design. *Industrial Crops and Products, 106*, 105–123. doi:10.1016/j.indcrop.2016.08.052

Parijat, P., & Bagga, S. (2014). Victor Vroom's expectancy theory of motivation–An evaluation. *International Research Journal of Business and Management, 7*(9), 1–8.

Parker, K., Horowitz, J. M., & Minkin, R. (2020, December 9). How coronavirus has changed the way Americans work. *Pew Research Center's Social & Demographic Trends Project*. https://www.pewresearch.org/social-trends/2020/12/09/how-the-coronavirus-outbreak-has-and-hasnt-changed-the-way-americans-work/

Parker, S. L., Jimmieson, N. L., & Amiot, C. E. (2017). The motivational mechanisms underlying active and high-strain work: Consequences for mastery and performance. *Work and Stress, 31*(3), 233–255. doi:10.1080/02678373.2017.1303551

PDEI. (2011). *Proyecto Desarrollo Económico Incluyente*. Programa de las Naciones Unidas para el Desarrollo (PNUD). Recuperado el 9 de septiembre de 2018 de:http://www.desarrolloeconomico.gov.co/sites/default/files/marcolegal/Proyecto-Desarrollo-Economico- Incluyente.pdf

Pearson, A., Ensley, M., & Amason, A. (2002). An assessment and refinement of Jehn's Intragroup Conflict Scale. *International Journal of Conflict Management, 13*(2), 110–126. doi:10.1108/eb022870

Peeters, M. C. W., Montgomery, A. J., Bakker, A. B., & Schaufeli, W. B. (2005). Balancing Work and Home: How Job and Home Demands Are Related to Burnout. *International Journal of Stress Management, 12*(1), 43–61. doi:10.1037/1072-5245.12.1.43

Pelta, R. (2020, September 21). *Survey: Productivity, work-life balance improves during pandemic*. FlexJobs Job Search Tips and Blog. https://www.flexjobs.com/blog/post/survey-productivity-balance-improve-during-pandemic-remote-work/

Penny, J. (2020, November 12). *Five ways buildings can improve mental health (Greenbuild 2020)*. Buildings. https://www.buildings.com/articles/42623/buildings-improve-mental-health

Pérez, J. (2013). Efecto del burnout y la sobrecarga en la calidad de vida en el trabajo. *Estudios Gerenciales, 29*, 445–455.

Persechino, B., Valenti, A., Ronchetti, M., Rondinone, B. M., Di Tecco, C., Vitali, S., & Iavicoli, S. (2013). Work-related stress risk assessment in Italy: A methodological proposal adapted to regulatory guidelines. *Safety and Health at Work, 4*(2), 95–99. doi:10.1016/j.shaw.2013.05.002 PMID:23961332

Petersen, A. H. (2020, December 23). Are you sure you want to go back to the office? *The New York Times*. https://www.nytimes.com/2020/12/23/opinion/covid-offices-remote-work.html

Peterson, S., Smith, P. B., Akande, A., Ayestaran, S., Bochner, S., Callan, V., Jesuino, J. C., D'Amorim, M., Francois, P.-H., Hofmann, K., Koopman, P. L., Mortazavi, S., Munene, J., Radford, M., Ropo, A., Savage, G., & Setiadi, B. (1995). Role conflict, ambiguity, and overload: A 21-nation study. *Academy of Management Journal, 38*(2), 429–452. doi:10.2307/256687

Piedrahita, H. (2006). Costs of work-related musculoskeletal disorders (MSDs) in developing countries: Colombia case. *International Journal of Occupational Safety and Ergonomics*, *12*(4), 379–386. doi:10.1080/10803548.2006.11076696 PMID:17156613

Pirschel, C. (2020, April 15). *Places matter: Best practices for working from home*. International WELL Building Institute. https://resources.wellcertified.com/articles/places-matter-best-practices-for-working-from-home/

Podsakoff, P. M., & Organ, D. W. (1986). Self-reports in organizational research: Problems and prospects. *Journal of Management*, *12*(4), 531–544. doi:10.1177/014920638601200408

Podsakoff, P., MacKenzie, S., Lee, J.-Y., & Podsakoff, N. (2003). Common Method Biases in Behavioral Research: A Critical Review of the Literature and Recommended Remedies. *The Journal of Applied Psychology*, *88*(5), 879–903. doi:10.1037/0021-9010.88.5.879 PMID:14516251

Potter, R. E., Dollard, M. F., Owen, M. S., O'Keeffe, V., Bailey, T., & Leka, S. (2017). Assessing a national work health and safety policy intervention using the psychosocial safety climate framework. *Safety Science*, *100*, 91–102. doi:10.1016/j.ssci.2017.05.011

Potter, R., O'Keeffe, V., Leka, S., Webber, M., & Dollard, M. (2019). Analytical review of the Australian policy context for work-related psychological health and psychosocial risks. *Safety Science*, *111*, 37–48. doi:10.1016/j.ssci.2018.09.012

Pradere, F. (2020). *Reimagining Human Experience* (No. 1). Jones Lang LaSalle.

PricewaterhouseCoopers (PwC). (2021, February). *Changing places: How hybrid working is reinventing the Australian CBD*. https://www.pwc.com.au/important-problems/future-of-work-design-for-the-future/changing-places-australian-cbd.html

PRODUCT | Crimson Dynamics431. (2020). https://www.c-dyn.com/product?

Prüss-Üstün, A., & Corvalán, C. (2006). *Preventing disease through healthy environments: Towards an estimate of the environmental burden of disease*. World Health Organization.

Psicopreven. (2018). *ISO 11228-1:2013*. Recuperado el 19 de Diciembre de 2020, de https://ergosoft.nextprevencion.com/bat/ajax.funciones.php

Pun, K. F., Chin, K. S., White, A. S., & Gill, R. (2004). Determinants of Manufacturing Strategy Formulation: A Longitudinal Study in Hong Kong. *Technovation*, *24*(2), 121–137. doi:10.1016/S0166-4972(02)00050-0

Punnett, L., & Wegman, D. H. (2004). Work-related musculoskeletal disorders: the epidemiologic evidence and the debate. *Journal of Electromyography and Kinesiology, 14*(1), 13-23.

Punnett, L. (2000). The costs of work-related musculoskeletal disorders in automotive manufacturing. *New Solutions*, *9*(4), 403–426. doi:10.2190/Y93Q-DEAQ-FEU2-8B26 PMID:17208891

Quintana, R., & Pawlowitz, I. (1999). A Poisson model for work-related musculoskeletal disorder cost estimation. *Safety Science*, *32*(1), 19–31. doi:10.1016/S0925-7535(99)00008-9

Raeve, L., Jansen, N., Brandt, P., Vasse, R., & Kant, I. (2009). Interpersonal conflicts at work as a predictor of self-reported health outcomes and occupational mobility. *Occupational and Environmental Medicine*, *66*(1), 16–22. doi:10.1136/oem.2007.037655 PMID:19095708

Raffo Lecca, E., Ráez Guevara, L., & Cachay Boza, O. (2013). *Riesgos psicosociales*. Industrial Data.

Raisinghani, M. S., Ette, H., Pierce, R., Cannon, G., & Daripaly, P. (2005). Six Sigma: Concepts, Tools, and Applications. *Industrial Management & Data Systems*, *105*(4), 491–505. doi:10.1108/02635570510592389

Realyvazquez, A., & Maldonado Macias, A. A. (2011). Selección de fresadoras con topsis usando ponderaciones de ahp. *CULCYT*, *8*(45), 95–102.

Reavley, N. J., Ross, A., Martin, A., LaMontagne, A. D., & Jorm, A. F. (2014). Development of guidelines for workplace prevention of mental health problems: A Delphi consensus study with Australian professionals and employees. *Mental Health & Prevention*, *2*(1–2), 26–34. doi:10.1016/j.mhp.2014.07.002

Reis, H. T., Sheldon, K. M., Gable, S. L., Roscoe, J., & Ryan, R. M. (2000). Daily well-being: The role of autonomy, competence, and relatedness. *Personality and Social Psychology Bulletin*, *26*(4), 419–435. doi:10.1177/0146167200266002

Rhee, J., Zhao, X., Jun, I., & Kim, C. (2017). Effects of Collectivism on Chinese Organizational Citizenship Behavior: Guanxi As Moderator. *Social Behavior and Personality*, *45*(7), 1127–1142. doi:10.2224bp.6128

Ribeiro, M. A., Teixeira, M. A. P., & Ambiel, R. A. M. (2019). Decent work in Brazil: Context, conceptualization, and assessment. *Journal of Vocational Behavior*, *112*, 229–240. doi:10.1016/j.jvb.2019.03.006

Richardsone, C., Sinha, L., & Yaapar, S. (2014). Work ethics from the Islamic and Hindu traditions: In quest of common ground. *Journal of Management, Spirituality & Religion*, *11*(1), 65–90. doi:10.1080/14766086.2013.801025

Ritz, A., Brewer, G. A., & Neumann, O. (2016). Public service motivation: A systematic literature review and outlook. *Public Administration Review*, *76*(3), 414–426. doi:10.1111/puar.12505

Rizzi, N. (2021, February 9). Salesforce to allow remote work for most staff permanently. *Commercial Observer*. https://commercialobserver.com/2021/02/salesforce-to-let-most-staff-work-remote-permanently/

Roadmap. (2015). We Bring Good Things to Life Impact. *Quality*.

Roberts, T. (2016, December 15). *We spend 90% of our time indoors: Says who?* BuildingGreen. https://www.buildinggreen.com/blog/we-spend-90-our-time-indoors-says-who

Roscoe, J. T. (1975). *Fundamental Research Statistics for the Behavioral Science*. Holt, Rinehart and Winston.

Rosone, M. (2019, April 8). *Office temperature and productivity in the workplace*. Arista. https://aristair.com/blog/office-temperature-and-productivity-in-the-workplace/

Ruotsalainen, J., Verbeek, J., Mariné, A., & Serra, C. (2014). Preventing occupational stress in healthcare workers. *Cochrane Database of Systematic Reviews*, *134*. Advance online publication. doi:10.1590/1516-3180.20161341T1

Russell, H., Maitre, B., & Watson, D. (2016). *Work-related Musculoskeletal Disorders and Stress, Anxiety and Depression in Ireland: Evidence from the QNHS 2002–2013. Economic and Social Research Institute (ESRI)* Research Series.

Ryan, R. M., & Deci, E. L. (2000). Self-Determination Theory and the facilitation of intrinsic motivation, social development, and well-being. *The American Psychologist*, *55*(1), 68–78. doi:10.1037/0003-066X.55.1.68 PMID:11392867

Ryan, R. M., & Deci, E. L. (2001). On Happiness and Human Potentials: A Review of Research on Hedonic and Eudaimonic Well-Being. *Annual Review of Psychology*, *52*(1), 141–166. doi:10.1146/annurev.psych.52.1.141

Ryan, R. M., & Deci, E. L. (2017). *Self-Determination Theory: Basic Psychological Needs in Motivation, Development, and Wellness*. Guilford Publications. doi:10.1521/978.14625/28806

Ryan, R. M., Huta, V., & Deci, E. L. (2008). Living well: A self-determination theory perspective on eudaimonia. *Journal of Happiness Studies*, *9*(1), 139–170. doi:10.100710902-006-9023-4

Ryan, R. M., Weinstein, N., Bernstein, J., Brown, K. W., Mistretta, L., & Gagné, M. (2010). Vitalizing effects of being outdoors and in nature. *Journal of Environmental Psychology*, *30*(2), 159–168. doi:10.1016/j.jenvp.2009.10.009

Sagnak, M., & Kazancoglu, Y. (2015). Integration of Green Lean Approach with Six Sigma: An Application for Flue Gas Emissions. *Journal of Cleaner Production, 127*, 112–118. doi:10.1016/j.jclepro.2016.04.016

Salazar, E. & Ruvalcaba, R. (2012). Factores psicosociales del trabajador en la industria manufacturera en México. *Trabajo y Sociedad, 20*, 119-129.

Salvendy, G. (2012). Handbook of Human Factors and Ergonomics (4th ed.). Wiley. doi:10.1002/9781118131350

Saniog, J., Karmakar, S., Patel, T., & Chowdhury, A. (2015). Towards virtual ergonomics: Aviation and aerospace. *Aircraft Engineering and Aerospace Technology Journal, 87*(3), 266–273. doi:10.1108/AEAT-05-2013-0094

Schaufeli, W. B., & Taris, T. (2014). A Critical Review of the Job Demands-Resources Model: Implications for Improving Work and Health. *Bridging Occupational, Organizational and Public Health, A Transdisciplinary Approach*, 43-65. , doi:10.1007/978-94-007-5640-3_4

Schaufeli, W. B., Leiter, M. P., Maslach, C., & Jackson, S. E. (1996). MBI-General survey. Mashlach Burnout Inventory, 3.

Schaufeli, W. B., & Bakker, A. B. (2004). Job demands, job resources, and their relationship with burnout and engagement: A multi-sample study. *Journal of Organizational Behavior, 25*(3), 293–315. doi:10.1002/job.248

Scruggs, G. (2021, February 28). Co-working companies tap into customers facing work-from-home fatigue. *Washington Post*. https://www.washingtonpost.com/road-to-recovery/2021/02/28/remote-work-flex-office-work-home/

Secretaría del Trabajo y Prevención Social. (2016). PROYECTO de Norma Oficial Mexicana PROY-NOM-035-STPS-2016, Factores de riesgo psicosocial-Identificación y prevención. *Diario Oficial de la Federación.*

Sekaran, U., & Bougie, R. (2016). *Research methods for business: A skill building approach*. John Wiley & Sons.

Selko. (2019). SLC: 2019 Toyota's Finding Success with Exoskeletons. *EHS Today*. https://www.ehstoday.com/safety-leadership-conference/article/21920474/slc-2019-toyotas-finding-success-with-exoskeletons

Shade, M. (2020, April 20). *Pro tips for working from home and staying healthy*. CNN. https://www.cnn.com/2020/04/20/health/staying-well-working-from-home/index.html

Shafer, S. M., & Moeller, S. B. (2012). The Effects of Six Sigma on Corporate Performance: An Empirical Investigation. *Journal of Operations Management, 30*(7–8), 521–532. doi:10.1016/j.jom.2012.10.002

Shahzadi, I., Javed, A., Pirzada, S. S., Nasreen, S., & Khanam, F. (2014). Impact of employee motivation on employee performance. *European Journal of Business and Management, 6*(23), 159–166.

Sharma, I., Pandit, B., Pathak, A., & Sharma, R. (2013). Hinduism, marriage and mental illness. *Indian Journal of Psychiatry, 55*(6, Suppl 2), S243–S249. doi:10.4103/0019-5545.105544 PMID:23858262

Sharpe, M., & Wilks, D. (2002). Fatigue. *BMJ (Clinical Research Ed.), 325*(7362), 480–483. doi:10.1136/bmj.325.7362.480 PMID:12202331

Siemsen, E., Roth, A., & Oliveira, P. (2010). Common Method Bias in Regression Models With Linear, Quadratic, and Interaction Effects. *Organizational Research Methods, 13*(3), 456–476. doi:10.1177/1094428109351241

Simanová, Ľ. (2015). Specific Proposal of the Application and Implementation Six Sigma in Selected Processes of the Furniture Manufacturing. *Procedia Economics and Finance, 34*(15), 268–275. doi:10.1016/S2212-5671(15)01629-9

Singelis, T. M., Triandis, H. C., Bhawuk, D. P., & Gelfand, M. J. (1995). Horizontal and vertical dimensions of individualism and collectivism: A theoretical and measurement refinement. *Cross-Cultural Research, 29*(3), 240–275. doi:10.1177/106939719502900302

Sivris, K. C., & Leka, S. (2015). Examples of holistic good practices in promoting and protecting mental health in the workplace: Current and future challenges. *Safety and Health at Work*, *6*(4), 295–304. doi:10.1016/j.shaw.2015.07.002 PMID:26929841

Skinner, W. (2007). Manufacturing Strategy: The Story of Its Evolution. *Journal of Operations Management*, *25*(2), 328–335. doi:10.1016/j.jom.2006.10.008

Slattery, P., Saeri, A. K., & Bragge, P. (2020). Research co-design in health: A rapid overview of reviews. *Health Research Policy and Systems*, *17*(1), 1–13.

Smith, J. (2020, November 23). *The workplace to become more human-centric than ever, as priorities change*. Workplace Insight. https://workplaceinsight.net/the-workplace-to-become-more-human-centric-than-ever-as-priorities-change/

Smith, J. (2021, February 19). *'Zoom rooms' and breakout space top of the agenda for post-COVID offices*. Workplace Insight. https://workplaceinsight.net/zoom-rooms-and-breakout-space-top-of-the-agenda-for-post-covid-offices/

Society for Human Resource Management (SHRM). (2020, March 25). *Reduction in force (RIF) strategy and selection checklist*. https://www.shrm.org/resourcesandtools/tools-and-samples/hr-forms/pages/downsizingchecklist.aspx

Spangler, A., & McLeod, V. (2020, April 24). *New rhythms of working: How to work WELL from home*. https://resources.wellcertified.comzh-cn//articles/working-well-from-home

Spector, P. E., & Jex, S. M. (1998). Development of four self-report measures of job stressors and strain: Interpersonal Conflict at Work Scale, Organizational Constraints Scale, Quantitative Workload Inventory, and Physical Symptoms Inventory. *Journal of Occupational Health Psychology*, *3*(4), 356–367. doi:10.1037/1076-8998.3.4.356 PMID:9805281

Spinelli, R., Aminti, G., & De Francesco, F. (2017). Postural risk assessment of mechanized firewood processing. *Ergonomics*, *60*(3), 375–383. doi:10.1080/00140139.2016.1172738 PMID:27215281

Sterculiaceae. (1789). Guazuma ulmifolia Lam. *Encyclopédie Méthodique*, *3*, 52.

Stevens, R., Petermans, A., & Vanrie, J. (2014). Converting happiness theory into (interior) architectural design missions. Designing for subjective well-being in residential care centers. *Proceedings of the Annual Architectural Research Symposium in Finland*, 53–67.

Stoetzer, U., Ahlberg, G., Johansson, G., Bergman, P., Hallsten, L., Forsell, Y., & Lundberg, I. (2009). Problematic Interpersonal Relationships at Work and Depression: A Swedish Prospective Cohort Study. *Journal of Occupational Health*, *51*(2), 144–151. doi:10.1539/joh.L8134 PMID:19225218

Suárez Amaya & Díaz Barrios. (2013). *Factores Criticos de Èxito En La Investigacion Universitaria Venezolana*. Academic Press.

Sultana, S., Salman, Y., & Irfan, S. (2020). Exploring the relationship of HRM Practices on Employee motivation in public organizations: A systematic Literature review. *Global Management Journal for Academic & Corporate Studies*, *10*(1), 143-163.

Sverdrup, U. (2021). *Compliance and styles of conflict management in Europe*. Arena Working Papers. https://www.sv.uio.no/arena/english/research/publications/arena-working-papers/2001-2010/2003/wp03_8.pdf

Sylla, N., Bonnet, V., Colledani, F., & Fraisse, P. (2014). Ergonomic contribution of ABLE exoskeleton in automotive industry. *International Journal of Industrial Ergonomics*, *44*(4), 475–481. doi:10.1016/j.ergon.2014.03.008

Tabb, P. J. (2021). *Biophilic urbanism: Designing resilient communities for the future*. Routledge.

Taherdoost, H. (2016). Sampling methods in research methodology; how to choose a sampling technique for research. *How to Choose a Sampling Technique for Research.*

Takala, J., Hämäläinen, P., Nenonen, N., Takahashi, K., Chimed-Ochir, O., & Rantanen, J. (2017). Comparative analysis of the burden of injury and illness at work in selected countries and regions. *Cent. Eur. J. Occup. Environ. Med*, *23*, 6–31.

Takala, J., Hämäläinen, P., Saarela, K. L., Yun, L. Y., Manickam, K., Jin, T. W., & Lin, G. S. (2014). Global estimates of the burden of injury and illness at work in 2012. *Journal of Occupational and Environmental Hygiene*, *11*(5), 326–337. doi:10.1080/15459624.2013.863131 PMID:24219404

Tayfur, O., & Arslan, M. (2013). The role of lack of reciprocity, supervisory support, workload and work–family conflict on exhaustion: Evidence from physicians. *Psychology Health and Medicine*, *18*(5), 564–575. doi:10.1080/13548506.2012.756535 PMID:23330970

Taysom, T. (2021, February 24). *Post-Covid offices will become cultural hubs and even art galleries to tempt staff back to the office.* CityAM. https://www.cityam.com/post-covid-offices-will-become-cultural-hubs-and-even-art-galleries-to-tempt-staff-back-to-the-office/

Thakore, R., Dave, R., Parsana, T., & Solanki, A. (2014). OPEN ACCESS A Review : Six Sigma Implementation Practice in Manufacturing Industries. *International Journal of Engineering Research and Applications*, *4*(11), 63–69.

Thaler, R. H. (2008). *Nudge: Improving decisions about health, wealth, and happiness.* Yale University Press.

Thatcher, A. (2012). Gr3en ergonomics: Definition and scope. *Ergonomics Journal*, *56*(1), 389–398. PMID:22928500

Thisera, T. J. R., & Nawaratne, N. N. J. (2018). Job demands and exposure to workplace bullying: A study of state universities in Sri Lanka. *Asian Journal of Empirical Research*, *8*(6), 195–207. doi:10.18488/journal.1007/2018.8.6/1007.6.195.207

Thompson, D. (2020, March 13). The Coronavirus experiment in working from home. *The Atlantic.* https://www.theatlantic.com/ideas/archive/2020/03/coronavirus-creating-huge-stressful-experiment-working-home/607945/

Thun, J. H. (2008). Empirical Analysis of Manufacturing Strategy Implementation. *International Journal of Production Economics*, *113*(1), 370–382. doi:10.1016/j.ijpe.2007.09.005

Thuynsma, C., & de Beer, L. T. (2016). Burnout, depressive symptoms, job demands and satisfaction with life: Discriminant validity and explained variance. *South African Journal of Psychology. Suid-Afrikaanse Tydskrif vir Sielkunde*, *47*(1), 46–59. doi:10.1177/0081246316638564

Timm, S., Gray, W. A., Curtis, T., & Chung, S. S. E. (2018). Designing for health: How the physical environment plays a role in workplace wellness. *American Journal of Health Promotion*, *32*(6), 1468–1473. doi:10.1177/0890117118779463b PMID:29972070

Tjahjono, B., Ball, P., Vitanov, V. I., Scorzafave, C., Nogueira, J., Calleja, J., Minguet, M., Narasimha, L., Rivas, A., Srivastava, A., Srivastava, S., & Yadav, A. (2010). Six Sigma: A Literature Review. *International Journal of Lean Six Sigma*, *1*(3), 216–233. doi:10.1108/20401461011075017

Tlapa, D., Limon, J., García-Alcaraz, J. L., Baez, Y., & Sánchez, C. (2016). Industrial Management & Data Systems Six Sigma Enablers in Mexican Manufacturing Companies: A Proposed Model"Six Sigma Enablers in Mexican Manufacturing Companies: A Proposed Model. *Industrial Management & Data Systems*, *116*(5), 926–959. doi:10.1108/IMDS-06-2015-0265

Toppinen-Tanner, S., Ojajärvi, A., Väänänen, A., Kalimo, R., & Jäppinen, P. (2005). Burnout as a Predictor of Medically Certified Sick-Leave Absences and Their Diagnosed Causes. *Behavioral Medicine (Washington, D.C.)*, *31*(1), 18–27. doi:10.3200/BMED.31.1.18-32 PMID:16078523

Triandis, H. C., & Gelfand, M. J. (1998). Converging measurement of horizontal and vertical individualism and collectivism. *Journal of Personality and Social Psychology*, *74*(1), 118–128. doi:10.1037/0022-3514.74.1.118

Triandis, H. C., & Singelis, T. M. (1998). Training to recognize individual differences in collectivism and individualism within culture. *International Journal of Intercultural Relations*, *22*(1), 35–47. doi:10.1016/S0147-1767(97)00034-5

Turnipseed, D. L. (1998). Anxiety and Burnout in the Health Care Work Environment. *Psychological Reports*, *82*(2), 627–642. doi:10.2466/pr0.1998.82.2.627 PMID:9621740

UK Green Building Council (UKGBC). (2017, September 21). *Health, wellbeing and productivity in offices: The next chapter for green building.* https://www.ukgbc.org/ukgbc-work/health-wellbeing-productivity-offices-next-chapter-green-building/

Umeda, M., McMunn, A., Cable, N., Hashimoto, H., Kawakami, N., & Marmot, M. (2015). Does an advantageous occupational position make women happier in contemporary Japan? Findings from the Japanese Study of Health, Occupation, and Psychosocial Factors Related Equity (J-HOPE). *SSM - Population Health*, *1*, 8–15. doi:10.1016/j.ssmph.2015.09.002 PMID:29349116

Unda, S., Uribe, F., Jurado, S., García, M., Tovalín, H., & Juárez, A. (2016). Elaboración de una escala para valorar los factores de riesgo psicosocial en el trabajo de profesores universitarios. *Revista de Psicología del Trabajo y de las Organizaciones*, *32*(2), 67–74. doi:10.1016/j.rpto.2016.04.004

Upasani, S., Franco, R., Niewolny, K., & Srinivasan, D. (2019). The Potential for Exoskeletons to Improve Health and Safety in Agriculture—Perspectives from Service Providers. *IISE Transactions on Occupational Ergonomics and Human Factors*, *7*(3–4), 222–229. doi:10.1080/24725838.2019.1575930

Uribe-Prado, J., Gutiérrez-Amador, J., & Amézquita-Pino, J. (2020). Crítica a las Propiedades Psicométricas de una Escala de Medición de Factores de Riesgo Psicosocial Propuesta en la NOM 035 de la STPS en México. *Contaduría y Administración*, *64*(1), 1–35.

Valbuena. (2017). *OVA Programa de Gestión para la prevención de los Desórdenes Músculo Esquelético*. Author.

Van der Klauw, M., Hengel, K. O., Roozeboom, M. B., Koppes, L. L., & Venema, A. (2016). Occupational accidents in the Netherlands: Incidence, mental harm, and their relationship with psychosocial factors at work. *International Journal of Injury Control and Safety Promotion*, *23*(1), 79–84. doi:10.1080/17457300.2014.966119 PMID:25531558

van der Kolk, B., van Veen-Dirks, P. M., & ter Bogt, H. J. (2019). The impact of management control on employee motivation and performance in the public sector. *European Accounting Review*, *28*(5), 901–928. doi:10.1080/09638180.2018.1553728

Van Dyne, L., Vandewalle, D., Kostova, T., Latham, M. E., & Cummings, L. (2000). Collectivism, propensity to trust and self-esteem as predictors of organizational citizenship in a non-work setting. *Journal of Organizational Behavior*, *21*(1), 3–23. doi:10.1002/(SICI)1099-1379(200002)21:1<3::AID-JOB47>3.0.CO;2-6

Vaughn, K. (2018, May 5). *You will spend 90,000 hours of your lifetime at work. Are you happy?* Medium. https://kassandravaughn.medium.com/you-will-spend-90-000-hours-of-your-lifetime-at-work-are-you-happy-5a2b5b0120ff

Vázquez, M. (2019). *El desarrollo sostenible a través de empresas sociales en comunidades indígenas de América Latina, Estudios Sociales*. Revista de Alimentación Contemporánea y Desarrollo Regional.

Velez-Calle, A., Robledo-Ardila, C., & Rodriguez-Rios, J.-D. (2015). On the Influence of Interpersonal Relations on Business Practices in Latin America: A Comparison with the Chinese Guanxi and the Arab Wasta. *Thunderbird International Business Review*, *57*(4), 281–293. Advance online publication. doi:10.1002/tie.21669

Vera-Calzaretta, A., Carrasco-Dájer, C., Da Costa, S., & Páez-Rovira, D. (2015). Factores psicosociales del presentismo en trabajadores del Sistema de Salud chileno. *Revista de Psicología del Trabajo y de las Organizaciones, 31*(2), 119–128. doi:10.1016/j.rpto.2015.03.004

Verweij, H., van Hooff, M. L. M., van der Heijden, F. M. M. A., Prins, J. T., Lagro-Janssen, A. L. M., van Ravesteijn, H., & Speckens, A. E. M. (2017). The relationship between work and home characteristics and work engagement in medical residents. *Perspectives on Medical Education, 6*(4), 227–236. doi:10.100740037-017-0364-y PMID:28677047

Víctor, Charria, Kewy, & Sarsosa. (2011). Factores de riesgo psicosocial laboral : Métodos e instrumentos de evaluación. *Revista Facultad Nacional de Salud Pública, 29*(4), 380–391.

Villalobos, G. (2005). *Diseño de un sistema de vigilancia epidemiológica de factores de riesgo psicosocial en el trabajo (Tesis de doctorado)*. Escuela Nacional de Salud Pública.

Vinod, M., Devadasan, S. R., Sunil, D. T., & Thilak, V. M. M. (2015). Six Sigma through Poka-Yoke: A Navigation through Literature Arena. *International Journal of Advanced Manufacturing Technology, 81*(1–4), 315–327. doi:10.100700170-015-7217-9

Vroom, V. H. (1964). *Work and motivation*. Wiley.

W.B. (2017). *Latinoamérica indígena en el siglo XXI. Banco Mundial*. Recuperado de: https://www.bancomundial.org/es/region/lac/brief/indigenous-latin-america-in-the-twenty-first-century-brief-report-page

Walsh, C. (2019, June 20). Harvard researchers outline steps to a healthy home. *Harvard Gazette*. https://news.harvard.edu/gazette/story/2019/06/harvard-researchers-outline-steps-to-a-healthy-home/

Wang, F.-K., Yeh, C.-T., & Chu, T.-P. (2016). Using the Design for Six Sigma Approach with TRIZ for New Product Development. *Computers & Industrial Engineering, 98*, 522–530. doi:10.1016/j.cie.2016.06.014

Waterman, A. S. (2013). *The best within us: Positive psychology perspectives on eudaimonia* (1st ed.). American Psychological Association. doi:10.1037/14092-000

Weber, M. (2008). *Economía y sociedad*. Fondo de Cultura Económica.

Weed, J. (2020, June 21). How to succeed in your office job when there is no office. *The New York Times*. https://www.nytimes.com/2020/06/21/business/work-home-coronavirus.html

Weerd, M. D., Tierney, R., Duuren-Stuurman, B. V., & Bertranou, E. (2014). *Estimating the cost of accidents and ill-health at work: a review of methodologies*. Academic Press.

Weiner, M. (2004). Six Sigma. *Communication World, 21*(1), 26–29.

Wellness Council of America (WELCOA). (2021). *The key to creating thriving organizations*. https://www.welcoa.org/blog/definition-of-wellness/

WHO. (2021, February 27). *WHO Coronavirus Disease (COVID-19) dashboard*. https://covid19.who.int

Wiberg, M. (2020, March-April). Interaction and architecture is dead: Long live architectural interactivity! *Interaction, 27*(2), 72–75. doi:10.1145/3378567

Wiig, A. (2015). IBM's smart city as techno-utopian policy mobility. *City, 19*(2–3), 258–273. doi:10.1080/13604813.2015.1016275

William, H. (2007). America's individualist culture influences the ability to view others' perspectives. *The University of Chicago Chronicles, 26*(19). doi:http://chronicle.uchicago.edu/070712/perspectives.shtml

Williams, R. B., Barefoot, J. C., & Schneiderman, N. (2003). Psychosocial Risk Factors for Cardiovascular Disease More Than One Culprit at Work. *Journal of the American Medical Association*, 2190–2192.

Wilson, J., Ryan, B., Schock, A., Ferreira, P., Smith, S., & Pitsopoulos, J. (2009). Understanding safety and production risks in rail engineering planning and protection. *Ergonomics Journal*, *52*(1), 774–790. doi:10.1080/00140130802642211 PMID:19562589

Wilson, M. G., DeJoy, D. M., Vandenbert, R. J., Richardson, H. A., & McGrath, A. L. (2004). Work characteristics and employee health and well-being: Test of a model of healthy work organization. *Journal of Occupational and Organizational Psychology*, *77*(4), 565–588. doi:10.1348/0963179042596522

Wong, W. P., & Wong, K. Y. (2014). Synergizing an Ecosphere of Lean for Sustainable Operations. *Journal of Cleaner Production*, *85*, 51–66. doi:10.1016/j.jclepro.2014.05.093

Work in Mind. (2020, November 19). *Safety concerns driving continued demand for remote working*. https://workinmind.org/2020/11/19/safety-concerns-driving-continued-demand-for-remote-working/

Work in Mind. (2021a, January 20). *Hybrid working: Hybrid model of work is being led by 18-24-year-olds*. https://workinmind.org/2021/01/20/hybrid-working-hybrid-model-of-work-is-being-led-by-18-24-year-olds/

Work in Mind. (2021b, February 10). *Workers report a cycle of fatigue when working from home*. https://workinmind.org/2021/02/10/pedalling-furiously-workers-report-a-cycle-of-fatigue-when-working-from-home/

Work in Mind. (2021c, February 16). *How do we really feel about working from home? – Microsoft explains*. https://workinmind.org/2021/02/16/how-do-we-really-feel-about-working-from-home-microsoft-has-the-answers/

World Green Building Council (WorldGBC). (2016). *Health, wellbeing and productivity in offices: The next chapter for green building*. World Green Building Council (WorldGBC).

World Health Organization (WHO). (2020, August). *World Health Organization Constitution*. https://www.who.int/about/who-we-are/constitution

Wu, Hu, & Zheng. (2019). Mental health in the workplace-Information sheet. World Health Organization.

Wu, G., Hu, Z., & Zheng, J. (2019). Role Stress, Job Burnout, and Job Performance in Construction Project Managers: The Moderating Role of Career Calling. *International Journal of Environmental Research and Public Health*, *16*(13), 2394. doi:10.3390/ijerph16132394

Wyon, D. P. (2004). The effects of indoor air quality on performance and productivity. *Indoor Air*, *14*(Suppl 7), 92–101. doi:10.1111/j.1600-0668.2004.00278.x PMID:15330777

Xanthopoulou, D., Bakker, A. B., Demerouti, E., & Schaufeli, W. B. (2007). The role of personal resources in the job demands-resources model. *International Journal of Stress Management*, *14*(2), 121–141. doi:10.1037/1072-5245.14.2.121

Yang, L.-Q., Spector, P., Sanchez, J., Allen, T., Poelmans, S., Cooper, C., Lapierre, L. M., O'Driscoll, M. P., Abarca, N., Alexandrova, M., Antoniou, A.-S., Beham, B., Brough, P., Çarikçi, I., Ferreiro, P., Fraile, G., Geurts, S., Kinnunen, U., Lu, C., ... Woo, J.-M. (2012). Individualism–collectivism as a moderator of the work demands–strains relationship: A cross-level and cross-national examination. *Journal of International Business Studies*, *43*(4), 424–443. Advance online publication. doi:10.1057/jibs.2011.58

Yunsoo, L., & Eissenstat, S. J. (2018). A longitudinal examination of the causes and effects of burnout based on the job demands-resources model. *International Journal for Educational and Vocational Guidance*, *18*(3), 337–354. doi:10.100710775-018-9364-7

Zárate, J. L. (2016). *Grupos étnicos de Sonora: territorios y condiciones actuales de vida y rezago Región y Sociedad.* Academic Press.

Zhang, M., & Iru, A. A. (2012). *Using Six Sigma To Achieve Sustianble Manufacturing*. Advance online publication. doi:10.1109/IDAM.2014.6912713

Zohar, D. (1999). Predicting burnout with a hassle-based measure of role demands. *Journal of Organizational Behavior, 18*(2), 101–115. doi:10.1002/(SICI)1099-1379(199703)18:2<101::AID-JOB788>3.0.CO;2-Y

Zoni, S., & Lucchini, R. G. (2012). *European approaches to work-related stress: A critical review on risk evaluation. Safety and Health at Work.* Elsevier Science B.V. doi:10.5491/SHAW.2012.3.1.43

Zu, X., Fredendall, L. D., & Robbins, T. L. (2006). Organizational Culture and Quality Practices in Six Sigma. *The 2006 Annual Meeting of the Academy of Management*, 1–40. 10.5465/ambpp.2006.27175447

Zu, X., Fredendall, L. D., & Douglas, T. J. (2008). The Evolving Theory of Quality Management: The Role of Six Sigma. *Journal of Operations Management, 26*(5), 630–650. doi:10.1016/j.jom.2008.02.001

Zu, X., Robbins, T. L., & Fredendall, L. D. (2010). Mapping the Critical Links between Organizational Culture and TQM/ Six Sigma Practices. *International Journal of Production Economics, 123*(1), 86–106. doi:10.1016/j.ijpe.2009.07.009

About the Contributors

Gabriela Jacobo-Galicia has a Master's degree with emphasis in quality and production systems. with professional experience in organizational production system improvements and working in socio-technical systems focus on psychosocial risks.

Samantha E. Cruz-Sotelo is a professor and researcher at the Autonomous University of Baja California (UABC). Member to the Mexican National Researcher System, Level I. She is a founding member of the Mexican Society of Science and Applied Technology Solid Waste (SOMERS) and member of the Ibero-American Network of Engineering in Environmental Sanitation (REDISA). She has published manuscripts in journals, books and book-chapters and participated as a guest editor of special issues in the international journals. Her research interests are in the areas of Optimization of Productive Processes, Sustainable Development, Life Cycle Assessment, Circular Economy, Sustainable Manufacture, Electronic Waste Management, Artificial Intelligence Tools.

* * *

Aide Aracely Maldonado-Macías completed her Bachelor Degree in Industrial Engineering, the MSc in Industrial Engineering by the Technological Institute of Ciudad Juárez and Ph. D. in Sciences in Industrial Engineering by the same Institute. She is currently a full-time Professor-Investigator at the Autonomous University of Ciudad Juárez (UACJ). Her research interests are the evaluation and ergonomic design, cognitive ergonomics anthropometric studies and work-related stress studies, Multicriteria and Multi-attribute decision-making with fuzzy logic and axiomatic design applications, as well as the ergonomic evaluation for the selection of technology of advanced manufacturing (AMT) and Structural Equation Models. She has published in indexed journals in English and Spanish; such as International Journal of Industrial Engineering and International Journal of Advanced Manufacturing Technology, Expert Systems with Applications, Work a Journal of Prevention, Assessment & Rehabilitation, International Journal of Environmental Research and Public Health, IEEE Access, Complexity, Sustainability among others. She has also collaborated with books and book chapters for Springer Editorial. She received the State Science and Technology Award 2018 and received the "Chihuahuense Destacada" distintion for the scientific merit of Mexico. She is actually recognized as an investigator SNI 2 by the National Science and Technology Institute.

Bikash Basnet is from Nepal. He has completed a Master of Business Administration from University of Agder, Norway and is currently studying a Master of Business Research at Excelsia College,

Australia. His main area of interest is organizational behavior and human resource management. This interest led him to conduct a thesis titled "Examining the determinants of employee motivation". Bikash also has an interest in finance and has worked in the finance sector for some years. For the MBA degree, Bikash conducted a study to explore predictive power of alternative forecasting model across multiple horizons in three asset classes.

Juan Alberto Castillo Martinez is a Full Professor of the School of Medicine and Health Sciences. Senior Researcher (Colciencias - 2019). Post-Doctor (T) in Movement Analysis (Politecnico di Milano, 2010), PhD in Cognitive Psychology (U. Lumiere Lyon II, 2004); Master in Ergonomics and Technological Changes (U. Lumiere Lyon II, 1998), Industrial Designer (Bogota, 1991). Researcher and consultant in Ergonomics and Cognitive Science since 1998, At Universidad del Rosario Scientific Director of projects in: Ergonomics, health and psychosocial aspects. Director of the Ergonomics and Movement Analysis Laboratory at Universidad del Rosario. Director of the National Ergonomics Seminar. Senior researcher specialized in Health and Work, Cognitive Science, Knowledge Modeling, Ergonomic development and technological change in organizations.

Sarah Eyaa has been an academic in the field of management for over fifteen years and is currently an academic staff at Excelsia College in Sydney, Australia. Previously, she taught at Makerere University Business School in Uganda, in the Department of Procurement and Logistics Management. She holds a Bachelor of Commerce (Marketing) from Makerere University (Uganda), a Master of Business Administration (Procurement) from Maastricht School of Management (The Netherlands), and a PhD (Management) from the University of Newcastle (Australia) and a Graduate Diploma in Purchasing and Supply from the Chartered Institute of Purchasing (United Kingdom). Her research interests are in various areas of management, specifically, communication, operations management, public procurement, supply chain management, logistics management, purchasing and supply chain management strategic management and marketing.

Victoria Moroyoqui Galaviz is a Marketing Engineer from the Universidad Tecnológica del Sur de Sonora and entrepreneur of various businesses related to the Mayo and Guarijio ethnic group located in the South of Sonora, Mexico.

Deanna Grant-Smith, PhD, is an Associate Professor in the QUT Business School and Deputy Director of the QUT Centre for Decent Work & Industry. Prior to an academic career, she worked in the government sector, where she had roles in policy development and implementation, public sector reform, integrated regional planning, inter-governmental program management, and community consultation and stakeholder engagement. Her research interests include stakeholder engagement with a focus on participatory planning with marginalized or disadvantaged groups, particularly young people and women, and cultural and political engagements with sustainability particularly those associated with waste.

Jesús Andrés Hernández Gómez has a PhD in Administration Sciences from the Universidad Autónoma de México. Professor-researcher in the programs of PhD in Technology, Master in Industrial Engineering and in the Industrial and Systems Engineering of the Universidad Autónoma de Ciudad Juárez. He is a Member of the National System of Researchers (SNI) in Mexico. His research interest on the study of critical success factors related to operational improvement strategies in the manufacturing industry. ORCID: 0000-0003-2325-2051.

Juan Luis Hernandez-Arellano is a researcher and a full-time teacher of the Design Department at the Autonomous University of Ciudad Juarez, Mexico. His research interests are about industrial ergonomics, ergonomic product design, statistics applied to research ergonomics, and biomechanics. Dr. Hernandez have published numerous articles, books and books chapters in indexed Journals and Internationals books. Currently, Dr. Hernandez is the coordinator of the Master of Product Design at the Autonomous University of Ciudad Juarez.

Aida López Guerrero has a bachelor degree in Industrial Engineer in 2006, the Master of Science in 2013, both at the Universidad Autónoma de Baja California and PhD degree in Technology at the Universidad Autónoma de Ciudad Juárez. From 2006 to 2008 she worked in manufacturing companies in the areas of continuous improvement and quality and since 2009 she works for the Universidad Autónoma de Baja California. Currently, she is a Full professor in the Faculty of Engineering, Department of Industrial Engineering and is responsible of Industrial Engineer program in Facultad de Ingeniería in UABC. She has participated in national and international conferences. Her research interest includes: administration, organizational culture, modeling of structural equations based on statistical analysis and application of statistical techniques for multivariate organizational phenomena. ORCID: 0000-0002-8856-0779.

Eusebio Jiménez López is a Doctor of Engineering and a Master in Mechanical Engineering from the National Autonomous University of Mexico. He works in robotics, artificial intelligence, reverse engineering, design, automation, manufacturing, and engineering education. He is currently a professor at the Universidad La Salle Noroeste and a researcher at the Universidad Tecnológica del Sur de Sonora, a member of the consolidated academic body CIAAM and belongs to the National System of Researchers Level 1.

Gustavo Lopez Badilla is a PhD in Chemical Engineering with experience in manufacturing processes with more than 15 years, analyzing the impact of atmospheric agents that generates deterioration of materials and impact in the operative of people and industrial equipment and machinery in industrial processes. The principal objective is evaluating the work conditions to avoid any negative effect in workers and industrial equipment and machinery, maintaining the ideal atmosphere in indoors of industrial companies. Have more than 35+ articles (technical and applied investigation) and 10+ book chapter and full books. Was participate in environmental, industrial, materials and innovation processes to improve work conditions in industries located in arid and marine atmospheres.

Aldo Augusto López Martínez is a Master in Mechatronics from CIDESI and a PhD student in Engineering. He is a project engineer at CIDESI (Centro de Ingeniería y Desarrollo Industrial).

Lilia Zulema Gaytán Martínez is a full-time teacher at the Universidad Tecnológica del Sur de Sonora, teaches English subjects and is a doctoral student in education at IDESA.

Raul Martinez-Balderrama received his degree in industrial engineering from the Facultad de Ingeniería, campus Mexicali at the Universidad Autónoma de Baja California in 2018. In 2019, he started his studies for a Master in Science Degree at the same university. His subject is in statistical analysis of psychosocial risk factors at work in a manufacturing context, and how they impact stress on workers that are involved in automatized processes. He is currently finishing his Master's dissertation. He has participated as a speaker at different conferences, talking about this issue. His interests are in Statistical analysis techniques and their use to evaluate soft problems.

Ismael Mendoza-Muñoz received his Doctorate of Science from the Universidad Autónoma de Baja California (UABC) in 2018. He is currently a Full-time Lecturer for the UABC and a member of the Sistema Nacional de Investigadores (SNI) as a National Researcher Candidate. He has a Desirable Profile from the Ministry of Public Education and is a member of the Academic Research Group in Consolidation: Manufacturing and Occupational Health. His areas of interest focus on Biomechanics, Design for Manufacturing, Product Development Process, Additive Manufacturing, Sustainable Manufacturing, Materials Science, and Ergonomics.

Jenna Mikus is a PhD candidate in the School of Architecture & Built Environment within the Faculty of Engineering at Queensland University of Technology (QUT). She is also a member of the Urban Informatics group within QUT's School of Design in the Creative Industries Faculty; a sessional academic in the Schools of Business and Architecture & Built Environment; and an affiliate of the Centre for Decent Work & Industry. Jenna received her BSc degree in Mechanical Engineering (with a minor in Entrepreneurship & Management) from the Johns Hopkins University in Baltimore, MD where she was a Beneficial Hodson Scholar and her MSc degree in Sustainable Environmental Design from the Architectural Association in London, UK where she was an AA bursary winner. With her background in engineering, architectural design, and business strategy, she has developed a specialty in "phygital" (physical + digital) transformation implementations (most recently within the built environment). Jenna comes to academia with 20 years' industry experience, during which she consulted at large firms, including Accenture and Booz Allen, and at smaller firms that specialize in curating transformational occupant experiences in the built environment. Before joining QUT, Jenna founded the consultancy firm Eudae Group to advise clients on how best to curate flourishing environments that enhance occupant health and precipitate organizational success. She continues to consult on designing for health and well-being with clients and to advise certification bodies on health and equity-related issues across North America, Europe, and Australasia.

Víctor Manuel Martínez Molina is a Master in Mechanical Engineering from the National Autonomous University of Mexico and is currently Director of Innovation and Liaison of the City of Cajeme, Sonora, Mexico.

Pablo Antonio Muñoz Gutierrez is an Industrial Designer and student of the Master in Product Design at the Universidad Autonoma de Ciudad Juarez, Mexico. His research is focused on the design, evaluation, and validation of exoskeletons.

Mydory Oyuky Nakasima López has a bachelor degree in Industrial Engineer in 2008 at Engineering Faculty of Universidad Autónoma de Baja California and PhD Engineering degree at Instituto de Ingeniería of Universidad Autónoma de Baja California in 2015. Since 2006 to 2008 she worked in Aerospace Industry in manufacturing area. From 2016 to date she is a full-time Research Professor in the Industrial Engineering education program at Faculty of Chemical Sciences and Engineering of Universidad Autónoma de Baja California where she is Environmental Responsible of the Faculty. She is an invited Professor at Cetys Universidad of Mexicali Baja California. Her research interests include: simulation of sustainable processes, renewable energies, sustainability and energy efficiency. ORCID: https://orcid.org/0000-0001-6508-5859.

Carlos Raul Navarro Gonzalez is currently part of the "Universidad Autónoma de Baja California" as a staff member of the Industrial Engineering area, as university professor. With many papers related to "Lean Manufacturing", "Six Sigma" and "process optimization"; also with research in "ergonomics and occupational health". He has many participation in investigations of applying technologies in Ergonomics, Anthropometrical and Biomechanics area with tracking sensors, visual processing and health monitoring devices. He's grades are Industrial Engineering, with a Master Degree in Engineering with Industrial Process and PhD in Engineering since 2008. As 2014 has been acting as full-time research professor in this University.

José Manuel Luna Nemecio is a research professor in the Department of Socioformation and Sustainable Development Studies of the CIFE University Center located in Cuernavaca Morelos, Mexico. He is a member of the National System of Researchers at the candidate level.

Nekpen Euodia Okhawere earned her Ph.D. degree in Management from the University of Newcastle, Australia, where she worked on academics' response to neoliberal practices in universities with Associate Professor Suzanne Erina Ryan and Dr. Richard Oloruntoba. She is currently an academic staff at the University of Newcastle, Australia and the University of Benin, Nigeria.

Luz del Consuelo Olivares Fong has a bachelor degree in Manufacturing Engineer by Centro de Enseñanza Técnica y Superior (CETYS – Universidad/Centro Politécnico Superior (Spain)); Master degree in Engineering with the project: "Eco-efficiency in SMEs in Mexicali, B.C. in the manufacturing sector" by Instituto de Ingeniería, UABC; Virtual Diplomate in "Competencies for Education for Sustainable Development" by Universidad Autónoma de San Luis Potosí; Diplomate in "Manufacturing Management" by Centro de Enseñanza Técnica y Superior (CETYS – Universidad). Since 2006, professor at Facultad de Ingeniería-UABC, in 2014 assigned as full-time professor in UABC. She has participated in projects of Innovation-Conacty. Interesting areas include engineering materials, manufacturing process, sustainable development and organizational behavior. She has participated in national and international conferences. She has work experience in industry, mainly in continuous improvement projects, training and process documentations for testing certification. ORCID: 0000-0003-3790-6810.

Judith M. Paz-Delgadillo is a professor of the Industrial Engineering area at the "Universidad Autónoma de Baja California". She graduated as Industrial Engineer, has a Master in Business Administration and a PhD in Engineering (semiconductors, microelectronics and nanotechnology area). She has experience in automotive products from Honeywell company where she obtained a green belt certification; since 2010 has been working as university professor, some of the areas are human resources, lean manufacturing, quality, operations research, materials engineering and nanotechnology. Most recent papers are about UV sensors of metal-oxide-semiconductor (MOS) structures with silicon nanoclusters.

María Elizabeth Ramírez Barreto is a Planning Engineer with a Masters-Degree in System Engineering and PHD in Antropology. Currently works as a researcher and professor at the Engineering Institute of Universidad Autónoma de Baja California (UABC). She has been involved in several environmental projects. Also teaches in the UABC Master and PHD in Sciences and Engineering programme. She has written articles in international magazines and book chapters, as well as various academic awards.

Mildrend Montoya-Reyes graduated from Autonomous University of Baja California (UABC); with a Master and a PhD of Science from UABC; and Master in Education degree with a specialty in Organizational Development from the Center for Technical and Higher Education. She has worked as an engineer and business consultant. Currently, she works as a full-time lecturer and researcher at the Industrial Engineering Department of UABC. She is a member of the Teacher Professional Development Program (PRODEP) and a member of the Academic and Research Group "Manufacture and Occupational Health". She has published manuscripts in journals, books, and book chapters and participated as a guest reviewer in international journals. Her research interests include method engineering, process optimization, materials, quality systems, organizational development, ergonomics, and sustainable development.

Janice Rieger is Associate Professor in the School of Architecture and Built Environment, Faculty of Engineering at Queensland University of Technology. She is a Chief Investigator with the Centre for Justice and Design Lab at QUT. Janice has served as a faculty member at the University of Calgary, (Calgary, Canada), York University (Toronto, Canada), Mount Royal University (Calgary, Canada), and the University of Alberta (Edmonton, Canada). She has been a visiting scholar at the University of Hasselt (Hasselt, Belgium) and L'Université Catholique de Lille (Lille, France). She is also a Board Member for the European Society for Disability Research in France, is on the Scientific Advisory Board for AHFE, USA and is a member of the European Institute for Design and Disability and the EIDD-DfA. Janice was a Fellow of the Canadian Federation of University Women, is a committee member of the Women in Leadership (QWIL) program at QUT and was awarded a Fellowship with the Social Sciences and Humanities Research Council of Canada (SSHRC). She is an expert reviewer for the ARC, TEQSA and has created a national certificate program in accessible housing design (CSAHD) in Canada. Janice has been awarded for her inclusive leadership through a Mayor's Award in Calgary, a State level award in Alberta and a National MAGNA award in Australia. Dr Rieger is currently working on an Australian Research Council (ARC) research project and is a Senior Fellow with the Higher Education Academy (UK).

Henry Milimu Shililu is an accountant by profession and holds a Master of Business Research degree from Excelsia College, Sydney Australia. He holds a Post-Graduate Diploma in Marketing from the Chartered Institute of Marketing UK. He is a Certified Public Accountant from Strathmore University, Kenya. Currently, he is a Business Development Consultant specializing in taxation based in Sydney, Australia.

Olivia Yessenia Vargas-Bernal studied Industrial Engineering, to later pursue a Master's and Doctorate in Engineering from the Universidad Autónoma de Baja California (UABC). She has participated in publications on process optimization, quality systems and analysis of ergonomic methods, in addition to having presentations at national and international conferences. She has served as head of the quality management system in local companies in the construction area. She has been a professor at the UABC since 2014 and has taught classes at the undergraduate and postgraduate levels, as well as administrative activities at: Universidad UNEA, Universidad Estatal de Sonora (UES), Universidad del Valle de México (UVM) as academic coordinator.

Karla Isabel Velázquez Victorica has a bachelor degree in Industrial Engineer by Cetys Universidad, Master degree in engineering focus on Industrial Process by Universidad Autónoma de Baja California (UABC) and PhD in Science research area in Optimization and Statistical Quality Control by UABC. Since 2001 professor at Facultad de Ingeniería-UABC, in 2014 assigned as full-time professor at same university. She has participated in research projects focus in optimization and improving productive processes and services through statistical methodologies. She has participated in national and international conferences. She has work experience in industry, mainly in continuous improvement projects. ORCID: 0000-0003-0353-7084.

Index

A

absenteeism 3, 41, 74, 131, 173-175, 179, 191, 194
aerospace industry 150-151, 208, 210, 221, 228
autonomy 2, 6, 9-10, 13-14, 18-21, 24-25, 27-28, 31-32, 49, 77

B

built environment 1-4, 7, 20, 24-25

C

case study 72-73, 78-79, 208
collectivism 50, 63, 130, 132-135, 137, 139, 142-145, 147-149
commercial 22, 25, 27-28, 112, 157, 193-195, 197, 212-214, 218, 236, 258
competence 2, 6, 9-10, 13-14, 18-21, 27-28, 31-32
competitiveness 65, 146-147, 152, 208-209, 211-214
continuous improvement 68, 116-117, 122-125, 156-158, 162, 171, 208-209, 211, 219, 221, 223, 229
correlation 45-46, 72-73, 80, 89-96, 102-103, 137, 141, 160-161, 222, 225-226
COVID-19 1-4, 11-12, 14, 19, 21-23, 30-32
Critical Success Factors 208-209, 216-217, 229-232
Cultural Dimensions 130, 132-134, 144
Cultural Dimensions Theory 132-134, 144

E

Economic Incidence 173
electronics industry 107, 112-116, 121, 124, 127
emotional exhaustion 33-46, 48-56, 60, 76
emotional ill health 33-35, 37, 39, 46, 48, 53-56
employee motivation 130-134, 142-144, 146-149
Ergonomics 74, 77, 103, 107, 109-111, 122, 125-129, 145, 150, 153, 158, 172-173, 178, 192, 196, 201, 206-207, 234, 237, 246-247, 258-260
ethnic groups 234, 237, 259
eudaemonia 1, 4-5, 9, 11, 18, 31
eudaemonic well-being 1, 4, 6, 31
Expectancy 130-135, 137, 142-148
Expectancy Theory 130-133, 143, 145-148
Exposome 24, 32

H

health 1-7, 11-14, 16, 19-24, 26, 28-37, 39-41, 44, 46, 48, 53-65, 67-76, 79, 103-117, 120-125, 128, 146, 150-157, 159-161, 167, 169, 171, 174-178, 191-192, 194, 207, 230, 236-237, 246, 248-249, 258-259
horizontal collectivism 130, 132, 134-135, 137, 139, 142-145
hybrid work 12, 14

I

industry 17, 27, 40, 65, 69, 72, 75, 103-104, 107-117, 120-121, 124-128, 145, 150-152, 156, 158-159, 165, 171, 175, 177, 179, 194, 199, 207-208, 210, 215, 221, 228-230, 261
instrumentality 132-135, 137, 142, 144-145
interpersonal conflict 33, 38, 55-58, 62

J

job demands 33-42, 45-48, 50-57, 59, 61-62, 75-77, 104-105

L

local economy 234

M

manufacture 72, 112, 152, 208, 214-215, 228, 234,

238, 242-243, 246, 249, 258
Miro 20, 32
musculoskeletal disorders 65, 104, 114, 151, 153-154, 173-174, 191-194, 206, 248

N

Near Home 2, 10, 14-15, 17-18, 22, 32

O

occupational 32, 41, 52, 56-59, 61-62, 64-65, 68-70, 75, 103, 105-106, 110-111, 113, 115, 126, 151, 153, 157-158, 167, 171, 174, 179-183, 189, 191-195, 206-207
occupational depression 41
Occupational Health 56-59, 62, 64, 68-70, 110-111, 153, 171
office 1-2, 9-10, 12-20, 22-25, 27-30, 32, 39, 127-128, 172, 176
optimization 150, 179

P

passive exoskeleton 193, 195
patents 193-194, 197
Personal Protective Equipment (PPE) 11, 32
Post-COVID-19 1-2, 11-14, 16-19, 21, 32
Post-COVID-19 workplace 13-14, 19
Pre-COVID-19 1-2, 10-12, 15-16, 32
prevention 4, 24, 65, 68, 71, 73, 77, 79, 105, 114-115, 173-174, 178-180, 189, 191-192, 194, 216, 230
production 10, 72-73, 77, 80, 104, 107, 115-119, 121, 124, 126, 128-129, 150-152, 159, 161, 163-165, 171-172, 174, 179, 194, 206, 211-213, 215, 228-238, 246, 248-249, 254, 256, 258-259
productivity 3, 8, 13-14, 20, 22, 26, 28, 30-31, 34, 65, 72-74, 77-78, 80, 89-99, 101-105, 108-109, 111-116, 122, 125-128, 131, 145, 147, 153, 156-166, 169-171, 173-179, 181, 183, 186-187, 194, 201, 209-210, 212-214, 234, 246, 260
Psychology 5, 13, 24, 26-31, 56-62, 72, 74, 106, 145-149, 153
psychosocial risk 64-70, 73-75, 77, 79-80, 84, 88-98, 106
psychosocial risk factors 64-69, 73-75, 79, 106

R

relatedness 6, 9-10, 13-14, 18-21, 27-28, 32
risk evaluation 64, 71
role ambiguity 33, 35, 38-40, 43, 47, 50-52, 55-56, 58-60
rustic furniture 234, 237-240, 259

S

Safety and health regulation 64
Self-Determination Theory (SDT) 2, 7-8, 32
Six Sigma 208-209, 211, 215, 229-233, 260
sustainability 11, 21-22, 26, 128, 208-210, 215-216, 229-232, 234, 236, 246-248
sustainable benefits 208-209, 216, 220-222, 226, 228-229

T

Trello 20, 32

U

upper body 193

V

valance 132-133, 135, 137, 142, 144
vertical collectivism 130, 132, 134, 139, 142-143

W

well-being 1-6, 9, 13-14, 16, 19-21, 24, 26, 28-29, 31-32, 39-40, 57-58, 61, 65, 69, 72, 74, 77-78, 106-107, 126, 150-151, 158, 169-171
Well-Being in Work Areas 150
wellness 1-8, 13, 16, 19-23, 25, 28-30, 32
work absenteeism 174
Work Climate 72
work disability 174
Work from Anywhere 1, 17, 19, 25, 32
work from home 2, 15, 17, 26-27, 32
Work home interference 33
work overload 33-34, 38-40, 43, 47-48, 51, 54, 56, 58, 79
worker 3, 9-11, 13-16, 18-21, 32, 68-69, 72, 74-77, 89, 101-104, 107, 111, 115, 122, 125-127, 146, 151, 156, 158, 174, 179, 181, 185-189, 201, 205, 242, 256
worker well-being 107
working conditions 15, 18, 34, 36, 48, 67, 107-111, 113-115, 117-118, 123-127, 131, 150-153, 156-158, 161-162, 164, 169, 171, 215, 245, 248-249, 255, 259
Working from Anywhere (WfA) 14, 17, 32
Working From Home (WfH) 14, 32

Working from Near Home (WfNH) 14-15, 32
Working from Office (WfO) 14, 16, 32
workplace 1-6, 9-15, 18-21, 23-25, 27-29, 32, 34-36, 39-40, 48, 50, 55-56, 58, 60, 62, 65, 70-72, 74-75, 77-78, 101-102, 105, 108, 110, 126, 131-135, 143-144, 174, 189, 191, 193-194, 201, 249
workplace wellness 2-3, 6, 13, 20, 29, 32
workspace 9-11, 14-15, 18-21, 25-26, 32, 178

Z

Zoom 10, 14, 16, 20, 25-26, 29, 32

www.ingramcontent.com/pod-product-compliance
Lightning Source LLC
LaVergne TN
LVHW060424300926
849162LV00006B/1517